THE GOLDSTONE REPORT

THE GOLDSTONE REPORT

*The Legacy of the Landmark
Investigation of the Gaza Conflict*

EDITED BY
Adam Horowitz, Lizzy Ratner, and Philip Weiss

NATION
BOOKS
New York

CONTENTS

FOREWORD:
A CALL TO THE COMMUNITY
OF CONSCIENCE

Desmond Tutu

Every so often, the world witnesses events of such naked brutality that concerned observers must recoil in outrage and demand an end to the madness. We saw this in my own country after the Sharpeville Massacre, a bloodletting that finally awakened the world to the evils of Apartheid. We saw it, too, when Chinese tanks turned on young protesters in Tiananmen Square. We have seen it in Northern Ireland, Iran, the Soviet Union, in so many places marked by historical injustices.

In the waning days of 2008, we saw it once again in the Middle East. Israel had launched a bloody assault on the Gaza Strip, what its military called Operation Cast Lead, and for three weeks one of the world's most sophisticated armies pummeled a captive Palestinian population. Here were soldiers firing willy-nilly at fleeing Palestinian civilians. Here were families obliterated in an instant, men forced to be human shields, farms and factories destroyed. Here, too, were Palestinian militants firing rockets indiscriminately against peaceful Israeli towns. Many times on my journeys in the region, I have observed the gangrenous ravages of the conflict. But the Gaza conflict exceeded our worst expectations and offended our deepest understanding of right and wrong.

Those of us who lived through the decades of Apartheid South Africa know the transforming power of truth-telling. The act of seeking, and then saying, the truth can help to right persistent wrongs and can even sow the seeds of reconciliation. We would have wished that Israel and Hamas might have taken on this vital task, but after years of regrettable silence, the international community has stepped into the breach.

The document at the center of this book, the report of the United Nations Fact-Finding Mission on the Gaza Conflict, better known as the Goldstone Report, is an historic attempt at seeking and then speaking the truth. It takes on one of today's most difficult conflicts and does not blink but delves deep beneath the rubble of the three-week war to find evidence of human rights abuses. No side escapes the report's censure. But the documented evidence of Israeli military misconduct—of reckless, perhaps even deliberate, destruction of life and property—creates a portrait of stunning aggression. For these acts of aggression, the report accuses Israel of likely war crimes and crimes against humanity, and calls on it to look deep into the actions of its military and undertake its own investigation. It also accuses Hamas, the party governing Gaza, of likely war crimes and possible crimes against humanity for firing rockets into southern Israel, and urges it to investigate its actions as well.

It is no accident that the report takes such an unflinching stand. This is a tribute to the chief of the Mission, Justice Richard Goldstone, as well as the other distinguished commissioners: Christine Chinkin, Hina Jilani, and Desmond Travers. I have known Justice Goldstone, a fellow South African, for nearly thirty years, and I have admired his integrity and courage even longer. As a judge presiding over trials of some of the most horrendous human rights violations in recent history, he has never taken the path of simple expedience but has hewed stubbornly to law and principle. Even in the face of death threats, he did not mince words about the violent history of South Africa's Apartheid-era government security forces when he chaired the South African Standing Commission of Inquiry Regarding the Prevention of Public Violence and Intimidation. Nor did he shrink from ugly truths when he served as chief prosecutor of the international criminal tribunals in the former Yugoslavia and in Rwanda. In investigating the Gaza conflict, he has once again brought the same rigorous philosophy to bear: the belief that truth is the first step toward reconciliation, and justice the first step toward peace.

Sadly, his message has not always been greeted kindly. Many powerful people have found it threatening, but rather than engage in reasoned debate they have tried to undermine it by attacking the report and even the judge himself. Yet these attacks, no matter how fierce, cannot alter the essential reality of what befell Gaza. They cannot change the fact that nearly 1,400 Palestinians and 13 Israelis died during twenty-two days of bombing and fighting. They cannot undo the destruction of Gaza's legislative complex and factories. They cannot lift the blockade that has held 1.5 million people hostage for three years. Above all, they cannot change the fact that ours is a moral universe and that injustice cannot have the last word.

The Goldstone Report is a solemn attempt to ensure that balance. But in order to do so, it needs to be read. Israelis and Palestinians must read it, but they are not the only ones. We in the international community of conscience must also read it. Then, once we have read it, we must pursue its most important recommendation, its call for accountability, because it is only through accountability that we can begin building a more just future in this weary region. It is only through accountability, and its attendant promise, justice, that we can begin moving toward a future in which both the violence of the invaders and the violence of resistance come to an end.

INTRODUCTION:
THE END OF ISRAELI EXCEPTIONALISM

Naomi Klein

A sprawling crime scene. That is what Gaza felt like when I visited in the summer of 2009, six months after the Israeli attack. Evidence of criminality was everywhere—the homes and schools that lay in rubble, the walls burned pitch black by white phosphorous, the children's bodies still unhealed for lack of medical care. But where were the police? Who was documenting these crimes, interviewing the witnesses, protecting the evidence from tampering?

For months it seemed that there would be no investigation at all. Many Gazans I met on that trip appeared as traumatized by the absence of an international investigation as by the attacks themselves. They explained that even in the darkest days of the Israeli onslaught, they had comforted themselves with the belief that, this time, Israel had gone too far. Mona al-Shawa, head of the Women's Unit at the Palestinian Centre for Human Rights, told me that Gazans took great solace from news of pro-Palestinian protesters filling the streets of London and Toronto. "People called it war crimes," she recalled. "We felt we were not alone in the world." It seemed to follow from these expressions of outrage that there would be serious consequences for the attacks—criminal trials for the perpetrators, sentences. And under the glare of international investigation, Israel would surely have to lift the brutal embargo that had kept Gaza sealed off from the world since Hamas came to power. Those who dared to really dream convinced themselves that, out of the lawlessness and carnage, a just peace would emerge at last.

But six months later, an almost unbearable realization had set in: The cavalry wasn't coming. Despite all the expressions of righteous indignation, Israel had not been forced to change its behavior in any way. Gaza's borders were still sealed, only now the blockade was keeping out desperately needed rebuilding supplies in addition to many necessities of life. (It would take Israel's lethal attack on a humanitarian aid flotilla in 2010 for a debate about the siege to begin in earnest.) Even worse, the people I met were acutely aware that they could find themselves trapped under Israeli air bombardment again tomorrow, for any arbitrary excuse of Israel's choosing. The message sent by the paralysis of the international legal system was terrifying: Israel enjoyed complete impunity. There was no recourse.

Then, out of nowhere, a representative of the law did show up. His name was Justice Richard Goldstone and he was leading a fact-finding mission for the United Nations. His mandate was to assess whether war crimes had been committed during the attack and to spur official legal remedies. I happened to be in Gaza City when Justice Goldstone was wrapping up his public hearings and met several people who had testified before him, as well as others who had opened their homes to the Mission, showing the scars left by Israeli weapons and sharing photographs of family members killed in the attacks. Finally some light seemed to be shining on this rubble-choked strip of land. But it was faint and many Gazans remained skeptical that justice would follow. If the attacks themselves had failed to provoke action, they reasoned, what hope was there that words in a report would awaken the world? This caution, it turns out, was a wise form of self-preservation.

The attempts to block, then sabotage, then bury the report you are holding began before a single word had been written. The Israeli government rejected the original decision by the United Nations Human Rights Council to investigate allegations of war crimes during the Gaza attack. The Council was hopelessly biased, Israel claimed, and the January 12, 2009, resolution creating the fact-finding mission was, according to Israel's Ministry of Foreign Affairs, "one-sided and irrelevant."

It is true that the original mandate of the UN fact-finding mission called only for an investigation of violations committed "by the occupying Power, Israel, against the Palestinian people." But when Justice Goldstone took the top job and announced that the Mission's mandate had been expanded to include possible crimes committed by Palestinians "whether before, during or after" the attacks, Israel flatly refused to acknowledge this new reality. "There is no formal expansion of the mandate," Ministry of Foreign Affairs spokesman Yossi Levy insisted, against abundant evidence to the contrary. He added, "We will not cooperate with the mission because its duty is not to find the truth, but to find semi-judicial ways to attack Israel."[1]

When it became clear that the Mission would proceed despite this obstructionism, the Israeli government switched to a new strategy: doing almost everything in its considerable power to sabotage Goldstone's work. To this end, the Israeli government refused to allow the UN team to travel inside Israel's borders. That meant that to get into Gaza, members had to go through Egypt. It also meant that Goldstone's investigators could not travel to Sderot and Ashkelon to hear from Israeli victims of Qassam rocket attacks—critical testimony if the Mission was to fulfill its mandate to investigate crimes on all sides. Israel's strategy was transparent enough: It would force Goldstone to produce a one-sided report, which it would then enthusiastically dismiss for being one-sided.

It didn't work. To get around the government roadblocks, Goldstone flew Israelis to Geneva so he could hear their testimony in person. When the report came out, it reflected the scale of the crimes committed by each side, concentrating mostly on Israel's actions, including attacks on houses, hospitals, and mosques that together killed scores of innocent people, as well as attacks on civilian infrastructure such as water installations, agricultural facilities, and factories. But the report did not give Hamas a pass. Goldstone concluded that the launching of rockets and mortars into populated areas "where there is no intended military target"—a practice used by Hamas's military wing as well as other armed Palestinian groups—"indicates the commission of an indiscriminate attack on the civilian population of southern Israel, a war crime, and may amount to crimes against humanity." He also accused Hamas of "extrajudicial executions" in the Gaza Strip and the Palestinian Authority of repression and possibly torture in the West Bank.

The Goldstone Report is a serious, fair-minded, and extremely disturbing document—which is precisely why the Israeli strategy since its publication has been to talk about pretty much everything except the substance of the report. Distractions have ranged from further posturing about the UN's bias, to smear campaigns about Justice Goldstone's personal history, to claims that the report is an integral part of a grand conspiracy to deny Israel's right to exist. Dore Gold, a former Israeli ambassador and top political adviser, said the report was "the most serious and vicious indictment of the State of Israel"[2] since the UN equated Zionism with racism in 1975 and "an assault on Israeli society as a whole,"[3] while Israeli Prime Minister Benjamin Netanyahu explained that "there are three primary threats facing us today: the nuclear threat, the missile threat and what I call the Goldstone threat."[4] The phrase *blood libel* was thrown around with great promiscuity, disgracefully equating the Goldstone Report with the anti-Semitic trials of the Middle Ages in which Jews were accused of drinking the blood of Christian children.

Given this kind of incitement from the top, it's little wonder that the seventy-one-year-old judge was very nearly prevented from attending his own grandson's bar mitzvah in a Johannesburg suburb, with the synagogue worried about violence breaking out. "I could not believe that political anger against him—which people had every right to express—had evolved into an uncontrolled and unconscionable rage that sought to violate the spirit of one of the most sacred aspects of formal Jewish tradition,"[5] observed the noted South African judge Albie Sachs.

Israel has no shortage of critics, many of them Jewish. So what was it about Goldstone that ignited this conflagration? The likeliest answer lies in the particular rhetorical techniques Israel's leaders reliably employ to defend their actions. For decades, Israeli officials have deflected any and all human rights criticisms by claiming that Israel was being unfairly "singled out" by those who claim to care about international law but who look the other way when equally serious crimes are committed by other states. The problem posed by Goldstone was that his record as a judge on the world stage made it impossible for Israel to make this claim with any credibility.

Goldstone began his judicial career as one of a handful of liberal judges serving on the South African bench during the Apartheid era. Though required to enforce the country's brutal discriminatory laws, these judges were also able to chip away at the system from within, helping to loosen the grip of Apartheid in its final years. A 1982 ruling by Goldstone, for instance, blocked judges from evicting blacks and "coloreds" from their homes to make way for whites-only neighborhoods without considering whether suitable alternative accommodations could be found, a requirement that made it virtually impossible to enforce the much-hated "Group Areas Act." As Apartheid weakened, Goldstone began playing a more activist role, exposing a system of extra-judicial death squads within South Africa's police and military—crimes that eventually came before the Truth and Reconciliation Commission.

Goldstone's contribution to building South Africa's first multiracial democracy eventually took him to the international arena, where he sought justice for war crimes, ethnic cleansing, and genocide as chief prosecutor of the United Nations International Criminal Tribunals for the former Yugoslavia and for Rwanda. It was here that Goldstone began to dedicate his life to the post-Holocaust pledge of "never again"—never again to anyone. "If future perpetrators of genocide, crimes against humanity, and serious war crimes are brought to justice and appropriately punished," he wrote in a 2001 essay, "then the millions of innocent victims who perished in the Holocaust will not have died in vain. Their memory will remain alive and they will be remembered when future war criminals are brought to justice. And, it is certainly not too much to hope that efficient justice will also serve to deter war crimes in the future and so protect the untold numbers of potential victims."[6] The judge was always clear that this quest for justice was deeply informed by his Jewishness. "Because of our history, I find it difficult to understand how any Jew wouldn't instinctively be against any form of discrimination,"[7] he told the *Jerusalem Report* in 2000.

It is this theory of justice—a direct response to the Nazi Holocaust—that Justice Goldstone brought to his work in Gaza in 2009, insisting that his fact-finding mission would examine the crimes committed by both Israelis and Palestinians. For Israel's leaders it was terrifying when Goldstone took on the Gaza assignment precisely because there was absolutely no way to claim that the judge was "singling out Israel" for special condemnation. Clearly and indisputably, Goldstone was applying the *same* principles to Israel that he had systematically applied to other countries for decades. The only thing left for Israel and its allies to do was to make sure the report's recommendations never made it before a judicial body with any teeth.

In the United States the job was easy: Pro-Israel lobbyists handily persuaded the U.S. House of Representatives to declare the report "irredeemably biased and unworthy of further consideration or legitimacy," with an anti-Goldstone resolution passing by a vote of 344 to 36. In the occupied territories, the job of burying Goldstone required some very ugly tactics. According to a January 17, 2010, report in *Haaretz*, Palestinian Authority president Mahmoud Abbas was informed that "if he did not ask for a deferral of the vote [at the Human Rights Council] on the critical report on last year's military operation, Israel would turn the West Bank into a 'second Gaza.'"

But while Western governments continue to protect Israel from accountability, insisting that economic sanctions are off the table, even welcoming Israel into the Organization for Economic Co-operation and Development (OECD), civil society around the world is filling the gap. The findings of the Goldstone Report have become a powerful tool in the hands of the growing movement for Boycott, Divestment and Sanctions, which is attempting to pressure Israel to comply with international law by using the same non-violent pressure tactics that helped put an end to Apartheid in South Africa. And thanks to this crucial book, many more people will be able to read the text of the report and make their own judgments about whether Israel has been unfairly "singled out"—or whether, on the contrary, it is finally being held to account.

One of the most remarkable responses to the report came in January 2010, when a coalition of eleven leading Palestinian human rights groups called on Hamas and the Palestinian Authority to investigate Goldstone's allegations that they were complicit in war crimes—despite the fact that the Israeli government had refused to launch an independent investigation of the far more numerous allegations leveled against it in the report. Theirs was a deeply courageous position, one that points to what may prove to be the Goldstone Report's most enduring legacy. While most of us profess to believe in universal human rights and oppose all crimes of war, for too long those principles have been applied in ways that are far from universal. Too often we make apologies for the crimes of "our" side; too often our empathy is selectively deployed. To cite just one relevant example, the United Nations

Human Rights Council has frequently failed to live up to its duty to investigate all major human rights abuses, regardless of their state origins. So while the Council boldly created the Goldstone Mission to investigate crimes in Gaza, it stayed scandalously silent about the massacres and mass incarcerations of Tamils in Sri Lanka that were alleged to have taken place within months of the Gaza attack.

This kind of selectivity is a gift to defiantly lawless governments like Israel's, since it allows states to hide behind their critics' hypocrisy. ("They should call us the day the Human Rights Council decides on a human rights inquiry on some other place around the globe,"[8] Israeli spokesman Yigal Palmor said, explaining away his government's refusal to cooperate with Goldstone.) But now a new standard has been set. The Goldstone Report, with its uncompromising moral consistency, has revived the old-fashioned principles of universal human rights and international law—enshrined in a system that, flawed as it is, remains our best protection against barbarism. When we rally around Goldstone, insisting that this report be read and acted upon, it is this system that we are defending. When Israel and its supporters respond to Goldstone by waging war on international law itself, characterizing any possible legal challenge to Israeli politicians and military officials as "lawfare," they are doing nothing less than recklessly endangering the human rights architecture that was forged in the fires of the Holocaust.

One of the people I met in Gaza was Ibrahim Moammar, chairman of the National Society for Democracy and Law. He could barely contain his disbelief that the crimes he had witnessed had not sparked some kind of an international legal response. "Israel needs to face war crimes trials," he said. He is right, of course; in a just world, the testimonies collected in this book would not merely raise our consciousness. They would be submitted as evidence. But for now, in the absence of official justice, we will have to settle for what the survivors of Argentina's most recent dictatorship have called "popular justice"—the kind of justice that rises up from the streets, educating friends, neighbors, and family, until the momentum of its truth-telling eventually forces the courts to open their doors.

It starts with reading the report.

NOTES

1. Quoted in Haviv Rettig Gur, "Goldstone to 'Post': Mandate of My Gaza Probe Has Changed," *Jerusalem Post*, July 17, 2009.

2. Brandeis University, "Justice Richard Goldstone and Former Israeli Ambassador Dore Gold Discuss the U.N. Gaza Report," November 6, 2009, http://www.brandeis.edu/now/2009/november/gazaforumcoverage.html.

3. Quoted in Miranda Neubauer, "Debate over UN Gaza report," *The Justice* (Brandeis University), November 10, 2009.

4. Prime Minister's Office, "PM Netanyahu's Speech at the Knesset Special Session," December 23, 2009, http://www.pmo.gov.il/PMOEng/Communication/PMSpeaks/speech 40sigh231209.htm.

5. Chris McGreal, "Goldstone Family Drawn into Row over Gaza Report," *The Guardian*, April 30, 2010.

6. Richard Goldstone, "From the Holocaust: Some Legal and Moral Implications," in *Is the Holocaust Unique? Perspectives on Comparative Genocide*, ed. Alan S. Rosenbaum (Boulder, CO: Westview Press, 2009), p. 52.

7. Peter Hirschberg, "Brief Encounter—Richard Goldstone, South African Judge and Ex–War Crimes Prosecutor," *Jerusalem Report*, July 3, 2000.

8. Ben Hubbard, "UN to Hold War Crimes Hearings in Gaza, Geneva," Associated Press, June 4, 2009.

EDITORS' NOTE

Adam Horowitz, Lizzy Ratner, and Philip Weiss

Reports come and go. This is one of the tragic truths of the literature of human rights violations. Hard-working researchers scour the rubble of war zones for fragments of evidence—of war crimes, crimes against humanity, other violations of life and freedom—only to watch their findings sink into the oblivion of forgotten documents.

The Goldstone Report, whose official title is the Report of the United Nations Fact-Finding Mission on the Gaza Conflict, has thus far managed to defy this fate. Since its publication in September 2009, it has spawned debates, rebuttals, defenses, editorials, resolutions, and protests, both for and against. Few reports have experienced such a thunderous reception. But as time passes, it too is at risk of disappearing. It is our hope that this book will help keep the report alive and its findings relevant.

To this end, we have created a book that seeks to showcase the report by reprinting its central findings followed by eleven essays that capture its ongoing impact. We do not reprint the entire report. That would run over five hundred pages. Instead, we have abridged the report to about half its original length to focus on the story the Mission tells of the Gaza war: the historical context of the blockade and rocket attacks, the rupture of the 2008 ceasefire, and the main events of the December 2008–January 2009 conflict, beginning with Israel's overwhelming air strikes and ending with the destruction of industry. We have indicated small cuts with bracketed ellipses—[. . .]—and longer ones with brackets stating which paragraphs were removed, using the paragraph numbers the report uses. In cutting the report, we have also removed all footnotes. Needless to say, these notes supply important detail and contain critical information about the Mission's sources, some of which have fanned controversy. Again, we were limited by space.

The report also includes extended legal discussions that we have eliminated because the same principles and ideas recur so often. We have sought to make up for the loss with the first four essays in Part II.

We recognize that we have lost much of the report's impact by making these cuts, and we urge readers to read the entire report online. It can be found at the website for this book: www.goldstonereportbook.com.

In more than a dozen places in the report, we have added to it by inserting oral testimonies that the Mission collected while conducting its investigation. Motivated by his experience of the effectiveness of the South African truth and reconciliation process, Justice Richard Goldstone arranged for public hearings in Gaza and Geneva so that victims on both sides might force the other side to reckon with the human toll. We have included excerpts from the testimonies at relevant points, marking them with the title *Testimony*, along with the speaker's name. The first one, by ninety-one-year-old Moussa al-Silawi, follows on page 17 and serves as the introduction to the report.

Readers will also notice some unfamiliar spellings of familiar words in the report. This is because we have preserved the report's British orthography as we have also done for Raji Sourani's essay, "The Right to Live in Dignity." In addition, the essays in our book contain a range of casualty figures, a reflection of the fact that official reports of deaths and injuries have varied widely.

We completed this book in July 2010, as the charges of the Goldstone Report continued to reverberate throughout Israel, the Occupied Palestinian Territory, and the broader international community. At the time, both Israel and Hamas were preparing to submit reports to the United Nations on their actions during Operation Cast Lead, and Israel had just announced indictments of four military personnel for their conduct during the war. Though these indictments did not approach the response the Goldstone Report called for, they were widely seen as vindication of some of the report's most troubling findings, as well as confirmation of its ongoing influence.

This influence now extends well beyond the report's publication, and we have tried to capture that quality with the essays in Part II of this book, almost all of which are original.

In "The Right to Live in Dignity," Raji Sourani, the head of the Palestinian Centre for Human Rights, describes the experience of the Gaza war from the standpoint of Gazans themselves and demonstrates the importance of international law as a means of preventing repetition of the carnage.

In "International Law and the Goldstone Report," Jules Lobel, a professor of international law, summarizes the legal principles invoked by the Goldstone Report and places them in the framework of post–World War II efforts to build global law enforcement mechanisms.

Lobel's interpretation is followed by "The Goldstone Illusion," by Israeli philosopher Moshe Halbertal, who describes the report as "a terrible document" that is based chiefly on Palestinian testimonies and leaves a society with no ability to fight terrorist threats. Halbertal's piece first appeared in the *New Republic* in December 2009 and is widely considered to be the most thoughtful criticism of the report.

In "The Attacks on the Goldstone Report," longtime scholar of Israeli history Jerome Slater takes on the leading criticisms of the report in both Israel and the United States (including Halbertal's). In particular, Slater shows how the recent effort to characterize traditional guerrilla warfare as "asymmetrical war," in which a state's army is at a supposed disadvantage, would justify attacks on civilians.

In "The U.S. Congress and the Goldstone Report," Brian Baird, a six-term Democratic congressman from Washington State who has visited Gaza more times since the conflict than any other American politician, supports the accuracy of the report and describes its political reception in Washington.

In "Palestinian Dispossession and the U.S. Public Sphere," Rashid Khalidi, a professor at Columbia University, describes the rapidly shifting discourse in the United States about the conflict as well as the ways in which Palestinian concerns are at last getting attention.

Henry Siegman, former director of the American Jewish Congress and veteran Middle East expert, explores the controversy over the Goldstone Report in "Discrediting Goldstone, Delegitimizing Israel" and discovers that it reveals more about Israel than about Goldstone.

In "Gaza, Goldstone, and the Movement for Israeli Accountability," Palestinian-American journalist Ali Abunimah discusses how Israeli militarism is eroding the country's liberal support in the West, leading to a crisis of legitimacy that some Israelis view as an existential threat, while many Palestinians and others feel it offers hope for a better future.

In "Israel's Siege Mentality," Israeli journalist Noam Sheizaf tells the story of the often-angry response to the report in Israeli society, and explains what this response has revealed about the country's international image and its siege mentality.

Journalist and peace activist Letty Cottin Pogrebin traces the organized Jewish community's response to the report in "The Unholy Assault on Richard Goldstone" and finds that, in their rush to condemn, Jewish leaders have violated some of Judaism's most deeply held principles.

And in "Messages from Gaza," Laila el-Haddad offers a wrenching account of her family's experience of the Gaza war, and the mix of hope and skepticism with which they greeted the Goldstone Report.

Each of these contributors—along with Naomi Klein and Archbishop Desmond Tutu, who, respectively, wrote the Introduction and Foreword to this book—labored under tight deadlines and with little remuneration to bring new understanding to this tangled subject. Their insights impart nuance to a document that has been too often misunderstood, depth to a conversation that has veered too often toward frenzy. Their dedication inspired us, and the elegance of their essays never ceased to thrill us. We thank them all.

Our gratitude as well goes to Alex Kane, our intrepid researcher; Carl Bromley, our editor at Nation Books, who possesses both courage and wisdom in equal measure; John Sherer, our champion at Basic Books; Melissa Veronesi, this book's calm, cool, and organized project editor; Albert Angulo, maker of beautiful maps; and Bill Clegg, our dauntless agent who recognized the promise of this project early on and used all his rebel magic to make it happen.

Profuse and profound thanks as well to Michael Ratner and Abdeen Jabara, who had the original inspired idea for this book. Quite simply, it would not exist without them. We are also deeply grateful to Michael for serving as adviser/guru throughout this project.

Finally, we wish to acknowledge the brave work of the team that brought us the original Goldstone Report: the researchers, the writers, and the commissioners, Christine Chinkin, Hina Jilani, Desmond Travers, and Richard Goldstone. Above all Richard Goldstone. Thank you.

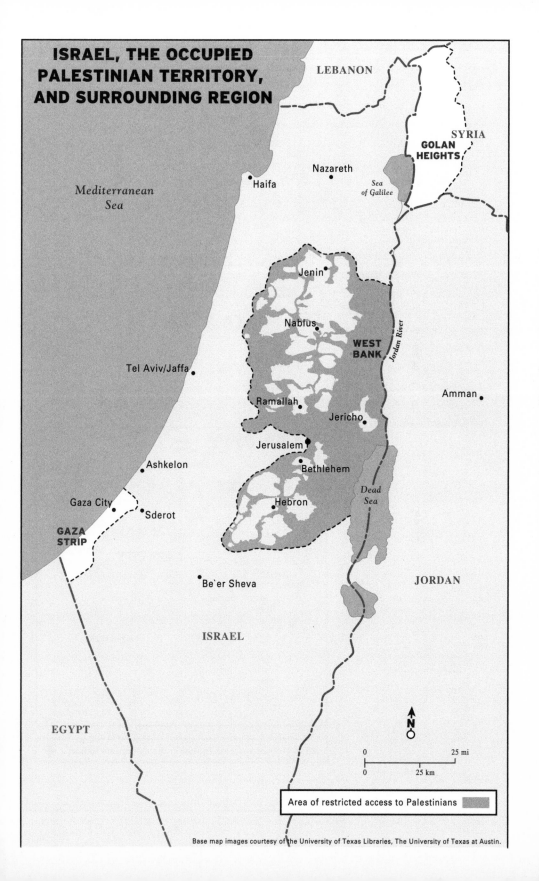

ISRAEL, THE OCCUPIED PALESTINIAN TERRITORY, AND SURROUNDING REGION

LEBANON

SYRIA

GOLAN HEIGHTS

Mediterranean Sea

Nazareth

Haifa

Sea of Galilee

Jenin

Nablus

WEST BANK

Jordan River

Tel Aviv/Jaffa

Ramallah

Jericho

Amman

Jerusalem

Bethlehem

Ashkelon

Dead Sea

Hebron

Gaza City

Sderot

GAZA STRIP

Be`er Sheva

JORDAN

ISRAEL

EGYPT

N

0   25 mi

0   25 km

Area of restricted access to Palestinians

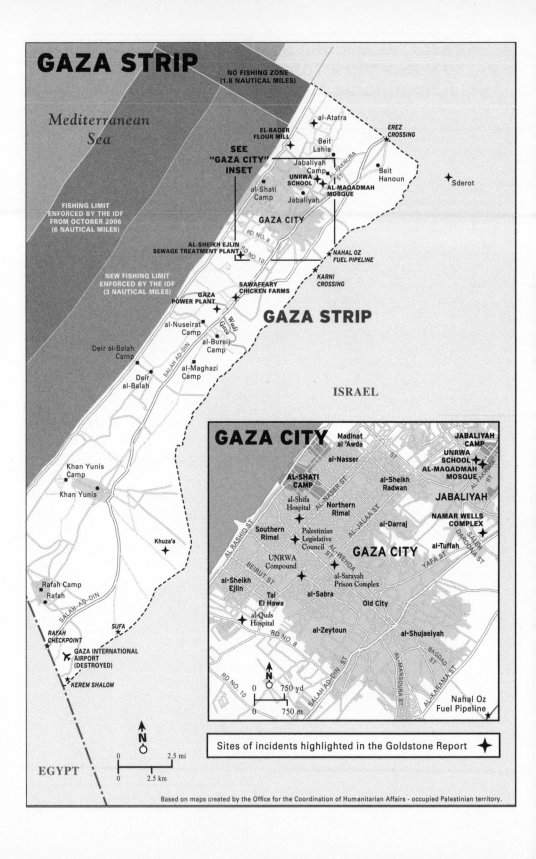

TIMELINE

1947: In November, the United Nations General Assembly approves a resolution calling for the partition of Palestine into two states, one Jewish, one Arab. Civil war breaks out between Jews and Palestinian Arabs.

1948: The State of Israel declares its independence in May, and the Arab states of Egypt, Transjordan, Iraq, Syria, and Lebanon invade the nascent state. Israel wins the war decisively. Both phases of war lead to the expulsion and flight of an estimated 750,000 Palestinians from their land to the West Bank, Gaza Strip, and surrounding Arab states.

1949: The United Nations negotiates an armistice line, referred to as the Green Line, creating interim borders between Israel and its neighbors. Jordan becomes the governing authority in the West Bank and East Jerusalem, and Egypt rules the Gaza Strip. UN Partition had granted the Jewish state 56 percent of Mandate Palestine; Israel now controls 78 percent.

1956: Egyptian leader Gamal Abdel Nasser nationalizes the Suez Canal, and Britain, France, and Israel respond by going to war against Egypt. A battleground is the Gaza Strip, a launching site for Palestinian fedayeen attacks inside Israel. Israel occupies Gaza and subsequently withdraws under international pressure.

1967: Egypt blocks Israel's access to the Straits of Tiran at the head of the Red Sea and begins mobilizing troops along the border with Israel. Israel responds by launching a preemptive strike. Thus begins the 1967 War. Egypt, Jordan, and Syria engage Israel, while other Arab states provide support. Israel captures the Gaza Strip, the West Bank, including East Jerusalem, the Sinai Peninsula, and the Golan Heights. Israeli settlement building, illegal under international law, soon begins in the captured territories.

1973: The 1973 War erupts on October 6. Egypt and Syria seek to regain their lands and initially succeed in driving Israel back. Helped by a United States airlift, Israel retains the occupied territories.

1979: Egypt and Israel sign the Camp David Accords. Israel withdraws from Egyptian territories in the Sinai. The Gaza Strip remains under Israeli occupation.

1987: The first intifada, or Palestinian uprising against the occupation, begins in the Jabaliya Refugee Camp in Gaza and spreads throughout the Occupied Palestinian Territory. Israel responds with force. Over the next several years, more than 1,000 Palestinians, including over 200 under the age of sixteen, are killed.

1993: Israel and the Palestinian Liberation Organization sign the Oslo Peace Accords, recognizing one another and leading to the creation of the Palestinian Authority in 1994 and the withdrawal of Israeli troops from parts of Gaza and the West Bank. Talks on "final status" issues—Jerusalem, refugees, settlements, borders, and resources—are put off until 1996 and then delayed until 2000. A final agreement is never reached.

1993: Palestinian militant groups begin using suicide bombings against Israeli civilian and military targets. According to the website of the Israeli Foreign Ministry of Foreign Affairs, upwards of 155 suicide bomb attacks take place between 1993 and 2008, killing nearly 800 people.

1994: Israel begins construction of a separation barrier between Israel and the Gaza Strip. Under the terms of a "general closure" instituted in 1993, and never lifted, it also continues to restrict Palestinian movement through the use of permits, checkpoints, and other mechanisms.

1995: Israeli Prime Minster Yitzhak Rabin is assassinated by Yigal Amir, a right-wing Israeli who opposed the Oslo Peace Accords.

2000: The second intifada, or the al-Aqsa intifada, begins after then–opposition leader Ariel Sharon embarks on a visit to the holy site of Haram al-Sharif/Temple Mount in Jerusalem, which both Jews and Muslims revere. Between 2000 to 2008, more than 5,000 Palestinians are killed, as well as over 1,000 Israelis.

2001: Palestinian militants begin firing homemade rockets at Israeli communities near the Gaza-Israel border. From 2001 to mid-June 2008, armed Palestinian groups fire over 3,400 rockets and over 3,700 mortar shells into Israel. From June 2004 to January 2009, 19 Israeli civilians die as a result of rocket and mortar fire, including 4 minors.

2002: The Arab League adopts a peace initiative to normalize relations with Israel if it will return to the 1967 borders and resolve the refugee crisis. Meanwhile, the United States, European Union, Russian Federation, and United Nations, collectively known as The Quartet, introduce a plan referred to as the "road map to peace." It calls on Israel to end settlement construction and accept a Palestinian government and calls on Palestinians to renounce violence and engage in democratic reforms before "final status" issues are resolved.

June 2002: Israel begins construction of the Separation Wall along the Green Line and in the West Bank. In 2004 the International Court of Justice issues an advisory opinion finding the Wall "contrary to international law," but its recommendations to cease construction and dismantle the portions of the wall in the West Bank are never enforced.

2005: Israel carries out a unilateral "disengagement plan" for the Gaza Strip, in which all soldiers and settlers leave Gaza. However, Israel erects a separation barrier between Gaza and Egypt and maintains control over Gaza's borders as well as its telecommunications, sewage, water, and electricity networks. In the year following disengagement, Israel fires approximately 15,000 artillery shells into Gaza and conducts more than 550 air strikes, killing approximately 525 Gazans. Over that same period at least 1,700 rockets are fired into Israel, injuring 41 Israelis.

2006: The Palestinian Authority holds legislative elections. The Islamist movement Hamas wins 74 seats out of 132, while the ruling party, Fatah, wins 45 seats. International observers say the election was conducted fairly, but Israel imposes economic sanctions, and the United States and the European Union withhold funds from the Palestinian Authority, saying that Hamas is a terrorist organization. Israel and the international community announce that the sanctions will end once Hamas adopts "the Quartet Principles": recognition of the state of Israel, recognition of previous agreements, and renunciation of violence.

June 2006: Palestinian militant groups attack an Israeli military post near Gaza, killing two soldiers and capturing Cpl. Gilad Shalit, who remains a prisoner in Gaza. In response, Israel conducts armed operations against Hamas in Gaza and further tightens its economic blockade of the territory.

July 2006: Hezbollah undertakes border raids into northern Israel, leading to the start of the Second Lebanon War. Israel invades Lebanon from the air and the ground. The war last 34 days and kills over 1,000 Lebanese, many of them civilians.

2007: Fatah and Hamas establish a unity government for the Palestinian territories in February, but it dissolves when Fatah attempts to take over the Gaza government with backing from the United States. Following skirmishes, Hamas retains control over Gaza while the Palestinian Authority sets up an "emergency" government in the West Bank with Mahmoud Abbas of Fatah as president. This paves the way for the United States, the European Union, and Israel to resume payments to the Palestinian Authority. Israel declares Gaza a "hostile entity" and intensifies its blockade of Gaza, placing greater restrictions over goods, fuel, and electricity that can enter the territory.

June 2008: Egypt brokers a ceasefire between Israel and Hamas. The ceasefire terms reportedly state that Hamas will halt attacks against Israel from groups inside Gaza, while Israel will cease military operations inside of Gaza and ease the blockade.

June–July 2008: Hamas insists that it is committed to keeping the truce, but other militant groups inside Gaza continue firing rockets. Israel fails to ease the blockade and conducts military operations inside Gaza and the West Bank aimed at Hamas. The UN Office for the Coordination of Humanitarian Affairs reports that the commodities being allowed into Gaza are "far below actual needs" and are "restricted to certain selected essential humanitarian items." As a result of the restrictions and a ban on exports, 95 percent of Gaza's industries are closed.

November 2008: After two months of relative calm, Israel breaks the truce with Hamas in a raid that kills six gunmen in Gaza. Hamas responds by firing rockets into Israel. Attacks by both Israel and armed groups in Gaza escalate in November and December. Nearly 200 rockets and mortar shells are fired into Israel in November, up from two in October. Israel closes the crossings into Gaza for most of November, forcing most of Gaza's bakeries to close and the United Nations Relief and Works Agency to suspend food distribution for five days to 750,000 Gazans.

December 2008: Gaza authorities declare an end to the truce with Israel following the continuing blockade on Gaza and multiple Israeli strikes during the first week of December, including one that kills two children and injures two others in Rafah. Israeli authorities say that Gazan forces fired 130 rockets and mortars into Israel in the first 18 days of the month.

December 27, 2008: The Israeli Air Force carries out a wave of attacks inside Gaza, starting "Operation Cast Lead." In the first day of the air assault, at least 225 Palestinians are killed and hundreds injured, making it the bloodiest day in decades of the conflict.

January 3, 2009: The ground phase of the assault begins. Israeli troops enter Gaza.

January 15, 2009: Israeli forces begin to withdraw from Gaza, but leave in their wake the systematic destruction of civilian infrastructure.

January 17, 2009: Israel declares a unilateral ceasefire, effectively ending the conflict. "The conditions have been created so that our targets, as defined when we launched the operation, have been fully achieved, and more so," then–Prime Minister Ehud Olmert says. In total, between 1,387 and 1,444 Palestinians die, the vast majority of them civilians, including over 300 children. More than 15,000 homes are destroyed or severely damaged, leaving 100,000 Palestinians homeless. Nearly half of Gaza's 122 health facilities are damaged or destroyed, and Gaza suffers more than $650 million in losses due to the Israeli destruction of housing, commerce, industry, and farming. Over the same three weeks, Palestinian rocket and mortar fire aimed at Israeli civilians kill 3.

April 2009: The United Nations Human Rights Council establishes a fact-finding mission on the Israeli invasion of Gaza to investigate all violations of human rights and international humanitarian law. Justice Richard Goldstone, a South African jurist who was the former prosecutor for the international tribunals in Yugoslavia and Rwanda, is named to head the mission.

September 2009: The "Report of the United Nations Fact-Finding Mission on the Gaza Conflict" is released. It states that both Israel and Palestinian armed groups, including Hamas, committed war crimes and possible crimes against humanity during the Gaza conflict. The report on the Israeli invasion concludes that the attack was "a deliberately disproportionate attack designed to punish, humiliate and terrorize a civilian population." The Mission calls on the UN Human Rights Council to address these "grave violations" of the Geneva Conventions by referring the report to the International Criminal Court in the Hague if the sides do not carry out appropriate, independent investigations.

October 2009: The UN Human Rights Council endorses the report by a 25–6 vote, with 11 abstentions.

November 2009: In a 114–18 vote, with 44 abstentions, the UN General Assembly endorses the Goldstone Report, urging Israel and the "Palestinian side" to conduct independent, credible investigations into the allegations of war crimes outlined in the report within three months. Secretary-General Ban Ki-moon is charged with monitoring the implementation of the resolution.

February 2010: A chorus of human rights organizations criticizes both Israel and the Palestinians for not conducting credible investigations. The General Assembly passes a second resolution, extending by five months the deadline for both Israel and the Palestinians to conduct credible investigations of the report's allegations. The resolution also calls on Secretary-General Ban to report to the Assembly within five months on the implementation of the resolution.

Report of the United Nations Fact-Finding Mission on the Gaza Conflict (Abridged)

UNITED NATIONS HUMAN RIGHTS COUNCIL

_____

HUMAN RIGHTS IN PALESTINE AND OTHER OCCUPIED ARAB TERRITORIES

Report of the United Nations Fact-Finding
Mission on the Gaza Conflict

CONTENTS

** All gray entries listed in the Contents are not included
in this abridged edition of the Report*

PART TWO
OCCUPIED PALESTINIAN TERRITORY

The Gaza Strip
Section A: Military Operations

CHAPTER VII. ATTACKS ON GOVERNMENT BUILDINGS AND POLICE　54

CHAPTER VIII. OBLIGATION ON PALESTINIAN ARMED GROUPS IN GAZA TO TAKE FEASIBLE PRECAUTIONS TO PROTECT THE CIVILIAN POPULATION　71

CHAPTER IX. OBLIGATION ON ISRAEL TO TAKE FEASIBLE PRECAUTIONS TO PROTECT CIVILIAN POPULATION AND CIVILIAN OBJECTS IN GAZA　81

TESTIMONY 4: Ziyad al-Deeb, describing the deadly mortar attack near the UNRWA school in al-Fakhura Street, 87

CHAPTER X. INDISCRIMINATE ATTACKS BY ISRAELI ARMED FORCES RESULTING IN THE LOSS OF LIFE AND INJURY TO CIVILIANS　106

PART THREE
ISRAEL

B.   Compensation and reparations to the Palestinian people in the
      Gaza Strip

PART FIVE
CONCLUSIONS AND RECOMMENDATIONS

*TESTIMONY 13: Sameh al-Sawafeary, describing the forced evacuation
of his neighborhood, 294*

*TESTIMONY 14: Rashad Mohammed Hamada, describing the
destruction of el-Bader Flour Mill, 306*

*TESTIMONY 15: Khaled Abd Rabbo, describing the death of his
two young daughters, 325*

Annexes

ACRONYMS AND ABBREVIATIONS

ACRI — Association for Civil Rights in Israel
BMC — Businessman Card
CLA — Coordination and Liaison Administration
CMWU — Coastal Municipalities Water Utility
COGAT — Coordinator of Government Activities in the Territories
DFLP — Democratic Front for the Liberation of Palestine
DIME — dense inert metal explosive
DSS — United Nations Department of Safety and Security
FAO — Food and Agriculture Organization of the United Nations
GIS — General Intelligence Service
HaMoked — Center for the Defense of the Individual
HCC — Humanitarian Coordination Centre
IAF — Israeli Air Force
ICCPR — International Covenant on Civil and Political Rights
ICESCR — International Covenant on Economic, Social and Cultural Rights
ICHR — Independent Commission for Human Rights
ICRC — International Committee of the Red Cross
IDF — Israeli Defense Forces
IED — improvised explosive device
IHL — international humanitarian law
IHRL — international human rights law
ILO — International Labour Organization
IOF — Israeli occupation forces
MADA — Palestinian Center for Development and Media Freedoms
NATO — North Atlantic Treaty Organization
NGO — non-governmental organization

OCHA — Office for the Coordination of Humanitarian Affairs
OHCHR — Office of the United Nations High Commissioner for Human Rights
PALTRADE — Palestine Trade Center
PCATI — Public Committee against Torture in Israel
PCHR — Palestinian Centre for Human Rights
PFLP — Popular Front for the Liberation of Palestine
PHR — Physicians for Human Rights–Israel
PLO — Palestine Liberation Organization
PRC — Popular Resistance Committee
PRCS — Palestinian Red Crescent Society
TAWTHEQ — Central Commission for Documentation and Pursuit of Israeli War Criminals
UAV — unmanned aviation vehicle
UNCTAD — United Nations Conference on Trade and Development
UNDP — United Nations Development Programme
UNFPA — United Nations Population Fund
UNHCR — Office of the United Nations High Commissioner for Refugees
UNICEF — United Nations Children's Fund
UNITAR — United Nations Institute for Training and Research
UNOSAT — United Nations Operational Satellite Applications Programme
UNRWA — United Nations Relief and Works Agency for Palestine Refugees in the Near East
WFP — United Nations World Food Programme
WHO — World Health Organization

EXECUTIVE SUMMARY

[Removed: Executive Summary (paragraphs 1–130)]

Moussa al-Silawi

Witness to the shelling of al-Maqadmah mosque,
describing the attack on January 3, 2009

In the name of God, the compassionate, the merciful, I am Moussa al-Silawi. I live in Jabaliyah Camp, on the eighth block. On the day of the event I went to the mosque to pray the evening prayer. And usually the prayers, if we hear any aircraft, any bullets, if we hear anything, usually we run to the mosque to take refuge. After evening prayer we heard a shell hit the mosque. And we have no idea what we saw at the moment. It was absolutely incredible and we started screaming. We screamed and we called for God. We . . . said, "Please, help us. Help us, God. Help us, God. Help us, God." And after that, I heard, I was told that [my] son . . . Ibrahim Moussa Isa Ibrahima al-Silawi, he was carried to the hospital and he became a martyr. He died. He has seven daughters, and they are ten. Altogether they are ten who became orphans, without anybody to give them assistance.

And moments later I heard and I was told, "Ahmed, Ahmed al-Silawi, he is also dead. He's a martyr." He was completely disintegrated in the mosque. A little bit later I was contacted again and I was told, "Your nephew, Mohammad Moussa al-Silawi, he has three daughters, he also is dead." And then I heard from another person, "Allahu akbar! Allahu akbar!" I was screaming. And thanks to God. And I was told, "Your grandchild, your grandchild the son of Moussa is also dead." His name is Mohammad. And then after a while I heard another news, and I was told, "Mohammad Moussa al-Silawi, your other grandchild is dead."

Allahu akbar. Allahu akbar. Where are the Arab countries? Where is Islam? Where is religion? Where is honor? And then I have to say: where is law? Where is the state? Where is justice? I am 91 years old. I was born in 1917. I lived at the time of the Turks, the time of the British, but we never saw anything of this sort. We've never seen something like that. I have lived 91 years, I have seen everything, but nothing of this sort. I have never seen such a catastrophe. We see our children dead. We transport them to the hospital, one to the Idwan Hospital, and then we carried them to the cemetery.

PART ONE

METHODOLOGY, CONTEXT AND APPLICABLE LAW

INTRODUCTION

On 3 April 2009, the President of the Human Rights Council established the United Nations Fact-Finding Mission on the Gaza Conflict with the mandate "to investigate all violations of international human rights law and international humanitarian law that might have been committed at any time in the context of the military operations that were conducted in Gaza during the period from 27 December 2008 and 18 January 2009, whether before, during or after." The appointment of the Mission followed the adoption on 12 January 2009 of resolution S-9/1 on the grave violations of human rights in the Occupied Palestinian Territory, particularly due to the recent Israeli military attacks against the occupied Gaza Strip, by the United Nations Human Rights Council at the end of its ninth special session.

The President appointed Justice Richard Goldstone, former judge of the Constitutional Court of South Africa and former Prosecutor of the International Criminal Tribunals for the former Yugoslavia and Rwanda, to head the Mission. The other three appointed members were: Professor Christine Chinkin, Professor of International Law at the London School of Economics and Political Science, who was a member of the high-level fact-finding mission to Beit Hanoun (2008); Ms. Hina Jilani, Advocate of the Supreme Court of Pakistan and former Special Representative of the Secretary-General on the situation of human rights defenders, who was a member of the International Commission of Inquiry on Darfur (2004); and Colonel Desmond Travers, a former Officer in Ireland's Defence Forces and member of the Board of Directors of the Institute for International Criminal Investigations.

[Removed: paragraphs 133–148]

Acknowledgments

The Mission is deeply grateful to the numerous Palestinians and Israelis, especially victims and witnesses of violations, who have shared with it their stories and views. It is equally grateful to the many Palestinian and Israeli civil society and NGOs, and to the Palestinian Independent Commission for Human Rights. They are at the forefront of the protection and promotion of human rights in the region and carry out their work with courage, professionalism and independence in very difficult circumstances. The Mission is also grateful to all the domestic and international NGOs that have supported its mandate and have provided a vast amount of relevant and well-documented information. Without the support and the assistance of United Nations agencies, programmes and other bodies, and particularly of the United Nations staff in Gaza, the Mission would have not been able to complete its work. Heartfelt thanks go to all of them. The Mission wishes to especially acknowledge the invaluable support received by the dedicated staff of UNRWA. The Mission expresses its gratitude to the United Nations security personnel and interpreters, who have professionally and sensitively accomplished their difficult tasks. In addition to the secretariat of the Mission appointed by OHCHR, a multinational team with a broad range of professional experience, the gratitude of the Mission goes also to the staff of OHCHR in Geneva, the Occupied Palestinian Territory and New York. A particular mention goes to all those who assisted with the daunting task of organizing at very short notice the public hearings in Gaza and in Geneva. The Mission wishes to formally thank the Government of Egypt and in particular the Permanent Mission of Egypt in Geneva. The Mission wishes to formally thank the Governments of Jordan and of Switzerland for facilitating the issuance of entry visas at short notice. The Mission also wishes to acknowledge the continued support received from the United Nations Secretary-General.

Finally, the Mission wishes to thank the people of Gaza for their warm welcome, their humanity and their hospitality in spite of such difficult and painful circumstances.

CHAPTER I.

METHODOLOGY

A. MANDATE AND TERMS OF REFERENCE

In his letter appointing the members of the Mission, the President of the Council entrusted the Mission with the following mandate: "to investigate all violations of international human rights law and international humanitarian law that might have been committed at any time in the context of the military operations that were conducted in Gaza during the period from 27 December 2008 and 18 January 2009, whether before, during or after."

To implement its mandate, the Mission determined that it was required to consider any actions by all parties that might have constituted violations of international human rights law or international humanitarian law. The mandate also required it to review related actions in the entire Occupied Palestinian Territory and Israel.

With regard to temporal scope, the Mission's broad mandate includes violations before, during and after the military operations that were conducted in Gaza between 27 December 2008 and 18 January 2009. The Mission considered that, while the Gaza events must be seen in the context of the overall conflict and situation in the Occupied Palestinian Territory, in view of the limited time and resources available, it would be beyond its abilities to focus on conduct or actions that took place long before the military operation of December–January. The Mission therefore decided to focus primarily on events, actions or circumstances occurring since 19 June 2008, when a ceasefire was agreed between the Government of Israel and Hamas. The Mission has also taken into consideration matters occurring after the end of military operations that constitute continuing human rights and international

humanitarian law violations related to or as a consequence of the military operation, up to 31 July 2009.

The Mission considered that the reference in its mandate to violations committed
in the context of the December–January military operations required it to go beyond violations that took place directly as part of the operations. Thus violations
within its mandate include those that are linked to the December–January military
operations in terms of time, objectives and targets, and include restrictions on
human rights and fundamental freedoms relating to Israel's strategies and actions
in the context of its military operations.

The normative framework for the Mission has been general international law, the
Charter of the United Nations, international humanitarian law, international human
rights law and international criminal law.

B. METHODS OF WORK

The Mission reviewed all allegations raised in connection with issues under its
mandate. The review included analysis of material in the public domain, including
the many reports produced after the military operations concluded, information
provided to the Mission through additional documentation and a series of meetings
with experts who had been to the area or studied matters of interest to the Mission.

In view of the time frame within which it had to complete its work, the Mission
necessarily had to be selective in the choice of issues and incidents for investigation. The report does not purport to be exhaustive in documenting the very high
number of relevant incidents that occurred in the period covered by the Mission's
mandate and especially during the military operations in Gaza. Nevertheless, the
Mission considers that the report is illustrative of the main patterns of violations.
The Mission also stresses that the exclusion of issues or incidents from the report
in no way reflects on the seriousness of the relevant allegations.

[Removed: paragraphs 158–165]

A note on the public hearings

The purpose of the public hearings, which were broadcast live, was to enable victims, witnesses and experts from all sides to the conflict to speak directly to as

many people as possible in the region as well as in the international community. The Mission is of the view that no written word can replace the voice of victims. While not all issues and incidents under investigation by the Mission were addressed during the hearings, the 38 public testimonies covered a wide range of relevant facts as well as legal and military matters. The Mission had initially intended to hold hearings in Gaza, Israel and the West Bank. However, denial of access to Israel and the West Bank resulted in the decision to hold hearings of participants from Israel and the West Bank in Geneva.

Participants in the hearings were identified in the course of the Mission's investigations, and had either first-hand experience or information or specialized knowledge of the issues under investigation and analysis. In keeping with the objectives of the hearings, the Mission gave priority to the participation of victims and people from the affected communities. Participants took part in the hearings on a voluntary basis. Some individuals declined to participate for fear of reprisal. The Mission received expressions of gratitude from participants, as well as members of the affected communities, for having provided an opportunity to speak publicly of their experiences.

[Removed: sections C and D (paragraphs 168–175)]

CHAPTER II.

CONTEXT

[Removed: paragraph 176]

[Removed: section A (paragraphs 177–197)]

B. OVERVIEW OF ISRAEL'S PATTERN OF POLICIES AND CONDUCT RELEVANT TO THE OCCUPIED PALESTINIAN TERRITORY, AND LINKS BETWEEN THE SITUATION IN GAZA AND IN THE WEST BANK

Since 1967, Israel has built hundreds of settlements in the West Bank, including East Jerusalem, and the Gaza Strip. Such settlements were recognized by its Ministry of Interior as Israeli "communities" subjected to Israeli law. The [. . .] Advisory Opinion by the International Court of Justice and "a number of United Nations resolutions have all affirmed that Israel's practice of constructing settlements—in effect, the transfer by an occupying Power of parts of its own civilian population into the territory it occupies—constitutes a breach of the Fourth Geneva Convention" (on the position of the Israeli High Court of Justice on the applicability of the Fourth Geneva Convention to the Occupied Palestinian Territory, see chapter IV). Sixteen settlements in the Gaza Strip and three in the northern West Bank were dismantled in 2005 during the implementation of the so-called Israeli disengagement plan, but the establishment of new settlements continued. In 2007, there were more than 450,000 Israeli citizens living in 149 settlements in the West Bank, including East Jerusalem. According to United Nations sources, almost 40 per cent of the West Bank is now taken up by Israeli infrastructure associated with the settlements, including roads, barriers, buffer zones and military bases. Data released by the Israeli Central Bureau of Statistics showed that construction in these settlements has increased in 2008 by a factor of 1.8 in comparison with the same period in 2007. The number of tenders in East Jerusalem has increased by 3,728 per cent (1,761 housing units, compared with 46 in 2007). Until the end of the 1970s, the Government of Israel claimed that the settlements were established on the grounds of military necessity and security, but it has since abandoned this position.

It is estimated that 33 per cent of the settlements have been built on private land owned by Palestinians, much of it expropriated by the State of Israel on asserted grounds of military necessity. Following a ruling of the Israeli High Court of Justice in 1979, the Government of Israel changed its policy of land confiscation on the asserted ground of military necessity and started having recourse to civil laws relating to land confiscation in place under Ottoman rule. According to these laws, land may be seized either because no one can prove ownership in accordance with the required standard of evidence or because the area in which it is situated is declared a closed military zone which farmers are prohibited from entering.

"Since 1967, the Israeli authorities have demolished thousands of Palestinian-owned structures in the [Occupied Palestinian Territory], including an estimated 2,000 houses in East Jerusalem." [According to a report by the U.N. Office for the Coordinator of Humanitarian Affairs.] During the first quarter of 2008, the Israeli authorities demolished 124 structures in the West Bank, including East Jerusalem, for lack of permits. Of those, 61 were residential buildings whose demolition caused the displacement of many Palestinians, including children. Demolition of structures and residential buildings has been a feature of the Israeli policy that has displaced Palestinians mainly in the Jordan Valley and in East Jerusalem, but also in other areas of the West Bank. The Israeli authorities justify the majority of these demolitions by claiming that the structures or buildings lack the necessary permits. The relevant Israeli authorities rarely issue building permits for Palestinians, frequently refusing them on the basis that the construction is in violation of the mandatory regional outline plans approved by the British Mandate Government of Palestine in the 1940s. Areas in East Jerusalem face the prospect of mass demolitions. Carrying out pending demolition orders would affect a combined total of more than 3,600 persons. The combined effects of the Israeli policies of expanding and establishing new settlements, the demolition of Palestinian-owned properties, including houses, the restrictive and discriminatory housing policies as well as the Wall have been described as a way of "actively pursuing the illegal annexation" of East Jerusalem.

The route of the Wall weaves between Palestinian villages and neighbourhoods and has contributed to the fragmentation of the West Bank into a series of enclaves separated from one another [. . .]. The Wall encircles settlements built around Jerusalem and within the West Bank and connects them to Israel. Eighty per cent of Israeli inhabitants of these settlements reside to the west of the Wall. The route of the Wall, which has created a demarcation, is to a great degree determined by the objective of incorporating settlements into the Israeli side and excluding Palestinians from these areas. If completed, 85 per cent of the Wall will be located inside the West Bank, and 9.5 per cent of West Bank territory, including East Jerusalem, will be cut off from the rest of the West Bank. It is estimated that 385,000 Israeli citizens in 80 settlements out of the total of 450,000 Israeli citizens in 149 settlements and 260,000 Palestinians, including in East Jerusalem, will be located between the Wall and the Green Line. In addition, approximately 125,000 Palestinians in 28 communities will be surrounded on three sides and 26,000 Palestinians in eight communities will be surrounded on four sides. A number of surveys compiled by United Nations agencies found that many Palestinian communities cut off by the Wall do not enjoy full access to emergency health services, posing severe challenges in medical emergencies and for expectant mothers. In addition, the Wall cuts off residents in closed areas from schools and universities, also having an impact on social relations and especially on traditional marriage patterns. The Wall isolates the land and water resources of a large number of Palestinians, having a negative impact on agricultural practices and on rural livelihoods.

Despite the claim by Israel that restrictions of movement within the West Bank are imposed on Palestinian residents for security purposes, most of those internal restrictions appear to have been designed to guarantee unobstructed travel to the Israeli inhabitants of the settlements. None of these restrictions applies to Israeli citizens travelling throughout the West Bank.

A two-tiered road system has been established throughout the West Bank in which main roads are reserved for the exclusive use of Israeli citizens while Palestinians are confined to a different (and inferior) road network. The Israeli-built roads in the West Bank form a network linking Israeli settlements with one another and to Israel proper. Palestinians are denied free access to approximately 1,500 km of roads within the West Bank. Travel on these roads by Palestinians is completely forbidden. Partially prohibited roads are those for which a special permit is required, while restricted roads are those on which individuals travelling on such roads who are not from the local area must have a permit.

The policy of "closure," i.e. closures of entire areas and restrictions on the movement for goods and people on the basis of alleged security threats to Israeli citizens, has been a characteristic of the Israeli control over the Gaza Strip and the West Bank since 1996 and has dramatically affected the lives of Palestinians. "Perhaps the most devastating effect of the heightened closure has been a dramatic rise in unemployment levels in the West Bank and Gaza Strip. Because the closure restricts the movement of all people (and goods) in and out of the Gaza Strip and West Bank, as well as movement within the West Bank itself, workers from these territories have been unable to reach their places of employment. According to the Palestinian Ministry of Labour, unemployment in Gaza has increased from 50 per cent to 74 per cent (and from 30 per cent to 50 per cent in the West Bank). Before the heightened closure, 22,000 Gazans (down from 80,000 in 1987) and 26,000 West Bankers had permits to work in Israel," [writes Sara Roy, senior research scholar at the Center for Middle Eastern Studies at Harvard University]. "Losses from unemployment amount to $1.04 million daily for the Gaza Strip alone—$750,000 from lost wages in Israel and $290,000 from lost wages in local sectors. The Palestinian Bureau of Statistics (PBS) estimates that from February 25 to April 4, the Gaza Strip and West Bank lost $78.3 million in wages and income." In June 2009, more than 40 United Nations and other humanitarian agencies urged Israel to lift its blockade of Gaza, where nearly everyone depends on international humanitarian assistance, and indiscriminate sanctions are affecting the entire population of 1.5 million (see also chap. V).

A number of Israeli policies and measures especially since 1996 have contributed to effectively separating Gaza from the West Bank, despite the commitments contained in the Oslo I Accord by which "the two sides view the West Bank and the Gaza Strip as a single territorial unit, whose integrity will be preserved during the interim period." The imposition of tight closures and limitations on movement has chiefly contributed to this separation. With the implementation of the "disengagement plan" and after Hamas secured control of the Gaza Strip, the imposition of an almost total closure has meant that direct contact is no longer possible with Palestinians from the West Bank. The arrest by Israel of members of the Palestinian Legislative Council and other Palestinian Authority officials has also resulted in the inability of many institutions to function properly and prevented Palestinians from the two areas to work together. In the past few years a new permit system has been imposed on Palestinians of the Gaza Strip living in the West Bank. Without such a permit they can be declared "illegal aliens." In addition, the Israeli authorities—who are in control of the population registry—have stopped updating the addresses of Palestinians who have moved from Gaza to the West Bank. The new requirement for a permit is based on a person's registered address, enabling Israel to bar Palestinians whose registered address is in Gaza from moving to the West Bank. This measure has also retroactively turned many Palestinians who already live in the West Bank into illegal residents. These policies have had a devastating impact on many families that were effectively forced to live apart or, in order to live together, move to the Gaza Strip with no possibility of returning to the West Bank. Israel has bureaucratically and logistically effectively split and separated not only Palestinians in the occupied territories and their families in Israel but also Palestinian residents of Jerusalem and those in the rest of the territory as well as Gazans and West Bankers/Jerusalemites.

Despite prohibitions under international humanitarian law (IHL), Israel has applied its domestic laws throughout the Occupied Palestinian Territory since 1967. Notably, existing planning and construction laws were annulled and replaced with military orders, and related civil powers transferred from local authorities to Israeli institutions, with ultimate discretion resting with military commanders. The application of Israeli domestic laws has resulted in institutionalized discrimination against Palestinians in the Occupied Palestinian Territory to the benefit of Jewish settlers, both Israeli citizens and others. Exclusive benefits reserved for Jews derive from the two-tiered civil status under Israel's domestic legal regime based on a "Jewish nationality," which entitles "persons of Jewish race or descendency" to superior rights and privileges, particularly in land use, housing, development, immigration and access to natural resources, as affirmed in key legislation. Administrative procedures qualify indigenous inhabitants of the Occupied Palestinian Territory as "alien persons" and, thus, prohibited from building on, or renting, large portions of land designated by the Government of Israel as "State land."

The two-tiered civil status under Israeli law, favouring "Jewish nationals" (*le'om yehudi*) over persons holding Israeli citizenship (*ezrahut*), has been a subject of concern under the International Covenant on Economic, Social and Cultural Rights, particularly those forms of discrimination carried out through Israel's parastatal agencies (World Zionist Organization/Jewish Agency, Jewish National Fund and their affiliates), which dominate land use, housing and development. The Committee on Economic, Social and Cultural Rights also has recognized that Israel's application of a "Jewish nationality" distinct from Israeli citizenship institutionalizes discrimination that disadvantages all Palestinians—in particular, refugees.

In 2007, the Committee on the Elimination of Racial Discrimination highlighted another discriminatory policy imposed by the Israeli authorities on Palestinian residents of the Occupied Palestinian Territory as well as those who are Israeli citizens (but denied a legal "nationality" status). The "Citizenship and Entry into Israel Law (Temporary Order)" of 31 May 2003 bars the possibility of granting Israeli citizenship and residence permits in Israel, including through family reunification, to residents of the Occupied Palestinian Territory. The Committee noted that such measures have a disproportionate impact on Arab Israeli citizens who marry Palestinians from the Occupied Palestinian Territory and wish to live together with their families in Israel. While noting the State party's legitimate objective of guaranteeing the safety of its citizens, the Committee expressed concern about the fact that these "temporary" measures have systematically been renewed and have been expanded to citizens of "enemy States."

Since 1967, about 750,000 Palestinians have been detained at some point by the Government of Israel, according to Palestinian human rights organizations. Currently, there are approximately 8,100 Palestinian prisoners in Israeli prisons and detention centres, roughly 550 of whom are administrative detainees. Administrative detention is detention without charge or trial, authorized by an administrative order rather than by judicial decree. The conditions of Palestinians in Israeli detention facilities have been the subject of considerable international criticism, including concerns of torture and other ill-treatment. Palestinian detainees can normally be visited only by first-degree relatives (see chapter XXI). However, following Hamas's seizure of full control in the Gaza Strip in June 2007, the Israeli authorities suspended visits from family members travelling from Gaza to Palestinian detainees in Israel, depriving more than 900 detainees of direct contact with their relatives.

[Removed: sections C and D (paragraphs 210–222)]

[Removed: Chapter III (paragraphs 223–267)]

CHAPTER IV.

APPLICABLE LAW

The Mission's mandate covers all violations of international human rights law (IHRL) and international humanitarian law (IHL) that might have been committed at any time, whether before, during or after, in the context of the military operations that were conducted in Gaza during the period from 27 December 2008 to 18 January 2009. The Mission has therefore carried out its task within the framework of general international law, in particular IHRL and IHL.

A. SELF-DETERMINATION

A fundamental element in the legal framework is the principle of self-determination of peoples, derived from the Charter of the United Nations, Article 1, accepted as constituting customary international law, and set out as a right of peoples in the two International Covenants on Human Rights (common article 1 of the International Covenant on Civil and Political Rights [ICCPR] and the International Covenant on Economic, Social and Cultural Rights [ICESCR]). The right of the Palestinian people to self-determination has been affirmed by the General Assembly and the International Court of Justice in its Advisory Opinion on the *Legal Consequences of the Construction of a Wall in the Occupied Palestinian Territory.* Self-determination has special prominence in the context of the recent events and military hostilities in the region, because they are but one episode in the long occupation of the Palestinian territory. The right to self-determination has an *erga omnes* character whereby all States have the duty to promote its realization. This is also recognized by the United Nations General Assembly, which has declared that peoples who resist forcible action depriving them of their right to self-determination have the right to seek and receive support from third parties. Those who take action amounting to military force must comply with IHL.

B. INTERNATIONAL HUMANITARIAN LAW

All parties to the armed conflict are bound by relevant rules of IHL, whether of conventional or customary character. International humanitarian law comprises principles and rules applicable to the conduct of military hostilities and provides for restraints upon the conduct of military action so as to protect civilians and those that are *hors de combat*. It also applies to situations of belligerent occupation.

Israel is a party to the four Geneva Conventions of 12 August 1949, but has not ratified their Additional Protocols I or II on the protection of victims of armed conflict. In addition, Israel is a party to the Convention on Prohibitions or Restrictions on the Use of Certain Conventional Weapons Which May be Deemed to be Excessively Injurious or to Have Indiscriminate Effects, as well as its Protocol I on Non-Detectable Fragments, both of 10 October 1980.

Many of the rules contained in the Fourth Hague Convention respecting the Laws and Customs of War on Land and the Regulations annexed to it, and the four Geneva Conventions and their Additional Protocols, are now part of customary international law. Israel's High Court of Justice has confirmed that Israel must adhere to those rules and principles reflected in the Fourth Geneva Convention, the Regulations annexed to the Fourth Hague Convention and the customary international law principles reflected in certain provisions of Additional Protocol I to the Geneva Conventions of 1949. The Government of Israel accepts that, although it is not a party to the Additional Protocol I, some of its provisions accurately reflect customary international law. Under the rules of State responsibility, Israel is responsible for any violations of international law attributable to it. Specifically, under the Fourth Geneva Convention, article 29, "the Party to a conflict in whose hands protected persons may be, is responsible for the treatment accorded to them by its agents, irrespective of any individual responsibility which may be incurred."

[Removed: paragraphs 273–275]

Israel has without doubt at all times relevant to the mandate of the Mission exercised effective control over the Gaza Strip. The Mission is of the view that the circumstances of this control establish that the Gaza Strip remains occupied by Israel. The provisions of the Fourth Geneva Convention therefore apply at all relevant times with regard to the obligations of Israel towards the population of the Gaza Strip.

Despite Israel's declared intention to relinquish its position as an occupying Power by evacuating troops and settlers from the Gaza Strip during its 2005 "disengagement," the international community continues to regard it as the occupying Power.

Given the specific geopolitical configuration of the Gaza Strip, the powers that Israel exercises from the borders enable it to determine the conditions of life within the Gaza Strip. Israel controls the border crossings (including to a significant degree the Rafah crossing to Egypt, under the terms of the Agreement on Movement and Access) and decides what and who gets in or out of the Gaza Strip. It also controls the territorial sea adjacent to the Gaza Strip and has declared a virtual blockade and limits to the fishing zone, thereby regulating economic activity in that zone. It also keeps complete control of the airspace of the Gaza Strip, inter alia, through continuous surveillance by aircraft and unmanned aviation vehicles (UAVs) or drones. It makes military incursions and from time to time hits targets within the Gaza Strip. No-go areas are declared within the Gaza Strip near the border where Israeli settlements used to be and enforced by the Israeli armed forces. Furthermore, Israel regulates the local monetary market based on the Israeli currency (the new shekel) and controls taxes and custom duties.

The ultimate authority over the Occupied Palestinian Territory still lies with Israel. Under the law and practice of occupation, the establishment by the occupying Power of a temporary administration over an occupied territory is not an essential requirement for occupation, although it could be one element among others that indicates the existence of such occupation. In fact, as shown in the case of Denmark during the Second World War, the occupier can leave in place an existing local administration or allow a new one to be installed for as long as it preserves for itself the ultimate authority. Although Israel has transferred to the Palestinian Authority a series of functions within designated zones, it has done so by agreement, through the Oslo Accords and related understandings, keeping for itself "powers and responsibilities not so transferred." When Israel unilaterally evacuated troops and settlements from the Gaza Strip, it left in place a Palestinian local administration. There is no local governing body to which full authority has been transferred. In this regard, the Mission recalls that the International Court of Justice, in its Advisory Opinion on the Legal Consequences of the Construction of a Wall in the Occupied Palestinian Territory, regards the transfer of powers and responsibilities by Israel under various agreements with the Palestine Liberation Organization (PLO) as having "done nothing" to alter the character of Israel as an occupying Power.

Although the essential elements of occupation are present in the Gaza Strip, account must be taken of the fact that inside Gaza there is a de facto local administration, which carries out the functions and responsibilities in various areas transferred to the Palestine Authority under the Oslo Accords, to the extent that it is able to do so in the light of the closures and blockade imposed by Israel.

[Removed: remainder of section B (paragraphs 281–285)]

C. INTERNATIONAL CRIMINAL LAW

International criminal law has become a necessary instrument for the enforcement of IHL and IHRL. Criminal proceedings and sanctions have a deterrent function and offer a measure of justice for the victims of violations. The international community increasingly looks to criminal justice as an effective mechanism of accountability and justice in the face of abuse and impunity. The Mission regards the rules and definitions of international criminal law as crucial to the fulfillment of its mandate to look at all violations of IHL and IHRL by all parties to the conflict.

Crimes under international law are defined in treaties and also in customary international law. Violations of fundamental humanitarian rules applicable in all types of conflict entail individual criminal responsibility under customary law. They encompass crimes against humanity, war crimes and genocide. Other crimes not necessarily committed as a war crime or crime against humanity are torture and enforced disappearance.

[Removed: paragraphs 288–290]

War crimes are serious breaches of international humanitarian law that apply to armed conflicts and entail individual criminal responsibility under treaty or customary law. War crimes can be committed in the context of armed conflicts of an international character as well as those of a non-international character. This category of crimes includes and/or overlaps with the grave breaches as defined in the four Geneva Conventions.

War crimes comprise crimes against protected persons (including wilful killing, torture or other inhuman acts, taking hostages, and collective punishments); crimes against property (including extensive destruction of property not justified

by military necessity and carried out unlawfully and wantonly, destroying or seizing property of the enemy, pillaging, and declaring abolished, suspended or inad-
missible in a court of law the rights and actions of the nationals of the hostile
party); crimes relating to the use of prohibited methods and means of warfare (including directing an attack against civilians or civilian objects, launching an attack
directed against legitimate targets if such attack causes excessive incidental civilian
casualties or damage to the environment, improper use of the protective emblems,
the use of starvation of civilians as a method of warfare, use of human shields and
acts of terror). In addition, article 8 (2) (b) (iii) of the Rome Statute defines as a
war crime the direct attack against protected personnel, installations, material,
units or vehicles involved in a humanitarian assistance or peacekeeping mission.

Crimes against humanity are crimes that shock the conscience of humanity. The
Statutes of the International Criminal Tribunal for the former Yugoslavia and of
the International Criminal Tribunal for Rwanda provided for the prosecution of
crimes against humanity. These crimes comprise murder, extermination, enslave-
ment, deportation, imprisonment, torture, rape, persecutions and other inhuman
acts when they are part of a widespread or systematic attack against any civilian
population. Although under the Statute of the International Criminal Tribunal for
the former Yugoslavia crimes against humanity must be committed in armed conflict, such a requirement is not part of the customary law definition of the crime.

D. INTERNATIONAL HUMAN RIGHTS LAW

Israel has ratified several of the most important international human rights treaties,
including the International Convention on the Elimination of All Forms of Racial
Discrimination, ICCPR, ICESCR, the Convention against Torture and Other Cruel,
Inhuman or Degrading Treatment or Punishment, the Convention on the Rights
of the Child, and the Convention on the Elimination of All Forms of Discrimination against Women.

It is now widely accepted that human rights treaties continue to apply in situations
of armed conflict. In its Advisory Opinion on the Legal Consequences of the Construction of a Wall in the Occupied Palestinian Territory, the International Court
of Justice considered that "the protection offered by human rights conventions
does not cease in case of armed conflict, save through the effect of provisions for
derogation. . . . "

[Removed: paragraphs 296–309]

To conclude, the Mission wishes to emphasize that all parties to an armed conflict have the obligation to respect the enjoyment of human rights by all.

TESTIMONY 2

Dr. Ahmad Abu Tawahina

Executive Director of the Gaza Community Mental Health Programme, explaining the psychological effects of the blockade on the people of Gaza

In fact and as I have mentioned, dealing with psychological problems that result from poverty is more difficult than dealing with mental problems related to war and violence. I recall one of the patients I treated. He's a 40-year-old man. He has a very large family. He lost his job because of the siege. His children continued to ask for their daily needs. One of his small children daily asked him for some money and the father daily answered, "I cannot, I cannot give you this money." So his child answered him one day, "So why did you bring me into this world since you cannot give me one shekel per day?" So the father went into a very severe state of depression. He tried to commit suicide twice. He was lucky because his family was following his situation up close and he was referred for treatment in the Gaza Health Programme. I started the treatment and I started with my patient talking about the best way of helping him. It was clear from the very beginning. He told me, "If you want to help me, find me a job. This will be the best treatment." I realized from the very beginning that all the techniques I have will not be useful in this situation or similar situations. The basic needs must be provided by giving job opportunities to people and, by the way, it is not sufficient to give people parcels of ready food. They have to work. . . .

PART TWO

OCCUPIED PALESTINIAN TERRITORY

The Gaza Strip
SECTION A: MILITARY OPERATIONS
SECTION B: INTERNAL VIOLENCE

The West Bank, Including East Jerusalem

CHAPTER V.

THE BLOCKADE:
INTRODUCTION AND OVERVIEW

The military operations of 28 December 2008 to 19 January 2009 and their impact cannot be fully evaluated without taking account of the context and the prevailing living conditions at the time they began. In material respects, the military hostilities were a culmination of the long process of economic and political isolation imposed on the Gaza Strip by Israel, which is generally described as a blockade. This chapter provides an overview of the blockade, while chapter XVII provides a detailed analysis of the cumulative impact of the blockade and the military operations on the people in Gaza and their human rights.

The series of economic and political measures imposed against the Gaza Strip began around February 2006 with the Hamas electoral victory in the legislative elections. This was also accompanied by the withholding of financial support for the Gaza Strip by some donor countries and actions of other countries that amounted to open or tacit support of the Israeli blockade. Hamas took over effective power in the Gaza Strip on 15 June 2007. Shortly thereafter Israel declared the Gaza Strip a "hostile territory," enacting a series of economic, social and military measures purportedly designed to isolate and strangle Hamas. These have made a deep impact on the population's living standards.

The blockade comprises measures such as the closure of border crossings, sometimes completely for a number of days, for people, goods and services, and for the provision of fuel and electricity. The closure has had severe effects on trade and general business activity, agriculture and industry in the Gaza Strip. Electricity and fuel that are provided from Israel are essential for a broad range of activities from business to education, health services, industry and agriculture. Further limits to the fishing area in the sea adjacent to the Gaza Strip were fixed and enforced by Israel, negatively impacting on fishing activities and the livelihood of the fishing community. Israel also established a buffer zone of variable and uncertain width along the border, together with a sizeable no-go area in the northern part of the Gaza Strip where some Israeli settlements used to be situated. This no-go area is in practice an enlarged buffer zone in the northern part of the Gaza Strip where people cannot go. The creation of the buffer zone has forced the relocation of a number of factories from this area closer to Gaza City, causing serious environmental concerns and potential health hazards for the population. People's movements have also been drastically restricted, with only a few businesspeople allowed to cross on a very irregular and unpredictable basis.

Because of the occupation, which created so many ties of dependence, and for other geographic, political and historical reasons, the availability of goods and services as well as the carrying-on of daily life in the Gaza Strip are highly dependent on Israel and its policies regarding the area. Food and other consumable items as well as fuel, electricity, construction materials and other items are traded from or through Israel. Israel also serves as the communication channel for the population of Gaza with the rest of the Occupied Palestinian Territory and the world, including for purposes of education and exchange programmes. There are five crossing points between Israel and the Gaza Strip: Erez (basically dedicated to the transit of people), Nahal Oz (for fuel), Karni (for grains), Kerem Shalom (for goods) and Sufa (for goods). Israeli control of these crossings has always been restrictive for the Gaza population. Since the beginning of the blockade, and particularly during and after the military operation, not only has the measure of restriction increased, but control has been exercised arbitrarily, resulting in uncertainty of access even for those items purportedly allowed entry by Israel.

Movement of people through the Erez crossing to Israel and the Rafah crossing to Egypt has been almost completely blocked. Exceptions include unpredictable and irregular permission for emergency medical evacuations, access to diplomats and international humanitarian staff and only limited access to some businesspeople.

The movement of goods has been restricted to imports of basic humanitarian supplies through the Kerem Shalom crossing point as well as to a limited quantity of fuel. The quantities of goods allowed into the Gaza Strip have not only been insufficient to meet local demands, they also exclude several items essential for the manufacturing of goods and the processing of food products, as well as many other goods that are needed. This is compounded by the unpredictable way in which crossings are managed. Neither the list of items allowed into the Gaza Strip nor the criteria for their selection are made known to the public.

Before the military operation, the blockade had resulted in a significant reduction in the number of trucks allowed through the crossings. The number of trucks is considered a fair measure of the amount of imports into or exports from the Gaza Strip. This number increased slightly during the period of calm between June and November 2008, but declined sharply again in November, due to the resumption of hostilities following the Israeli military incursion. The daily average of truckloads crossing the border in November–December 2008 was between 23 and 30, but it increased after the start of military hostilities to up to five times that number during January 2009. However, at no time was it close to what it had been prior to June 2007 or to the amount actually necessary to meet the needs of the population.

The 2005 Agreement of Movement and Access called for a daily flow of some 400 trucks in and out of Gaza by the end of 2006, which was already lower than before the second intifada, but not even that level was ever reached. Information supplied to the Mission reveals that imports into and exports from the Gaza Strip before the closure in 2007 reached a monthly average of 10,400 and 1,380 truckloads, respectively. This declined to about 2,834 truckloads of imports and no exports after the recent military operations. Immediately after the operations, there was only one isolated instance in which exports of flowers were allowed from the Gaza Strip in March 2009. Some 134 truckloads of cash crops were exported in total between June 2007 and May 2009.

In effect, economic activity in the Gaza Strip was severely affected because of the blockade. Since the military operation, the economy has almost come to a standstill. The private sector, particularly the manufacturing industry, has suffered irreparable damage.

The blockade and freeze on the movement of goods imposed by Israel have spurred a black market economy in the Gaza Strip that provides basic consumables but is unreliable and unaffordable for the majority of the people. The tunnels built under the Gaza-Egypt border have become a lifeline for the Gaza economy and the people. Increasing amounts of fuel (benzine and diesel) come through those tunnels, as well as consumables. While for the Gaza population this is a necessary means of survival in the circumstances, the black market is likely to hold back economic recovery and sustainability, even when the blockade is lifted.

The blockade has also included measures relating to access to the sea and airspace. Under the Oslo Accords, the fishing zone limit was set at 20 nautical miles. However, Israel set the limit unilaterally at 6 nautical miles and maintained this limit from October 2006 to January 2009, when it further restricted it to 3 nautical miles. The only airfield in Gaza has been closed and a project to rebuild the small airport was suspended after the seizure of power by Hamas. Israel keeps total control over Gaza's airspace.

In mid-December 2008, following an Israeli military incursion into the Gaza Strip and rockets fired into Israel by Hamas, all the crossings were totally closed for eight days. Other military or militant activities in areas near the crossings have also led to total closures over certain periods of time. Total and partial closures have significantly contributed to an emergency situation that became a full-fledged humanitarian crisis after the military operations of December 2008–January 2009. During December 2008, UNRWA had to suspend its delivery of food assistance due to the total depletion of its food stocks. Other humanitarian agencies had to reduce or postpone delivery of food and other forms of assistance. The unavailability of banknotes as a result of an Israeli prohibition also prevented humanitarian agencies from implementing "cash for work" or similar programmes over lengthy periods of time.

The implementation of the restrictive measures as part of the blockade of the Gaza Strip created not only an emergency situation but also significantly weakened the capacities of the health, water and emergency sectors in Gaza to adequately respond to a worsening situation. The impact on the local economy further reduced the resilience and coping capacities of the local population and has aggravated the effects of the war on livelihoods and living standards (see below, chap. XVII).

The Mission asked the Government of Israel to provide information in relation to the blockade on the Gaza Strip. It requested information on the criteria applied to determine which goods are or are not allowed to enter the Gaza Strip, the reasons for restricting or preventing cash and bank transfers, the reasons for imposing restrictions on the ability of Gazans to leave the Gaza Strip, including for urgent medical reasons, the reasons for the highly restrictive policy permit applied to international donors, humanitarian and human rights organizations wishing to enter the Gaza Strip, and the reasons and legal basis for establishing a limited fishing zone. No reply was received on any of these questions.

The legality of some of the measures imposed by the Government of Israel (the reduction in the supply of electricity and fuel) was the subject of a petition to the Supreme Court of Israel. The petitioners comprised a group of NGOs operating within Israel together with Palestinian citizens and groups who argued that the planned cuts in the supply of fuel and electricity were inconsistent with the obligations of Israel under the Fourth Geneva Convention relating to the protection of civilians. The Court's ruling recognizes that Israel has obligations under humanitarian law vis-à-vis the Gaza Strip under which the intended supply of fuel and electricity was considered "capable of satisfying the essential humanitarian needs of the Gaza Strip at the present." The Court, however, did not indicate what would constitute "essential humanitarian needs" and appears to have left those details for the authorities to determine.

The Mission holds the view that Israel continues to be duty-bound under the Fourth Geneva Convention and to the full extent of the means available to it to ensure the supply of foodstuff, medical and hospital items and others to meet the humanitarian needs of the population of the Gaza Strip without qualification. Furthermore, the Mission notes the information it received regarding the lack of compliance by the Government of Israel even with the minimum levels set by the Israeli Court, and in this regard observes that the Government retains wide discretion about the timing and manner of delivering fuel and electricity supplies to the Gaza Strip, and that this discretion appears to have been exercised capriciously and arbitrarily.

CHAPTER VI.

OVERVIEW OF MILITARY OPERATIONS CONDUCTED BY ISRAEL IN GAZA BETWEEN 27 DECEMBER 2008 AND 18 JANUARY 2009 AND DATA ON CASUALTIES

[Removed: paragraph 327]

[Removed: section A (paragraphs 328–332)]

B. THE PHASES OF THE HOSTILITIES

1. Air phase

The Israeli armed forces began the military operations with a week-long air attack, from 27 December 2008 until 3 January 2009. One study suggests that they had drawn up a list of 603 targets to be hit as they belonged to Hamas suspects or were part of what Israel viewed as the Hamas infrastructure. The study claims that a senior Israeli officer reported that all 603 targets had been hit before the end of the fourth day of the aerial operations in the first week. Officially, the spokesman of the Israeli forces claimed that 526 targets had been hit by 31 December 2008.

An analysis of the strikes in a report of the Palestinian Centre for Human Rights gives the following breakdown.

> IOF [Israeli occupation forces] have launched at least 300 air and sea strikes against the Gaza Strip. These strikes have targeted 37 houses; 67 security and training sites; 20 workshops; 25 public and private institutions; seven

mosques; and three educational institutions. The public institutions that have been bombarded are: the compound of ministries, the building of the Palestinian Legislative Council, the building of the cabinet in Gaza City; the buildings of the agricultural control department and the Municipality of Bani Suhaila in Khan Yunis; the buildings of Rafah Municipality and Governorate. The air strikes have targeted also four money exchange shops, a clinic, three fishing harbours, the Islamic University and two schools.

Of the incidents addressed in detail in this report, the following occurred during this phase:

- The attack on Arafat City Police Station;
- Attacks on four other police stations, one in Deir al-Balah and three in Gaza City;
- The attack on the Palestinian Legislative Council building and the Ministry of Justice;
- The attack on Gaza main prison in the al-Sarayah complex, Gaza City.

Israeli air force activities continued throughout the military operations. In total, it has been suggested that between 2,300 and 3,000 sorties were flown.

2. The air-land phase

Around 3 January 2009 Israeli ground troops entered Gaza from the north and east. One study suggests that "the war was fought largely by the Southern Command using brigade teams that operated with a high degree of independence and freedom to adapt and innovate."

One of the key initial objectives described by one soldier involved was to divide the Gaza Strip into two parts, i.e. to split and fragment it, with Nitzarim constituting the midpoint. The division therefore ran from the Karni crossing point to the coast in a south-westerly direction. After creating the split, the Israeli armed forces concentrated all of their ground forces in the north. Targets in the south were hit from the air, such as in Rafah.

At least in the initial phase it appears forces from the Givati Brigade entered from the east and approached Gaza City from the south. It is understood that forces from the Armoured Corps Brigade also operated in this area but probably at a later stage. Zeytoun, on the southern outskirts of Gaza, took the brunt of these brigade operations, with incidents of attacks on the civilian population.

It appears that those with primary responsibility in the north of Gaza, especially around Beit Lahia and al-Atatra, included forces from the Golani Brigade.

The forces focusing on the area between Gaza City and the northern section, especially in Jabaliyah, appear to have been drawn largely from the Paratrooper Brigade.

The movement into the south of Gaza City reached at least as far as Zeytoun on 3 January 2009. Some of the troops entering there on that day appear to have been brought in by helicopter rather than arriving by land. Israeli armed forces maintained a presence in Zeytoun until the final withdrawal. It is understood that the original forces that entered Zeytoun were at least partially replaced by other troops at some point, but it is not known if any of the original forces remained in the area throughout the period.

In the other brigade areas regular troops were augmented or replaced by reservists who were called up after the initial ground attacks.

Zeytoun was an area of particularly intense action by Israeli forces, yet there are almost no indications of armed resistance in the area at the time.

Among the issues of particular concern to the Mission in Zeytoun are the killings of the al-Samouni family, the mass destruction in the area, including the systematic demolition of the Sawafeary chicken farms, and the air strike that killed 22 members of the al-Daya family.

The forces in Zeytoun also appear to have been responsible for the push towards the area around Tal el-Hawa and Rimal in the south-west of Gaza City, about three kilometres from Zeytoun. The Mission has information that indicates that tanks took up positions in and around Tal el-Hawa around 4 and 5 January. Sources indicate that there was a presence there throughout the hostilities, as also evidenced by the artillery fire from around this area on 14 and 15 January on the compound of the United Nations Relief and Works Agency for Palestine Refugees in the Near East (UNRWA) and al-Quds hospital, both of which the Mission addresses in detail.

The forces responsible for the execution of the Israeli plan in the north-east of the Gaza Strip included the Golani Brigade. Among the areas of special concern in this regard are al-Atatra and Beit Lahia. Various witnesses indicate that in the past there has at times been some armed presence in the area. Information taken from websites apparently belonging to Palestinian armed groups indicates that these were areas of some resistance. The Mission heard from several witnesses about the scale of the destruction that occurred there as a result of artillery fire after the ground phase began on 3 January. Information indicates a sustained attack with aerial and artillery fire from 3 to 8 January. The Mission addresses a number of particular cases that occurred in this context, such as the alleged use of human shields, the alleged widespread mistreatment of civilians, including detentions, and transfers of large numbers to Israeli prisons in unlawful circumstances.

In the Jabaliyah area, located between Beit Lahia and Gaza City, the Mission understands that at least for part of the time there was a significant presence of the Paratrooper Brigade. At the beginning of the ground phase it is noted that an Israeli projectile struck the al-Maqadmah mosque, killing at least 15 civilians. A few days later the al-Fakhura Street incident occurred in the same area when a series of mortars fired by the Israeli armed forces killed at least 35 people.

Around 15 January the Israeli armed forces began withdrawing from their positions in the main areas described above. As they did so, there appeared to be a practice of systematically demolishing a large number of structures, including houses, water installations, such as tanks on the roofs of houses, and of agricultural land. A renewed aerial phase in Rafah was also conducted in the last few days of the military operations. Whereas the strikes in the first week appear to have been relatively selective, the last few days saw an increase in the number of strikes with several hundred targets hit, causing not only very substantial damage to buildings but also, according to some, underground structural damage.

C. DATA ON CASUALTIES DURING THE ISRAELI MILITARY OPERATIONS IN GAZA FROM 28 DECEMBER 2008 TO 17 JANUARY 2009

1. Palestinian casualties

The Mission received statistics on the fatalities of the military operations from the Gaza authorities, specifically from the Central Commission for Documentation and Pursuit of Israeli War Criminals (TAWTHEQ), as well as from PCHR, Al Mezan and B'Tselem. The first three also provided lists of all the persons killed in the military operations, with their names, sex, age, address, occupation, and place and date of the fatal attack. Another NGO, Defence for Children International–Palestine Section, provided a list of all the children killed.

The three lists give different numbers. According to TAWTHEQ, 1,444 persons were killed. The two Palestinian NGOs provide a lower number, 1,417 victims according to PCHR and 1,409 according to Al Mezan, while B'Tselem mentions 1,387 victims. The Mission has not cross-checked the three lists. TAWTHEQ, PCHR, Al Mezan and B'Tselem also provide disaggregated data.

TAWTHEQ reports that 341 of those killed were children (under 18), 248 members of the police, 11 members of the Internal Security Service and 5 members of the National Security Service. It provides no figures for the number of combatants killed.

PCHR divides the overall 1,417 victims into 926 civilians, 255 police and 236 combatants. It reports that 313 of the dead were children and 116 women.

Al Mezan reports that overall 1,409 persons were killed during the military operations, of whom 237 were combatants (including 13 under-age combatants) and 1,172 non-combatants, including 342 children, 111 women and 136 members of the police. Thus, according to PCHR and Al Mezan, fewer than 17 per cent of the Palestinians killed during the military operations were combatants.

B'Tselem states that, of the 1,387 Palestinians who were killed, 773 did not take part in the hostilities, including 320 minors and 109 women over the age of 18. Of those killed, 330 took part in the hostilities and 248 were Palestinian police officers, most of whom were killed in aerial bombings of police stations on the first day of the operations. For 36 people B'Tselem could not determine whether they had participated in the hostilities or not.

According to Defence for Children International, 348 children were killed during the military operations.

The Israeli armed forces claim that 1,166 Palestinians were killed during the military operations "according to the data gathered by the Research Department of the Israel Defense Intelligence." They allege that "709 of them are identified as Hamas terror operatives," 295 are "uninvolved Palestinians," while the remaining 162 are "men that have not yet been attributed to any organization." Of the 295 "uninvolved Palestinians," 89 were children under the age of 16 and 49 women. According to these figures, at least 60 per cent, and possibly as many as three out of four, of those killed were combatants. The Mission notes, however, that the Israeli Government has not published a list of victims or other data supporting its assertions, nor has it, to the Mission's knowledge, explained the divergence between its statistics and those published by three Palestinian sources, except insofar as the classification of policemen as combatants is concerned.

The Mission, not having investigated all incidents involving loss of life in the Gaza Strip, will not make findings regarding the overall number of persons killed nor regarding the percentage of civilians among those killed. The incidents it did investigate, and on which it will make findings based on the information it gathered, involve the death of more than 220 persons, at least 47 of them children and 19 adult women.

The Mission notes that the statistics from non-governmental sources are generally consistent. Statistics alleging that fewer than one out of five persons killed in an armed conflict was a combatant, such as those provided by PCHR and Al Mezan as a result of months of field research, raise very serious concerns about the way Israel conducted the military operations in Gaza. The counterclaims published by the Government of Israel fall far short of international law standards.

The Mission also notes that—as the Government of Israel argues at length—there are circumstances under international humanitarian law in which military actions resulting in the loss of civilian life would not be unlawful. These include attacks directed against military objectives that comply with the principles of discrimination and proportionality, but nonetheless kill civilians. They also include the killing of persons who, though not members of an armed group, participate directly in the hostilities. The reportedly exceedingly high percentage of civilians among those killed raises concerns about the precautions taken by Israel in launching attacks as well as the legality of many of the attacks, as elaborated further in this report with regard to the specific incidents investigated by the Mission.

The Mission finally notes that it cannot entirely discount the possibility that Palestinian civilians may have been killed as a result of fire by Palestinian armed groups in encounters with the Israeli armed forces, as argued in a submission to the Mission, although it has not encountered any information suggesting that this was the case.

2. Israeli casualties

The Israeli Ministry of Foreign Affairs reported that, during the military operations from 27 December 2008 to 18 January 2009, there were four Israeli casualties in southern Israel (all adults), of whom three were civilians and one was a soldier. In addition, nine Israeli soldiers were killed during the fighting inside the Gaza Strip, four of whom by friendly fire. B'Tselem confirmed these numbers, stating that during the operations Palestinians killed nine Israelis, of whom three were civilians, who were reportedly killed by Qassam and Grad rocket fire, and six members of the security forces, while another four soldiers were killed by friendly fire.

Dr. Rony Berger

Clinical psychologist, director of community services for NATAL: Israel Trauma Center for Victims of Terror and War, explaining the psychological impact of Qassam rocket attacks on the people of Sderot

Dear members of the committee, distinguished members, as I speak to you now and when I speak to you in a moment, what would happen if each of you were under threat of a Qassam rocket falling on you in a few minutes, what would you feel when you were listening to me? How could you concentrate on what I'm saying if you knew that a rocket could be falling on you at any moment? How would you function? How would you concentrate? Would you remember what had been said? This is actually the experience, the phenomenological experience of people who are in Sderot.

It's not only a matter of the number of casualties, the number of those wounded. It's the constant feeling that at any given moment a rocket can land on you or on your children and you live in constant anxiety.

How does this translate into facts? Let me begin with exposure. What do I mean by exposure? How many rockets are there? I am now writing an article and I found that over the past 3-½ years the number of rockets that have landed in Sderot itself is around 1,000; 1,000 rockets. The number of rockets that have fallen in the periphery of Gaza is around 2,885; 1,700 of a different type of rocket, warhead, have also fallen. So try to imagine a day when constantly rockets are falling and threatening your life. How does this exposure affect people subjectively? Ninety percent of people said that they had been near a rocket falling and 68 percent said that they knew someone who had been injured or wounded or killed. This is extraordinary exposure. The question is, what are the effects?

When we measured the influence of the post-traumatic disorders, and when I speak of a disorder I'm not only speaking about anxiety or sleep disorders, I'm speaking about the inability to function. I'm speaking about a whole collection of syndromes that cause you not to function as a student, as a child at school, as a worker. We find that 28.4 percent of the inhabitants of Sderot suffer from PTSD. This is a figure which can be seen as about five times the proportion of people who suffer from post-trauma elsewhere, even after the terrorist attacks in Israel as a whole. In other words, eight years of constant bombardments create five times as many inhabitants suffering from trauma and this will continue for a long time.

CHAPTER VII.

ATTACKS ON GOVERNMENT BUILDINGS AND POLICE

A. DELIBERATE ATTACKS ON GAZA GOVERNMENT INFRASTRUCTURE

1. Overview of damage to Gaza government buildings

In its early recovery and reconstruction plan for Gaza, the Palestinian Authority states that "seven government institutions were either completely or partially levelled (including the Government Palace, the Archives building, the General Personnel Council, and the Presidential Compound), and the Ministries of Interior, Justice and Culture were either partially or entirely destroyed, along with their associated compounds. In addition, 19 municipal facilities were damaged and 11 were totally destroyed, including commercial centres such as markets, slaughterhouses and stores."

2. The Israeli air strikes on the Gaza main prison and on the Palestinian Legislative Council building

The Mission visited two locations where government buildings were destroyed by Israeli air strikes: the Palestinian Legislative Council building and the main prison in the al-Sarayah complex in Gaza City. In addition, the Mission visited six police stations, which will be discussed separately below.

The Mission visited the remains of the Gaza City main prison and interviewed two senior police officers who were, according to their testimony, eyewitnesses to the attack. The Mission also reviewed reports on the attack from other sources based on the testimony of prisoners. It furthermore addressed questions to the Government of Israel regarding the military advantage pursued in attacking the

Palestinian Legislative Council building and the main prison in Gaza City, but received no reply.

The main prison was located in a densely built-up area of Gaza City in the al-Sarayah complex of buildings occupied by government departments, including the Ministries of Education, Transport and the Interior. The prison itself was an old building, several stories high, reportedly used as a prison by successive authorities in charge of Gaza during the previous and present centuries. It held both common offenders and political detainees.

While there were some discrepancies in the different accounts of this incident, the Mission was able to ascertain that the complex was attacked at 11 A.M. on 28 December 2008, on the second day of the air strikes by Israel. At the time of the attack between 200 and 300 prisoners were held in the facility, most of the almost 700 prisoners having been released in the days before the strike. The accounts given by officials regarding the number of fatalities and injured among the prisoners are contradicted by NGO reports, and the Mission heard allegations of extrajudicial executions of escaping prisoners by, or at the behest of, the Gaza authorities,* which the Mission deals with in chapter XIX. Police officials told the Mission that one prison guard was killed and several injured by the Israeli strike, as the first missile hit the guards' quarters, and that no prisoners were seriously injured. The guards had opened the prison doors immediately after the first strike. Others reported that "some prisoners were killed in the bombing, while others escaped the destroyed building." A number of prisoners injured in the attack went to al-Shifa hospital in Gaza City for treatment after escaping from the prison.

Despite the limited number of casualties that may have occurred, the high probability of more serious loss of life and of injuries in an attack on a populated prison facility could not have been discounted by the Israeli forces. The Mission has taken note of the assessment of the Israeli Air Force that 99 per cent of the strikes it carried out were accurate. In the light of this claim and in the absence of explanations to the contrary from the Israeli Government, it can only be concluded that the prison was the intended target of the strike. There is no indication from the information gathered on the incident and an inspection of the site that there was any cause for considering the prison building a "military objective."

---

* The mission uses the term "Gaza authorities" to refer to the Hamas–led authorities in Gaza since June 2007. [Eds.]

The Palestinian Legislative Council building in central Gaza City was, according to information provided by the Israeli armed forces on their official website, attacked on 31 December 2008. Mr. Ahmad Bahr, then Acting Speaker of the Palestinian Legislative Council in Gaza, stated to the Mission that it was hit by three missiles launched from fighter planes. The Mission visited the damaged assembly room. It also saw the rubble of the severely damaged three-storey building of the Parliament, which had been completed two years before. It was explained to the Mission that the new building contained a videoconferencing room which allowed the Gazan parliamentarians to hold joint sessions with the members of Parliament based in Ramallah. No casualties as a result of the strike on the Legislative Council building were reported to the Mission.

The Mission notes that the Israeli armed forces acknowledged in their "Summary of overnight events" of 1 January 2009 that:

> The IAF and Israel Naval Forces struck around 20 Hamas targets throughout the Gaza Strip during late night and early morning hours (Dec. 31).

> Among the sites targeted were:

> The buildings housing Hamas's Ministry of Justice and Legislative Assembly, both located in the Tel El-Hawwa government complex. Hamas Government sites serve as a critical component of the terrorist groups' infrastructure in Gaza.

The Israeli army spokesperson further elaborated: "The attack on strategic government objectives, which constitute part of Hamas's mechanism of control, is a direct response to the continued firing on communities in southern Israel by the Hamas terrorist organization."

3. The position of the Government of Israel

The Mission observes that the Government of Israel is not alleging that any Hamas military activity, such as launching of rockets, storage of weapons or planning of operations, was carried out in the Legislative Council building, the Ministry of Justice or the main prison. The justification of the Government of Israel for the strike on the Palestinian Legislative Council is that it is a "Hamas Government site," and that such sites "serve as a critical component of the terrorist groups' infrastructure in Gaza" and "constitute part of Hamas's mechanism of control."

This explanation posted on the Israeli armed forces' official website is integrated and elaborated on by numerous statements made by current and former senior Government officials to the media. Major Avital Leibovich, a spokesperson of the Israeli armed forces, reportedly argued that "anything affiliated with Hamas is a legitimate target." The deputy chief of staff, Maj. Gen. Dan Harel, reportedly told a meeting with heads of local authorities in southern Israel that:

> This operation is different from previous ones. We have set a high goal which we are aiming for. We are hitting not only terrorists and launchers, but also the whole Hamas government and all its wings. . . . We are hitting government buildings, production factories, security wings and more. We are demanding governmental responsibility from Hamas and are not making distinctions between the various wings. After this operation there will not be one Hamas building left standing in Gaza, and we plan to change the rules of the game.

Israeli armed forces' spokesman Captain Benjamin Rutland reportedly stated: "Our definition is that anyone who is involved with terrorism within Hamas is a valid target. This ranges from the strictly military institutions and includes the political institutions that provide the logistical funding and human resources for the terrorist arm."

Mr. Matti Steinberg, a former senior adviser to the Israeli General Security Services, argued that "Hamas's civilian infrastructure is a very, very sensitive target. If you want to put pressure on them, this is how." Less than three months before the hostilities in Gaza began, Col. Gabriel Siboni similarly argued that:

> . . . the IDF will be required to strike hard at Hamas and to refrain from the cat and mouse games of searching for Qassam rocket launchers. The IDF should not be expected to stop the rocket and missile fire against the Israeli home front through attacks on the launchers themselves, but by means of imposing a ceasefire on the enemy.

The Mission understands all these statements to imply that, in the view of their authors, in order to be effective, military operations have to be directed not only against military targets but also against the non-military infrastructure.

The Israeli Government's discussion of the "targeting of Hamas terrorist infrastructure" asserts that, "consistent with the principle of distinction, IDF forces attacked military targets directly connected to Hamas and other terrorist organizations' military activities against Israel." This statement is followed by a list of examples of objectives, such as command posts of al-Qassam Brigades, alleged weapons storage sites and training camps, rocket and mortar launch sites, and tunnels. The list also refers twice to a location identified as the office of Ismail Haniyah, "head of the Hamas administration." This list is followed, however, by a statement reiterating and elaborating the argument that there is really no distinction to be made between military and civilian objectives as far as government and public administration in Gaza are concerned:

> While Hamas operates ministries and is in charge of a variety of administrative and traditionally governmental functions in the Gaza Strip, it still remains a terrorist organization. Many of the ostensibly civilian elements of its regime are in reality active components of its terrorist and military efforts. Indeed, Hamas does not separate its civilian and military activities in the manner in which a legitimate government might. Instead, Hamas uses apparatuses under its control, including quasi-governmental institutions, to promote its terrorist activity.

[Removed: section 4 (paragraphs 380–381)]

5. Legal analysis

In assessing the Israeli strikes against the Legislative Council building and the main prison, the Mission first of all notes that Hamas is an organization with distinct political, military and social welfare components.

Since July 2007 Hamas has been the de facto government authority in Gaza. As recognized by the Israeli Government, the Hamas-led authorities in Gaza have been responsible for the civilian administration of Gaza. For instance, they employ civil servants and workers, run schools, hospitals, traffic police and the administration of justice. The fact that these institutions and the buildings housing them have been administered by authorities led by Hamas since July 2007, and no longer by a government composed of both Hamas and Fatah members, has, in the view of the Mission, no bearing on the continued civilian character of these institutions. Regarding the prison, the Mission finds the consequences of the attack aptly described in the answer to its questions received from the Gaza authorities: "As a result of this targeting, great numbers of those who were detained pending trial in criminal cases and of those convicted of major crimes such as murder escaped. This has caused disorder and chaos, encouraged 'family revenge' cases and people taking the law into their own hands." As far as the Palestinian Legislative Council building is concerned, it served representatives from all Palestinian parties who won seats in the 2006 elections (which were recognized as free and fair by international observers).

The Mission met with Gaza-based Legislative Council members belonging to Hamas, to Fatah and to the Popular Front for the Liberation of Palestine (PFLP). While Hamas constitutes the de facto authority in Gaza, the buildings attacked and destroyed served a public purpose that cannot be regarded as "promoting Hamas terrorist activity."

[Removed: paragraph 385]

The statement by the Israeli Government concerning the attack on the Legislative Council building and the Ministry of Justice does not suggest any "effective contribution to military action" that the buildings might have been making. No reference is made to any "definite military advantage" that their destruction would offer. Instead, the explanation is that government buildings constitute "part of Hamas's mechanism of control," that they "serve as a critical component of the terrorist groups' infrastructure in Gaza" and that "ostensibly civilian elements of [the Hamas] regime are in reality active components of its terrorist and military efforts."

The Mission observes that there is nothing unique in the fact that in Gaza ministries and prisons are part of the government's "mechanism of control" and that the legislature's assembly hall and administrative buildings are a critical component of the government infrastructure. That is not, however, the test applied by international humanitarian law and accepted State practice to distinguish between civilian and military objects. The Mission reviewed, for instance, the tentative list of military objectives drawn up by Major General A.P.V. Rogers, a former Director of the British Army Legal Services, and a proposed list of military objectives drawn up by the International Committee of the Red Cross (ICRC). There is nothing in this comprehensive list of military objectives that comes close to a legislative assembly's building or a prison. As far as ministries are concerned, both lists limit the definition of military objective to "war ministries."

[Removed: paragraph 388]

There is an absence of evidence or, indeed, any allegation from the Israeli Government and armed forces that the Legislative Council building, the Ministry of

Justice or the Gaza main prison "made an effective contribution to military action." On the information available to it, the Mission finds that the attacks on these buildings constituted deliberate attacks on civilian objects in violation of the rule of customary international humanitarian law whereby attacks must be strictly limited to military objectives.

[Removed: paragraph 390]

The Mission rejects the analysis of present and former senior Israeli officials that, because of the alleged nature of the Hamas government in Gaza, the distinction between civilian and military parts of the government infrastructure is no longer relevant in relation to Israel's conflict with Hamas. This analysis is accompanied, in the statements of Col. Gabriel Siboni and Mr. Matti Steinberg, by an explicit argument that Israel should "put pressure" on Hamas by targeting civilian infrastructure to attain its war aims.

The Mission is of the view that this is a dangerous argument that should be vigorously rejected as incompatible with the cardinal principle of distinction. International humanitarian law prohibits attacks against targets that do not make an effective contribution to military action. Attacks that are not directed against military (or dual-use) objectives are violations of the laws of war, no matter how promising the attacker considers them from a strategic or political point of view. As a recent academic contribution to the discussion on whether "new wars" require "new laws" has noted, "if this argument [that attacks against political, financial or psychological targets may prove more effective than those against military or dual-use objectives] was decisive, in some societies—in particular in democracies—it may be hospital maternity wards, kindergartens, religious shrines, or homes for the elderly whose destruction would most affect the willingness of the military or of the government to continue the war."

B. DELIBERATE ATTACKS ON THE GAZA POLICE

Information received by the Mission indicates that 248 members of the Gaza police were killed in the course of Israel's military operations. In other words, more than one out of every six casualties was a member of the Gaza police.

[Removed: paragraphs 394–395]

The Arafat City police headquarters and three of the five police stations visited were attacked during the first minutes of the Israeli military operations in Gaza, between 11.20 and 11.35 A.M. on 27 December [2008]. According to witnesses, the attacks were carried out primarily with bombs and missiles launched from fighter jets. Missiles launched by naval forces might also have been used.

According to the information received by the Mission from TAWTHEQ, 29 other police stations were targeted by the Israeli armed forces in addition to the five police stations visited by the Mission. Twenty-four were targeted on 27 December 2008 (mostly during the first minutes of the attack), the first day of the military operations, nine on the following day and one on 14 January 2009.

1. Information regarding the attacks on the police headquarters and police stations visited by the Mission

Arafat City police headquarters occupy a large compound in central Gaza. They are used by the civil police (shurta), one of the police forces operating in Gaza, as office space and for training courses. The Mission visited three sites in the compound in which missiles or bombs had struck. In one large yard, three missiles struck the participants of a police training course. Forty-eight policemen were killed on the spot, five more were wounded, two of whom subsequently succumbed to their injuries.

While it appears that all the policemen killed in this location were taking part in a training course, there is conflicting information on the details. Most reports by NGOs are to the effect that these were police "cadets" in the midst of a graduation ceremony. The Gaza police spokesperson, however, told the Mission that they were serving policemen, who had been taking a three-week course and who were, at the time of the strike, doing "morning sport exercise." The contents of the training course reportedly were "protocol," i.e. how to deal with representatives of foreign Governments and international delegations, and rescue operations. An obituary of one of the policemen killed, published on the website of al-Qassam Brigades, claims that he was attending "a military refreshing course."

The police gave the Mission small cube-shaped ($4\times4\times4$ mm^3 and $2\times4\times4$ mm^3) metal fragments allegedly from the missiles fired at this location. Information provided by NGOs that visited the site soon after the strike and collected samples of the munitions fragments confirm that they were found there. Laboratory analysis of the cubes establishes that they are made of tungsten.

In a second location at Arafat City police headquarters, two projectiles fired by Israeli fighter jets left two craters. No one was present in the area at the time of the strike. The third location visited by the Mission was near the north gate of the police headquarters where a projectile, most likely a missile, killed police chief Tawfiq Jabr. Reports indicate that other sites at the police headquarters, not visited by the Mission, were also targeted.

A second police training course targeted was reportedly attended by around 50 policemen. Twenty-eight of them were killed in the strike. According to the police spokesperson, the training course was designed to instruct police officers on how to deal with police officers who abused their power as well as on cultural and economic issues relevant to police work. Moreover, as the survivors were trying to flee through the western gate of the police city, they were reportedly targeted by two anti-personnel missiles, which caused deaths and injuries. While the Mission did not receive official information from the Gaza authorities on the number of policemen killed at the police headquarters on 27 December 2008, a report by an NGO submitted to the Mission states that 89 policemen died as a result of this attack.

Abbas police station in central Gaza City was, according to the station commander, hit by three missiles on 27 December 2008 at 11.35 A.M. Officials at the police station had just been informed of the attack on Arafat City police a few minutes earlier and immediate evacuation of the station had begun. Nine policemen were killed, 20 more reportedly injured. There were, according to the station commander, five detainees (common criminal suspects) in the police cells, who were released before the attack. There were members of the public going about their normal business at the police station at the time of the strike, including women and children. TAWTHEQ estimates the material damage caused by the attack at US$80,000.

The police station in the al-Tuffah neighbourhood of Gaza City, a recently completed three-storey building, was struck by three missiles around 11.30 A.M. on 27 December [2008]. Also according to the station commander, no policemen were killed, as it had been possible to evacuate the police station very rapidly after another target in the neighbourhood had been hit. Many civilian bystanders were, however, allegedly injured. The station was hit again in the course of the hostilities. TAWTHEQ estimates the material damage caused by the attack at US$150,000.

The Deir al-Balah investigative police station was attacked between 11.30 and 11.45 A.M. on 27 December 2008. According to a police officer interviewed by the

Mission, the police station was hit by a missile fired from an F-16. Other witnesses interviewed by the Mission recalled several explosions, the first of them most likely on a plot adjacent to the police station. Police officers who were inside the station at the time of the attack reported that routine police activities were taking place. Suspects were being interrogated (there were four or five persons held in the station's jail) and residents of the area were filing complaints. One police officer, Ashraf Hamadah Abu Kuwaik, was killed in the strike, and five other officers and one civilian were also injured.

The attack on the Deir al-Balah investigative police station cost the lives of six members of the public, who were in the vicinity. As a result of the explosions at the police station and of the debris, walls at the house of the al-Burdini family next to the police station collapsed, killing the 10-year-old Kamelia al-Burdini and injuring several other members of the family. At a wholesale fruit and vegetable market next to the police station on Salah ad-Din Street, where between 50 and 100 persons were trading at the time, debris from the police station killed five persons, among them Abd al-Hakim Rajab Muhammad Mansi, 32, and his son, Uday Hakim Mansi, and injured many others.

The strikes on al-Shujaeiyah and Zeytoun police stations, on 28 December 2008 and 14 January 2009, did not result in the deaths of any policemen, as after the 27 December attacks the police stations had been evacuated. In the attack on al-Shujaeiyah police station, however, two women, a man and a child, standing on the opposite side of the road, were reportedly killed by debris. TAWTHEQ estimates the material damage caused by the attacks on al-Shujaeiyah and Zeytoun police stations at US$210,000 and US$900,000, respectively.

2. Conflicting characterizations of the Gaza security forces
(a) The approach of the Government of Israel

The position of the Government of Israel is that "due to their military functions, these internal security forces were not accorded the immunity from attack generally granted to civilians." It alleges that, in May 2006, Hamas formed the Executive Force as a loyal militia, "[drawing] this paramilitary force largely from its military wing, the Izz al-Din al-Qassam Brigades, and armed the members with anti-tank missiles, mortars, machine guns and grenades. The newly recruited commanders and subordinates were not obliged to give up their military wing affiliation, and continued to operate simultaneously in both functions." It further alleges that after the June 2007 seizure of full control over Gaza, Hamas restructured the

Executive Force and subdivided it into several units, including the police, who "assumed many traditional law enforcement functions." It goes on to say that its members, however, remained members of Hamas's military wing and their weaponry continued to include machine guns and anti-tank weapons. ". . . [T]he former Executive Force continued to be closely integrated with—although not formally part of—the al-Qassam Brigades. . . . [M]any members of the internal security services also served directly in the al-Qassam Brigades." Regarding the military operations, the Israeli Government alleges that "Hamas intended to, and did, in fact, employ its internal security forces for military activities during the Gaza Operation." It further alleges that the "collective role of the Gaza 'police' as an integral part of Hamas armed forces is further evidenced by the fact that many Gaza 'policemen' were also members of the al-Qassam Brigades." To support this allegation, an Israeli Government paper shows pictures of four men killed during the military operations. Each of the men is shown in two pictures purportedly downloaded from Palestinian websites, one identifying the man as a policeman, the other as a member of al-Qassam Brigades. Finally, the paper refers to [a] . . . study of the Orient Research Group Ltd., stating that it found that "more than nine out of every ten alleged 'civilian police' were found to be armed terrorist activists and combatants directly engaged in hostilities against Israel."

(b) The approach of the Gaza authorities

The characterization of the Gaza internal security forces by the Government of Israel differs sharply from the tasks of the police as they are described on the official website of the Gaza Ministry of Interior, in orders to the police issued by the Minister of Interior which the Mission has reviewed, and in the interviews with the Director of Police and the police spokesman conducted by the Mission.

The Director of Police, Gen. Jamal al-Jarrah, also known as Abu Obeidah, stated that "the role of the police is to solve problems of the population, combat drug trafficking, arrest criminals." He reported that they are equipped with Kalashnikov firearms and batons, as the authorities have not been able to obtain other police equipment, such as tear gas and small guns. Gen. Abu Obeidah acknowledged that there were complaints about the "harsh" methods of the Gaza police, but showed pride in their success in reducing lawlessness in the Gaza Strip. This assessment was shared by many whom the Mission interviewed in the course of its investigations. The police orders and the Ministry's website similarly describe the police as a law enforcement agency. As to allegations that the police and al-Qassam

Brigades were "interchangeable," the Director of Police asserted that they were "absolutely not true."

According to the police spokesperson, during the military operations the mandate of the police was firstly to "protect the internal front," i.e. ensure that the relationship between the civilian population and the authorities stayed "intact." Secondly, the police were to monitor the distribution of humanitarian goods to the civilian population. Thirdly, they were to continue regular law enforcement duties, with a particular focus on combating looting and speculation on prices.

3. The Mission's assessment of the role and composition of the police

In order to shed some light on where the truth might lie between these two conflicting descriptions of the police, the Mission finds it necessary to examine the development of the security forces linked to Hamas after its election victory in January 2006. When Mr. Said Seyam, a senior Hamas representative, took office as the Palestinian Authority's Minister of Interior in April 2006, he found that he had little or no control over the Palestinian Authority's security forces, which were put under the control of the President of the Palestinian Authority and of officials loyal to him. On 20 April 2006, he announced the formation of a new security force reporting directly to him. This was the Security Forces Support Unit, also known as the Executive Force (al-Quwwa al-Tanfiziyya). The new security force appears to have had a double function as both a law enforcement agency and, at least potentially, a military force. It was officially charged with enforcing public security and protecting property. At the same time, he appointed Mr. Jamal Abu Samhadana, commander of the Popular Resistance Committees, as the head of the Executive Force and announced that it would be composed of 3,000 new recruits from various Palestinian armed groups, including al-Qassam Brigades. The newly appointed commander reportedly declared: "[The Executive Force] will be the nucleus of the future Palestinian army. The resistance must continue. We have only one enemy. . . . I will continue to carry the rifle and pull the trigger whenever required to defend my people. We are also a force against corruption. We are against thieves, corrupt officials and law breakers."

In August 2007, following the June 2007 Hamas seizure of full control over Gaza, the current Director of the Gaza authorities' civil police, then head of the Executive Force, Gen. Abu Obeidah, described the planned reorganization of the security services in Gaza. Executive Force members were to be integrated into the civil police. He reportedly stated that Hamas was "working hard to retrain Executive

Force members to perform police duties" and that the "Force will be in charge of chasing drug dealers and lawless residents." At the same time, he stated that "members of the Force are religious, and are resistance fighters."

In October 2007, the security services operating in Gaza were reorganized. The previous Palestinian Authority's police agencies in Gaza were merged with the Executive Force. The security forces under the control of the Ministry of Interior emerging from this reorganization comprise the Civil Police, the Civil Defence, the Internal Security (an intelligence agency) and the National Security. Their mandates, according to the Gaza authorities' Ministry of Interior's website, are differentiated.

The National Security force is given specific military tasks, such as "the protection of the State from any foreign aggression" and "responsibility for the defence of the Palestinian homeland in the face of external and internal threats." It is thus plainly a military force whose members are, under international humanitarian law, combatants. The functions of the police have been outlined above.

On 1 January 2009, during the Israeli military operations in Gaza, the police spokesperson, Mr. Islam Shahwan, informed the media that the police commanders had managed to hold three meetings at secret locations since the beginning of the armed operations. He added that "an action plan has been put forward, and we have conducted an assessment of the situation and a general alert has been declared by the police and among the security forces in case of any emergency or a ground invasion. Police officers received clear orders from the leadership to face the enemy, if the Gaza Strip were to be invaded." Confirming to the Mission that he had been correctly quoted, Mr. Shahwan stated that the instructions given at that meeting were to the effect that in the event of a ground invasion, and particularly if the Israeli armed forces were to enter urban settlements in Gaza, the police was to continue its work of ensuring that basic foodstuffs reached the population, of directing the population to safe places, and of upholding public order in the face of the invasion. Mr. Shahwan further stated that not a single policeman had been killed in combat during the armed operations, proving that the instructions had been strictly obeyed by the policemen.

The Mission notes that there are no allegations that the police as an organized force took part in combat during the armed operations. On the basis of the information provided by the Gaza authorities and of the above-mentioned study of the

Orient Research Group Ltd., it would appear that 75 per cent of its members killed in the course of the military operations died as a result of the air strikes carried out during the first minutes of the Israeli attack. These men had not engaged in combat with the Israeli armed forces.

The Mission also notes that while the then commander of the Executive Forces and now Director of Police did reportedly say in August 2007 that members of the Executive Force were "resistance fighters," he stressed in the same interview the authorities' intention to develop it into a law enforcement force. The Mission notes that a situation in which a recently constituted civilian police force integrates former members of armed groups would not be unique to Gaza. That prior membership in itself would not be sufficient to establish that the police in Gaza is a part of al-Qassam Brigades or other armed groups.

Except for the statements of the police spokesperson, the Israeli Government has presented no other basis on which a presumption can be made against the overall civilian nature of the police in Gaza. It is true that the police and the security forces created by Hamas in Gaza may have their origins in the Executive Force. However, while the Mission would not rule out the possibility that there might be individuals in the police force who retain their links to the armed groups, it believes that the assertion on the part of the Government of Israel that "an overwhelming majority of the police forces were also members of the Hamas military wing or activists of Hamas or other terrorist organizations" appears to be an overstatement that has led to prejudicial presumptions against the nature of the police force that may not be justified.

In his meeting with the Mission, the Director of Police was very open in acknowledging that many of his men were Hamas supporters, but insisted at the same time there are others who supported other Palestinian factions. Police station commanders interviewed by the Mission stated that most of their men (70 per cent according to the estimates of one station commander, 95 per cent in another station) had joined the police after June 2007. The Mission understands that most, if not all, of the post–June 2007 recruits into the civil police will have been recruited from the Executive Force, which was strongly loyal to Hamas.

The Mission also notes, however, that in senior positions in the police, the representation of non-Hamas men appears to have been broader. The Director of Police killed on 27 December 2008, Mr. Tawfiq Jabr, was generally known as not being affiliated with Hamas. Several of the station commanders interviewed by the Mission were also not Hamas affiliates but men who had joined the Palestinian Authority's police after the Oslo Accords allowed the Palestinians to constitute their own law enforcement agencies. They had thus served in the Palestinian police in Gaza for more than 10 years before Hamas seized control of it in June 2007.

The Mission further notes that the study conducted by the Orient Research Group Ltd. names policemen killed during the attack, whom it identifies as members of Hamas, al-Qassam Brigades, other armed Palestinian groups or "terror operatives" whose affiliation is not known. In 78 out of 178 cases the policemen are alleged to be members of al-Qassam Brigades on the sole basis that they were allegedly Hamas members.

Furthermore, it appears from the response to the Mission from the Orient Research Group Ltd. describing its methodology that its information on police members' alleged affiliation with armed groups was based to a large extent on the websites of the armed groups. In this respect, the Mission is mindful of a recent report by a Palestinian human rights NGO drawing attention to the "issue of the 'adoption' of killed persons by resistance groups; i.e. declaration by a political or armed group that the person killed was one of their members. Often, when persons, including children, are killed by actions of the Israeli armed forces, political and/or armed groups 'adopt' them as 'martyrs,' placing their photographs on their websites and commending their contribution to resisting occupation. This does not mean that those persons killed were involved in resistance activities in any way. The families accept this 'adoption' of deceased family members for various reasons including the willingness of resistance groups to provide financial support to the families and pay for funeral costs of the persons killed." As the NGO concludes, "these cases require in-depth investigation on a case-by-case basis in order to determine every person's status according to his actual affiliation."

4. Factual findings
[Removed: paragraphs 424–426]

From the facts gathered by it, the Mission finds that there is insufficient information to conclude that the Gaza police as a whole had been "incorporated" into the armed forces of the Gaza authorities. The statement by the police spokesperson on 1 January 2009 (after the attacks of 27 December 2008 had been carried out) cannot, on its own, justify the assertion that the police were part and parcel of the armed forces.

The Mission could not verify the allegations of membership of armed groups of policemen. In half the cases, moreover, the allegations appear to be based merely on an equation of membership in Hamas (in itself alleged on the basis of unverifiable information) with membership in al-Qassam Brigades, which in the view of the Mission is not justified. Finally, even according to the study referred to by the Israeli Government, 34 policemen without any affiliation to Hamas or a Palestinian armed group were killed in the armed operations, the great majority of them in the bombardment of police stations on the first day of the military operations.

[Removed: paragraph 429]

5. Legal analysis
(a) The applicable rules of
international humanitarian law

The general rule of international humanitarian law is that members of law enforcement agencies are considered part of the civilian population, unless they have been incorporated into the armed forces of a party to the conflict. This principle is accepted by the Israeli Government. The obligation to distinguish at all times between the civilian population and combatants and to direct attacks only against military objectives (the principle of distinction) therefore generally prohibits attacks against members of the law enforcement agencies. In its Advisory Opinion of 8 July 1996 on the Legality of the Threat or Use of Nuclear Weapons, the International Court of Justice recognized the principle of distinction as an "intransgressible" principle of customary international law.

[Removed: paragraph 431]

(b) Conclusion
[Removed: paragraph 432]

First, as already noted above, the Mission finds that there is insufficient information to conclude that the Gaza police as a whole had been "incorporated" into the armed forces of the Gaza authorities. Accordingly, the policemen killed cannot be considered to have been combatants by virtue of their membership in the police.

Second, the Mission finds that the policemen killed on 27 December 2008 cannot be said to have been taking a direct part in hostilities. Thus, they did not lose their civilian immunity from direct attack as civilians on this ground.

Third, the Mission examined whether the attacks on the police stations could be justified on the basis that there were, allegedly, members of Palestinian armed groups among the policemen. The question would thus be one of proportionality. The principle of proportionality is reflected in Additional Protocol I, which prohibits launching attacks "which may be expected to cause incidental loss of civilian life, injury to civilians, damage to civilian objects, or a combination thereof, which would be excessive in relation to the concrete and direct military advantage anticipated."

The Mission has earlier accepted that there may be individual members of the Gaza police that were at the same time members of al-Qassam Brigades or other Palestinian armed groups and thus combatants. Even if the Israeli armed forces had reliable information that some individual members of the police were also members of armed groups, this did not deprive the whole police force of its status as a civilian law enforcement agency.

From the facts available to it, the Mission finds that the deliberate killing of 99 members of the police at the police headquarters and three police stations during the first minutes of the military operations, while they were engaged in civilian tasks inside civilian police facilities, constitutes an attack which failed to strike an acceptable balance between the direct military advantage anticipated (i.e. the killing of those policemen who may have been members of Palestinian armed groups) and the loss of civilian life (i.e. the other policemen killed and members of the public who would inevitably have been present or in the vicinity). The attacks on the Arafat City police headquarters and the Abbas Street police station, al-Tuffah police station and the Deir al-Balah investigative police station constituted disproportionate attacks in violation of customary international humanitarian law.

From the facts available to it, the Mission further believes that there has been a violation of the inherent right to life of those members of the police killed in the attacks of 27 December [2008] who were not members of armed groups by depriving them arbitrarily of their life in violation of article 6 of the International Covenant on Civil and Political Rights.

CHAPTER VIII.

OBLIGATION ON PALESTINIAN ARMED GROUPS IN GAZA TO TAKE FEASIBLE PRECAUTIONS TO PROTECT THE CIVILIAN POPULATION

[Removed: paragraph 439]

In its efforts to gather more direct information on the subject, during its investigations in Gaza and in interviews with victims and witnesses of incidents and other informed individuals, the Mission raised questions regarding the conduct of Palestinian armed groups during the hostilities in Gaza. The Mission notes that those interviewed in Gaza appeared reluctant to speak about the presence of or conduct of hostilities by the Palestinian armed groups. Whatever the reasons for their reluctance, the Mission does not discount that the interviewees' reluctance may have stemmed from a fear of reprisals.

The Mission also addressed questions regarding the tactics used by Palestinian armed groups to the Gaza authorities. They responded that they had nothing to do, directly or indirectly, with al-Qassam Brigades or other armed groups and had no knowledge of their tactics. To gather first-hand information on the matter, the Mission requested a meeting with representatives of armed groups. However, the groups were not agreeable to such a meeting. The Mission, consequently, had little option but to rely upon indirect sources to a greater extent than for other parts of its investigation.

[Removed: paragraph 442]

The Mission focused on allegations that Palestinian fighters had launched attacks from within civilian areas and from protected sites (such as schools, mosques and medical units); used civilian and protected sites as bases for military activity; misused medical facilities and ambulances; stored weapons in mosques; failed to distinguish themselves from the civilian population and, in so doing, used the Gazan civilian population as a shield against Israeli attack. The Mission further sought information concerning allegations that Palestinian armed groups had booby-trapped civilian property.

The significance of these allegations is twofold. First, the alleged conduct might constitute a violation by the Palestinian armed groups of their obligation of care to prevent harm to the civilian population or the prohibition against the deliberate use of civilians to shield from military activity. Second, the Government of Israel and others argue that certain attacks by Israeli armed forces on civilian objects or protected sites were justified by the unlawful use that Palestinian armed groups made of them. In the words of a report by the Israeli armed forces on its shelling of a United Nations compound in which at least 600 Palestinian civilians had taken refuge, such attacks were "the unfortunate result of the type of warfare that Hamas forced upon the IDF, involving combat in the Gaza Strip's urban spaces and adjacent to facilities associated with international organizations."

[Removed: paragraph 445]

A. LAUNCHING ATTACKS FROM WITHIN CIVILIAN AREAS AND FROM WITHIN OR IN THE IMMEDIATE VICINITY OF PROTECTED SITES

The Mission investigated two incidents in which the Government of Israel alleged that Palestinian combatants had fired on the Israeli armed forces from within a United Nations protected site or its immediate vicinity in densely populated urban areas. In the case of the shelling in al-Fakhura Street by the Israeli armed forces on 6 January 2009 (chap. X), the Mission accepted, on the basis of information in the reports it had seen, the possibility of mortar attacks from Palestinian combatants in the vicinity of the school.

In the incident at the UNRWA compound in the neighbourhood of Rimal, in the centre of Gaza City, senior international UNRWA staff indicate that they were unaware of any sustained fire at the relevant time from anywhere in the nearby areas. In that case the Mission was unable to make a finding as to whether any combat activity was being conducted by Palestinian armed groups against the Israeli armed forces in that area at that time.

The Mission spoke with two witnesses who testified to the launching of rockets from urban areas. One witness stated seeing rockets being launched from a narrow street and from a square in Gaza City without providing further details as to when this occurred. A second witness told the Mission that rockets may have been fired from within the Sheikh Radwan neighbourhood north of Gaza City during the military operations in Gaza.

The Mission found corroboration of these witness accounts in a number of reports from international NGOs. In reports issued following Israel's military operations in Gaza, Amnesty International, the International Crisis Group and Human Rights Watch each determined that the rocket units of the Palestinian armed groups operated from within populated areas. Human Rights Watch and the International Crisis Group gathered reports from civilians about instances in which armed groups had launched or had attempted to launch rockets near residential areas. Human Rights Watch quoted a resident of northern Gaza as stating that, on 1 January 2009, residents of the area prevented Palestinian fighters, who they believed were preparing to launch rockets, from entering a garden next to the building in which they lived. The International Crisis Group interviewed a resident of Beit Lahia who stated that fighters used his land to fire rockets, which he did not dare to resist, as his father had previously been shot in the leg by a member of such an armed group when he had tried to prevent them from using his land as a rocket launching site. Amnesty International conducted interviews with residents of Gaza who stated that they had observed Palestinian fighters firing a rocket from a courtyard of a Government school in Gaza City at a time when the schools were closed. In another area of Gaza City, another resident reportedly showed an Amnesty International researcher a place from which a rocket had been launched, 50 metres from a residential building. Amnesty International also reported, however, that it had seen no evidence that rockets had been launched from residential houses or buildings while civilians were still in them.

Both the International Crisis Group and Human Rights Watch found that the practice of firing close to or within populated areas became more prevalent as the Israeli armed forces took control of the more open or outlying areas.

[Removed: paragraph 451]

In view of the information communicated to it and the material it was able to re-view, the Mission believes that there are indications that Palestinian armed groups launched rockets from urban areas. In those instances in which Palestinian armed groups did indeed fire rockets or mortars from urban areas the question remains whether this was done with the specific intent of shielding the combatants from counter-attack. The Mission has not been able to obtain any direct evidence on this question; nor do reports from other observers provide a clear answer.

According to the International Crisis Group, for instance, a fighter for Islamic Jihad stated in an interview that "the most important thing is achieving our military goals. We stay away from the houses if we can, but that's often impossible," which suggests the absence of intent. The same NGO also reports an interview with three Palestinian combatants in January 2009 in which the fighters reportedly stated that rockets and mortars were launched in close proximity to homes and alleyways "in the hope that nearby civilians would deter Israel from responding."

[Removed: paragraphs 454–455]

The Mission received a submission from a colonel of the reserve of the Israeli armed forces that seeks to illuminate the "combat principles" of Palestinian armed groups. His report is based on material published by Palestinian armed groups on their websites. The report describes alleged tactics such as "seizing houses as mil-itary positions for the purpose of staging ambushes against IDF forces" and "de-ploying explosive charges of various types (IEDs, penetrating, bounding, anti personnel etc.) in the vicinity of residences and detonating them," "booby-trapping houses . . . and detonating the charges," and "conducting fighting and sniper fire at IDF forces operating in the built-up areas."

This submission provides useful information. It tends to show, for instance, that ground engagements between Israeli forces and Palestinian armed groups were most intense in areas of mixed urban-rural character on the outskirts of Gaza City, Jabaliyah and Beit Lahia.

The Mission notes, however, that the one incident described in the submission which it has investigated itself illustrates the unreliability of some of the sources the report relies on. In this incident, the source claimed that three Palestinian com-batants had laid an ambush in a house in Izbat Abd Rabbo, hurled explosives at the Israeli armed forces and managed to drag a wounded Israeli soldier into the house. From the facts it has itself gathered, the Mission can exclude that in this incident the Palestinian combatants managed to capture an Israeli soldier. This example suggests that some websites of Palestinian armed groups might magnify the extent to which Palestinians successfully attacked Israeli forces in urban areas.

Other sources reviewed by the Mission confirm scepticism about the intensity of attacks on the Israeli armed forces by Palestinian armed groups in built-up areas. The Mission notes that a thread running through many of the Israeli soldiers' testimonies collected by the Israeli NGO Breaking the Silence is that they had no encounters with Palestinian combatants. According to another NGO report, "Hamas fighters plainly were frustrated by their inability to engage in street battles." Generally, the Mission received relatively few reports of actual crossfire between the Israeli armed forces and Palestinian armed groups. This would also appear to be reflected in the low number of Israeli soldiers killed or injured during the ground offensive. The Mission also notes that in none of the incidents it investigated was there any indication that civilians were killed in crossfire between Palestinian armed groups and the Israeli armed forces.

While the Mission is unable to form an opinion on the exact nature or the intensity of combat activities carried out by the armed groups in urban residential areas that would have placed the civilian population and civilian objects at risk of attack, their presence in these areas as combatants is established from the information that has come to the attention of the Mission.

B. BOOBY-TRAPPING OF CIVILIAN HOUSES

In chapter XIV the Mission will report on different incidents in which witnesses have described the circumstances in which they had been used by the Israeli armed forces during house searches and forced at gunpoint to enter houses ahead of the Israeli soldiers. These witnesses testified that they had been used in this way to enter several houses. None of them encountered a booby trap or other improvised explosive devices during the house searches. The Mission is also mindful of other incidents it has investigated that involved entry into civilian houses by Israeli soldiers in different areas in Gaza. None of these incidents showed the use of booby traps.

The Mission, however, recalls the allegations levelled in the reports that it has reviewed. The Government of Israel alleges that Hamas planted booby traps in "homes, roads, schools and even entire neighbourhoods." It adds, "in essence, the Hamas strategy was to transform the urban areas of the Gaza Strip into a massive death trap for IDF forces, in gross disregard for the safety of the civilian population." The Mission notes that the existence of booby-trapped houses is mentioned in testimonies of Israeli soldiers collected by Breaking the Silence. One soldier recounts witnessing the detonation of a powerful explosion inside a house as a bulldozer approached it. A second soldier stated "many explosive charges were found, they also blew up, no one was hurt. Tank Corps or Corps of Engineers units blew them up. Usually they did not explode because most of the ones we found were wired and had to be detonated, but whoever was supposed to detonate them had run off. It was live, however, ready. . . . " Also the reports published by Palestinian armed groups, on which the submission to the Mission on the tactics of Palestinian combatants by the Jerusalem Center for Public Affairs is based, suggest that booby-trapped civilian houses were a frequently used tactic. According to the Israeli Government, "because roads and buildings were often mined, IDF forces had to target them to protect themselves."

While, in the light of the above reports, the Mission does not discount the use of booby traps by the Palestinian armed groups, it has no basis to conclude that civilian lives were put at risk, as none of the reports record the presence of civilians in or near the houses in which booby traps are alleged to have been set.

C. USE OF MOSQUES TO LAUNCH ATTACKS AGAINST THE ISRAELI ARMED FORCES OR TO STORE WEAPONS

The Israeli Government alleges that "Hamas abused the protection accorded to places of worship, making a practice of storing weapons in mosques." This assertion is supported by pictures of Israeli soldiers in a room amid weaponry, including anti-tank weapons, which are alleged to have been taken upon discovery of a weapons cache in a Jabaliyah mosque during the military operations. The Mission notes that Israeli soldiers speaking at the Rabin Academy "Fighters' Talk" recount coming under fire from Palestinian combatants positioned in a mosque.

Although the Mission was not able to investigate the allegation of the use of mosques generally by Palestinian groups for storing weapons, it did investigate the incident of a missile attack by the Israeli armed forces against al-Maqadmah mosque on the outskirts of Jabaliyah camp, in which at least 15 people were killed and 40 injured on 3 January 2009 (see chap. XI). The Mission found no evidence that this mosque was used for the storage of weapons or any military activity by Palestinian armed groups. As far as this mosque is concerned, therefore, the Mission found no basis for such an allegation. However, the Mission is unable to make a determination regarding the allegation in general nor with respect to any other mosque that was attacked by the Israeli armed forces during the military operations.

D. MISUSE OF MEDICAL FACILITIES AND AMBULANCES
1. Use of hospitals for military purposes
The Government of Israel alleges that

> Hamas systematically used medical facilities, vehicles and uniforms as cover for terrorist operations, in clear violation of the Law of Armed Conflict. This included the extensive use of ambulances bearing the protective emblems of the Red Cross and Crescent . . . and the use of hospitals and medical infrastructure such as headquarters, situation rooms, command centres and hiding places.

As described in detail in chapter IX, the Mission investigated the attacks against al-Quds hospital in Tal el-Hawa, one of the hospitals which were allegedly used for military purposes by Palestinian armed groups. This hospital was directly hit by white phosphorous shells and at least one high explosive shell on 15 January 2009. The Mission conducted extensive interviews with al-Quds hospital staff and others who were in the area at the time of the attack and concluded that it was unlikely that there was any armed presence in any of the hospital buildings at that time. The Mission also investigated the attacks against al-Wafa hospital in eastern Gaza City. As in the case of al-Quds hospital, after hearing credible testimony from doctors at that hospital, the Mission excluded the possibility that there were combatants inside the hospital at the time of the attack. However, the Mission did not make any findings with respect to the possible presence of Palestinian combatants in the surroundings of the hospital.

In its report, the Government of Israel states that Hamas used two units and a ground-floor wing of al-Shifa hospital, the largest in the Gaza Strip, as a military base. As its sources, it cites an interview with a "Hamas activist" captured by Israel and an Italian newspaper article, which in turn bases this assertion on a single anonymous source. The Mission did not investigate the case of al-Shifa hospital and is not in a position to make any finding with regard to these allegations.

On the basis of the investigations it has conducted, the Mission did not find any evidence to support the allegations made by the Israeli Government.

2. Ambulances

The Government of Israel alleges that "Hamas made particular use of ambulances, which frequently served as an escape route out of a heated battle with IDF forces."

The Mission investigated cases in which ambulances were denied access to wounded Palestinians. Three cases in particular are described in chapter XI: the attempts of the Palestinian Red Crescent Society (PRCS) to evacuate the wounded from the al-Samouni neighbourhood south of Gaza City after the attack on the house of Ateya al-Samouni and after the shelling of the house of Wa'el al-Samouni; the attempt of an ambulance driver to rescue the daughters of Khaled and Kawthar Abd Rabbo in Izbat Abd Rabbo; and the attempt of an ambulance driver to evacuate Rouhiyah al-Najjar after she had been hit by an Israeli sniper. In all three cases the Mission found, on the facts it gathered, that the Israeli armed forces must have known that there were no combatants among the people to be rescued or in the immediate vicinity.

The Mission is aware of an interview reportedly given by an ambulance driver to an Australian newspaper, in which he describes how Palestinian combatants unsuccessfully tried to force him to evacuate them from a house in which they were apparently trapped. The same driver reportedly told the journalist that "Hamas made several attempts to hijack the ambulance fleet of al-Quds Hospital." He also describes how the PRCS ambulance teams managed to avert this misuse of ambulances. According to this report, relied on by the Israeli Government, the attempts of Palestinian combatants to exploit ambulances as shields for military operations were not successful in the face of the courageous resistance of the PRCS staff members.

This is consistent with the statements of representatives of the Palestinian Red Crescent Society in Gaza who, in interviews with the Mission, denied that their ambulances were used at any time by Palestinian combatants. Finally, in a submission to the Mission, Magen David Adom (MDA) stated that "there was no use of PRCS ambulances for the transport of weapons or ammunition . . . [and] there was no misuse of the emblem by PRCS."

While it is not possible to say that no attempts were ever made by any armed groups to use ambulances during the military operations, the Mission has substantial material from the investigations it conducted and the enquiries it made to convince it that, if any ambulances were used by Palestinian armed groups, it would have been the exception, not the rule. None of the ambulance drivers that were directly interviewed by the Mission reported any attempt by the armed groups to use the ambulances for any ulterior purpose. Moreover, of the ambulance staff members and their volunteer assistants that were killed or injured in the course of their duties, none was a member of any armed groups, so far as the Mission is aware.

E. FORCING CIVILIANS TO REMAIN IN AN AREA FOR THE SPECIFIC PURPOSE OF SHELTERING THAT AREA OR FORCES IN THAT AREA FROM ATTACK

As discussed in more detail in other parts of the report, the Mission asked numerous witnesses in Gaza why they had stayed in their homes in spite of the shelling, bombing and Israeli ground invasion. They stated that they had decided to stay put either because they had experienced previous incursions and, based on past experience, did not think they would be at risk as long as they remained indoors or because they had no safe place to go. In addition, some witnesses stated that they had chosen to stay because they wished to watch over their homes and property. The Mission did not find any evidence of civilians being forced to remain in their houses by Palestinian armed groups.

The Mission's attention has been drawn to a well-known incident in which women and children followed calls to gather on the roof of the house of a Palestinian man who had been informed by the Israeli authorities that his house would be targeted. This incident has been documented in video footage in the public domain and is referred to in submissions received by the Mission as evidence of the use of human shields. The Mission notes, however, that the incident occurred in 2007. No such incidents are alleged by the Israeli Government with regard to the military operations that began on 27 December 2008. The Mission received no reports of such incidents from other sources. On the contrary, in one case investigated by the Mission, a Hamas official received a phone call from the Israeli armed forces to the effect that his house would soon be targeted. He evacuated the house with his family and alerted the neighbours to the imminent threat so that they, too, were able to leave their homes before the missile did indeed strike.

The Mission is also aware of the public statement by Mr. Fathi Hammad, a Hamas member of the Palestinian Legislative Council, on 29 February 2009, which is adduced as evidence of Hamas's use of human shields. Mr. Hammad reportedly stated that

> . . . the Palestinian people has developed its [methods] of death seeking. For the Palestinian people, death became an industry, at which women excel and so do all people on this land: the elderly excel, the mujahideen excel and the children excel. Accordingly, [Hamas] created a human shield of women, children, the elderly and the mujahideen, against the Zionist bombing machine.

Although the Mission finds this statement morally repugnant, it does not consider it to constitute evidence that Hamas forced Palestinian civilians to shield military objectives against attack. The Government of Israel has not identified any such cases.

F. MINGLING WITH THE CIVILIAN POPULATION TO SHIELD COMBATANTS AGAINST ATTACK

When military operations take place in areas in which civilians are present, the importance of military dress and distinctive signs to distinguish combatants from civilians is all the greater. The Mission notes that only one of the incidents it investigated clearly involved the presence of Palestinian combatants. In that incident, the witness told the Mission that three fighters trapped in his neighbour's house were "wearing military camouflage and headbands of the al-Qassam Brigades."

Reports on the military operations by NGOs suggest that in general members of Palestinian armed groups did not wear military uniforms. One report states that after the destruction caused by the Israeli air strikes at the start of the military operations, members of al-Qassam Brigades abandoned military dress and patrolled streets "in civilian clothes." A second report states that members of the Palestinian armed groups "also mixed with the civilian population, although this would be difficult to avoid in the small and overcrowded Gaza Strip, and there is no evidence that they did so with the intent of shielding themselves."

Finally, on this issue, it is relevant to mention that the Israeli Government has produced no visual or other evidence to support its allegation that Palestinian combatants "mingle routinely with civilians in order to cover their movements."

[Removed: sections G and H (paragraphs 482–498)]

CHAPTER IX.

OBLIGATION ON ISRAEL TO TAKE FEASIBLE PRECAUTIONS TO PROTECT CIVILIAN POPULATION AND CIVILIAN OBJECTS IN GAZA

This chapter focuses on incidents where the Mission considered compliance by Israel with its obligations under the Fourth Geneva Convention and customary rules of international law in relation to taking feasible precautions. In particular, it considers whether everything feasible was done to verify that objectives to be attacked were neither civilians nor civilian objects and were not subject to special protection, whether all feasible precautions were taken in respect of the choice of weapons used and whether the military advantage sought was excessive in relation to the expected loss of civilian life or civilian objects. Before entering into specific incidents, it considers the obligation to provide warnings in relation to attacks.

A. WARNINGS

The Israeli Government has stated that it took the following steps to warn the civilian population of Gaza:

- The Israeli armed forces made 20,000 calls on 27 December and 10,000 on 29 December 2008;
- 300,000 warning notes were dropped over the whole of the Gaza Strip on 28 December;
- 80,000 leaflets were dropped in Rafah on 29 December;

- In the context of the beginning of ground operations on 3 January, 300,000 leaflets were dropped in the entire Gaza Strip, especially in the northern and eastern parts;
- On 5 January, 300,000 leaflets were dropped in Gaza City, Khan Yunis and Rafah;
- In total some 165,000 telephone calls were made throughout the military operations;
- In total some 2,500,000 leaflets were dropped.

In addition to these measures, the Israeli Ministry of Foreign Affairs explains that the telephone calls were both direct calls and pre-recorded messages, that it made radio broadcasts, and that it developed a practice of dropping apparently light explosives on rooftops (referred to by some as "roof-knocking").

[Removed: paragraph 502]

1. Telephone calls

The Mission received first-hand information about some of these methods in its interviews with witnesses in Gaza. In the report on the attack at al-Fakhura Street junction (see chap. X), the Mission notes the credible account of Mr. Abu Askar of the telephone warning he received as a result of which he was able to evacuate up to 40 people from his and other houses. He received that call at around 1.45 A.M. and Israeli forces destroyed his house with a missile strike seven minutes later.

The Mission is also aware of circumstances in which telephone warnings may have caused fear and confusion. El-Bader Flour Mill Co. (see chap. XIII) received two recorded messages indicating the mill was to be destroyed, but neither of these was acted upon. Five days later the mill was struck in the early hours of the morning with no warning whatsoever. The owners of the business and their staff suffered anxiety by having to evacuate the premises on two occasions as a result of receiving such messages when no strikes took place.

Israel's Ministry of Foreign Affairs states that more than 165,000 telephone calls were made issuing warnings. The Mission has received information that there were at least two types of telephone calls. One was a direct and specific warning, as was received by Mr. Abu Askar. The other was a more generic, recorded message, such as the type received by el-Bader Flour Mill. The Mission does not know and, as far as it can determine, Israel has not indicated what proportion of the 30,000 telephone calls was pre-recorded and more generic and what proportion was specific.

2. Roof-knocking

The Israeli Government describes that in certain circumstances its armed forces fired "warning shots from light weapons that hit the roofs of the designated targets"—a practice referred to as roof-knocking. The Israeli Government indicates that this practice was used when it appeared that people had remained in their houses despite being given some previous warning. It is not clear whether this was the only circumstance in which this method was employed. The Mission heard that in the al-Daya incident the Israeli Government claims to have made such a warning shot, albeit to the wrong house. The Mission also saw in the Sawafeary house (see chap. XIII) that a missile had penetrated the rear of the house on the wall near the ceiling, gone through an internal wall and exited through the wall at the front of the house near the windows. At the time (around 10 P.M. on 3 January 2009) there were several family members in the house, who happened to be lying down. The Mission cannot say what size of weapon was used on this occasion, although it was sufficiently powerful to penetrate three walls, or whether it was intended as a warning.

3. Radio broadcasts and leaflet dropping

The radio broadcasts that the Mission listened to appeared to be generic. For example, on 3 January 2009 a radio broadcast made the following points:

- Gaza residents are welcome to receive food and medical supplies, delivered via the Rafah, Karni and Kerem Shalom passages, at the UNRWA centres throughout the Gaza Strip;
- Israel calls on the population to move to city centres for its own safety.

This warning preceded the ground phase of the military operations. Its language clearly indicates that UNRWA centres should be regarded as places of safety and civilians may collect food from them.

Leaflets dropped appear to fall into a number of categories. One leaflet did not deal with attacks on a particular place but on the storage of weapons and ammunition:

To the residents of the Gaza Strip,

- The IDF will act against any movements and elements conducting terrorist activities against the residents of the State of Israel;
- The IDF will hit and destroy any building or site containing ammunition and weapons;
- As of the publication of this announcement, anyone having ammunition and/or weapons in his home is risking his life and must leave the place for the safety of his own life and that of his family;
- You have been warned.

In some areas specific warnings were sometimes given. One example of a sufficiently specific warning is that issued to the residents of Rafah:

Because your houses are used by Hamas for military equipment smuggling and storing, the Israeli Defense Forces (IDF) will attack the areas between Sea Street and till the Egyptian border. . . .

All the Residents of the following neighbourhoods: Block O—al-Barazil neighbourhood—al-Shu'ara'-Keshta-al-Salam neighbourhood should evacuate their houses till beyond Sea Street. The evacuation enters into force from now till tomorrow at 8 A.M.

For your safety and for the safety of your children, apply this notice.

4. Factual findings

Whether a warning is deemed to be effective is a complex matter depending on the facts and circumstances prevailing at the time, the availability of the means for providing the warning and the evaluation of the costs to the purported military advantage.

Israel was in a strong position to prepare and issue effective warnings. The preparations for its military operations were "extensive and thorough." Israel had intimate knowledge and sophisticated up-to-date intelligence in its planning. It had the means to use the landlines and mobile telephone networks. It had complete domination of Gaza's airspace. In terms of the practical capabilities of issuing warnings, it is perhaps difficult to imagine more propitious circumstances.

The Mission accepts that the element of surprise that was sought in the initial strikes might well have provided a degree of justification for not giving any advance notice of the time the strikes would take place or the buildings that would be struck.

(a) The question of whether civilians could be expected to respond to the warnings to leave their homes

The Mission recognizes that leaflets dropped from the air can have some direct benefit in assisting the civilian population to get out of harm's way. The effectiveness will depend on three considerations: the clarity of the message, the credibility of the threat and the possibility of those receiving the warning taking action to escape the threat.

The Mission has already cited one kind of leaflet which referred to the likelihood of attacks on locations storing weapons and ammunitions. At the beginning of the land-air phase of the operations, the Israeli armed forces also dropped leaflets and made broadcasts advising people to move towards city centres.

There had been an intense aerial campaign from 27 December 2008 until 3 January 2009 that had seen hundreds of buildings destroyed in built-up areas of city centres. Civilians not living in city centres were being asked to leave their homes to go to places that as far as they could reasonably assess were already in much more danger than they were in their own homes. In order for the warning to be effective there had to be an objective basis to believe that they would be safer elsewhere. The Mission does not consider that such an objective evaluation could reasonably have been made by civilians in the Gaza Strip.

During its meetings with people in Gaza the Mission was told on several occasions of the sense that there was "nowhere to go." The nature of the attacks in the first week had caused deep shock. The widespread attacks created a dilemma not only about where to go but about whether it was safe to leave at all.

Even if in the minds of the Israeli armed forces it would have been safer, from 3 January onwards, for civilians to go to city centres, nothing that had happened in the preceding week could lead those civilians to the same conclusion given the widespread destruction of areas and buildings. The events that occurred in those locations after 3 January appear to support the view that going to the city centres offered little guarantee of safety.

(b) Events in the city centre after
the warning to go there was issued

On 3 January 2009 the attack on al-Maqadmah mosque took place in a built-up area in central Jabaliyah. Three days after the 3 January warning was given to move to central locations and attend United Nations centres there was the Israeli mortar attack immediately outside a large United Nations shelter, killing at least 35 people in Jabaliyah at al-Fakhura Street.

Following the attack in al-Fakhura Street, the Director of Operations in Gaza of UNRWA, John Ging, stated in a press conference on 7 January 2009: "There is nowhere safe in Gaza. Everyone here is terrorized and traumatized."

On 15 January the UNRWA compound in Tal el-Hawa (Gaza City) was seriously damaged when it was struck by white phosphorous. Between 600 and 700 civilians were sheltering there at the time and were put in grave danger. The same day, the nearby al-Quds hospital was struck directly by a number of missiles, including white phosphorous shells, again putting staff and patients in great danger (see sect. C, p. 98).

The day after the UNRWA compound was hit, John Ging repeated that what had happened there had happened throughout Gaza. He said that the United Nations and the civilian population were "all in the same boat" and that nobody could be said to be safe in Gaza.

(c) The inference that those who did not
go to the city centres must be combatants

The warning to go to city centres came at the start of the ground invasion. In the Mission's view it was unreasonable to assume, in the circumstances, that civilians would indeed leave their homes. As a consequence, the conclusion that allegedly formed part of the logic of soldiers on the ground that those who had stayed put had to be combatants was wholly unwarranted. There are many reasons why people may not have responded. In several cases the Mission heard from witnesses about people who were physically disabled, too frail or deaf so that it was difficult or impossible to respond to the warning. In other cases, as outlined above, civilians who could have responded may have had legitimate reasons not to do so. The issuance of warning is one measure that should be taken wherever possible. The fact that a warning was issued does not, however, relieve a commander or his subordinates from taking all other feasible measures to distinguish between civilians and combatants.

TESTIMONY 4

Ziyad al-Deeb

University student in his final year, describing the deadly mortar attack near the UNRWA school in al-Fakhura Street on January 6, 2009

Let me first start by describing the house. We have two floors—one ground floor and first floor, and most of the family members were in the patio of the house where everybody gathers. There was about 16 of them at that time. And at 3:30 we were together, including my father, the women and the children and my grandma. And everybody was actually in a joyful mood. And there was bombardment near us. So we were trying to solace each other and to support each other.

And at that moment we felt, somehow, relative security because of the togetherness of the family. Also we felt security because we were just near the UNRWA school, because the people who witnessed the land incursion which was about [a] few kilometers from our house, some of them were in a real condition of fear. But we felt more secure being closer to the school.

And all of a sudden we heard the explosion and that was the impact of an explosion very close to the wall of our house. So panic gripped us all, because of the closeness of the explosion. And at that time there was no time for us to think. And before we could think what happened, another shell fell, just in the midst of our gathering. And that led to 11 martyrs that were killed instantly. And I was with them. I had my uh, both legs truncated because of the explosion. . . .

So I just waited for the fallout to rest. I waited for about five minutes. When the fallout rested, I started looking around. I looked at my own self. I found that I lost my legs and my legs were exploded away and I was sprawled over the body of my own brother. I looked for my father and the rest of my relatives. I found them motionless and most of them were killed, except for the crying of small children, of two small children.

Israeli armed forces had created the circumstances in which civilians could not reasonably believe the city centres were safe. An effective warning had to make clear why, even in those circumstances, it was better for civilians to leave than to stay in their homes.

5. Israel's review

According to press reports, military sources, including representatives from the military prosecution's international law department, have agreed that more specific information, such as more accurate timetables for strikes to be carried out and escape routes, should be given in warnings. The press report goes on to say: "Fliers distributed by the IDF from now on will also be more detailed in order to make it clear to civilians that their lives are in danger and give them a chance to flee. It was also determined in the hearing that the military made multiple efforts to prevent civilian casualties in January's offensive."

The Mission cannot confirm if such press reports are accurate but notes two things. Firstly, any improvements in practice in this regard are to be welcomed. Secondly, the changes, if reported correctly, appear to address the matters that have been touched on in this section. Those were matters that could not be considered in any way as unforeseeable in the circumstances at the time the warnings were in fact issued. While improvements are welcome in this case, it would also appear to indicate that circumstances almost certainly permitted much better warnings to be given than was the case.

[Removed: sections 6 and 7 (paragraphs 526–542)]

B. UNRWA COMPOUND, GAZA CITY

The field office compound of UNRWA is situated in the southern Rimal area of Gaza City. On the morning of 15 January 2009 it came under sustained shelling from the Israeli armed forces. At least three high explosive shells and seven white phosphorous container shells struck the workshop and warehouse area of the compound, causing massive damage as a result of ensuing fires. Five of the shells exploded in the compound including all three high explosive shells. Two complete container shells of white phosphorous were retrieved. Five additional white phosphorous shells were retrieved but not in their complete form. These five shells deposited large amounts of the phosphorus wedges contained in the shells into the compound, if not in fact all of the wedges. At least three shells hit the Gaza Training Centre and caused light injuries to one staff member. At the time of the attack there were between 600 and 700 civilians sheltering in the compound. The remaining shells hit the area in and around the fuel depot and workshop.

[Removed: paragraph 544]

The Mission will not here repeat all of the details of the attack that are recounted accurately in a number of other reports. It will, however, join with others in noting the bravery of two staff members in particular in dealing with the white phosphorous in close proximity to thousands of litres of fuel stored in tankers. Had the fuel depot exploded, it would have caused untold deaths and damage. The swift and courageous actions of these two people at huge personal risk may have prevented a disaster of gigantic proportions and their efforts should be so recognized.

In this particular case, the Mission's interest lay in what was known by the Israeli armed forces at the time, what steps were feasible to reduce the massive risk to civilian life and why were these steps not taken.

1. The immediate context

Shelling had been ongoing since the night of 14 January. The areas of Tal el-Hawa and southern Rimal had come under attack. There had been shelling close to the UNRWA compound at various points during the night. In the morning of 15 January staff in the UNRWA compound were instructed to remain inside as much as possible.

2. The risks

The UNRWA compound contained, among other things, a substantial fuel depot. The depot has an underground storage facility, which at the time had about 120,000 litres of fuel. Fuel tankers parked above ground had around 49,000 litres of fuel in them. In addition to the obvious and immediate risk of fire in these circumstances, the compound also stored large quantities of medical supplies, food, clothing and blankets in the warehouses.

Conservative estimates suggest that between 600 and 700 civilians were taking shelter in the compound at that time.

The principal and immediate risk was, therefore, of what might have been a catastrophic fire caused by the ignition of the fuel in the direct vicinity of the site where hundreds of civilians had sought shelter directly in response to the Israeli warnings of 3 January 2009.

3. The strikes

The Mission considers the witnesses it interviewed about this incident to be reliable and credible.

After careful analysis of the information it received, the Mission finds that the following can be established with a high degree of certainty:

Three high explosive shells hit the compound. Two landed on the Gaza Training Centre and one landed in the car park. Complete or substantial parts of seven white phosphorous container shells landed in the compound. The wedges in these container shells were either discharged totally or very substantially in the compound. One shell, which was seen directly by a senior international staff member with many years' of active military service, detonated on impact or only a very short distance from the ground.

One high explosive shell struck the Gaza Training Centre's yard and was witnessed by at least two guards and left a crater.

Two high explosive shells landed on the roof of the education building. There are two large holes in the roof and shrapnel all around.

A white phosphorous container shell struck the Project and Logistics Division Building.

One white phosphorous container shell hit the back of a vehicle in the spare parts store, coming through a wall on the south side at a high point. This is believed to have caused the fire to start in the workshop area.

One white phosphorous container shell or a substantial part thereof came through a wire fence at the top of the southern boundary of the compound near the spare parts and workshop area, causing damage to a vehicle there.

One white phosphorous container shell landed in the workshop embedding itself in the concrete.

One white phosphorous container shell or a substantial part thereof came through the roof of the painting bay.

One white phosphorous container shell or a substantial part thereof struck a manhole cover near small warehouses storing food.

One white phosphorous container shell struck near a generator on concrete ground.

Seven of the ten strikes occurred in an area smaller than a standard football pitch. The whole area, including the three other strikes on or near the Gaza Training Centre, would be no more than two football pitches.

The precise moment when each of the strikes occurred cannot be stated with certainty but all occurred between 8 A.M. and 12 noon.

4. Communications and responses

For the purposes of liaison with the Israeli authorities, the counterpart of the United Nations Department of Safety and Security (DSS) is the Coordinator of Government Activities in the Territories (COGAT). This is a unit within the Israeli Ministry of Defense. In Gaza the day-to-day liaison and coordination activity with COGAT is carried out by the Coordination and Liaison Administration (CLA), located on the Israeli side of the Erez crossing. CLA is the military unit responsible for the coordination of access to and from Gaza in connection with the facilitation of civilian and humanitarian needs. DSS at the time routinely liaised with COGAT through CLA.

From 27 December until 2 January DSS communicated with COGAT/CLA by telephone and by e-mail. The Mission is in possession of the names of the Israeli officers with whom such contact was established and maintained. In the second phase of the conflict, COGAT intervention increased and new personnel added to their capacity. Two new contacts were added to those already established.

The most comprehensive list of relevant data was forwarded to COGAT/CLA on 3 April 2008, including all United Nations installations. As of 29 December 2008 COGAT/CLA had been provided with an updated list of the coordinates of all United Nations offices, international residences and pre-identified possible emergency shelters. Throughout the military operations DSS was in almost daily communication, providing detailed information on coordinates of relevant emergency shelters and distributions centres. The Mission has been shown the relevant log of all such communications.

On the day in question DSS made at least seven phone calls to COGAT/CLA counterparts between 8.14 A.M. and 1.45 P.M. These conversations addressed, for instance, the proximity of Israeli fire, the damage done to UNRWA installations, requests that fire be redirected or withdrawn, and coordination for the removal of fuel tankers.

Despite calls beginning at 8.14 A.M., it does not appear that COGAT/CLA was able to confirm that contact had been established with the relevant brigade until 11.06 A.M.

Other information available to the Mission shows that the Deputy Director of Operations of UNRWA, who was in Jerusalem at the time, was engaged in frequent calls to senior Israeli officials. He had received a call at 9 A.M. from John Ging, the Director of Operations at UNRWA, advising him of the shelling near the compound and had been asked to demand that the shelling be stopped by calling the Israeli armed forces' Humanitarian Coordination Centre (HCC) in Tel Aviv. He made a total of 26 calls to the head of HCC or to his assistant as well as to members of COGAT/CLA. He was assured on a number of occasions by the head of HCC that shelling had stopped, but it was clear when he relayed this message back to Gaza that shelling was continuing. The Deputy Director had warned of the immediate risk to the fuel depot and those seeking shelter.

5. Weapons used

Analysis of the shells used in the strikes that hit the UNRWA compound indicates clearly that at least seven shells were white phosphorous shells, three of which were complete and four of which were very substantial components of the shells. Military experts indicate that in all probability these shells were fired from a 155 mm Howitzer.

Three other missiles were determined clearly by UNRWA military experts to have been high explosive missiles.

6. The Israeli response

On 15 January the Israeli Defence Minister, Ehud Barak, said the attack had been a "grave error" and apologized, according to the United Nations Secretary-General, who had spoken with him earlier in a meeting in Tel Aviv. The same day the Israeli Prime Minister said that it was "absolutely true that we were attacked from that place, but the consequences are very sad and we apologize for it." The Israeli Welfare and Social Services Minister made subsequent statements suggesting there had been gunfire directed at Israeli troops from adjacent premises. He said it was shrapnel from the return fire that entered the UNRWA compound, causing the blaze.

On 22 April the summary of the conclusions of the Israeli armed forces' investigations reported as follows:

> . . . [T]he IDF deployed a smoke screen in order to protect a tank force operating in the neighbourhood from Hamas anti-tank crews who had positioned themselves adjacent to the UNRWA headquarters. The smoke screen was intended to block the terrorists' field of view. Information received by the IDF shows that the smoke screen did assist in protecting the force and prevented precise anti-tank fire against IDF forces. The smoke projectiles were fired at an area a considerable distance from the UNRWA headquarters, and were not intended to cause damage to either person or property. However, it appears that fragments of the smoke projectiles did hit a warehouse located in the headquarters, causing it to catch fire.

> During the incident, claims were also made that an explosive shell or shrapnel hit the UNRWA headquarters. The investigation showed that these were shells, or shell fragments that were fired at military targets within the battle zone.

> The damage caused to the UNRWA headquarters during the fighting in the Tal el-Hawa neighbourhood is the unfortunate result of the type of warfare that Hamas forced upon the IDF, involving combat in the Gaza Strip's urban spaces and adjacent to facilities associated with international organizations. These results could not be predicted.

> Nevertheless, it is clear that the forces did not intend, at any stage, to hit a UN facility. Following UN complaints that an explosive shell had hit the headquarters, the forces were ordered to cease firing explosive shells in the region in question. Following the receipt of reports about the fire in the warehouse, all firing in the area was stopped. The entry of fire-fighting trucks to

the area was coordinated with the IDF in order to assist in extinguishing the fire.

In its report of July 2009 on the military operations, the Israeli Government explains that the "primary rationale" for firing white phosphorous was to "produce a smokescreen to protect Israeli forces from the Hamas anti-tank crews operating adjacent to the UNRWA headquarters." The report goes on to assert:

> The IDF sought to maintain a safety distance of several hundred metres from sensitive sites, including the UNRWA compound. Despite the maintenance of a safety distance, some felt wedges and other components of the projectiles apparently landed in the compound after the release of felt wedges in the air. The IDF neither anticipated [nor]intended this outcome.

The Mission has a number of observations about the conclusions of the Israeli Government. First, it does not share the circumspect or indeed understated representation of the nature and extent of the strikes in the compound. There were ten strikes: three high explosive shells landed and exploded in the compound; seven white phosphorous container shells discharged completely or very substantially in the confines of a very limited space around particularly vulnerable areas of the UNRWA compound. This is not a matter of a limited number of wedges falling inside the compound or shrapnel or parts of shells landing in the compound as the shells exploded elsewhere. It is important to emphasize that we are dealing with shells exploding or discharging inside the compound in areas where hazardous material was stored.

Secondly, the claim that this result was neither intended nor anticipated has to be reviewed carefully. In the first place the Mission affirms the result to be reviewed is not fragments and wedges landing in the compound but ten shells landing and exploding inside the compound. It is difficult to accept that the consequences were not appreciated and foreseen by the Israeli armed forces.

Those in the Israeli army who deploy white phosphorous, or indeed any artillery shells, are expertly trained to factor in the relevant complexities of targeting, including wind force and the earth's curvature. They have to know the area they are firing at, possible obstacles in hitting the target and the other environmental factors necessary to ensure an effective strike. It is also clear that, having determined that it was necessary to establish a safety distance, the presence of the

UNRWA installations was a factor present in the minds of those carrying out the shelling.

The question then becomes how specialists expertly trained in the complex issue of artillery deployment and aware of the presence of an extremely sensitive site can strike that site ten times while apparently trying to avoid it.

The Mission's scepticism that the result was not anticipated is confirmed by the fact that from around 8 A.M. on 15 January UNRWA officials began a series of calls to a number of officials explaining precisely what was going on. These calls were made to the appropriate people at COGAT/CLA as a result of prearranged coordination and further reinforced by the numerous calls by the Deputy Director of UNRWA to senior Israeli military officials in Tel Aviv.

In particular, the Israeli military officials were informed that shells had indeed struck inside the compound by the series of phone calls made by UNRWA officials.

The Mission is in possession of information that indicates a senior UNRWA official called the head of HCC in Tel Aviv and a number of his immediate subordinates several times. In particular a call was made at 10.31 A.M. by the official to the Israeli armed forces to explain that white phosphorous had landed in the compound and had set fire to the warehouse. He was told "by Tel Aviv" that the firing had stopped. To be clear, this means that by 10.30 A.M. at the latest, channels of communication had been opened between Tel Aviv and those on the ground in Gaza City responsible for the firing of the shells, albeit not necessarily directly, but sufficient to be receiving reports of what was going on from Israeli troops on the ground.

At 10.30 A.M. staff at the UNRWA compound noted five white phosphorous container shells had discharged in the confines of the compound. At 10.40 A.M. the UNRWA official was again in direct communication with Tel Aviv, explaining specifically that "the targeting is taking place in the vicinity of the workshop" and requiring that the Israeli armed forces desist immediately. In particular, he pointed out that what was required was a cessation of the firing for a sustained period of time to allow staff to bring the fire under control.

At 11.17 A.M. the same senior UNRWA official was informed in a phone call from UNRWA staff in the compound that a further two rounds had impacted "within the last ten minutes."

At 11.53 A.M., in a further telephone call, the senior UNRWA official indicated to the COGAT/CLA contact person that the firing had been unforgivable and unacceptable. He noted that efforts had been made since 9.30 A.M. to get the firing to stop and that UNRWA had been told in several calls that the firing had been ordered to be stopped at higher levels, yet it continued. The UNRWA official noted that it was incomprehensible that, with the amount of surveillance and geographic positioning system (GPS) information, the most vulnerable part of the compound had been repeatedly struck.

In all the circumstances the Mission rejects the Israeli armed forces' assertion to the effect that it was not anticipated that the shells would land in the compound. The Israeli armed forces were told what was happening. It no longer had to anticipate it. The Israeli armed forces' responses in Tel Aviv and in COGAT/CLA indicate quite clearly that they understood the nature and scale of what was happening. Their responses in particular indicate that orders had been given to stop the firing.

7. Factual and legal findings

The Mission considers that Israeli armed forces had all of the information necessary to appreciate the danger they were creating as a result of their firing at the UNRWA installations, in particular the fuel depot, and to the civilians gathered there. Orders were said to have been issued to cease firing in the vicinity of the UNRWA premises.

[Removed: paragraphs 587–588]

Even if the Israeli armed forces were under fire from anti-tank missiles from Palestinian armed groups at the time, all of the information referred to above indicates that the commanders in question did not take all feasible precautions in the choice of methods and means of warfare with a view to avoiding or, in any event, to minimizing incidental civilian casualties or civilian property damage.

The Mission is not attempting to second-guess with hindsight the decisions of commanders. The fact is that the events in question continued over a period of some three hours. In these circumstances the Israeli armed forces were not confronted by surprise fire to which they had to respond with whatever materiel was available to them at the time. If they were faced with anti-tank missiles, that was hardly something of which they had been unaware for an appreciable time.

Statements made to the Mission by senior UNRWA international staff indicate that they were unaware of any sustained fire at the relevant time from anywhere in the nearby areas. The Mission notes that official statements made on 15 January by Israel's Prime Minister had indicated with complete certainty that firing by Palestinian armed groups had occurred from within the UNRWA compound. This was later contradicted and corrected to state that the armed groups occupied positions near to but outside the compound. The Mission considers it important to record that the initial allegation was incorrect and this appears now to be accepted as such by the Israelis.

The Mission concludes that the Israeli commanders knew of the location of the UNRWA premises and indeed of the layout of the compound in terms of the most vulnerable areas and especially the fuel depot before the shelling took place around 8 A.M.

Even if the Israeli Government's position regarding the position of Palestinian armed groups is taken at face value, the Mission concludes that, given the evident threat of substantial damage to several hundred civilian lives and to civilian property in using white phosphorous in that particular line of fire, the advantage gained from using white phosphorous to screen Israeli armed forces' tanks from anti-tank fire from armed opposition groups could not be deemed proportionate.

Having been fully alerted not to the risks but to the actual consequences of the course of action, Israeli armed forces continued with precisely the same conduct as a result of which further shells hit the compound. Such conduct, in the Mission's view, reflects a reckless disregard for the consequences of the choice of the means adopted in combating the anti-tank fire the Israeli authorities claim they were facing. The decision to continue using the same means in the face of such knowledge compounds that recklessness. It deprived the UNRWA staff of the ability to contain the fires that had been caused and led to millions of dollars worth of damage that could have been avoided. It also put in danger some 700 lives, including staff and sheltering civilians.

The Mission, therefore, concludes on the basis of the information it received and in the absence of any credible refuting evidence that Israeli armed forces violated the customary international law requirement to take all feasible precautions in the choice of means and method of attack with a view to avoiding and in any event minimizing incidental loss of civilian life, injury to civilians and damage to civilian objects as reflected in article 57 (2) (a) (ii) of Additional Protocol I to the Geneva Conventions.

C. AL-QUDS HOSPITAL, TAL EL-HAWA, GAZA CITY

Al-Quds hospital belongs to the Palestinian Red Crescent Society (PRCS). It consists of three buildings facing west towards the sea and occupying the corner of Jami'at ad-Duwal al-Arabiyah Street and al-Abraj Street in the area of Tal el-Hawa. The building nearest the corner is seven storeys high. Its principal purposes were administrative and cultural rather than medical. It stored a huge quantity of PRCS archives. The middle building contains the accident and emergency treatment area as well as other offices. The building furthest from the corner is the main medical building, with operating theatres in the basement. About 200 metres eastwards on al-Abraj Street is the Palestinian Red Crescent ambulance depot. These buildings all suffered significant damage in the course of an Israeli bombardment on 15 January 2009, which included the use of white phosphorous. The attacks endangered the lives of the staff and more than 50 patients in the hospital. There was no warning given for any of the attacks.

The Mission met staff from the hospital on six separate occasions, three of them on site visits. Two extended site visits included inspections not only of the hospital premises, but also of the ambulance depot, of the damage done to apartment buildings on that street and of the area opposite the hospital to assess the damage done by fighting in that area. Three long interviews were carried out with one doctor individually, another was carried out with two doctors together and there were two group meetings with four and five doctors, respectively. The Mission also received a considerable body of photographs and digital video footage of the events of the day in question. It furthermore addressed questions to the Government of Israel regarding the use of white phosphorous munitions against al-Quds hospital and the direct military advantage pursued by their use under the circumstances, but received no reply.

The doctors with whom the Mission spoke all occupied senior positions but also witnessed the events that occurred throughout that day. The Mission was impressed with their objectivity and the genuine distress several of them showed at being unable to help or protect the sick and wounded who had come to the hospital. Throughout that day many of the staff, including the doctors, took exceptional risks to stop fire spreading, including by removing white phosphorous wedges from near diesel tanks. One doctor in particular showed remarkable courage. He left the hospital to drive an ambulance through artillery shelling as he sought to bring an eight-year-old girl to al-Shifa hospital for treatment which he was no longer able to provide in al-Quds. Having taken the girl there, he drove back to the hospital in the same conditions to continue assisting the efforts to fight the fires.

1. The facts

When the Israeli air offensive began on 27 December a government building opposite the al-Quds administrative building on al-Abraj Street was almost totally destroyed. The building had previously served as a criminal detention centre and is still referred to locally by that designation although it had recently been used for other purposes, including customs administration. The same building was reportedly struck on a number of other occasions after 27 December. When the Mission visited in June 2009, the site was completely demolished.

Diagonally opposite al-Quds hospital on Jami'at ad-Duwal al-Arabiyah Street was another building rented to the Government and used primarily for public registry functions. Today only the ground floor of the building remains. Witnesses indicate that the upper floors had been destroyed, probably by artillery fire, around 6 and 7 January.

Three senior doctors at the hospital and two residents from al-Abraj Street indicated that at some point between 3 and 6 January several tanks were stationed several hundred metres east of al-Quds hospital, visible from the ambulance depot. Throughout the days of 5, 6, 7 and 8 January there was significant artillery fire on a number of civilian apartment buildings on al-Abraj Street. On 8 January 2009 the seventh-floor apartment of Dr. Jaber Abu al-Naja was struck. His wife and son-in-law were killed immediately as they sat on the balcony of the apartment eating pastries. His wife was cut in half by the explosion and his son-in-law was thrown from the balcony onto the street below. His daughter, Ihsan, was seriously injured and taken to al-Quds hospital for treatment. Dr. Jaber Abu al-Naja is the former Ambassador of the PLO to Senegal and a well-known Fatah politician.

By 15 January the area immediately to the south of al-Quds hospital (the customs building and the registry building) had been totally or very substantially destroyed. The area to the east on al-Abraj Street had been significantly attacked by artillery fire.

By this time a large number of civilians (several hundreds) had also gathered in the hospital buildings seeking safety.

During the night of 14 January Israeli armed forces began an extended barrage of artillery fire over the area. It continued into the morning of 15 January. Between 8 and 9 A.M. doctors in the main building were in the principal meeting room when shells landed on either side of the building. They saw white phosphorous wedges burning near a container of diesel and efforts were successfully made to move those away. The initial explosions had blown out the office windows. At about the same time it became apparent that the administrative building on the corner had also been hit. The hospital building next to it has a large timber-built component. The risk of fire spreading was immense and a witness described how hospital staff, including senior doctors, all sought to break, by hand, the wooden bridge way that linked the administrative building to the hospital building to prevent the fire from spreading.

Shortly after the initial explosions and fire were observed, a tank shell directly penetrated the rear of the middle hospital building. That part of the building is made of corrugated iron and the entry point of the shell is easily detectable. The shell then penetrated the inner concrete wall of the hospital where the pharmacy was located. The pharmacy was completely destroyed as a result. An eyewitness described that, through the holes made in the corrugated iron, he observed a tank on a road between two buildings about 400 metres eastwards. Although he could not say whether it was this tank that had struck the hospital directly, it was in a direct line in relation to the entry point of the shell.

Throughout the day the hospital was unable to procure the assistance of civil defence forces or other fire-fighting support. As a result, the staff of the hospital were almost entirely consumed with the task of saving the buildings and ensuring the safety of patients.

It was not until around 4 P.M. that it was possible to coordinate an evacuation of hospital patients with the assistance of ICRC, which made clear upon arrival that it would be able to carry out this procedure only once. Those not evacuated at this point were relocated to the operating theatres of the hospital.

At around 8 P.M. another fire broke out, causing serious damage to the main hospital building. As a result of this fire it was decided to carry out a total evacuation of the remaining patients as well as a number of local residents who had sought refuge in the hospital. It was at this stage that one of the senior doctors took an eight-year-old girl who had been struck by a bullet in the jaw and was critically ill to al-Shifa hospital, where she later died. At that point he says he felt that there was very heavy fire in the area and that there appeared to be some attempts to aim directly at or near to the ambulance.

Meanwhile, 200 metres to the east in al-Abraj Street the PRCS ambulance depot had also been severely damaged. One of its principal buildings was entirely destroyed. The Mission also saw the remnants of three PRCS ambulances that had been parked at the entrance to the depot. Two had been crushed by tanks but not burned out. The other ambulance showed signs of having been struck directly in the front below the windscreen by a missile of some description and having been burned out.

The devastation caused to both the hospital buildings, including the loss of all archives in the administrative building, and the ambulance depot was immense, as was the risk to the safety of the patients.

[Removed: paragraph 611]

2. The Israeli position

[Removed: paragraph 612]

In its report of July 2009 (para. 173) the Israeli Government quotes part of an article from *Newsweek* magazine:

> One of the most notorious incidents during the war was the Jan. 15 shelling of the Palestinian Red Crescent Society buildings in the downtown Tal-al Hawa part of Gaza City, followed by a shell hitting their Al-Quds Hospital next door; the subsequent fire forced all 500 patients to be evacuated. Asked if there were any militants firing from the hospital or the Red Crescent buildings, hospital director general Dr. Khalid Judah chose his words carefully. 'I am not able to say if anyone was using the PRCS buildings [the two Palestine Red Crescent Society buildings adjacent to the hospital], but I know for a fact that no one was using the hospital.' In the Tal-al Hawa neighborhood nearby, however, Talal Safadi, an official in the leftist Palestinian People's Party, said that resistance fighters were firing from positions all around the

hospital. He shrugged that off, having a bigger beef with Hamas. 'They failed to win the battle.' Or as his fellow PPP official, Walid al Awad, put it: 'It was a mistake to give Israel the excuse to come in.'

While the Israeli Government does not comment further on the specific attack, it would appear to invoke these comments to justify the strikes on the hospital and surrounding area.

The Mission understands that the Israeli Government may consider relying on journalists' reporting as likely to be treated as more impartial than reliance on its own intelligence information. The Mission is nonetheless struck by the lack of any suggestion in Israel's report of July 2009 that there were members of armed groups present in the hospital at the time.

3. Factual findings

The Mission finds that on the morning of 15 January the hospital building and the administrative building were struck by a number of shells containing white phosphorous and by at least one high explosive shell. The fires these caused led to panic and chaos among the sick and wounded, necessitated two evacuations in extremely perilous conditions, caused huge financial losses as a result of the damage and put the lives of several hundred civilians including medical staff at very great risk.

The Mission also notes that, as a result of the conditions the attack created, the hospital was unable to provide the necessary care for an eight-year-old girl. Despite heroic attempts to save her, she died later in another hospital. The girl had been shot by an Israeli sniper. The Mission finds the Israeli armed forces responsible for her death.

On the issue of armed groups being present in the hospital buildings, the Mission does not agree that anything in the extract cited above from *Newsweek* magazine justifies the conclusion that the hospital premises were being used by armed groups. The fact that Dr. Judah spoke with certainty about matters within his knowledge cannot be presumed to mean that he believed other parts of the hospital premises were being used by armed groups. That may be journalistic gloss and is tantamount to putting words in the mouth of Dr. Judah. The comments attributed to Mr. Safadi that "resistance fighters were firing from positions all around the hospital" can mean either that people were inside the hospital firing or were in positions outside but near to the hospital. The journalist did not clarify precisely what was meant.

The Mission, having carried out over eight hours of interviews with senior and junior staff, and having sought to verify the matter with others, including journalists who were in the area at that time, has concluded that it is unlikely there was any armed presence in any of the hospital buildings at the time of the attack.

The Mission finds that no warning was given at any point of an imminent strike and at no time has the Israeli Government suggested such a warning was given.

Reviewing the scene at the time of the strikes on al-Quds hospital, it is important to bear in mind that a great deal of destruction had already occurred and that buildings with an apparent connection to the local government had been attacked and largely destroyed. As such, Israeli tanks had a relatively clear view of the area immediately to the south of the hospital. The Mission also notes that as a result of the attacks on al-Abraj Street by tanks for several days, the scope for resistance, if any, from that particular quarter had been significantly reduced.

The Mission is aware of reports that there was significant resistance from Palestinian armed groups in the Tal el-Hawa area on the night of 14 January. Information available alleges that on the night of 14 January Israeli troops had entered buildings on al-Abraj Street, used human shields to check if there was any presence of enemy combatants or explosive devices and found none. Reports do not specify the nature, scale or precise location of resistance in Tal el-Hawa. The Mission notes that in the buildings directly opposite al-Quds hospital on Jami'at ad-Duwal al-Arabiyah Street there is very little sign of damage to any of the buildings on that side of the street, and certainly nothing that compares to the damage to the buildings on al-Abraj Street.

The Mission takes into account the damage that had already occurred between 27 December and 8 January on al-Abraj and Jami'at ad-Duwal al-Arabiyah Streets, and the lack of apparent damage to the buildings directly opposite the hospital on Jami'at ad-Duwal al-Arabiyah Street. It also takes account of the sighting of at least one tank whose direct line of fire, bearing in mind that it was surrounded by tall buildings on both sides, was the hospital itself. It also notes the credible sightings of Israeli aircraft in the area at various points throughout the day. It further notes the extensive damage to the ambulance depot at the same time as the strikes on the hospital occurred and the apparently unexplainable crushing of ambulances parked outside the depot.

In the light of all these considerations, the Mission finds that there are reasonable grounds to believe that the hospital and the ambulance depot, as well as the ambulances themselves, were the object of a direct attack by the Israeli armed forces in the area at the time and that the hospital could not be described in any respect at that time as a military objective.

4. Legal findings

Article 18 of the Fourth Geneva Convention provides that civilian hospitals may in no circumstances be the object of attack but shall at all times be respected and protected by the parties to the conflict.

Article 19 provides that the protection to which civilian hospitals are entitled shall cease "only after due warning has been given, naming, in all appropriate cases, a reasonable time limit and after such warning has remained unheeded."

Even in the unlikely event that there was any armed group present on hospital premises, there is no suggestion even by the Israeli authorities that a warning was given to the hospital of an intention to strike it. As such, the Mission finds on the information before it that Israeli armed forces violated articles 18 and 19 of the Fourth Geneva Convention.

On considering the information before it, the Mission takes the view that there was intent to strike the hospital, as evidenced in particular by the high explosive artillery shell that penetrated the rear of the hospital and destroyed the pharmacy.

Even if it is suggested that there was no intent to directly strike the hospital but that Palestinian armed groups had taken up positions near al-Quds hospital, the Israeli armed forces would still have been bound to ensure that risk of death, injury or damage to the people in the hospital or the hospital itself would not be excessive in relation to the military advantage anticipated in attacking the hospital.

Taking into account the weapons used, and in particular the use of white phosphorous in and around a hospital that the Israeli armed forces knew was not only dealing with scores of injured and wounded but also giving shelter to several hundred civilians, the Mission finds, based on all the information available to it, that in directly striking the hospital and the ambulance depot the Israeli armed forces in these circumstances violated article 18 of the Fourth Geneva Convention and violated customary international law in relation to proportionality.

[Removed: section D (paragraphs 630–652)]

CHAPTER X.

INDISCRIMINATE ATTACKS BY ISRAELI ARMED FORCES RESULTING IN THE LOSS OF LIFE AND INJURY TO CIVILIANS

A. THE SHELLING IN AL-FAKHURA STREET BY ISRAELI ARMED FORCES

In the afternoon of 6 January at least four mortar bombs fired by Israeli armed forces exploded near the al-Fakhura junction in the al-Fakhura area of the Jabaliyah camp in northern Gaza.

The Mission interviewed Mr. Muhammed Fouad Abu Askar on three occasions. His brother and two sons were killed in the attack. It also met surviving members of the al-Deeb family on two occasions. The Mission interviewed four men who had lost family members in the attack, the Director of the UNRWA premises that were being used as a shelter for civilians and a number of journalists who covered the story. In addition, the Mission has seen a number of statements provided to organizations in Gaza in the form of affidavits. The Mission has also considered to the degree possible the information available from Israeli sources on the circumstances of the strike.

B. THE FACTS SURROUNDING THE ISRAELI ARMED FORCES' MORTAR SHELLING

On 5 January 2009 UNRWA had opened the elementary school on al-Fakhura Street to provide shelter to civilians fleeing the areas where the Israeli armed forces had entered.

The Mission spoke on two occasions with the Director of the shelter about its management. He said that about 90 per cent of those in the shelter had come from outside of Jabaliyah camp, largely from the al-Atatra area. He explained that the shelter was guarded by security staff at its entry points and that all people coming in were registered by name and searched to ensure no weapons were being taken into the premises.

UNRWA has confirmed to the Mission that the Israeli armed forces were fully aware that the school was being used as a shelter from 5 January 2005. UNRWA materials indicate that there were 1,368 people in the shelter at the time.

About 16 hours prior to the shelling on the afternoon of 6 January 2009, Israeli armed forces had already carried out at least one strike, destroying the house of Mr. Abu Askar. At around 1.45 A.M. on 6 January 2009, Mr. Abu Askar received a personal telephone call from the Israeli armed forces advising him that he should evacuate the house and everyone in it because it was going to be destroyed by an air strike. The building housed not only his immediate family but a large number of his extended family, about 40 in all. Mr. Abu Askar responded quickly, evacuating not only his own extended family but also advising neighbours of the imminent strike. The survivors of the al-Deeb family confirm they were advised at this time by Mr. Abu Askar of the call he had received.

The house was struck by a missile from an F-16 according to Mr. Abu Askar about seven minutes after the call was received. Several hours later, at around 6 A.M., he returned to the site of the house with members of his family hoping to retrieve some items of furniture. There he noticed that a number of other houses in the area also appeared to have been hit at some time in the intervening four hours. In the course of that day Mr. Abu Askar and members of his family took various steps to prepare the move of the family to rented accommodation nearby.

Mr. Abu Askar was in the street at around 4 P.M., when several mortars landed. He believes that there were about 150 people in the street at the time. The Director of the shelter confirmed that the street outside the school was generally busy. It had become busier than usual due to the large influx of people into the school looking for shelter. Some relatives were coming to the school to visit those who had recently arrived and new people were arriving to seek shelter, including with belongings on donkey carts.

Witnesses indicate that all of the explosions were over within around two minutes. One shell landed directly in the courtyard outside the al-Deeb house, where most of the family was gathered. Surviving family members interviewed by the Mission explained that nine members of the family were killed immediately. Ziyad Samir al-Deeb lost both legs as a result of the blast. Surviving family members and neighbours carried the dead and injured one after another to hospital. Ambulances came, but most casualties were transported in private cars. Alaa Deeb, a daughter of Mo'in Deeb, was taken to al-Shifa hospital and thereafter to Egypt, where she died of her injuries. In total, 11 members of the family died, including four women and four girls.

Apart from the shell that landed in the al-Deeb courtyard, three other shells landed in the street outside. The total spread of the four mortars was a little over 100 metres. The Mission cannot specify in which order the mortars fell, but proceeding southwards from the al-Deeb house along al-Fakhura Street, the Mission saw the impact of another mortar, 45 metres away, a third was seen a further 50 metres south and a fourth a further 10 metres south.

The three other shells that the Mission could identify as having landed at different places on al-Fakhura Street killed at least 24 people. The witnesses estimate that up to another 40 were injured by the blasts. The Mission has not been able to verify those figures, but having inspected the site and viewed the footage, it does not consider these numbers to be exaggerated.

Among those killed immediately were two sons of Mr. Abu Askar, Imad, aged 13, and Khaled Abu Askar, aged 19. Mr. Abu Askar's brother Arafat was also killed.

The Director of the UNRWA school shelter confirmed to the Mission that the blasts had damaged the part of the school building facing onto al-Fakhura Street. Up to nine people were injured. One boy of 16, who was sheltering in the school but was in the street at the time, was killed. No one inside the school was killed. He confirmed that no shell had directly hit the United Nations premises either inside or outside.

Witnesses have described the scene of chaos and carnage caused by the bombs. They indicate that people were ferried to hospitals in private cars because of the difficulties in reaching ambulance services at the time, although some ambulances did arrive.

C. THE ISRAELI POSITION

Contradictory accounts emerge from official Israeli statements. The initial position accepted that Israeli forces had struck inside the UNRWA school, claiming to be in response to Hamas fire. A later response accepted that Hamas had not been in the UNRWA school but had allegedly fired from 80 metres away from the school. Finally, the Israeli Government claimed that in fact Hamas operatives were launching mortars at Israeli armed forces for around one hour, firing every few minutes until the Israeli armed forces identified them and returned fire, killing a number of them.

On 6 January the Israeli armed forces posted the following statement on their website:

> An initial inquiry by forces on operating in the area of the incident indicates that a number of mortar shells were fired at IDF forces from within the Jebaliya school. In response to the incoming enemy fire, the forces returned mortar fire to the source.

> This is not the first time that Hamas has fired mortars and rockets from schools, in such a way deliberately using civilians as human shields in their acts of terror against Israel. This was already proven several months ago by footage from an unmanned plane showing rockets and mortars being fired from the yard of an UNRWA school.

> Again, we emphasize that this announcement is based on an initial inquiry.

> After an investigation that took place over the past hour it has been found that among the dead at the Jebaliya school were Hamas terror operatives and a mortar battery squad who were firing on IDF forces in the area. Hamas operatives Immad Abu Iskar and Hassan Abu Iskar were among terrorists identified killed.

Further statements from spokespersons for the Prime Minister, the Foreign Ministry and the Israeli armed forces all adhered to the position set out in the statement cited above. In two interviews the Prime Minister's spokesman, Mr. Regev, emphasized that he considered Hamas were mounting a cover-up in relation to the fact the senior operatives had been killed by the Israeli armed forces in its strike and in particular that two persons, Imad and Hassan Abu Askar, were "well-known members of the Hamas military machine—part of the rocket network."

[Removed: paragraph 670]

On 15 and 19 February 2009 *The Jerusalem Post* published reports quoting Colonel Moshe Levi of CLA. He indicated that the stories of 40 or more dying as a result of the attack were the result of distortions and that in fact the Israeli armed forces had killed 12 people, including nine Hamas operatives and three non-combatants. The report of 19 February lists 7 of the 12 he said were killed. He also pointed out that the Israeli surveillance footage showed only a "few stretchers were brought in to evacuate people."

On 22 April 2009 the Israeli armed forces published the results of their preliminary investigations, stating a completely different position from that previously expressed:

> Regarding the UNRWA school in Jabaliya, the Fahoura school, the investigation concluded that the IDF used minimal and proportionate retaliatory fire, using the most precise weapons available to them. Hamas made this necessary, as it fired mortar shells at Israeli forces 80 metres from the school. Additionally, it was concluded that all of the shells fired by IDF forces landed outside of the school grounds.

In July 2009 the Israeli Government stated:

> Soon after the source of fire was detected, a scouting unit was dispatched to confirm the location. Approximately 50 minutes after the mortar attack had begun, two independent sources cross-verified the location of the mortars. Only subsequent to this, and after verification of a safety margin of at least 50 metres between the target (i.e. the identified source of the mortar fire) and the UNRWA school, did the force respond to the ongoing barrage, by using the most accurate weapon available to it—120-mm mortars.

D. OTHER REPORTS

The Mission carried out nine interviews with people who were present in al-Fakhura Street, in the al-Deeb yard or in the UNRWA school. No witness stated that he had heard any firing prior to the Israeli armed forces' mortars landing. On the other hand, the Mission is aware of at least two reports that indicate local residents had heard such fire in the area.

The Mission notes that the statement of the Israeli armed forces on 22 April did not indicate where the Hamas fire came from, only stating it was 80 metres away. The Mission finds it difficult to understand how the Israeli armed forces could have come to this view without having the information at the same time that Hamas operatives had been firing mortars for almost one hour. It regards these new allegations as lacking credibility. However, the Mission accepts, for the purposes of this report, that some firing may have occurred that gave rise to the Israeli armed forces' response.

It seems clear to the Mission that Israel's Government developed a position justifying the striking of an UNRWA school as a result of the immediate outcry generated by initial erroneous reports that the school had been hit. That effort included a number of statements, in particular those by Mr. Regev and Major Leibovich, which turned out to be erroneous.

The Mission notes the comment of Colonel Moshe Levi in *The Jerusalem Post* on 15 February 2009 casting doubt on the numbers of dead, noting that Israeli surveillance saw only a few stretchers being used to lift the dead and injured. If Israel had that capacity of surveillance in the immediate aftermath of the shelling, it must have been able to see that the shells had hit on the street outside the school and not inside the school. Furthermore, if such surveillance was recorded, in the face of serious allegations levelled against the Israeli armed forces by several sources after the military operation in Gaza, the Government could have made this footage public in order to establish the truth of its claims regarding this incident.

Finally, the Mission comes to the repeated assertion of the Israeli authorities as to the identities of those killed in the strikes. The most detailed attempt to name these come in Col. Levi's statement of the 12 dead, including nine militants and three non-combatants. On 19 February *The Jerusalem Post* published seven of the names given to them by CLA. The Mission notes that CLA did not provide any information to explain where the information on the dead came from. None of the seven names corresponds with any the Mission has so far established died in the attack.

The position assumed by Colonel Levi of CLA is problematic in the light of the relatively uncomplicated case of the al-Deeb family, of whom nine members died immediately and two died later. Four of these were women and four were children. Given these figures alone, and the relative ease with which the victims could be identified, the Mission considers the CLA assertions as to the total numbers and identities of those killed in the Israeli armed forces' mortar strikes to be unreliable. Even if the Israeli authorities were to be correct in saying that nine combatants were killed, they are, in the considered view of the Mission, incorrect in stating that only three non-combatants were killed.

A further assertion made several times by Israeli spokespersons on 6 and 7 January and confirmed again on 12 January was that the strikes had not only managed to hit the militant rocket launchers but had also killed two senior Hamas militants, namely Imad Abu Askar and Hassan Abu Askar. Again, for the most part these early assertions indicated that both had been killed in the UNRWA school. It is noticeable that the Israeli armed forces' summary of their own preliminary investigations does not repeat this claim.

What is now clear is that, if any Hamas operatives were killed by the Israeli strike, they were not killed in the school premises. It is difficult for the Mission to understand how the Israeli authorities could establish with such certainty within a matter of hours the identities of two of the Hamas operatives it had killed but could not establish within a week that the alleged firing had not come from the school and that the Israeli armed forces had not hit the school.

The Mission is satisfied that three Abu Askar family members were killed: Imad, aged 13, his brother Khaled, aged 19, and their uncle, Arafat, aged 33. Mr. Mark Regev indicated that Imad Abu Askar was a well-known member of Hamas's militant operation and of some significance in the rocket-launching operations. Major Leibovich and Captain Rutland also named Imad as one of the two operatives killed.

The Mission does not deny the possibility of children being recruited by Palestinian armed groups. However, in the case of Imad Abu Askar, the Mission is satisfied that he was not a Hamas operative. Apart from his father's vehement and, in the Mission's view, credible rejection of any such claim, two other factors appear relevant. Firstly, since it has become clear that Imad was a 13-year-old boy it is noticeable that Israel has not commented further on the allegation of his alleged Hamas activity in general or the allegation in particular that on the day in question he had launched mortars at Israel.

Secondly, the Israeli armed forces directly called Mr. Abu Askar early in the morning of 6 January notifying him that his house would be attacked imminently. If Imad Abu Askar was as notorious and important as alleged, despite his young age, the Mission presumes that the Israeli authorities would have known where he lived and, in particular, that he lived in the very house they were about to destroy. It is extremely doubtful that the Israeli armed forces, having identified the house where alleged Hamas militants of some significance lived, would warn them so that they may escape and then bomb the house.

There is no indication that anyone of the name of Hassan Abu Askar was killed in the attacks as far as the Mission can determine. The Mission notes that the two Hamas operatives Israeli reports refer to were at least on one occasion referred to as brothers. Mr. Abu Askar confirms that there is no one of such a name in his family.

It would appear that shortly after the attack the Israeli armed forces received some information that two Abu Askar brothers had been killed. That much is indeed true. However, the use made of that information appears to the Mission to have been knowingly distorted. The brothers were Imad and Khaled, not Imad and Hassan as asserted. One was a 13-year-old boy, the other was a recently married 19-year-old. The certainty and specificity with which the Israeli authorities spoke at the time make it very difficult for them to suggest now that they had simply mixed up the names.

[Removed: sections E and F (paragraphs 687–703)]

CHAPTER XI.

DELIBERATE ATTACKS AGAINST THE CIVILIAN POPULATION

According to the Israeli Government, the Israeli armed forces' rules of engagement for the military operation in Gaza emphasized the principle of distinction as one of four "guiding principles that applied in an integrated and cumulative manner: military necessity, distinction, proportionality and humanity." It defines the principle of distinction in the following terms: "Strikes shall be directed against military objectives and combatants only. It is absolutely prohibited to intentionally strike civilians or civilian objects (in contrast to incidental proportional harm)."

The Mission investigated 11 incidents in which serious allegations of direct attacks with lethal outcome were made against civilians. There appears to have been no justifiable military objective pursued in any of them. The first two incidents concern alleged attacks by Israeli armed forces against houses in the al-Samouni neighbourhood of Gaza during the initial phase of the ground invasion. The following group of seven incidents concern the alleged shooting of civilians who were trying to leave their homes to walk to a safer place, waving white flags and, in some of the cases, following an injunction from the Israeli armed forces to do so. In the last of these seven cases, a house was allegedly shelled with white phosphorous, killing five and injuring others. Two further members of the family were allegedly shot by Israeli troops as they tried to evacuate the wounded to a hospital. In the following incident, a mosque was targeted during the early evening prayer, resulting in the death of 15. In many of the incidents, the Israeli armed forces allegedly obstructed emergency medical help to the wounded. A further incident concerns the bombing of a family house, killing 22 family members. In the last of the incidents described, a crowd of family and neighbours at a condolence tent was attacked with flechettes.

A. ATTACKS ON THE HOUSES OF ATEYA AL-SAMOUNI AND WA'EL AL-SAMOUNI IN ZEYTOUN, RESULTING IN THE DEATH OF 23 MEMBERS OF THE AL-SAMOUNI FAMILY

To investigate the attacks on the houses of Ateya and Wa'el al-Samouni, which killed 23 members of the extended al-Samouni family, the Mission visited the site of the incidents. It interviewed five members of the al-Samouni family and several of their neighbours on site. Two members of the extended al-Samouni family, who were eyewitnesses to the incident, Messrs. Wa'el and Saleh al-Samouni, testified at the public hearing in Gaza. The Mission also interviewed PRCS ambulance drivers who went to the area on 4, 7 and 18 January 2009, and obtained copies of PRCS records. The Mission finally reviewed material on this incident submitted to it by TAWTHEQ as well as by NGOs.

The so-called al-Samouni area is part of Zeytoun, south of Gaza City, bordered to the east by al-Sekka Street, which in that part of Gaza runs parallel and very close to Salah ad-Din Street. It is inhabited by members of the extended al-Samouni family, which gives its name to the area, as well as by other families, such as the Arafats and the Hajjis. Al-Samouni area is more rural than urban; houses used to stand next to small olive and fig groves, chicken coops and other small plots of agricultural land. A small mosque stood in the centre of the neighbourhood. These no longer existed at the time of the Mission's visit in June 2009. The Mission saw very few buildings left and a few tents standing amidst the rubble of collapsed houses and bulldozed land.

The Israeli ground offensive from the east reached al-Samouni neighbourhood around 4 A.M. on 4 January 2009. In addition to the ground forces moving in from the east, there were, in all likelihood, heliborne troops that landed on the roofs of several houses in the area. Residents told the Mission that there was shooting in the neighbourhood in the night of 3 to 4 January and again the following night, but denied having seen any Palestinian fighters.

1. The killing of Ateya al-Samouni and his son Ahmad

During the morning of 4 January 2009, Israeli soldiers entered many of the houses in al-Samouni area. One of the first, around 5 A.M., was the house of Ateya Helmi al-Samouni, a 45-year-old man. Faraj, his 22-year-old son, had already met Israeli soldiers some minutes earlier as he stepped outside the house to warn his neighbours that their roof was burning. The soldiers entered Ateya al-Samouni's house by force, throwing some explosive device, possibly a grenade. In the midst of the smoke, fire and loud noise, Ateya al-Samouni stepped forward, his arms raised, and declared that he was the owner of the house. The soldiers shot him while he was still holding his ID and an Israeli driving licence in his hands. The soldiers then opened gunfire inside the room in which all the approximately 20 family members were gathered. Several were injured, Ahmad, a boy of four, particularly seriously. Soldiers with night vision equipment entered the room and closely inspected each of those present. The soldiers then moved to the next room and set fire to it. The smoke from that room soon started to suffocate the family. A witness speaking to the Mission recalled seeing "white stuff" coming out of the mouth of his 17-month-old nephew and helping him to breathe.

At about 6.30 A.M. the soldiers ordered the family to leave the house. They had to leave Ateya's body behind but were carrying Ahmad, who was still breathing. The family tried to enter the house of an uncle next door, but were not allowed to do so by the soldiers. The soldiers told them to take the road and leave the area, but a few metres further a different group of soldiers stopped them and ordered the men to undress completely. Faraj al-Samouni, who was carrying the severely injured Ahmad, pleaded with them to be allowed to take the injured to Gaza. The soldiers allegedly replied using abusive language. They also said "You are bad Arabs." "You go to Nitzarim."

Faraj al-Samouni, his mother and others entered the house of an uncle in the neighbourhood. From there, they called PRCS. As described below, at around 4 P.M. that day a PRCS ambulance managed to come into the vicinity of the house where Ahmad was lying wounded, but was prevented by the Israeli armed forces from rescuing him. Ahmad died at around 2 A.M. during the night of 4 to 5 January. The following morning those present in the house, about 45 persons, decided to leave. They made themselves white flags and walked in the direction of Salah ad-Din Street. A group of soldiers on the street told them to go back to the house, but the witness said that they walked on in the direction of Gaza. The soldiers shot at their feet, without injuring anyone, however. Two kilometres further north on Salah ad-Din Street, they found ambulances which took the injured to al-Shifa hospital in Gaza.

2. The attack on the house of Wa'el al-Samouni

In other cases, the entry of soldiers was less violent than in Ateya al-Samouni's home. In one instance, the soldiers landed on the roof and descended the stairs to the ground floor, separated men from women, searched and handcuffed the men. In another case they broke into a house by knocking a hole in the wall with a sledgehammer. At the house of Saleh al-Samouni, the Israeli soldiers knocked on the door and ordered those inside to open it. All the persons inside the house stepped out one by one and Saleh's father identified each of the family members in Hebrew for the soldiers. According to Saleh al-Samouni, they asked to be allowed to go to Gaza City, but the soldiers refused and instead ordered them to go to Wa'el al-Samouni's house across the street.

The Israeli soldiers also ordered those in other houses to move to Wa'el al-Samouni's house. As a result, around 100 members of the extended al-Samouni family, the majority women and children, were assembled in that house by noon on 4 January. There was hardly any water and no milk for the babies. Around 5 P.M. on 4 January, one of the women went outside to fetch firewood. There was some flour in the house and she made bread, one piece for each of those present.

In the morning of 5 January 2009, around 6.30–7 A.M., Wa'el al-Samouni, Saleh al-Samouni, Hamdi Maher al-Samouni, Muhammad Ibrahim al-Samouni and Iyad al-Samouni, stepped outside the house to collect firewood. Rashad Helmi al-Samouni remained standing next to the door of the house. Saleh al-Samouni has pointed out to the Mission that from where the Israeli soldiers were positioned on the roofs of the houses they could see the men clearly. Suddenly, a projectile struck next to the five men, close to the door of Wa'el's house and killed Muhammad Ibrahim al-Samouni and, probably, Hamdi Maher al-Samouni. The other men managed to retreat to the house. Within about five minutes, two or three more projectiles had struck the house directly. Saleh and Wa'el al-Samouni stated at the public hearing that these were missiles launched from Apache helicopters. The Mission has not been able to determine the type of munition used.

Saleh al-Samouni stated that overall 21 family members were killed and 19 injured in the attack on Wa'el al-Samouni's house. The dead include Saleh al-Samouni's father, Talal Helmi al-Samouni, his mother, Rahma Muhammad al-Samouni, and his two-year-old daughter Azza. Three of his sons, aged five, three and less than one year (Mahmoud, Omar and Ahmad), were injured, but survived. Of Wa'el's immediate family, a daughter and a son (Rezqa, 14, and Fares, 12) were killed, while two smaller children (Abdullah and Muhammad) were injured. The photographs of all the dead victims were shown to the Mission at the home of the al-Samouni family and displayed at the public hearing in Gaza.

After the shelling of Wa'el al-Samouni's house, most of those inside decided to leave immediately and walk to Gaza City, leaving behind the dead and some of the wounded. The women waved their scarves. Soldiers, however, ordered the al-Samounis to return to the house. When family members replied that there were many injured among them, the soldiers' reaction was, according to Saleh al-Samouni, "go back to death." They decided not to follow this injunction and walked in the direction of Gaza City. Once in Gaza, they went to PRCS and told them about the injured that had remained behind.

TESTIMONY 5

Wa'el al-Samouni

Witness to the Israeli ground offensive in Zeytoun,
describing an Apache helicopter attack that killed numerous
members of his extended family on January 5, 2009

What I have seen myself was seen by nobody else. It was an appalling massacre. Nobody had expected that massacre to happen. A hundred and five persons were gathered in my house. . . . They were our dearest, my sons, my cousins. I lost the dearest to my heart. We were blockaded, we were rounded up, 105 persons were rounded up in one room; children, women, elderly, all of whom were rounded and gathered at the house. . . .

The Israeli Mossad, uh, personnel were rounding up all the persons, bringing them back to our house at gunpoint. My cousin's house was about 100 meters to the east of my house. They brought them all to my house, gathered them inside the house. When I looked at them I saw that there were so many of them. So I talked to my mother and I said, "What am I going to do with all these persons? How am I going to cater for them? How am I going to bring and put food on the table for them?" So my mother baked about 100 loaves. Everybody had enough to eat. But we didn't have any drinking water. The reservoirs, the tanks were destroyed. None of us was able to leave the house.

It became dark and the night was falling. None of us was able to leave the house. We didn't have any drinking water. We had children. We couldn't do anything for them. So when the night fell I was wondering

3. The attempts of PRCS and ICRC to rescue
the civilians in the al-Samouni area

PRCS had made its first attempt to evacuate the injured from the al-Samouni area on 4 January 2009 around 4 P.M. after receiving a call from the family of Ateya al-Samouni. PRCS had called ICRC, asking it to coordinate its entry into the area with the Israeli armed forces. A PRCS ambulance from al-Quds hospital managed to reach the al-Samouni area. The ambulance had turned west off Salah ad-Din Street when, at one of the first houses in the area, Israeli soldiers on the ground

---

Testimony 5 (*continued*)

how am I going to provide them with covers, with blankets, with mattresses? But thank God, I mean we managed to provide cover and blankets for everyone.

So it was pitch dark. We heard shooting and we were afraid. In the morning we got ready for the prayers and along with the call for the prayers at the dawn time, we kissed each other goodbye and we were expecting to die. So my mother said, "How about if we prepare some breakfast for the children? At least they will not die hungry." So I, my cousin, a number of my cousins, we went out to find some firewood to prepare the breakfast. As we were leaving the house we were targeted by an Apache missile. Two of my cousins died immediately. I was wounded. I was brought into the house. Someone was trying to cater for my wounds but the house was targeted with another Apache missile right inside the house. Ten persons were killed immediately.

So we didn't understand why we were targeted. We tried to talk to the Israelis. We told them, "You gathered us all inside that house, all the children, women, and elderly. Why did you target us?" The Apache targeted us again with another missile. Fifteen other people were killed. So we couldn't do anything. We were helpless. All the survivors were shouting and screaming. Everybody was saying, "Let's leave the house. It's better to die outside than inside." We couldn't do anything. We were helpless. . . .

I lost my mother. I lost my son. I lost my daughter. I lost my sister-in-law, my nephew, my cousins. I lost so many people. I'm not talking about one or two. Twenty-nine members of my family were killed. It was an appalling massacre. No one had expected that thing to happen.

and on the roof of one of the houses directed their guns at it and ordered it to stop. The driver and the nurse were ordered to get out of the vehicle, raise their hands, take off their clothes and lie on the ground. Israeli soldiers then searched them and the vehicle for 5 to 10 minutes. Having found nothing, the soldiers ordered the ambulance team to return to Gaza City, in spite of their pleas to be allowed to pick up some wounded. In his statement to the Mission, the ambulance driver recalled seeing women and children huddling under the staircase in a house, but not being allowed to take them with him.

As soon as the first evacuees from the al-Samouni family arrived in Gaza City on 5 January, PRCS and ICRC requested permission from the Israeli armed forces to go into the al-Samouni neighbourhood to evacuate the wounded. These requests were denied. On 6 January around 6.45 P.M., one ICRC car and four PRCS ambulances drove towards the al-Samouni area in spite of the lack of coordination with the Israeli armed forces, but were not allowed to enter the area and evacuate the wounded.

On 7 January 2009, the Israeli armed forces finally authorized ICRC and PRCS to go to the al-Samouni area during the "temporary ceasefire" declared from 1 to 4 P.M. on that day. Three PRCS ambulances, an ICRC car and another car used to transport bodies drove down Salah ad-Din Street from Gaza City until, 1.5 km north of the al-Samouni area, they found it closed by sand mounds. ICRC tried to coordinate with the Israeli armed forces to have the road opened, but they refused and asked the ambulance staff to walk the remaining 1.5 km.

Once in the al-Samouni neighbourhood, PRCS looked for survivors in the houses. An ambulance driver who was part of the team told the Mission that in Wa'el al-Samouni's house they found 15 dead bodies and two seriously injured children. One of the children had a deep wound in the shoulder, which was infected and giving off a foul odour. The children were dehydrated and scared of the PRCS staff member. In a house close by, they found 11 persons in one room, including a dead woman.

The rescue teams had only three hours for the entire operation and the evacuees were physically weak and emotionally very unstable. The road had been damaged by the impact of shells and the movement of Israeli armed forces, including tanks and bulldozers. The rescuers put all the elderly on a cart and pulled it themselves for 1.5 kilometres to the place where they had been forced to leave the ambulances.

The dead bodies lying in the street or under the rubble, among them women and children, as well as the dead they had found in the houses had to be left behind. On the way back to the cars, PRCS staff entered one house where they found a man with two broken legs. While they were carrying the man out of the house, the Israeli armed forces started firing at the house, probably to warn that the three-hour "temporary ceasefire" was about to expire. PRCS was not able to return to the area until 18 January.

On 18 January 2009, members of the al-Samouni family were finally able to return to their neighbourhood. They found that Wa'el al-Samouni's house, as with most other houses in the neighbourhood and the small mosque, had been demolished. The Israeli armed forces had destroyed the building on top of the bodies of those who died in the attack. Pictures taken on 18 January show feet and legs sticking out from under the rubble and sand, and rescuers pulling out the bodies of women, men and children. A witness described to the Mission family members taking away the corpses on horse carts, a young man sitting in shock beside the ruins of his house and, above all, the extremely strong smell of death.

4. Factual findings

The Mission found the foregoing witnesses to be credible and reliable. It has no reason to doubt their testimony.

With regard to the context in which the attacks on the houses of Ateya al-Samouni and Wa'el al-Samouni took place, the Mission notes that there is some indication that there might have been a presence of Palestinian combatants in the al-Samouni neighbourhood during the first hours of the Israeli ground attack. A witness told the Mission that when he heard the first shots in the vicinity of his house in the night of 3 to 4 January, he at first thought it was Palestinian fighters. An NGO report submitted to the Mission states that a Palestinian combatant, reportedly a member of the Islamic Jihad, was killed in the al-Samouni area around midnight between 3 and 4 January.

The Mission considers, however, that the testimonies of the witnesses strongly suggest that already before daybreak on 4 January 2009 the Israeli armed forces were in full control of the al-Samouni neighbourhood. The Israeli soldiers had taken up position on the roofs of the houses in the area. According to several witnesses, the soldiers on the street spoke to residents who had ventured out of their houses. In some cases (for instance, at the house of Saleh al-Samouni and at the house Iyad al-Samouni was in, see below), they entered the houses non-violently after knocking on the door. According to Saleh al-Samouni, the prolonged identification of all the persons present in his house (his father identifying each family member in Hebrew for the soldiers) took place outside. The soldiers appear to have been confident that they were not at immediate risk of being attacked.

The Mission also reviewed the submission it received from an Israeli researcher, arguing generally that statements from Palestinian residents claiming that no fighting took place in their neighbourhood are disproved by the accounts Palestinian armed groups give of the armed operations. The Mission notes that, as far as the al-Samouni neighbourhood is concerned, this report would appear to support the statements of the witnesses that there was no combat.

Regarding the attack on Ateya al-Samouni's house, the Mission finds that the account given to it by Faraj al-Samouni is corroborated by the soldiers' testimonies published by the Israeli NGO Breaking the Silence. The assault on Ateya al-Samouni's house appears to be the procedure of the Israeli armed forces referred to as a "wet entry." A "wet entry" is, according to the soldier's explanation, "missiles, tank fire, machine-gun fire into the house, grenades. Shoot as we enter a room. The idea was that when we enter a house, no one there could fire at us." This procedure was, according to the soldier, thoroughly practised during recent Israeli armed forces manoeuvres.

The Mission notes that considering the generally calm circumstances that appear to have prevailed in the al-Samouni neighbourhood at the time (as evidenced by the way the soldiers entered other houses after knocking on the door) and the fact that the soldiers had already spoken to Faraj al-Samouni, one of the persons in Ateya al-Samouni's house, the Mission cannot see any circumstance justifying the violent entry into the house.

With regard to the attack on the five men who stepped out of Wa'el al-Samouni's house to fetch firewood in the early morning of 5 January 2009 and to the subsequent shelling of the house, the Mission notes that the members of the other families who had been moved by the Israeli forces into Wa'el al-Samouni's house had been searched by Israeli soldiers, as recounted by Saleh al-Samouni. Everything indicates that the Israeli forces knew that there were about 100 civilians in the house. Indeed, the families had asked to be allowed to leave the area towards a safer place, but had been ordered to stay in Wa'el al-Samouni's house. The house must have been under constant observation by the Israeli soldiers, who had complete control over the area at the time.

The Mission was not able to determine whether the attack was carried out by missiles launched from Apache helicopters, as Saleh and Wa'el al-Samouni told the Mission at the public hearing in Gaza, or by other munitions. Nevertheless, the fact that a first projectile struck next to the five men soon after they had left the house (at a time at which there was no combat in the area), and two or three projectiles struck the house after the survivors had retreated into the house, indicates that the weaponry used allowed a high degree of precision with a short response time and that the five men and then the house were the intended targets of the attack.

The Mission notes that, four days later, the Israeli armed forces denied that the attack on the house of Wa'el al-Samouni had taken place. On 9 January 2009, an Israeli army spokesman, Jacob Dallal, reportedly told the Reuters news agency that "the IDF did not mass people into any specific building. . . . Furthermore, we checked with regard to IDF fire on the 5th. The IDF did not target any building in or near Zeitun on the 5th." The Mission is not aware of any subsequent statement from the Israeli Government which would contradict this blanket denial or suggest that the allegations have been the subject of further investigation.

With regard to the obstruction of emergency medical access to the wounded in the al-Samouni neighbourhood, the Mission notes that four-year-old Ahmad al-Samouni was still alive at 4 P.M. on 4 January 2009, when the PRCS ambulance called by his relatives managed to arrive within what the Mission estimates to be 100 to 200 metres from the house where he was. In fact, he died about 10 hours later, which suggests that he might have had a good chance of survival. Israeli soldiers stopped the ambulance and thoroughly searched the driver, nurse and vehicle. Although they did not find anything indicating that the ambulance staff was not on a genuine emergency mission to evacuate a wounded civilian, they forced the ambulance to return to Gaza City without the injured Ahmad.

On 5 and 6 January 2009, following the arrival in Gaza City hospitals of survivors of the attack on Wa'el al-Samouni's house, PRCS and ICRC requested permission from the Israeli armed forces to go into the al-Samouni neighbourhood to evacuate the wounded. These requests were denied. According to the information available to PRCS, the Israeli armed forces told ICRC that there were combat operations going on in the area. A PRCS ambulance driver, who was part of the PRCS convoy which went to the area in spite of the refusal of the Israeli armed forces to grant permission, reported that there were no clashes at the time. PRCS and ICRC were not able to evacuate the wounded from the area until 7 January in the afternoon.

The information before it leads the Mission to believe that the Israeli armed forces arbitrarily prevented the evacuation of the wounded from the al-Samouni area, thereby causing at least one additional death, worsening of the injuries in others, and severe psychological trauma in at least some of the victims, particularly children.

These findings are corroborated by the press release ICRC issued on 8 January 2009:

> The ICRC had requested safe passage for ambulances to access this neigh-bourhood [the al-Samouni area in Zeytoun] since 3 January but it only re-ceived permission to do so from the Israel Defense Forces during the afternoon of 7 January.

> The ICRC/PRCS team found four small children next to their dead mothers in one of the houses. They were too weak to stand up on their own. One man was also found alive, too weak to stand up. In all there were at least 12 corpses lying on mattresses.

> In another house, the ICRC/PRCS rescue team found 15 other survivors of this attack including several wounded. In yet another house, they found an additional three corpses. Israeli soldiers posted at a military position some 80 metres away from this house ordered the rescue team to leave the area which they refused to do. There were several other positions of the Israel Defense Forces nearby as well as two tanks.

B. KILLING OF CIVILIANS ATTEMPTING TO LEAVE THEIR HOMES TO WALK TO SAFER AREAS

[Removed: sections 1 through 4 (paragraphs 736–755)]

5. The shooting of Ibrahim Juha

The Juha family lives in a house on al-Sekka Street a few meters north of where al-Samouni Street goes off Salah ad-Din Street to the west. The house was struck by several missiles during the night of 3 to 4 January 2009, which had caused significant destruction. In the early morning of 4 January, Israeli soldiers entered the house and fired into the room where the Juha family, consisting of Mr. Juha, his two wives, his mother and 13 children, was assembled. Photographs of the scene taken by Mr. Juha show that numerous rounds were discharged. The family was made to assemble in the upper part of the house. They were then ordered to leave the house and walk towards Rafah.

The Juha family and their neighbours, the Sawafeary family, walked down al-Sekka Street for 100 metres in the direction of Rafah. When they reached the house of another neighbour, Mr. Abu Zur, they were invited into that house and decided to stay there. The three families spent 4 January in the house. On the morning of 5 January the house was the subject of intense firing from Israeli troops in the vicinity. After some time Israeli soldiers approached the house and ordered everyone to come out. The men were separated from the women. From the group of men four were separated and required to strip to their underwear. They were held in a house opposite the Abu Zur house, belonging to Mr. Subhi al-Samouni. The remaining group was told once again to leave the area and walk towards Rafah. Mr. Juha recounts that walking down al-Sekka Street the group came to a point where a large crater blocked the way ahead and the surrounding rubble provided a difficult obstacle for some members of his family, including his ageing mother, who had fainted shortly before outside the Abu Zur house.

In the face of these obstacles the group of three families walked east towards Salah ad-Din Street. There they entered the house of another family, the Mughrabis. With the arrival of the Juha, Sawafeary and Abu Zur families, there were now more than 70 persons assembled in the house.

Mr. Juha told the Mission that, after taking a little rest in the Mughrabi house, he came to the view that it was impossible for them all to stay there, given their substantial numbers and the earlier experience of the intense firing at the Abu Zur house. He decided that they should seek to go back into the street and move to another place. Mr. Mughrabi strongly advised against this.

The Juha, Abu Zur and Sawafeary families went back into the street in the afternoon of 5 January. Mr. Juha had his mother in front of him propped up on a two-wheeled trolley as she was unable to walk. Mr. Sawafeary was near to him at the front of the group. Behind him, towards the middle of the group, was his 15-year-old son,

Ibrahim, carrying a white flag. Mr. Juha believes he heard two shots. One of the shots hit his son in the chest. The group immediately sought cover once again in the Mughrabi house. They tried to care for Ibrahim in the workshop at the front of the house. His mother tried to sew the wound with a needle and thread and sterilize the materials with eau de cologne. Ibrahim died some six hours after he was shot.

The group of over 70 persons remained in the house until 8 January in the afternoon, when ICRC and PRCS representatives came to the neighbourhood and they managed to leave the area and walk to Gaza City.

6. Factual findings

The testimonies of Mr. Mu'een Juha and Mrs. Juha, Mr. Sameh Sawafeary and Mr. Rajab Darwish Mughrabi, as well as of Mrs. Abir Hajji, all establish that there were no combat operations in the area at the time of the incident. The Israeli armed forces had attacked Mr. Juha's house and that of Mr. Abu Zur, where the Juhas and other families had taken refuge, forcing them to leave the area. It was the Israeli armed forces that ordered these families to take the road to Rafah. In sum, the Israeli armed forces deliberately opened fire on a group of persons they had interacted with during the preceding 24 hours and therefore knew to be civilians, killing the child Ibrahim Juha.

[Removed: sections 7 through 10 (paragraphs 764–779)]

11. The shooting of Rouhiyah al-Najjar

The Mission visited the site of the shooting of Rouhiyah al-Najjar in Khuza'a. It interviewed two eyewitnesses of the shooting and six other witnesses to the events, including Yasmine al-Najjar, Nasser al-Najjar, Rouhiyah al-Najjar's husband, and their daughter Hiba.

The Israeli armed forces launched the attack against Khuza'a, a small town about half a kilometre from the border (Green Line) with Israel east of Khan Yunis, around 10 P.M. on 12 January 2009. During the night, they used white phosphorous munitions, causing fires to break out in the al-Najjar neighbourhood on the eastern fringe of Khuza'a. Families in the neighbourhood, including the family of Nasser al-Najjar, his first wife Rouhiyah and their daughter Hiba, spent much of the night trying to extinguish fires in their houses. Israeli armed forces, possibly heliborne troops, had taken position on the roofs of some houses in the neighbourhood and observed the residents as they attempted to fight the fires. Around 3 A.M. residents also began to hear the noise of approaching tanks and bulldozers, with which they were well familiar, as in 2008 there had been several Israeli incursions into the farmland to the north and east of Khuza'a, in the course of which bulldozers flattened fields, groves, chicken coops and greenhouses.

In the early morning hours, some of the residents, including Rouhiyah al-Najjar, climbed on the roofs of their houses and hoisted improvised white flags. Using megaphones, the Israeli armed forces asked the men of the neighbourhood to come out of the houses and walk towards the tanks. There the men were separated into two groups which were then held in different houses under the control of the soldiers.

At some point between 7 and 7.45 A.M., Rouhiyah al-Najjar and the women in her immediate neighbourhood decided to leave their homes and walk with their children to the town centre. The group of women was headed by Rouhiyah al-Najjar and her 23-year-old neighbour and relative Yasmine al-Najjar, both carrying white flags. Rouhiyah's daughter Hiba was right behind her. Other women were holding up babies in their arms, shouting "God is great!" and "We have children!" The group of women and children started moving down a straight alley, about six or seven metres wide, flanked on both sides by houses. At the other end of the alley, a little more than 200 metres away, was the house of Faris al-Najjar, which had been occupied by numerous Israeli soldiers (around 60 according to one witness). The soldiers had made a hole in the wall of the first floor of the house, giving them a good view down the alley into which the group of women and children were advancing. When Rouhiyah al-Najjar was about 200 metres from Faris al-Najjar's house, a shot fired from that house hit her in the temple (she had just turned her head towards her neighbour next to her to encourage her). Rouhiyah al-Najjar fell to the ground; Yasmine was struck in her leg. This single shot was followed by concentrated gunfire, which forced the group of women and children to scramble back into the houses of Osama al-Najjar and Shawki al-Najjar, though it did not cause further injury. Because of the fire from the Israeli soldiers, they did not dare to leave the house and look after Rouhiyah al-Najjar. They stayed inside until around noon the same day, when they made a second, successful attempt to leave the neighbourhood and walk to a safer part of Khuza'a.

An ambulance driver from Khan Yunis hospital, Marwan Abu Reda, received a phone call from Khuza'a asking for emergency help for Rouhiyah al-Najjar at around 7.45 A.M. He immediately drove to Khuza'a and arrived in the neighbourhood shortly after 8 A.M., i.e. within no more than an hour from the shooting. He was already in the alley where Rouhiyah al-Najjar was lying on the ground when soldiers opened fire from houses or rooftops, forcing him to make a U-turn and take the ambulance to a nearby alley. He called PRCS and asked it to seek access to the injured woman, through ICRC and in coordination with the Israeli armed forces, without success. Marwan Abu Reda was not able to pick up Rouhiyah al-Najjar's (by then lifeless) body until the evening of that day. He confirmed to the Mission that she had received a bullet in the temple.

12. Factual findings

The Mission has no reason to doubt the veracity of the main elements of the testimony of the witnesses it heard with regard to the shooting of Rouhiyah al-Najjar.

The Mission's site inspection and the testimony of several witnesses appear to establish that the group of women and children led by Rouhiyah al-Najjar had slowly walked for at least 20 metres before the shot that killed Rouhiyah was fired. During that time, Israeli soldiers standing on the roofs of the houses in the neighbourhood had ample time to observe the group. The fact that, after shooting Rouhiyah and Yasmine al-Najjar, the soldiers directed warning fire at the group without injuring anyone, but forcing them to retreat to a house, is further indication that the soldiers had not observed any threat to them from the group. Indeed, a few hours later the same group was allowed to walk past the soldiers to a safer area of Khuza'a. The Mission accordingly finds that Rouhiyah al-Najjar was deliberately shot by an Israeli soldier who had no reason to assume that she was a combatant or otherwise taking part in hostilities.

The Mission also observes that, while it is unclear whether the ambulance from Khan Yunis hospital could have saved Rouhiyah al-Najjar's life, the Israeli forces prevented the evacuation of the wounded woman without any justification.

13. The Abu Halima family case

The Mission interviewed three members of the Abu Halima family who were eyewitnesses to the events described below. The Mission also spoke to the doctor who treated some of the family members. The Mission reviewed a report by Physicians for Human Rights–Israel and the Palestinian Medical Relief Society which includes analysis by doctors who observed the wounds of the surviving victims at the beginning of March 2009 and also has medical reports confirming the injuries they suffered. Finally, the Mission reviewed information received from TAWTHEQ.

On 3 and 4 January 2009, the initial days of the ground invasion, there was heavy aerial bombardment and shelling by tanks of the open areas around Siyafa village, in al-Atatra neighbourhood west of Beit Lahia. Most residents are farmers and, although the Israeli armed forces had dropped leaflets warning civilians to leave the area, most had chosen to stay. Based on their previous experiences of ground invasions, they reportedly believed that they were not in danger.

On 4 January 2009, the bombardment reportedly increased as Israeli troops moved into and took control of al-Atatra neighbourhood. The Abu Halima family was sheltering in the home of Muhammad Sa'ad Abu Halima and Sabah Abu Halima in Sifaya village. The house has two floors; the ground floor is used for storage and the living quarters are on the upper floor. According to Sabah Abu Halima, 16 members of her immediate family were sheltering on the upper floor.

In the afternoon, after hearing that a shell had hit the adjacent house of Sabah Abu Halima's brother-in-law, most of the family moved from the bedroom into a hallway in the middle of the upper floor, where they thought they would be better protected. At around 4.30 P.M., a white phosphorous shell came through the ceiling into the room where they were sheltering.

According to family members who survived, there was intense fire and white smoke in the room, the walls of which were glowing red. Five members of the family died immediately or within a short period: Muhammad Sa'ad Abu Halima (aged 45) and four of his children, sons Abd al-Rahim Sa'ad (aged 14), Zaid (aged 12) and Hamza (aged 8), and daughter Shahid (aged 18 months). Muhammad Sa'ad and Abd al-Rahim Sa'ad were decapitated, the others burnt to death. Five members of the family escaped and suffered various degrees of burns: Sabah Abu Halima, her sons Youssef (aged 16) and Ali (aged 4), daughter-in-law Ghada (aged 21), and Ghada's daughter Farah (aged 2).

Family members tried to call an ambulance, but the Israeli armed forces had declared the area a closed military zone and ambulances were not permitted to enter. Two cousins put Sabah Abu Halima in the back of a tractor trailer and drove her to Kamal Idwan hospital in Beit Lahia. The driver reported that he reached the hospital despite coming under fire from Israeli soldiers posted inside the Omar Bin Khattab school for girls on the road to al-Atatra. One cousin remained with Sabah Abu Halima, while the other returned to help the rest of the family.

The remaining survivors and the injured were placed on a second tractor trailer to take them to Kamal Idwan hospital. The remains of Shahid Abu Halima were also taken. The tractor was driven by a cousin, Muhammad Hekmat Abu Halima (aged 16). Another cousin, Matar Abu Halima (aged 17), his brother Ali (aged 11) and his mother, Nabila, accompanied them.

When they reached the crossroads next to the Omar Bin Khattab school in al-Atatra, Israeli soldiers positioned on the roof of a nearby house, some ten metres away, ordered them to stop. Muhammad Hekmat, Matar, Ali and Nabila got down and stood beside the tractor. One or more soldiers opened fire, hitting Muhammad Hekmat Abu Halima in the chest and Matar Abu Halima in the abdomen. Both died as a result of their injuries. Ali, Omar and Nabila Abu Halima fled. Omar was shot in the arm, but they eventually reached Kamal Idwan hospital.

The remaining family members were ordered to abandon the tractors and walk. They were not permitted to take the bodies of the two dead boys, or the remains of Shahid Abu Halima, which were recovered four days later, on 8 January. Ghada Abu Halima, who had burns on 45 per cent of her body, had great difficulty walking. After some 500 metres, a vehicle picked up several members of the family, including Ghada and Farah, and took them to al-Shifa hospital in Gaza City.

Dr. Nafiz Abu Shaban, Chief of Plastic Surgery at al-Shifa hospital, confirmed that Sabah, Ghada and Farah Abu Halima were admitted there with serious burns and were transferred to Egypt for treatment. The doctor believed that the burns were caused by contact with white phosphorous.

14. Factual findings

The Mission found Sabah Abu Halima, Muhammad Sa'ad Abu Halima and Omar Sa'ad Abu Halima to be credible and reliable witnesses. It has no reason to doubt the veracity of the main elements of their testimonies, which were corroborated by the testimony of Dr. Nafiz Abu Shaban of al-Shifa hospital.

With regard to the white phosphorous shelling of the Abu Halima family house, the Mission notes that the house is located in a village in a rural area. The shelling occurred on 4 January 2009 at a time when Israeli ground forces were apparently advancing into al-Atatra. Moreover, the Israeli armed forces had dropped leaflets warning civilians to leave. Under the circumstances, the Mission cannot make any determination as to whether the shelling of the Abu Halima house was a direct attack against a civilian objective, an indiscriminate attack or a justifiable part of the broader military operation.

With regard to the shooting of Muhammad Hekmat Abu Halima and Matar Abu Halima, the Mission notes that the Israeli soldiers had ordered the tractor on which they were transporting the wounded to stop and had ordered the two cousins (aged 16 and 17) to come down. They had complied with those instructions and were standing next to the tractor, when the Israeli soldiers standing on the roof of a nearby house opened fire on them. The soldiers cannot have been mistaken about the circumstance that these were two civilians taking gravely wounded persons to a hospital. The shooting of Muhammad Hekmat Abu Halima and Matar Abu Halima was a direct lethal attack on two under-age civilians. The fact that they were hit in the chest and the abdomen, respectively, indicates that the intention was to kill them.

The Mission further notes that in this case the Israeli armed forces denied the ambulances access to the area to evacuate the wounded and then opened fire on the relatives of the wounded who were trying to take them to the nearest hospital.

C. INFORMATION CONCERNING THE INSTRUCTIONS GIVEN TO THE ISRAELI ARMED FORCES WITH REGARD TO THE OPENING OF FIRE AGAINST CIVILIANS

The Mission found in the above incidents that the Israeli armed forces repeatedly opened fire on civilians who were not taking part in the hostilities and who posed no threat to them. These incidents indicate that the instructions given to the Israeli armed forces moving into Gaza provided for a low threshold for the use of lethal fire against the civilian population. The Mission found strong corroboration of this trend emerging from its fact-finding in the testimonies of Israeli soldiers collected by the Israeli NGO Breaking the Silence and in the Protocol of the Rabin Academy's "Fighters' Talk." These testimonies suggest in particular that the instructions given to the soldiers conveyed two "policies." Both are an expression of the aim to eliminate as far as possible any risk to the lives of the Israeli soldiers.

The first policy could be summarized, in the words of one of the soldiers: "[I]f we see something suspect and shoot, better hit an innocent than hesitate to target an enemy." Another soldier attributed the following instructions to his battalion commander: "If you are not sure—shoot. If there is doubt then there is no doubt." The first soldier summarized the briefing from the battalion commander as follows: "[T]he enemy was hiding behind civilian population. . . . [I]f we suspect someone, we should not give him the benefit of the doubt. Eventually, this could be an enemy, even if it's some old woman approaching the house. It could be an old woman carrying an explosive charge." A third soldier explained "you don't only shoot when threatened. The assumption is that you constantly feel threatened, so anything there threatens you, and you shoot. No one actually said 'shoot regardless' or 'shoot anything that moves.' But we were not ordered to open fire only if there was a real threat."

The Mission notes that some soldiers stated that they agreed with the instructions to "shoot in case of doubt." One of them explained "this is the difference between urban warfare and a limited confrontation. In urban warfare, anyone is your enemy. No innocents." Another told of his profound discomfort with the policy and of how he and his comrades had attempted to question their commander about it after a clearly harmless man was shot. While they disagreed about the legitimacy and morality of the policy, they had little doubt about the terms of the instructions: each soldier and commander on the ground had to exercise judgement, but the policy was to shoot in case of doubt.

The second policy clearly emerging from the soldiers' testimonies is explained by one of the soldiers as follows: "One of the things in this procedure [the outpost procedure, which is being applied in areas held by the Israeli armed forces after the Gaza ground invasion] is setting red lines. It means that whoever crosses this limit is shot, no questions asked. . . . Shoot to kill." In one incident highly relevant to the cases investigated by the Mission because of factual similarities, a soldier recounted an event he witnessed. A family is ordered to leave their house. For reasons that remain unclear, probably a misunderstanding, the mother and two children turn left instead of right after having walked between 100 and 200 metres from their house. They thereby cross a "red line" established by the Israeli unit (of whose existence the mother and children could have no knowledge). An Israeli marksman on the roof of the house they had just left opens fire on the woman and her two children, killing them. As the soldier speaking at the Rabin Academy's "Fighters' Talk" a month later observes, "[F]rom our perspective, he [the marksman] did his job according to the orders he was given."

"Incessant" alerts about suicide bombers meant that even civilians clearly identified by the soldiers as carrying no arms were perceived as a threat as soon as they came within a certain distance from the soldiers—a threat to be eliminated, also without warning fire, as a second might be enough for the "suicide bomber" to get close enough to harm the soldiers.

The Mission notes that many of the persons interviewed in Gaza described incidents in which they were, individually, as part of a group or in a vehicle, exposed to intense gunfire from Israeli soldiers—but without being hit or injured. This was the case, for instance, of an ambulance driver attempting to drive into an area which the Israeli armed forces had decided he should not enter. In the Khuza'a case, after the lethal shooting of Rouhiyah al-Najjar and wounding of Yasmine al-Najjar, the other women and children were exposed to fire from the Israeli soldiers, which forced them to retreat to the houses they had been trying to leave. These incidents suggest that the Israeli armed forces made ample use of gunfire to "communicate" with the civilian population, to issue injunctions to civilians not to walk or not to drive any further in a certain direction or to immediately retreat to a building they were about to leave. The terrifying effect this sort of non-verbal communication had on those at the receiving end is evident, as is the likelihood of lethal consequences.

The Mission also read testimony from soldiers who recounted cases in which, although a civilian had come within a distance from them which would have required opening fire under the rules imparted to them, they decided not to shoot because they did not consider the civilian a threat to them.

[Removed: section D (paragraphs 809–821)]

E. THE ATTACK ON THE AL-MAQADMAH MOSQUE, 3 JANUARY 2009

1. The facts gathered by the Mission

The al-Maqadmah mosque is situated near the north-west outskirts of Jabaliyah camp, close to Beit Lahia. It is located less than 100 metres from the Kamal Idwan hospital, in the al-Alami housing project. At least 15 people were killed and around 40 injured—many seriously—when the Israeli armed forces struck the entrance of the mosque with a missile.

The Mission heard five eyewitnesses who had been in the mosque at the time it was struck. Two of them had been facing the door as the explosion occurred. Three of them had been kneeling facing the opposite direction and had been seriously injured. The Mission also heard from a number of relatives of those who died in the attack and has seen a number of sworn statements signed by them testifying to the facts they witnessed. The Mission also heard again from three witnesses it had interviewed earlier at the public hearings in Gaza. Finally, the Mission reviewed information received from TAWTHEQ.

On the evening of 3 January 2009, between 5 and 6 P.M., a large number of people had gathered in the mosque for evening prayers. Witnesses indicate that between 200 and 300 men had gathered on the first floor. A number of women had also congregated in the basement at that time. Witnesses explained that in time of fear or emergency it was the tradition to combine sunset and evening prayers. In addition, the Mission heard that, while some time normally elapses between the muezzin calling the faithful to prayer and the prayers beginning, at this time it was the practice to begin prayers almost immediately.

The witnesses indicated that prayers had ended and the sermon was just beginning. At that point there was an explosion in the doorway to the mosque. One of the two wooden doors was blown off its hinges and all the way across the prayer area to the opposite wall.

As a result of the explosion at least 15 people died. Almost all were inside the mosque at the time. One of the casualties was a boy who had been sitting at the entrance. His leg was blown off by the missile strike and found afterwards on the roof of the mosque. A large number, around 40, suffered injuries. Many were taken to the Kamal Idwan hospital for treatment.

On visiting the mosque, the Mission was able to observe the damage done to it. Its immediate entrance is on a raised level from the external pavement and is reached via a ramp. There are a number of stairs below the doorway, now covered by the raised entrance at the end of the ramp. The stairs underneath the ramp were damaged and the concrete had been pierced. There was a scorch mark on the ground and stairs.

The Mission has also viewed a number of photographs taken shortly after the strike and considers them to be reliable. They showed that something had penetrated the concrete (about three inches thick) immediately outside of the mosque doorway and then hit the pavement at the bottom of the stairs below the concrete covering.

The ramp and entrance level structure had a wall about one metre high built on its outer side. The part of the wall opposite the mosque door was blown away.

The Mission observed that the interior walls of the mosque and part of the exterior wall around the doorway appeared to have suffered significant damage as a result of a spray of small metal cubes. A good number of these were lodged in the wall even at the time of the Mission's visit to the site in June 2009. Several of these were retrieved and the Mission could see how deeply embedded they were in the concrete walls.

Apart from the aforementioned visit to the mosque, the Mission has interviewed its sheikh on three occasions, its imam twice, its muezzin, several members of the sheikh's family, several of those injured in the blast and a number of the relatives who lost family members and who assisted in the immediate aftermath of the attack. It has seen medical certificates that bear out the nature of those injuries related by the young men it interviewed. The Mission questioned all of the witnesses and sought to clarify any doubts it may have had.

2. The position of the Israeli Government and the Israeli armed forces
The Israeli armed forces' response to the allegations states:

> ... [R]elating to a strike against the "Maqadme" mosque in Beit-Lahiya on January 3rd, 2009, it was discovered that as opposed to the claims, the mosque was not attacked at all. Furthermore, it was found that the supposed uninvolved civilians who were the casualties of the attack were in fact Hamas operatives killed while fighting against the IDF.

Apart from the apparent contradictions it contains, the Mission notes that the statement does not indicate in any way the nature of the inquiry, the source of its information or the reliability and credibility of such sources.

In July 2009 the Israeli Government repeated the same position.

3. Factual findings
The Mission has established that the Israeli armed forces fired a missile that struck near the doorway of the mosque. The penetration pattern witnessed on the concrete ramp and stairs underneath is consistent with that which would be expected of a shrapnel fragmentation sleeve fitted onto an air-to-ground missile. Shrapnel cubes

Moteeh al-Silawi

Sheikh of al-Maqadmah mosque, describing the attack on the mosque on January 3, 2009. He lost five members of his family, including a brother.

Because we were so afraid, we would send our elderly, our wives, our children to the mosque, because we believed—and you know very well that when you are fearful, any person, when you are scared, you would go to the church, because church is a safe place, there is no safer place than a church.

We therefore went to the mosque and sent our people to the mosque. On the upper floor there were over 300 men. In the basement were plenty of women. My father was on the ground floor and my mother was in the basement. As usual we started the prayer. . . . And as soon as the imam finished the prayer, then I stood up to preach to the people, to give a lesson, to talk about peacefulness.

And after two words, there was a loud explosion in the mosque. Everybody was looking towards the qiblah, towards Mecca. I was the only one who was looking towards the door. And there I saw fragments like rain falling at the door of the mosque. At that moment we were all very, very fearful. Everybody was screaming, everybody was yelling: men, women, children. The electricity was out. My father is blind, therefore I took his hand and I was leading him out. . . . It was a terrible, terrible shock. I cannot describe to you what I saw: a safe place, and people go to the mosque for safety, and we saw bloodshed. There was blood in the mosque. I saw legs, I saw legs and arms, I saw the leg of a small child, and I stepped on it, even. . . . I saw this blood being shed in the mosque. The mosque, the safe place where everybody should feel safe. Can you imagine such a shock happening? I never thought this would be possible. Nobody, nobody would expect that the house of God, the place of worship would be targeted by missiles. Where are we going to go?

that the Mission retrieved from the rear inside wall of the mosque are consistent with what would be expected to be discharged by a missile of this nature.

The strike killed at least 15 people attending the mosque for prayers and very seriously injured several others.

The Mission is not in a position to say from which kind of aircraft or air-launch platform the missile was fired. It believes the testimony of the witnesses regarding the circumstances of the attack, finding it plausible and consistent not only with the other witnesses but also with the physical evidence at the scene. The Mission also notes that a number of local organizations sent representatives to the site of the attack very shortly after it occurred and they witnessed the scene for themselves. The Mission has also spoken with them and notes that their accounts are consistent with the testimony provided by the witnesses it heard.

There has been no suggestion that the al-Maqadmah mosque was being used at that time to launch rockets, store weapons or shelter combatants. Since it does not appear from the testimonies of the incident or the inspection of the site that any other damage was done in the area at that time, the Mission concludes that what occurred was an isolated strike and not in connection with an ongoing battle or exchange of fire.

[Removed: section 4 (paragraphs 838–843)]

[Removed: section F (paragraphs 844–866)]

G. ATTACK ON THE ABD AL-DAYEM CONDOLENCE TENTS

1. The facts gathered by the Mission

On 4 January 2009 the Israeli armed forces struck an ambulance in the Beit Lahia area with a flechette missile as it was attending a number of wounded persons who had been hit in an earlier attack. Those wounded in the first attack had also been hit by a flechette missile. As a result of the attack on the ambulance, one of the first-aid volunteers in the ambulance crew, Arafa Abd al-Dayem, suffered severe injuries. He died later the same afternoon.

The following day, as is the custom, the family set up condolence tents where family and friends would pay their respects and comfort the grieving relatives. The family home is in Izbat Beit Hanoun, a built-up area in the north-east corner of the Gaza strip. It is located between Jabaliyah and Beit Hanoun, about 3 kilometres from the border with Israel both to the north and to the east. Although the Israeli armed forces had entered Gaza at the time of the incident, in this area they remained on the Israeli side of the "Green Line" border. Two tents were set up—one for male visitors and one for female visitors. They were positioned at about ten metres from each other. The male tent was outside the house of Mohammed Deeb Abd al-Dayem, the father of the ambulance driver.

The tents were struck three times in two hours, again with flechette missiles.

The Mission spoke to several of the witnesses who had attended and survived the attacks on the condolence tents. The Mission noted the great pride Arafa Abd al-Dayem's father had in his son and the deep sense of loss he clearly felt.

As regards the attacks on the condolence tents, witnesses stated that at around 7.30 A.M. on 5 January, the house of Mohammed Deeb Abd al-Dayem was hit by a shell. The shell struck the fourth floor of the five-storey building, causing the roof to collapse. Three men at the gathering, including the father of the deceased, were slightly wounded and taken to the Kamal Idwan hospital in Beit Lahia for treatment. They returned to the house at around 8.15 A.M. where a decision was taken by the mourners to end the condolence ceremony for fear of further attacks.

The witness stated that at around 8.30 A.M. when the people were leaving the house of Mohammed Deeb Abd al-Dayem and moving towards the women's condolence tent, two flechette missiles struck within a few metres of the tent and less than half a minute apart. Around 20 to 30 persons assembled there were injured. The injured include a 13-year-old boy who received a flechette injury to the right side of his head and a 33-year-old man who sustained injuries to the chest and head, his body punctuated with little holes according to a witness who saw his corpse being prepared for burial. A 22-year-old man was wounded in the abdomen, the chest and the head. A 16-year-old boy sustained injuries to the head and the neck. A 26-year-old man sustained injuries to his chest, head and left leg. These five persons died of their injuries. Another 17 persons present at the scene, including 14 men, two children (aged 17 and 11) and one woman, were injured.

IK/12, who survived the attack, still has several flechettes embedded in his body, including in his chest, and is unable to move freely without pain.

Witnesses described that their sense of loss was aggravated by the fact that they could not access the injured or dead in hospitals as movement was restricted owing to continued shelling in and around the neighbourhood. Only two families out of the five families of the dead were able to conduct the burial according to their traditional customs and practices.

2. The Israeli position

The Israeli Government does not appear to have made any public comment on the allegations surrounding the Abd al-Dayem case, despite information about it being in the public domain for some time. It has, however, recalled that the Israeli High Court of Justice has rejected the argument that flechette munitions are by their nature indiscriminate and maintains that subject to the general requirements of the rules of armed conflict their use is legal.

3. Factual findings

The Mission visited the area and the house of the Abd al-Dayem family. It spoke with the father of Arafa Abd al-Dayem, who had died as a result of the injuries received while working as a first-aid volunteer, and with several of the witnesses who had attended the condolence ceremonies.

The account of the incidents was consistent and plausible. The fact that it was mainly men who were killed near the women's tent is explained by the fact that the strikes occurred precisely when the men were making their way across the road.

The Mission can see nothing at all that points to the house of Mohammed Deeb Abd al-Dayem, or the condolence tents, constituting a military objective. The repeated nature of the strikes indicates that there was a deliberate attempt to kill members of the group or the entire group, but no information about the purpose of the strikes has been forthcoming from the Israeli authorities.

The Mission inspected the sites of the attacks and was left in no doubt that they had been entirely deliberate. There was a tent at each side of the wide road. The particular area is relatively open.

[Removed: section 4 (paragraphs 880–885)]

CHAPTER XII.

THE USE OF CERTAIN WEAPONS

In the course of its inquiries, the Mission was made aware of the use of certain weapons by the Israeli armed forces. This chapter does not intend to present a comprehensive analysis of all the aspects raised on the kinds of weaponry used during the military operations. It is rather a summary of the Mission's views on a number of issues that arise from the foregoing chapters in relation to the obligation to take all feasible precautions in the choice of the means and methods of warfare. Many of the issues brought to the Mission's attention had already received scrutiny in the press or as a result of analysis carried out by a number of organizations. Among these issues was the use of white phosphorous, the use of flechette missiles, the use of so-called dense inert metal explosive (DIME) munitions, and the use of depleted uranium.

A. WHITE PHOSPHOROUS

White phosphorous was used throughout the ground phase of the operations. The Israeli Government has set out its reasons for doing so, emphasizing that it is not only not a proscribed weapon under international law but that it was deployed with a high degree of success.

It has explained that it used white phosphorous in two forms. One was as exploding munitions used as mortar shells by ground and naval forces. It says that in this form it was deployed only in unpopulated areas for marking and signalling purposes, and not in an anti-personnel capacity. It claims that, as a result of international concerns, it decided to stop using these munitions on 7 January 2009, although this was not required by international law. It also acknowledges the use of smoke projectiles containing felt wedges dipped in white phosphorous.

The Mission understands the means of deploying these smoke projectiles was that they were fired as a canister shell by 155 mm howitzers. The projectile was timed or programmed to air-burst over its designated target. The canister shell then discharged a quantity of felt wedges impregnated with white phosphorous, usually in the order of 160 wedges in a fan-like dispersion earthwards. These wedges with white phosphorous, which is a pyrophoric chemical (that is, self-igniting when in contact with the air), emit smoke and continue to do so until the chemical is exhausted or deprived of air. Wedges of white phosphorous therefore remain active and have done so in Gaza for up to 21 and 24 days after discharge. It is technically possible that there are still active white phosphorous wedges in Gaza—in water tanks or in sewage systems, for example. Children have subsequently been injured by coming in contact with such wedges.

The Mission has recounted a number of incidents where it has particular concern about the choice to use white phosphorous. These incidents have been addressed in detail elsewhere and include the incidents at the UNRWA compound in Gaza City, the attacks on al-Quds and al-Wafa hospitals, also in Gaza City, and the use of white phosphorous in the attack on the Abu Halima family to the north of al-Atatra and in Khuza'a.

The Mission notes that, at least in the case of Abu Halima, it appears that the white phosphorous was deployed by means of an exploding shell and not as a smoke projectile. This occurred several days after the apparent decision to stop using the munitions on 7 January 2009.

The Mission has also spoken at some length to a number of local and international medical experts who treated patients in Gaza who suffered burns as a result of exposure to white phosphorous.

The Mission need not repeat much of what it has already concluded on the choice to use white phosphorous in specific circumstances. It has already made clear that the risks it posed to the civilian population and civilian objects in the area under attack were excessive in relation to the specific military advantages sought.

The Israeli Government has frequently pointed out the difficulties posed by fighting in built-up areas. One of the difficulties is the proximity of civilian premises to possible military targets. Commanders have no choice but to factor in the risk to such premises and the people inside them in deciding which weapons to use.

The Mission finds that the Israeli armed forces were systematically reckless in determining to use white phosphorous in built-up areas and in particular in and around areas of particular importance to civilian health and safety.

In addition to the reckless use of white phosphorous, the Mission must emphasize that it is concerned not only with the inordinate risks the Israeli armed forces took in using it but also the damage it caused in fact. In speaking with medical experts and practitioners, it was impressed by the severity and sometimes untreatable nature of the burns caused by the substance.

Several doctors told of how they believed they had dealt with a wound successfully only to find unexpected complications developing as a result of the phosphorous having caused deeper damage to tissue and organs than could be detected at the time. Several patients died, according to doctors, as a result of organ failure resulting from the burns.

A senior doctor at al-Shifa hospital in Gaza City confirmed that Sabah, Ghada and Farah Abu Halima were admitted with serious burns and transferred to Egypt for treatment. The doctor believed that the burns were caused by contact with white phosphorous.

The doctor commented that, before the military operations, the hospital was not familiar with white phosphorous burns. Staff became concerned when patients who had been sent home after treatment of apparently minor burns would come back in the following days with more serious wounds. They found that when they removed the bandages that had been applied to a wound that still contained fragments of white phosphorous, smoke would come from the wound, even hours after the injury. White phosphorous continues to burn as long as it is in contact with oxygen.

International doctors working with al-Shifa staff, some of whom had worked in Lebanon during the 2006 war, identified white phosphorous as the cause of these injuries and the treatment was adapted accordingly. Any apparent white phosphorous burn was immediately covered with a wet sponge and the particles extracted. White phosphorous sticks to tissue, so all flesh and sometimes the muscle around the burn would have to be excised.

In addition, the highly toxic substance, used so widely in civilian settings, posed a real health threat to doctors dealing with patients. Medical staff reported to the

Mission how even working in the areas where the phosphorous had been used made them feel sick; their lips would swell and they would become extremely thirsty and nauseous.

While accepting that white phosphorous is not at this stage proscribed under international law, the Mission considers that the repeated misuse of the substance by the Israeli armed forces during this operation calls into question the wisdom of allowing its continued use without some further degree of control. The Mission understands the need to use obscurants and illuminants for various reasons during military operations and especially in screening troops from observation or enemy fire. There are, however, other screening and illuminating means which are free from the toxicities, volatilities and hazards that are inherent in the chemical white phosphorous. The use of white phosphorous in any form in and around areas dedicated to the health and safety of civilians has been shown to carry very substantial risks. The Mission therefore believes that serious consideration should be given to banning the use of white phosphorous as an obscurant.

B. FLECHETTES

Flechettes are small, dart-like pieces of composite metal and are usually fired in salvo from canister projectiles or shells. Those fired and retrieved in Gaza were 4 cm long and approximately 2–4 mm wide, having a pointed end and a fletched end.

Flechettes are used in an anti-personnel role and are discharged in such quantities that they cover an area forward of the canister shell. As an area weapon, on impact the darts will hit whatever is within a certain zone. They are incapable of discriminating between objectives after detonation. They are, therefore, particularly unsuitable for use in urban settings where there is reason to believe civilians may be present.

Flechettes were fired during the military operations on several occasions by tanks and on at least one occasion from an air-to-surface missile of the "Hellfire" type. In all cases those hit by these devices were civilians and in one case were attending a condolence tent following the loss of a family member who was also killed by flechettes.

Flechettes are known to bend, break or "tumble" on impact with human flesh. Such performances are often part of the flechettes' design characteristic and are marketed as such. "Tumbling" in particular is adjudged to be a further determination of the projectiles' "incapacitation" effect. The Mission notes, however, that flechettes can be designed to be free of these post-impact characteristics if it is desired that they should do so.

C. ALLEGED USE OF MUNITIONS CAUSING A SPECIFIC TYPE OF INJURY

The Mission received reports from Palestinian and foreign doctors who operated in Gaza during the military operations of a strikingly high percentage of patients with severed legs as a result of the impact of projectiles launched by the Israeli armed forces. Dr. Mads Gilbert, a Norwegian anaesthetist, and Dr. Eric Fosse, a Norwegian surgeon, who carried out surgery in al-Shifa hospital from 31 December 2008 to 10 January 2009, described to the Mission the characteristics of the wounds. The amputations mostly occurred at waist height in children, generally lower in adults, and were combined with skin-deep, third-degree burns, four to six fingers upward from the amputation. Where the amputation took place, the flesh was cauterized as a result of the heat. The patients with these amputations had no shrapnel wounds, but red flashes on the abdomen and chest. The excision of large pieces of flesh was not infrequent in these patients. Dr. Gilbert added that the patients also suffered internal burns. This description was confirmed to the Mission by Palestinian surgeons.

The Mission understands such injuries to be compatible with the impact of DIME weapons. DIME weapons consist of a carbon-fibre casing filled with a homogeneous mixture of an explosive material and small particles, basically a powder, of a heavy metal, for instance, a tungsten alloy. Upon detonation of the explosive, the casing disintegrates into extremely small, non-lethal fibres. The tungsten powder tears apart anything it hits. The impact of such weapons in general causes very severe wounds within a relatively limited diameter (compared to other projectiles) from the point of detonation. As the small heavy metal particles can slice through soft tissue and bone, survivors close to the lethal zone may have their limbs amputated and tungsten alloy particles embedded in their bodies. The probabilities of injuries to persons at a greater distance from the detonation point are reduced compared to more conventional projectiles. It is therefore also referred to as a "focused lethality munition."

The materials submitted to the Mission, including by the expert witness Lt. Col. Lane, point to specific medical concerns with regard to survivors of DIME weapon injuries. The tungsten alloy particles are suspected to be highly carcinogenic and so small that they cannot be extracted from the patient's body. Dr. Gilbert noted that there had been no follow-up studies on the survivors of this type of amputation observed in Gaza and Lebanon since 2006 following Israeli military operations. There is some research suggesting that these patients might be at increased risk of cancer. These concerns apply equally to missile or projectile shrapnel of heavy metal such as tungsten or tungsten alloy which was used in at least two occasions in Gaza. The carcinogenic hazards are the same no matter the delivery means or the size or shape of the pieces of the metal that enter human flesh.

D. FACTUAL FINDINGS ON THE USE OF MUNITIONS CAUSING A SPECIFIC TYPE OF INJURY

From the facts it gathered, the Mission finds that the allegations that DIME weapons were used by the Israeli armed forces in Gaza during the military operations require further clarification with regard to their use and, particularly, the health-care needs of survivors of the amputations attributed to DIME weapons.

The Mission notes that DIME or heavy metal shrapnel weapons and weapons armed with heavy metal are not prohibited under international law as it currently stands. The "focused lethality" reportedly pursued in the development of DIME weapons could be seen as advancing compliance with the principle of distinction. The Mission also observes, however, that there remains a very high risk of harming civilians when using these weapons in built-up areas and that concerns have been expressed that DIME weapons could have a particularly adverse impact on the enjoyment of the right to health of survivors, which would go beyond the impact generally associated with being affected by anti-personnel weapons in an armed conflict.

[Removed: section E (paragraphs 911–912)]

CHAPTER XIII.

ATTACKS ON THE FOUNDATIONS OF CIVILIAN LIFE IN GAZA: DESTRUCTION OF INDUSTRIAL INFRASTRUCTURE, FOOD PRODUCTION, WATER INSTALLATIONS, SEWAGE TREATMENT PLANTS AND HOUSING

A. THE DESTRUCTION OF EL-BADER FLOUR MILL

The Mission visited the site of the air strikes and surveyed the surrounding area in Sudaniyah, west of Jabaliyah. It met and interviewed the Hamada brothers, joint owners of the el-Bader Flour Mill, on four occasions. It spoke with representatives of the business community about the context and consequences of the strike on the flour mill. Mr. [Rashad] Hamada also testified at the public hearings in Gaza. The Mission also addressed questions to the Government of Israel with regard to the military advantage pursued in attacking the el-Bader Flour Mill, but received no reply.

The Hamada brothers are well-established businessmen and hold *Businessman Cards*, issued by the Israeli authorities to facilitate business travel to and from Israel. The flour mill is one of several businesses owned by the brothers on this site, including a tomato-canning factory and a factory for the production of nappies [diapers]. These last two businesses were closed down sometime before the beginning of the Israeli military operations in Gaza, as the blockade led to a lack of supplies. According to Mr. Rashad Hamada, the tomato-canning business failed primarily because of the Israeli authorities' refusal to allow tins for canning into Gaza. The owners had transferred many employees from the businesses that had closed down to the flour mill so that these employees would continue to draw a salary. At the time of its destruction, the flour mill employed more than 50 people.

The el-Bader Flour Mill began operations in 1999. By 27 December 2008, it was the only one of Gaza's three flour mills still operating. The others had ceased operations owing to a lack of supplies. The el-Bader mill was able to continue in part because of its greater storage capacity.

On 30 December 2008, a recorded warning was left on the flour mill's answering machine to the effect that the message was from the Israeli armed forces and that the building should be evacuated immediately. The approximately 45 workers in the mill at the time were evacuated at around 9.30 A.M.

Following the evacuation, Mr. Hamada called a business associate in Israel, explained what had happened and asked him for advice. The business associate called him back, indicating that he had spoken with contacts in the Israeli armed forces on Mr. Hamada's behalf, and had been told that, although the mill had been on a list of proposed targets, they had decided not to proceed with the strike. Mr. Hamada did not receive any information as to why his mill might have been targeted.

As a result of these conversations and the fact that there had been no strike, the employees returned to work the next day. Work continued for a number of days until a second recorded warning was received on or around 4 January 2009. The flour mill was again evacuated and Mr. Hamada again contacted his business associate in Israel. The same scenario unfolded whereby Mr. Hamada received a call later on to the effect that the Israeli armed forces had informed his associate that the mill would not be hit. The employees returned to work in the light of this information and the fact that the warnings had not been put into effect.

On 9 January, at around 3 or 4 A.M., the flour mill was hit by an air strike, possibly by an F-16. The missile struck the floor that housed one of the machines indispensable to the mill's functioning, completely destroying it. The guard who was on duty at the time called Mr. Hamada to inform him that the building had been hit and was on fire. He was unhurt. In the next 60 to 90 minutes the mill was hit several times by missiles fired from an Apache helicopter. These missiles hit the upper floors of the factory, destroying key machinery. Adjoining buildings, including the grain store, were not hit. The strikes entirely disabled the factory and it has not been back in operation since. A large amount of grain remains at the site but cannot be processed.

The Israeli armed forces occupied the disabled building until around 13 January. Hundreds of shells were found on its roof after the soldiers left. They appeared to be 40 mm grenade machine-gun spent cartridges.

The Hamada brothers rejected any suggestion that the building was at any time used for any purpose by Palestinian armed groups. They pointed out that all of the buildings and factories were surrounded by a high wall and manned by at least one guard at night. In addition, the Israeli authorities knew them as businessmen and they would not have been given Businessman Cards had there been any reason for the Israeli Government to suspect that they were involved with or supported armed groups. They were both adamant that their interest was and always had been industrial and commercial, and that the last thing they were prepared to do was put their business at risk.

1. Factual findings

The Mission found the Hamada brothers to be credible and reliable witnesses. It has no reason to doubt the veracity of their testimony. The information they provided was corroborated by other representatives of the Gaza business community with whom the Mission discussed the context and consequences of the strike on the flour mill.

The owners and employees of the flour mill were forced to evacuate the building twice because of the two recorded warnings left on the answerphone, which were not followed by air strikes. They were put into a state of fear as a result of the false alarms. When the mill was hit on 9 January, the strike happened without prior warning, raising questions about the efficacy or seriousness of the warnings system used by the Israeli armed forces.

The consequences of the strike on the flour mill were significant. Not only are all the employees out of work, the capacity of Gaza to produce milled flour, the most basic staple ingredient of the local diet, has been greatly diminished. As a result, the population of Gaza is now more dependent on the Israeli authorities' granting permission for flour and bread to enter the Gaza Strip.

Available information does not suggest that the Israeli authorities have investigated the destruction of the flour mill. The Mission finds the version of the Hamada brothers to be credible and in line with the Israeli practice of leaving telephone warnings of impending attacks.

[Removed: sections 2 and 3 (paragraphs 926–941)]

B. THE DESTRUCTION OF THE SAWAFEARY CHICKEN FARMS

On or around the night of 3 January 2009 Israeli troops arrived at a number of houses on al-Sekka Road in Zeytoun. The Mission interviewed four people who were direct witnesses to and victims of the events that occurred in the aftermath of their arrival. One witness was interviewed three times for a total of five hours and testified at the public hearings in Gaza. Another three were interviewed for an hour each. The Mission also visited the site of the Sawafeary chicken farms. Finally, the Mission addressed questions to the Government of Israel with regard to the military advantage pursued in attacking Mr. Sawafeary's chicken farms, but received no reply. The following narrative reflects the eyewitness accounts.

Sameh Sawafeary is a chicken farmer. His family has been in the egg production business for many years. He indicated that he, his brothers and his children owned 11 chicken farms in Zeytoun as of December 2008. The farms housed more than 100,000 chickens.

On 3 January, Mr. Sawafeary, who was in his home on al-Sekka Road in the al-Samouni neighbourhood of Zeytoun with his family, was alerted by an al-Jazeera television news broadcast at around 8 P.M. that an Israeli ground invasion was imminent. As a result, he took a number of precautions, including hiding money and other valuables. He then gathered around 11 members of his family on the upper floor of the two-storey concrete house. At around 10 P.M. a missile struck the house, entering through the rear of the upper floor and exiting near the window of the living room opposite. The missile passed over several of Mr. Sawafeary's children and grandchildren, who were lying on the floor. No one was injured.

At around 11 P.M., Mr. Sawafeary heard the sound of helicopters flying over his house followed by soldiers landing on his roof. The soldiers remained there until

7 A.M. the next morning, firing what he described as "a rain of bullets." The family stayed, terrified, on the floor of an upstairs room.

At around 7.15 A.M. on 4 January, soldiers came into the upstairs room where the family was sheltering. They separated the men from the women and put the women in another room. The hands of the men and the boys were tied behind their backs, except for one of Mr. Sawafeary's sons who has only one arm. After some time the commander told Mr. Sawafeary that they should walk south and "go to Rafah." The soldiers then searched the house. The 11 members of the household there at the time left the house as instructed.

The Sawafeary family spent the following five days in terror. Together with neighbouring families they spent one night in the Abu Zur house and the following three in the nearby house of Mr. Rajab Mughrabi. During that time they suffered a number of violations at the hands of the Israeli armed forces, including the killing of the child Ibrahim Juha (see chap. XI).

For the purposes of this section the Mission refers to the information it received about the systematic destruction that occurred for several days and which the witnesses were able to see during the time they were forced by the circumstances to remain in the house of Mr. Mughrabi.

Mr. Sawafeary and Mr. Mughrabi informed the Mission that they had watched Israeli armoured bulldozers systematically destroy land, crops, chickens and farm infrastructure. Mr. Mughrabi stated that he watched the bulldozers plough through fields with crops and trees, destroying everything in their path. Mr. Sawafeary stated that he saw less, as he was watching through a small opening because he was afraid of being seen and shot. He stated that he saw only two or three "tanks," but was not in a position to say whether there were more. He watched as the armoured bulldozers destroyed the chicken farms, crushing the wire mesh coops with the chickens inside. He could not see his own farms and the chickens he could see being destroyed were not his. He noted that the drivers of the tanks would spend hours flattening the chicken coops, sometimes stopping for coffee breaks, before resuming their work.

When he left Mr. Mughrabi's house on 8 January, Mr. Sawafeary was able to see that his own farms did not appear to have been subjected to the destruction he had witnessed from inside the house. However, when he was able to return to his home after the Israeli withdrawal all 31,000 of his chickens had been killed and the coops systematically flattened.

The Mission visited the site and saw the still flattened mesh coops, which had been covered with corrugated iron, as well as the remains of water tanks and machinery. The Mission was also shown the remnants of a small mosque near the end of one of the lines of the coops that had been destroyed. The remains of some dead chickens were still visible and Mr. Sawafeary stated that it had been a mammoth task to clean up the area when he returned. He pointed out that, in addition to the loss of livestock, the farm had been completely automated with significant investment in machinery, all of which had been destroyed, as had the plant for packaging the eggs. In short, the business had been razed to the ground. A protective grille, believed to be part of a D-9 armoured bulldozer, was found at the site.

The Mission notes comments from one soldier to Breaking the Silence that appear to broadly corroborate the destruction in Zeytoun, probably at the hands of the Givati Brigade.

The Mission inspected the inside of Mr. Sawafeary's house and noted damage to the upper floor, where a missile had penetrated. It also observed a number of graffiti that appeared to have been written by Israeli troops. One said "424 Givati." There were others apparently written in Russian.

Mr. Sawafeary told the Mission that he and his family together supplied approximately 35 per cent of the egg market in Gaza. His own farms supplied over 10 per cent. He noted that it was not only his farms that had been destroyed but also most of his family's farms had been destroyed in the same way as his. He estimated that close to 100,000 chickens were killed in the process.

The Mission has reviewed the relevant UNOSAT report and satellite imagery. One satellite image shows the Sawafeary chicken farms in June 2007 and another shows the area in January 2009. The images depict clearly the size of the farms and the surrounding area. The destruction is plainly visible in the second image.

1. Factual findings

The systematic destruction along with the large numbers of killings of civilians suggest premeditation and a high level of planning. Even in the context of a campaign that had many serious violations of international humanitarian law, the events in Zeytoun at this time stand out.

The Mission finds that the destruction of the land and farms in the area was not justified by the pursuit of any military objective. The Israeli armed forces that arrived took control of the area within a matter of hours. They remained there until 18 January. The destruction of the land was not necessary to move the tanks or equipment or gain any particular visual advantage.

An inspection of the scene indicates that the area is relatively sparsely populated. The Mission rejects the idea that the Sawafeary farm was destroyed in the pursuit of any military objective.

The destruction of the farms appears to have been wanton and not militarily necessary. Not only were the coops with the chickens destroyed, but all of the plant and machinery of the farms as well.

From the facts ascertained by it, the Mission finds that the Sawafeary chicken farms, the 31,000 chickens and the plant and material necessary for the business were systematically and deliberately destroyed, and that this constituted a deliberate act of wanton destruction not justified by any military necessity.

[Removed: section 2 (paragraph 961)]

C. THE DESTRUCTION OF WATER AND SEWAGE INSTALLATION

1. The Gaza wastewater treatment plant, Road No. 10, al-Sheikh Ejlin, Gaza City

The Mission visited the site of al-Sheikh Ejlin treatment plant on 3 and 17 June 2009. While there it interviewed the Director of the Coastal Municipalities Water Utility (CMWU), Mr. Munther Shublaq, inspected the plant, the site of lagoon No. 3 and the location where a large pipe carrying raw sewage had been ruptured. On 3 June, the Mission also visited a nearby farm that had been inundated with raw sewage and spoke to the farmer. The Mission interviewed Mr. Munther Shublaq a second time at length on 14 June 2009. The Mission took photographs of the area, and obtained plans and diagrams of the plant. Finally, the Mission addressed questions to the Government of Israel with regard to the military advantage pursued in attacking al-Sheikh Ejlin treatment plant, but received no reply.

The Gaza wastewater treatment plant is located in the coastal area south-west of Gaza City in the al-Sheikh Ejlin neighbourhood. It was built in 1977 and expanded with support from development cooperation. It consists of a number of installations, including offices, tanks and lagoons to store raw sewage.

At some point between 3 and 10 January, a large missile hit the northernmost wall of lagoon No. 3, causing a massive outflow of raw sewage, which travelled a distance of 1.2 kilometres and damaged 5.5 hectares of land, including agricultural land, according to UNOSAT satellite imagery.

The chief of the plant, Mr. Jaoudat al-Dalou, explained to the Mission that when the Israeli ground offensive started around 3 January, all staff left for security reasons, as did the local residents of the sparsely populated area. Around 14 January, he received a phone call from someone in the vicinity of the plant reporting the strike on lagoon No. 3 and the flooding of neighbouring farmland by sewage. He contacted ICRC and PRCS to seek permission from the Israeli armed forces to go to the plant and carry out urgent repairs. Permission was denied on the grounds that the area was a "military zone."

After the withdrawal of the Israeli armed forces, Mr. al-Dalou and his colleagues returned to al-Sheikh Ejlin to inspect the damage. They also saw what they believed to be unexploded bombs nearby and called the police to contact UNRWA to clear the area. Mr. al-Dalou found a crater five metres deep on the north-east side of lagoon No. 3. The damaged wall took over four days to repair at a cost of some US$158,000. More than 200,000 cubic metres of raw sewage had flowed into neighbouring farmland.

In addition, a number of items, including an incubator, had been taken out of the plant and used by Israeli soldiers to make a barricade or protection wall. The damage done by the impact of bullets could still be seen on interior walls. Shattered windows had still not been replaced as glass was not available. Other damaged equipment included distillation equipment (damaged beyond repair) and a nitrogen ammonium machine.

In interviews with the Mission, Mr. Munther Shublaq, who issued a CMWU report of the damage in January 2009, confirmed that staff had left upon the arrival of Israeli ground forces and did not return until their withdrawal. He also indicated that on hearing news of the rupture of lagoon No. 3 he made several unsuccessful efforts to obtain permission to access the area to stop the damage caused by the outflow.

The Mission noted breaks in a large raw-sewage pipe which ran to the north of lagoon No. 3. Plant officials suggested that clearly visible markings on the pipe had been made by tanks. The routes of such pipes are marked by 1.5-metre-high, red and white poles to ensure that care is taken not to damage the pipes. The damage is very close to one such pole.

The precise date of the strike on Lagoon No. 3 is uncertain because there were no witnesses in the area at the time. With satellite images it is, however, possible to establish that the strike must have occurred before 10 January 2009, as the images clearly show the massive outflow of sewage from the lagoon on that date.

It is also possible to ascertain from the satellite images that the strike on the lagoon wall's eastern side created a breach of about 22 metres, through which the sewage flowed. The same images show the route of the outflow and where it stopped. The United Nations Environment Programme carried out a ground survey of the site on 30 January 2009 and data from that survey were added to the UNOSAT image interpretation.

The plant occupies a position at the top of a hill and provides a view over a considerable area of open land, which is mainly farmland. As such, it might reasonably be considered to be of strategic interest.

Factual findings

The plant was effectively abandoned by staff when the ground invasion began. The strike on lagoon No. 3 must have occurred after the Israeli armed forces had taken control of the plant and the surrounding area as the employees interviewed confirmed that it was intact when they left the area. Although the damage to the raw-sewage pipe may have been caused by a tank stopping or passing over it, the Mission is not in a position to conclude that this was in fact what occurred.

Notwithstanding the possible military advantage offered to the Israeli armed forces by the plant's location, the Mission cannot find any justification for striking the lagoon with what must have been a very powerful missile, sufficient to cause a breach 5 metres deep and 22 metres wide. It is highly unlikely that Palestinian armed groups could have taken up positions in or around the lagoon after the initial occupation of the area by Israeli armed forces: any such groups would have been exposed in the open area. The fact that the lagoon wall was struck precisely there where it would cause outflow of the raw sewage suggests that the strike was deliberate and premeditated.

2. Namar wells group, Salah ad-Din Street, Jabaliyah refugee camp

The Mission visited the site of the Namar wells group on 17 June 2009. It interviewed engineer Ramadan Nai'm, CMWU water production and storage manager, and Ibrahim al-Ejjla, CMWU media coordinator. The Mission took photographs of the site. The Mission also addressed questions to the Government of Israel with regard to the military advantage pursued in attacking the Namar wells group, but received no reply.

The wells group stood approximately 50 metres from the Jabaliyah refugee camp's administration building, which was also destroyed. A crater (approximately five metres wide) was still visible in the grounds belonging to the civil administration, with at its bottom the case of a rocket.

This was a complex of two water well pumps, one in operation and another next to it as standby. Mr. Ramadan Nai'm told the Mission how proud CMWU had been of this water well, which produced more than 200 cubic metres per hour of the best-quality water in the area. The well supplied water to some 25,000 people in eastern and central Jabaliyah. The standby well pump was capable of pumping some 100 cubic metres of water. Both were completely destroyed on 27 December by an air strike.

In the Namar water wells complex there were not only pumping machines but also a 180 kg generator, a fuel store, a reservoir chlorination unit, buildings and related equipment. These were also destroyed.

The operator, Mr. Abdullah Ismail al-Zein, was killed in the air strike while he was working at the station. He was employed by the Municipality rather than by CMWU and had been working in the station for four years. He was blown to pieces and his identity was established when his shoes were found three days later.

The strike also blew up the pipes connecting the wells to other water wells; incoming water spilled into the area for some 10 days before the pipes could be shut off.

Mr. Nai'm informed the Mission that he tried through the mediation of ICRC to get permission from the Israeli armed forces to repair the supply pipes, but permission was not granted and he was obliged to wait until the withdrawal of the Israeli armed forces.

It was calculated that repairs to this group of water wells would cost around US$200,000, excluding the ancillary but necessary civil engineering works.

Mr. Nai'm stated that at least 10 bombs were used to destroy the complex. Not a single wall was left intact.

Factual findings

From the facts ascertained by it, the Mission finds that the Namar wells were destroyed by multiple air strikes on the first day of the Israeli aerial attack and that civil administration buildings located at approximately 50 metres were also destroyed.

The question remains as to whether the Israeli air strikes on the Namar wells group were deliberate or made in error. The Mission notes that the deployment systems and aircraft used in the strikes of 27 December (principally F-16 fighter jets and UAVs) are capable of a high degree of precision. It notes also that, by all accounts, a great deal of preparation had been put into determining and designating the targets of air strikes. The Mission considers it unlikely that a target the size of the Namar wells could have been hit by multiple strikes in error, given the nature of the deployment systems and the distance between the wells and any neighbouring buildings. The facts thus indicate that the strikes on the Namar wells group were intentional.

The Mission found no grounds to suggest that there was any military advantage to be gained from hitting the wells. There was no suggestion that Palestinian armed groups had used the wells for any purpose.

[Removed: section 3 (paragraphs 987–989)]

D. THE DESTRUCTION OF HOUSING

The Mission received information about the extensive destruction of houses and private property during the military operations. During its own visits to the Gaza

Strip, the Mission witnessed the extent of the destruction caused by air strikes, mortar and artillery shelling, missile strikes, the operation of bulldozers and demolition charges. Some areas of the Gaza Strip were more heavily affected than others, but the Mission saw many piles of rubble where, prior to the military operations, there had been multi-storey houses.

In many, if not most, of the incidents investigated by the Mission, described in chapters X, XI, XIV and XV, the victims it interviewed not only suffered the loss of loved ones (or were used as human shields or detained) but also saw their homes severely damaged or completely destroyed. For present purposes, the Mission will recall a few of the incidents relating to the destruction of housing.

In some cases, the damage to or destruction of housing was arguably related to the conduct of military operations against Palestinian combatants. The houses of Majdi Abd Rabbo and of his neighbour, HS/08, for instance, were destroyed in combat against the three Palestinian fighters hiding in HS/08's house (see chap. XIV).

In many others, such as the shelling of the houses of Mahmoud Abd Rabbo al-Ajrami (chap. XIV), of the Sawafeary family (see above and chap. XI) and of the Abu Halima family (chap. XI), the houses were in the general path of the advancing Israeli ground troops.

In a third group of cases, however, the facts ascertained by the Mission strongly suggest that housing was destroyed without their having any direct link to combat operations. On 6 January 2009 at 1.45 A.M., Mr. Abu Askar received a phone call from the Israeli armed forces informing him that his family should evacuate their house as it was going to be targeted by an air strike. This warning was put into practice a few minutes later, when the home of about 40 members of the extended Abu Askar family was destroyed by a missile (see chap. X).

In Juhr ad-Dik, after the killing of Majda and Rayya Hajaj, the Israeli armed forces directed machine-gun fire at the house of the al-Safadi family for the entire afternoon of 4 January 2009. The soldiers firing at the house had seen the Hajaj and al-Safadi families taking refuge there after their failed attempt to flee to Gaza City. When the Hajaj family managed to leave Juhr ad-Dik the following day, Israeli troops apparently took up position in Mr. Youssef Hajaj's house, which they rendered completely uninhabitable, as the Mission saw for itself during a visit. His brother Saleh Hajaj was even less fortunate. His house was reduced to a pile of rubble.

Other neighbourhoods were destroyed during the last few days of the military operations as the Israeli armed forces were preparing to withdraw. For example, in an incident described below, after an attempt to demolish a cement-packaging plant in east Gaza, soldiers also destroyed the surrounding houses of the owner and the employees. The factory owner, Mr. Abu Jubbah, had hidden in the house for two days with seven members of his family. Suddenly, a direct strike on the side of the house warned them that the house was to be destroyed and they should leave. Waving a white flag, Mr. Abu Jubbah left the house in a rush, put his family in a car and drove off. On their way they saw tanks and soldiers in the area. Their house was destroyed by shelling. It took several strikes to destroy it, while the factory facilities and the fence were demolished by bulldozers. Housing for 55 factory workers was also demolished with bulldozers.

Two further cases investigated by the Mission also exemplify the deliberate demolition of residential housing. The house of Wa'el al-Samouni, in which 21 family members died, was damaged but still standing when PRCS and ICRC extracted the wounded survivors in the afternoon of 7 January 2009 (chap. XI). When the family and rescuers returned to the area on 18 January, the house was completely demolished. As the Mission could see for itself during its visit to the area as well as on photographs taken on that day, the manner in which the house had collapsed strongly indicated that this was the result of deliberate demolition and not of combat.

Similarly, when Khaled Abd Rabbo [see Testimony 15] returned to the home of his extended family in Izbat Abd Rabbo (which he had abandoned intact after the shooting of his daughters) after the withdrawal of the Israeli armed forces, he found it completely demolished, as were the other houses in the vicinity. Khaled Abd Rabbo drew the Mission's attention to what appeared to be an anti-tank mine visible under the rubble of his neighbour's house, which had reportedly been used by the Israeli armed forces to cause the controlled explosion which brought down the building. As in the case of Wa'el al-Samouni's house, the way the buildings had collapsed strongly suggests that both Khaled Abd Rabbo's house and that of his neighbour were deliberately demolished by explosives experts, rather than damaged during combat. Khaled Abd Rabbo added that, to his knowledge, his house had been demolished by the Israeli armed forces shortly before they withdrew from Gaza.

1. Factual findings

From the facts gathered, the Mission concludes that, in a number of cases it investigated, the Israeli armed forces launched direct attacks against residential houses, destroying them. Although the Mission does not have complete information on the circumstances prevailing in Juhr ad-Dik, al-Samouni neighbourhood and Izbat Abd Rabbo when the houses of the Hajaj, al-Samouni and Khaled Abd Rabbo families were destroyed, the information in its possession strongly suggests that they were destroyed outside of any combat engagements with Palestinian armed groups. Nor were these houses otherwise making any effective contribution to military action. These attacks deprived the extended families living there of shelter and of a significant part of their property.

In other cases, residential neighbourhoods were subjected to air-launched bombing and to intensive shelling apparently in the context of the advance of Israeli ground forces. In these cases, although the facts gathered by the Mission do not suggest that the residential houses were directly targeted, it doubts whether there were military objectives pursued by the shelling.

2. Corroboration of Mission's factual findings and widespread nature of housing destruction

Testimonies of Israeli soldiers deployed in Gaza during the military operations corroborate what the Mission saw for itself and heard from the witnesses it interviewed. Several of the soldiers interviewed by Breaking the Silence spoke of the unprecedented scale of destruction of houses and of "intentional, systematic destruction." The testimonies of the soldiers appear to distinguish between three phases in or types of destruction of residential housing. First, there is the destruction which is incidental to the actual combat between the advancing Israeli forces and the Palestinian combatants or to Israeli forces directing fire at locations from which rockets were launched. Second, there is destruction of houses for what is termed "operational reasons." This is the deliberate destruction of houses from which fire had been opened on Israeli soldiers or which were suspected of being booby-trapped, containing tunnels or being used for weapons storage. "Operational necessity" also embraced the destruction of houses which obstructed visibility for the Israeli armed forces or had a "strategic advantage" for them. "In case of any doubt, take down houses. You don't need confirmation for anything, if you want" were the instructions of one commander to his troops.

The third phase of destruction of housing was no longer tied to the "operational necessities" of the ongoing military operations. It was in view of "the day after" the Israeli armed forces withdrew from Gaza. In the words of one Israeli soldier:

> . . . [T]hen we were told there are houses to be demolished for the sake of
> "the day after." The day after is actually a thought that obviously we're going

in for a limited period of time which could be a week and it might also be a few months. But it's not a longer span of time without defining what it is. And the rationale was that we want to come out with the area remaining sterile as far as we're concerned. And the best way to do this is by razing. That way we have good firing capacity, good visibility for observation, we can see anything, we control a very large part of the area and very effectively. This was the meaning of demolition for the sake of the day after. In practical terms this meant taking a house that is not implicated in any way, that its single sin is the fact that it is situated on top of a hill in the Gaza Strip.

Satellite imagery provided by UNOSAT at the Mission's request is consistent with the soldiers' testimonies. It shows, for instance, that 65 per cent of the destruction/damage of buildings in Rafah was caused by air strikes between 11 and 18 January. By contrast, 54 per cent of the destruction/damage in Izbat Abd Rabbo (east Gaza) occurred between 6 and 10 January as the Israeli troops advanced into the city.

The UNOSAT reports on the destruction of buildings in al-Samouni neighbourhood and al-Atatra, two areas that suffered particularly heavy destruction of civilian housing and other buildings, show that most were destroyed during the last three days of the Israeli armed forces' presence on the ground in Gaza. In al-Samouni, out of 114 severely damaged or completely destroyed buildings, 60 were destroyed between 27 December 2008 and 10 January 2009 (i.e. the air phase and the advance of the ground invasion), only 4 between 10 and 16 January and 50 between 16 and 19 January 2009. Similarly, in al-Atatra, out of 94 severely damaged or completely destroyed buildings, 36 were destroyed between 27 December 2008 and 10 January 2009, only 6 between 10 and 16 January 2009, and 52 between 16 and 19 January 2009.

These figures confirm that a first phase of extensive destruction of housing for the "operational necessity" of the advancing Israeli forces in these areas was followed by a period of relative idleness on the part of the Israeli bulldozers and explosives engineers. But during the last three days, aware of their imminent withdrawal, the Israeli armed forces engaged in another wave of systematic destruction of civilian buildings.

[Removed: section 3 (paragraphs 1005–1007)]

E. ANALYSIS OF THE PATTERN OF WIDESPREAD DESTRUCTION OF ECONOMIC AND INFRASTRUCTURAL TARGETS

The Mission interviewed Mr. Amr Hamad, the Deputy General-Secretary of the Palestinian Federation of Industries, on three separate occasions, including at the public hearings in Gaza. The Mission also met a number of businessmen involved in fishing, strawberry farming, construction, including concrete and cement production and packaging, food and drinks production, car mechanics and repairs, livestock farming and refrigeration. While much of the information provided to the Mission focused on the effect of the restrictions Israel had imposed on the Gaza Strip for a considerable time before 27 December 2008, significant information was also provided on the effect of the attacks during the Israeli military operations in Gaza.

Amr Hamad indicated that 324 factories had been destroyed during the Israeli military operations at a cost of 40,000 jobs. In its detailed written report on the impact of the Israeli military activities, the Palestinian Federation of Industries points out that 200 businesses and factories were destroyed in Gaza City, 101 in northern Gaza and 20 in southern Gaza. Of the total 324 premises damaged, almost 30 per cent were linked to the metals and engineering sector, over 20 per cent to construction and 16 per cent to furniture businesses. Other sectors with significant losses were aluminium, food, sewing textiles, chemicals and cosmetics, plastics and rubber, paper and carton, and handicrafts. The Federation states that more than half were totally destroyed. The Federation emphasized that "the Gaza Strip's most crucial industries, and ones which require the greatest investment, were most severely hit." Eleven of the 324 premises struck by the Israeli armed forces were linked to the food industry and the losses incurred amount to some US$37 million, i.e. over one third of all the losses to the industrial sector. Similarly, while the construction sector suffered 69 of the 324 strikes, this represented just under 30 per cent of the total damage. The report notes that the majority of the losses resulting from the strikes on the 324 premises related to machinery costs (50 per cent), while just over a quarter relate to the buildings themselves.

The Mission found the information provided by Mr. Hamad, as well as the report produced by the Palestinian Federation of Industries, to be credible and reliable. The Mission discussed and was satisfied by the methodology used in compiling the report, which was produced with the support of the Konrad Adenauer Foundation.

TESTIMONY 7

Amr Hamad

Deputy General-Secretary of the Palestinian Federation of Industries, explaining the effect on workers of the destruction of Gaza's industrial sector

There is no doubt that the biggest loser[s] of the destruction of such factories are the workers themselves. We know that the industrial sector was home to more than 120,000 workers. Most of them have been laid off. Regretfully, however, those laid-off workers will have to seek humanitarian aid from international organizations or charity organizations. So these workers will become simply a burden on the society. They will have to seek work within the armed militias or will have to work in the black market or in the informal economy or will work in the tunnels. So those are the steps that will probably be made by such workers, which will lead to losing their skills.

The Mission also found that the testimony of businessmen whose premises had been struck or destroyed by the Israeli armed forces corroborate information provided by Mr. Hamad and the Palestinian Federation of Industries.

1. Construction industry

One of the incidents Mr. Hamad referred to at the public hearing relates to the destruction of the only cement-packaging plant in Gaza. The Mission also interviewed its owner, Mr. Atta Abu Jubbah. According to the reconstruction of the events, the Israeli armed forces began striking the plant from the air, damaging it significantly. Later ground forces—equipped with bulldozers and tanks—moved in and used mines and explosives to destroy the silo that used to contain 4,000 tons of cement. Helicopters launched rockets to destroy the main manufacturing line and fired holes into the cement containers. Bulldozers were used to destroy the factory walls. Over four days the factory was systematically destroyed. The Mission spoke with a number of other witnesses able to verify this account and considers it to be reliable. Among those witnesses was a civil engineer who inspected the site and confirmed that certain aspects of the destruction could have been achieved only by placing explosives inside the building. The silo had not been entirely destroyed in the aerial attacks, so explosives were attached to its supporting columns.

The plant was an important part of Gaza's construction industry. It produced cement in bags, selling 200 tons per day with a profit of US$15 per ton. The company is valued at some US$12 million. As mentioned above, the owner's house was also destroyed by rocket fire.

The owner is one of fewer than 100 businessmen who are in possession of the Businessman Card issued by Israel. The Mission notes that the plant was not destroyed during the aerial phase but was systematically reduced to rubble in a concerted effort over several days at the end of the military operations.

The destruction of Mr. Atta Abu Jubbah's plant forms part of what appears to have been a very deliberate strategy of attacking the construction industry. The Palestinian Federation of Industries also provides details on the systematic and total destruction of the Abu Eida factories for ready-mix concrete. They were established in 1993. Nineteen of the 27 concrete factories were reported to have been destroyed, representing 85 per cent of the productive capacity.

The ability to produce and supply concrete in a context where external supplies are entirely controlled by Israel is a matter not only of economic importance but arguably one of human necessity to satisfy the basic need for shelter. Even if the population can get by in makeshift accommodation or by living in cramped conditions with their extended families, the capacity to repair the massive damage done to buildings without internally produced concrete is severely reduced. To the extent that concrete is allowed to enter at all, it is significantly more expensive than domestically produced concrete.

There appears to have been no military reason or justification for destroying the factory. This conclusion is borne out by the long-established trading history of the owners and their recognition through the Businessman Cards.

[Removed: section 2 (paragraphs 1018–1021)]

3. Destruction of water installations

Finally, in relation to the supply and treatment of water, the Mission analysed a limited number of cases. The strikes on the al-Sheikh Ejlin plant and on the Namar water wells have been described in some detail. The Mission also spoke at length with Mr. Munther Shublaq, who was responsible for the CMWU Damage Assessment Report. That report indicates that all types of water installations appeared to have been damaged to some extent during the Israeli operations, but

notes especially that in some areas, particularly Beit Lahia, Jabaliyah, Beit Hanoun, part of Zeytoun, south of Rafah and the villages in the east, buildings, water
and wastewater infrastructure and other facilities have been totally destroyed.
"Those areas need a complete water and wastewater infrastructure which may require re-designing the networks based on the new population in the area."

Mr. Munther Shublaq noted that, although a number of wells had been struck, the
worst effects had been as a result of the damage to water-treatment plants and
sewage pipes. The Mission heard a number of reports that indicated that the strikes
on plants, pipes, wells and tanks had put considerable pressure on the sanitation
and water-supply system.

[Removed: remainder of section 3 (paragraphs 1024–1025)]

4. Conclusions

The facts ascertained by the Mission indicate that there was a deliberate and systematic policy on the part of the Israeli armed forces to target industrial sites and
water installations. In a number of testimonies given to Breaking the Silence, Israeli soldiers have described in detail the way in which what is at one point eu-
phemistically referred to as "infrastructure work" was carried out. The deployment
of bulldozers for systematic destruction is graphically recounted. Soldiers confirm
in considerable detail information provided to the Mission by witnesses.

[Removed: remainder of section 4 (paragraph 1027)]

[Removed: section 5 (paragraphs 1028–1031)]

CHAPTER XIV.

THE USE OF PALESTINIAN CIVILIANS AS HUMAN SHIELDS

The Mission received allegations that in two areas in north Gaza Israeli troops used Palestinian men as human shields whilst conducting house searches. The Palestinian men were allegedly forced to enter houses at gunpoint in front of or, in one case, instead of soldiers. The Mission investigated four cases. One incident took place in the Izbat Abd Rabbo neighbourhood and another in al-Salam neighbourhood, both east of Jabaliyah, close to the border with Israel.

Two incidents took place in al-Israa neighbourhood, west of Beit Lahia. The Mission visited each of the locations and interviewed a number of witnesses. In each case, the Mission found the allegations to be credible.

A. THE CASE OF MAJDI ABD RABBO

To investigate this case, the Mission visited Izbat Abd Rabbo. The Mission interviewed Mr. Majdi Abd Rabbo and several of his neighbours. It also obtained two sworn statements Majdi Abd Rabbo had given to two NGOs.

Majdi Abd Rabbo, a man aged 39 at the time of the incident, is married and the father of five children aged between 16 years and 14 months. He is an intelligence officer of the Palestinian Authority. He lived with his family in a house on the main street of Izbat Abd Rabbo, al-Quds Street, which in this section is commonly known as Izbat Abd Rabbo Street. His family house stood next to Salah ad-Din mosque. The home of the family of Khaled and Kawthar Abd Rabbo [see Testimony 15] is less than 500 metres east of the Majdi Abd Rabbo family home.

Majdi Abd Rabbo recounted that, at around 9.30 A.M. on 5 January 2009, he heard loud banging on the outer door of the house. He asked who was at the door and someone responded in Arabic, ordering him to open the door. He opened the door and saw in front of him a handcuffed Palestinian man, whom he later found out to be HS/07, aged 20. A group of around 15 Israeli soldiers stood behind HS/07. One of the soldiers was holding a weapon to HS/07's head. The soldiers pushed HS/07 to one side and four soldiers pointed their weapons at Majdi Abd Rabbo. They ordered him to undress down to his underwear. He was then told to dress again and they pushed him into the house.

The soldiers ordered him to call his children one by one. He started with his eldest son, aged 16, who was ordered by the soldiers to strip naked. The same process was followed with the two other sons, aged nine and eight. He then called his daughter, aged 14, who was told to press her clothes to her body and turn around. His wife, who was holding their baby daughter, was also told to press her clothes to her body, and then to take the baby's trousers off.

Majdi Abd Rabbo stated that the soldiers then forced him to walk in front of them as they searched the house, room by room, holding a firearm to his head. They questioned him about the house behind his. He told them that the house was empty and the owner, HS/08, had been absent for four years working in the Sudan. There was a small gap between the two houses, but they were joined at the roof. The soldiers gave him a sledgehammer, the kind used to break stones, and told him to break a hole through the dividing wall into HS/08's house. This took around 15 minutes.

From the roof, the soldiers entered HS/08's house, pushing Majdi Abd Rabbo ahead of them down the stairs while they watched over his shoulders. They had descended only a few steps, however, when the soldiers apparently detected some movement in the house, started shouting, pulled Majdi Abd Rabbo back and rushed back into his house over the roof. Majdi Abd Rabbo heard some gun shots.

The soldiers ran out into the street, forcing Majdi Abd Rabbo and HS/07 with them while they were shooting. Both were taken into the adjacent mosque, where there were a large number of soldiers with military equipment. They were forced to sit down and then handcuffed.

The soldiers used the raised area of the mosque, from where the imam leads prayers, to fire at Majdi Abd Rabbo's house and the houses next to it. He shouted at the soldiers to stop, as his family was still in the house. A soldier told him to shut up or they would shoot him. The shooting continued for around 30 minutes. After a lull, the soldiers warned that there would be a huge explosion and, indeed, about three minutes later there was a huge explosion. The explosion was followed by intensive gunfire and artillery shells. Majdi Abd Rabbo could not identify the source of the explosion.

In the meantime, he had been forced to break a hole in the wall of the mosque on the south side and into the neighbouring house. He had then been interrogated about his knowledge of Hamas and the location of tunnels. Subsequently, he was taken and detained together with a group of neighbours, men and women, in another house in the neighbourhood (the HS/09 family home).

When the shooting stopped, soldiers came to fetch him. He was taken to the road next to his house, to an empty area behind HS/08's house. He saw that HS/08's house and the entrance area of his house had been damaged. There were numerous soldiers standing next to the house, including some officers. He saw a senior officer talking to the soldiers who raided his house, and the officer then came to speak to him, through an Arabic-speaking soldier. The soldier said that they had killed the fighters inside the house and told him to go into the house and come back with their clothes and weapons. He protested, saying that he just wanted to find out if his family was safe. The officer told him to obey their orders if he wanted to see his family again. He refused to go, and was kicked and beaten by soldiers with their weapons until he gave in.

He approached HS/08's house from the street. The entrance was destroyed and blocked by rubble. He went back to the officer and told him that he could not get in. The officer told him to go through the roof instead. He went into his own house, which he found empty, except for a soldier. This reinforced his anxiety about the fate of his family. At this point, there was no major damage to his house. He crossed the roof and went down the stairs into HS/08's house. He was scared that the fighters would shoot at him and shouted, "I am a Palestinian, a neighbour. I am being forced to come into this house." In a room at the bottom of the stairs he found three armed young men wearing military camouflage and headbands of al-Qassam Brigades. They pointed their weapons at him. He told them that the Israeli soldiers thought that they had been killed and had sent him to check. He said that he was helpless as the soldiers had taken his wife and children. The armed men told him that they had seen everything, and asked him to go back to the soldiers and tell them what he had seen.

He went back outside, again crossing over the roof of his house. As he approached the soldiers, they pointed their weapons at him and ordered him to stop, strip naked and turn around. After he dressed again, he told them what he had seen. Initially, the soldiers did not believe him. They asked how he knew that they were Hamas militants and he explained about their headbands. The soldiers asked about their weapons. He replied that they were carrying Kalashnikovs. The officer told him that, if he was lying, he would be shot dead.

He was handcuffed and taken back to the HS/09 family house for detention. At around 3 P.M., he heard gunfire for around 30 minutes. The soldiers came back for him and took him to the same officer. This time he noticed different soldiers present with different military equipment. Through the translator, the officer told him that they had killed the militants, and told him to go in and bring back their bodies. Again he refused, saying "this is not my job, I don't want to die." He lied to them, saying that the three militants had told him that if he came back, they would kill him. The officer told him that, as they had already killed the militants, he should not worry. He added that they had fired two missiles into the house, which must have killed the militants. When he still resisted, he was beaten and kicked again, until he went into HS/08's house via the roof again.

He found the house very badly damaged. The bottom part of the stairs was missing. He again went in shouting, to alert the militants if they were still alive. He found them in the same room as before. Two were unharmed. The third was badly injured, covered in blood, with wounds to his shoulder and abdomen. They asked him what was going on outside and he told them that the area was fully occupied and the soldiers had taken numerous hostages, including his family.

The wounded man gave him his name (HS/10) and asked him to tell his family what had happened. Majdi Abd Rabbo promised to do so if he survived and later did so. Another of the three told him to tell the Israeli officer that, if he was a real man, he would come to them himself.

Majdi Abd Rabbo returned to the soldiers, who again forced him to strip naked before they approached him. He told the officer that two of the militants were unharmed. The officer swore at him and accused him of lying. Majdi Abd Rabbo then repeated the message from the militant, at which the officer and four other soldiers assaulted him with their weapons and insulted him.

The officer asked Majdi Abd Rabbo for his identity card. He replied that it was in his house but gave him the ID card number. The officer checked the number via an electronic device. Three minutes later the officer asked him if it was true that he worked with the head of Palestinian Authority's intelligence services, which he confirmed. The officer asked him if he was with Abu Mazen and a Fatah affiliate. He said he was.

The soldiers brought Majdi Abd Rabbo a megaphone and told him to use it to call the militants. He initially refused but did so under threat. As instructed, he told the militants to surrender, that ICRC was present and they could hand themselves over. There was no response.

By then, night had fallen. Majdi Abd Rabbo was again handcuffed and taken back to the house of the HS/09 family. Thirty to forty minutes later, he heard shooting and a huge explosion. Soldiers came to tell him that they had bombed HS/08's house and ordered him to go in again and check on the fighters.

The Israeli armed forces had floodlit the area. Majdi Abd Rabbo found both his and HS/08's house very badly damaged. He could not use the roof of his house to enter HS/08's house, as it had collapsed. He went back to the soldiers, who again made him strip, this time to his underwear. He asked where his family was and said that he could not reach the fighters because of the damage to the houses. He accused the soldiers of destroying his house. The officer said that they had only hit HS/08's house. Majdi Abd Rabbo was then handcuffed. Until this time, he had been given no food or water, and it was very cold. After a while, his handcuffs were removed, he was told to dress and taken back to the HS/09 family house, to the room where he found that other people were being held. All the men and boys in this room were handcuffed and their ankles were tied. A soldier came with some drinking glasses and smashed them at the entrance to the room where they were being held. After smashing the glasses, he left again. Majdi Abd Rabbo had developed a severe headache. Another detainee, who spoke Hebrew, called a soldier to say that Majdi Abd Rabbo was sick and needed medicine. The soldier told him to keep quiet or he would be shot. A woman tied a scarf around Majdi Abd Rabbo's head to ease the pain.

At around 7 A.M., Majdi Abd Rabbo was taken back to the soldiers outside. He was questioned about the number of fighters in the house. He confirmed that he had seen only three.

Two young Palestinian men from the neighbourhood were brought over. A soldier gave them a camera and told them to go into the house and take photos of the fighters. The two tried to refuse, and were beaten and kicked. The soldier showed them how to use the camera and they went into HS/08's house through the damaged main entrance. About 10 minutes later, they came back with photos of the three fighters. Two appeared to be dead, under rubble. The third was also trapped by rubble but appeared to be alive and was still holding his firearm. A soldier showed Majdi Abd Rabbo the photos and asked if these were the same people. He confirmed they were.

A soldier took the megaphone and told the fighters that they had 15 minutes to surrender, that the neighbourhood was under the control of the Israeli armed forces and that, if they did not surrender, they [the Israeli armed forces] would hit the house with an air strike.

Fifteen minutes later, a soldier came with a dog, which had electronic gear attached to its body and what looked like a camera on its head. Another soldier had a small laptop. The dog handler sent the dog into the house. A few minutes later, shots were heard and the dog came running out. It had been shot and subsequently died.

At around 10.30 A.M. on 6 January 2009, a bulldozer arrived and started to level the house. The bulldozer moved from east to west, demolishing everything in its way. Majdi Abd Rabbo watched it demolish his own house and HS/08's house. He and the two young men were told to go back to the HS/09 house. They heard shooting.

At around 3 P.M., he was taken back close to the site of his and HS/08's house. He told the Mission that he saw the bodies of the three fighters lying on the ground in the rubble of the house.

The soldiers then forced him to enter other houses on the street as they searched them. All the houses were empty. The soldiers forced him to go into the house alone initially and, when he came out, sent in a dog to search the house. During the house searches he managed to find some water to drink, the first drink he had had for two days. At midnight, the soldiers took him back to the HS/09 family house.

On 7 January, all the men and boys were taken from the HS/09 family house and transferred to the house of a cousin of Majdi Abd Rabbo's in the same neighbourhood. There were more than 100 men and boys, including members of his extended family, aged between 15 and 70. The women were being held elsewhere. Majdi Abd Rabbo's immediate family members were not there, and he learnt that no one had seen them. He remained extremely anxious about their safety.

At around 11 P.M., the men and boys in that house were told that they were going to be released, and that they should all walk west towards Jabaliyah, without turning left or right, on threat of being shot. They found Izbat Abd Rabbo Street severely damaged. Majdi Abd Rabbo went to his sister's house in Jabaliyah, where he was reunited with his wife and children on 9 January 2009. His wife then told him that they had stayed for some hours in the house, during the first shooting on 5 January, and had then fled with a white flag to a neighbour's house.

Majdi Abd Rabbo told the Mission that he and his family were traumatized by what had happened to them and did not know what to do now, having lost their home and all their possessions. His children were all suffering psychologically and performing poorly at school. Five months later, in June 2009, Majdi Abd Rabbo was still having nightmares.

The Mission notes that his account to it implies that there were at least three other Palestinian men compelled by the Israeli armed forces to search houses. A journalist's account indicates that the author "spoke with eight residents of Izbat Abd Rabbo neighbourhood, who testified that they were made to accompany IDF soldiers on missions involving breaking into and searching houses. . . . The eight estimated that about 20 local people were made to carry out 'escort and protection' missions of various kinds, . . . between January 5 and January 12."

B. THE CASE OF ABBAS AHMAD IBRAHIM HALAWA

When hostilities started on 27 December 2008, Abbas Ahmad Ibrahim Halawa, aged 59, asked his family to leave the home and stayed behind alone. On 9 January 2009, after a day of shelling, the ground forces invaded the north-west of his neighbourhood. At around 0.05 A.M. on 5 January 2009, the Israeli armed forces stormed into his house. He was hiding under the staircase and screamed when they reached him, putting his hands in the air. The soldiers had torch lights on their rifles and helmets, and their faces were painted black.

At gunpoint, the soldiers ordered him to take off his clothes, which he did except for his underwear. They made him turn around and ordered him to dress again.

By this time there were some 40 soldiers in the house. His hands were tied behind his back, his legs were tied and he was blindfolded. He was severely beaten. He was then taken to a neighbour's house. He told the soldiers that he had bad asthma, but they would not allow him to take his inhaler.

In the neighbour's house, he was questioned by an Israeli officer about the whereabouts of Gilad Shalit and the location of Hamas tunnels and rocket launch sites. The soldiers threatened to blow up his house if he did not tell them. He insisted that he did not know the answers to their questions. He pleaded that he had worked in Israel for 30 years and had built hundreds of houses there. He speaks fluent Hebrew and communicated with the soldiers in Hebrew.

After about 30 minutes, he was taken to a different location in the vicinity and made to sit down. After another 15 minutes, he was again made to walk to a different location. He was still blindfolded; the ties binding his legs had been loosened slightly, but walking was difficult. One of the soldiers was directing his footsteps while holding him at gunpoint.

In a house that he subsequently recognized as that of a neighbour, one of the soldiers untied his legs and the blindfold. His hands remained tied. He saw a number of soldiers in the house and around 15 officers sitting in the living room. They had maps and radios in front of them. One of the officers (there were three stripes on the shoulder of his uniform) asked him to identify his house on the map, and then asked him about the location of tunnels and rocket launching sites. He answered that he did not know. He was blindfolded again but he could see a little through the blindfold.

He was then taken out of the house and onto the road. As previously, he was held from behind, a weapon pressed against his back or the back of his head. Due to the damage to the roads caused by the tanks and other military equipment, walking was difficult. For about two hours he walked around as directed by the soldiers. They would stop and call: "Who is in the house?" They would then open fire, force Abbas Ahmad Ibrahim Halawa to go into the house while they were gathering behind him, and then leave the house again after the search. He was made to go into five houses in this way. They did not find anyone in any of the houses.

Thereafter, they walked and stopped for about an hour without any shooting. Finally, he was ordered to sit down on the ground and covered with a blanket. He was held for two days at this location, which he identified to be near the American

School in north Gaza, close to an Israeli armed forces' tank position. During the two days he was given neither food nor water.

He was then transported, blindfolded, in what he believes was a tank, for about 90 minutes to another location which he believes was Netsalim (Nitzarim), where he was thrown on the ground. He was kept there for two days and nights in the open, during which time the soldiers refused to give him a blanket. During the two days he was again interrogated several times about the location of Hamas tunnels and rockets, and about Gilad Shalit's whereabouts. He was beaten and threatened with death if he did not provide the information.

At around 5 P.M. on the second day he was taken in a closed vehicle, which he believes was a truck, to a detention centre inside Israel, which he heard a soldier refer to as Telmund. He was fingerprinted and taken to see a doctor, whom he told that he was suffering from acute asthma and severe pain from a back injury caused by the beating. The doctor did not give him medication. He was placed in a cell, where he was again refused a blanket.

He was interrogated again at the detention centre, this time by civilians and then transferred to another location, where he was held together with some 50 Arabs. After two days, he was taken to the Erez border crossing and told to walk back into Gaza. Soldiers shot around his feet and over his head as he walked. He managed to reach his sister's house, where he collapsed and was taken to al-Shifa hospital.

When he returned to his house, he found it vandalized. When the Mission spoke to him, he was still traumatized from the treatment he had undergone at the hands of the Israeli armed forces.

[Removed: sections C and D (paragraphs 1076–1088)]

E. DENIAL OF THE ALLEGATIONS BY THE ISRAELI ARMED FORCES

Reacting to reports of the use of civilian men as human shields in Izbat Abd Rabbo, the Israeli armed forces' Spokesperson's Unit told an Israeli journalist:

> The IDF is a moral army and its soldiers operate according to the spirit and values of the IDF, and we suggest a thorough examination of the allegations

Mahmoud Abd Rabbo al-Ajrami

Assistant to the Foreign Minister, describing the search and occupation of his house in Sudaniyah by the Israel Defense Forces on January 10, 2009. He is 60 years old.

Now, the soldiers came through the kitchen door. They had already exploded the door and they came inside the house while shooting, and the shooting was continuous and they asked my wife to stand up. The soldiers were using their guns with laser beams.

So at one point we were facing them, so I started talking to them in a loud voice, telling them, we are here, we are the owners of this house, we are civilians, and my wife was saying more or less the same. My wife was speaking to them in classical Arabic and this made us laugh later, much later on when remembered those delicate moments.

So, one of them—actually there were about 20 to 25 soldiers inside the house, and like I said, we were in the corner, although we tried to get closer to them, and one of them yelled at us in broken Arabic and I couldn't understand him, and I didn't understand exactly what he said. In broken Arabic, he said something to the extent that I must get closer to him, so I did, but actually, I had misunderstood him. So when I got closer to him, he pointed his gun at me with the laser beam, of course, pointing at me, so I moved my hands and said, please, just stop, stop, don't shoot. I don't understand what you need, what you want.

So I started in English, do you speak English. I asked even in French, parlez vous Français, so which language do you speak, I'm ready to talk to you and so on and so forth. And so I spoke to him in English and French and then he said, okay, okay, let's speak English. So we spoke in English and that was the case until the end of my ordeal.

His first question was, "What are you doing here?" and I said, this is my house, this is my home and it's quite natural to be at home, and I don't know, frankly speaking, what are you doing here, because my presence here is natural, your presence is not natural. So he insulted me, using extremely crude words and he said, you have to remove your shirt, turn around. I did, and he—maybe he expected me to be carrying a bomb, although like I said, there was not one single bullet fired from my house or from my neighborhood. Then he asked me to move ahead.

Some soldiers went to the first floor, then they came back after a moment. When all the soldiers were gathered while pointing their guns at our heads, one of them pushed me and pushed my wife on the shoulder and said just go. So we left from the kitchen door, that is, from where they came in, and we went to our neighbor's house, Hassan Dahman's house, while they were still pointing their guns at our heads. . . .

Of course, the Israeli soldier asked me for my I.D., and I think because of the lighting I could tell that he was checking the serial number of my I.D. on his laptop, but this is, I think, what happened. And then he said, well, you're going to stay with us and he started then asking a question, I'm gonna give you five minutes and then you will have to tell us in detail where is Gilad Shalit, Corporal Gilad Shalit. Where are the Hamas tunnels located and where are the Hamas militants, where are the rockets and so on.

So I immediately responded, I don't know, and I'm telling you I don't know. So he said, well, I'll come back to you. A few minutes later the Israeli officer came back and—they were calling him major actually. I don't know who it is because on their faces there was painting and I couldn't, you know, see them clearly. So he came back five minutes later. He told me, if you don't speak we will take you and we will kill you, and I remember exactly what he said: if you don't talk we will take you and shoot you. And he repeated the same sentence over and over again. So I said, I don't have any information. I don't know what I can tell you.

So he said, what do you do? I said, I work as the assistant of the . . . Foreign Minister. So he said, then you're the assistant of Dr. Mahmoud al-Zahar, the Foreign Affairs Minister. I said, well, I worked with all of the ministers of Foreign Affairs. We stopped there and then he said, you're a Hamas member, and I said, no, that this is my job as a diplomat at the Foreign Affairs Minister. I don't belong to any party.

Then he said, well, you don't want to speak, and I said, no, so he yelled at me and he was extremely angry. He started insulting me, he insulted my mother, using words, extremely offensive words that nobody can imagine. So I said, look, you can take me wherever you want, I can't do anything about it. You're an Army, you have your forces, your tanks are stationed here, and you can take me of course. . . .

He left me for a few minutes, then came back. Give me your hands, and he tied me up this way, from the front, and then he blindfolded me and they did the same to my wife, tied her hands and blindfolded her and then asked us to stand up. So I stood up and one of the soldiers came and pushed me from my shoulder with force. So my wife had her hands tied, was hanging to my robe, and she said please take me with him and she was screaming and she said, I'm not gonna leave him, take me with him.

One of the soldiers pushed her back, so she fell on the ground and he said, no, you are not to move. So I left. Time back then was around 1:30 A.M. or 2:00 A.M., I don't remember clearly. The soldiers pushed me from the shoulders, pushed me and I walked for a few minutes and all of a sudden, I don't know how things happened. I realized that they were carrying me and throwing me off from the second floor. I fell on the ground and I felt there were rocks underneath me. I fell on the right side—of course, I didn't expect that I was going to be thrown out of the second floor, and of course, it goes without saying, I couldn't do anything about it. I remember that it was almost impossible for me to breathe.

Postscript: Badly bruised, his ribs broken, Ajrami was handcuffed and blindfolded and made to walk. Holding a gun to his head, the Israeli soldiers forced him to enter several houses while they took cover behind him. He was finally released more than a day later.

of Palestinian elements with vested interests. The IDF troops were instructed unequivocally not to make use of the civilian population within the combat framework for any purpose whatsoever, certainly not as "human shields."

Following an examination with the commanders of the forces that were in the area in question, no evidence was found of the cases mentioned. Anyone who tries to accuse the IDF of actions of this kind creates a mistaken and misleading impression of the IDF and its fighters, who operate according to moral criteria and international law.

F. FACTUAL FINDINGS

The Mission found the foregoing witnesses to be credible and reliable. It has no reason to doubt the veracity of their accounts and found that the different stories serve to support the allegation that Palestinians were used as human shields.

The Mission notes in particular that Mr. Majdi Abd Rabbo has told the story of his experience from 5 to 7 January 2009 to several NGOs, to several journalists and to the Mission without any material inconsistencies. There are some minor inconsistencies, which are not, in the opinion of the Mission, sufficiently weighty to cast doubt on the general reliability of Majdi Abd Rabbo. There are also, not surprisingly, some elements of the long account which appear in some versions and not in others. The Mission finds that these inconsistencies do not undermine the credibility of Majdi Abd Rabbo's account.

The Mission further notes that one of the Israeli soldiers interviewed by the NGO Breaking the Silence recounts the case of Majdi Abd Rabbo. The soldier describes the case in great detail and mentions having personally met Majdi Abd Rabbo. Finally, the Mission notes that the submission it has received from the Jerusalem Center for Public Affairs, while not containing a summary of Majdi Abd Rabbo's role in the incident in which the three Palestinian fighters were killed, also refers to the incident.

In more general terms, the Mission notes that the statements of the men used as human shields by the Israeli armed forces during house searches are corroborated by statements made by Israeli soldiers to the NGO Breaking the Silence. The soldier providing Testimony 1 speaks of the "Johnnie procedure": "It was the first week of the war, fighting was intense, there were explosive charges to expose, tunnels in open spaces and armed men inside houses. . . . Close in on each house. The method used has a new name now—no longer 'neighbour procedure.' Now people are called 'Johnnie.' They're Palestinian civilians, and they're called Johnnies. . . . To every house we close in on, we send the neighbour in, 'the Johnnie,' and if there are armed men inside, we start, like working the 'pressure cooker' in the West Bank." This soldier then mentions that some commanders were "bothered" by the fact that "civilians were used to a greater extent than just sending them into houses." A second soldier interviewed by Breaking the Silence, Testimony 17, appears to have discussed the "Johnnie procedure" at length, but his testimony was censored or otherwise cut in that respect, so that we can only read: "They [civilians found in houses] were used as 'Johnnies' (at a different point in the interview the witness described the 'Johnnie' procedure, using Palestinian civilians as human shields during house searches), and then released, and we're finding them in later searches."

[Removed: remainder of section F (paragraphs 1094–1095)]

[Removed: section G (paragraphs 1096–1106)]

CHAPTER XV.

DEPRIVATION OF LIBERTY: GAZANS DETAINED DURING THE ISRAELI MILITARY OPERATIONS OF 27 DECEMBER 2008 TO 18 JANUARY 2009

According to information that the Mission received, hundreds of Gazans, including women and children, were detained by the Israeli armed forces during the military operations. Their exact number is not known. Some were held for hours or days in homes, other buildings or sandpits in the Gaza Strip; others were taken into detention in Israel, either immediately or after an initial period of detention in the Gaza Strip. A number of people were held in army bases (e.g. Sde Teiman), others were held in prison, and some released detainees do not know where they were held. Some detainees have reported abuse during detention, including beatings, and being kept in unsanitary conditions, without any or with only inadequate food or toilet facilities. Some released persons have reported that they were used as human shields during their detention, for example, forced to walk in front of soldiers and enter buildings ahead of soldiers.

On 28 January 2009, seven Israeli human rights organizations appealed to the Israeli Military Judge Advocate General and to the Attorney General, concerning the "appalling conditions in which Palestinians arrested during the fighting in Gaza were held, and the humiliating and inhuman treatment to which they were subjected from the time of their arrest until their transfer to the custody of the Israel Prison Service."

The number of detainees that were eventually taken to Israeli prisons has been estimated at around 100. Some of them have since been released. It often took the families and lawyers several weeks to find out that their loved ones or clients were being detained. Some lawyers have alleged that Israel deliberately did not disclose the number of detentions, even to ICRC. Human rights organization Adalah has filed a freedom of information request to the Government, but at the time of writing this report has yet to receive a response. Eventually many were released by the Israeli Prison Service but the Mission is not in a position to determine the exact number.

[Removed: paragraph 1110]

The Mission has interviewed a number of persons who were detained by the Israeli armed forces for substantial periods of time during the military operations in Gaza and thereafter. In the course of that detention they were in some cases held without trial or respect for basic due process guarantees, and were mentally and physically abused. The Mission has also heard directly from legal representatives of several people who were detained at this time, including some of those referred to above. Moreover, the Mission addressed questions to the Government of Israel with regard to the number of persons from Gaza detained by Israel during the military operations and the duration of their detention, including how many remain in custody. The Mission asked how many persons detained in Gaza were charged with being "unlawful combatants" and on what basis, how many were subjected to trial and what due process guarantees were afforded to them. No reply was received.

A. AL-ATATRA SANDPITS

Al-Atatra is located 10 kilometres north of Gaza City, west of Beit Lahia and three to four kilometres south of the Green Line. The neighbourhood is largely agricultural with orange and lemon orchards. On the morning of 5 January, it suffered heavy aerial bombardment, which was followed by a ground incursion by Israeli troops. The Mission met six people, members of the same extended family and residents of al-Atatra, three of whom were direct witnesses and victims of the events that occurred in the aftermath of the ground incursion. Their testimonies are supported by those of three others, also residents of al-Atatra, submitted to the Mission by an NGO.

On the morning of 5 January, shortly after the ground operations began, an estimated 40 Israeli soldiers broke into several homes, including that of AD/01, who described to the Mission how 65 persons, several of whom were holding white flags, were made to assemble in the street. The soldiers separated the men from the women. The men were made to line up against a wall and strip to their underwear.

AD/01 indicated that any attempt to resist the soldiers was met with physical force, resulting in injuries.

Approximately 20 minutes later, they were taken into a house owned by Mr. Khalil Misbah Attar, where they were detained for a day, the men still separated from the women. The house had been struck by a number of missiles that morning and was badly damaged. Witnesses indicated to the Mission that the house was at that time being used by the Israeli armed forces as a military base and sniper position.

At around 10 P.M., all of the men were handcuffed behind their backs with plastic restraints and blindfolded. The men, 11 women and at least seven children below the age of 14, were taken on foot to al-Kaklouk located south of the American School, one to two kilometres away. Many of the men remained in their underwear, exposed to the harsh winter weather. Al-Kaklouk is very close to Israeli military artillery and tank positions, and while the detainees were held here at least one tank was engaged in frequent firing.

AD/01 told the Mission that, on arrival at al-Kaklouk, everyone was asked to clamber down into trenches, which had been dug to create a pit surrounded by a wall of sand, about three metres high. There were three such pits, each of which was surrounded by barbed wire. They were estimated to cover about 7,000 square metres ("six or seven *dunums*") each. AD/01 described how they were assembled in long single files, rather than massed together, and held in these pits, in the open air and exposed to cold temperatures for three days (till 8 January). Each pit accommodated approximately 20 people. They were forced to sit in stress positions, on their knees and leaning forward keeping their heads down. They were monitored by soldiers and were not allowed to communicate with each other. They had no access to food or water on the first day of their internment, and were given a sip of water and an olive each to eat on the second and third days of their detention (6 and 7 January). They had limited access to toilet facilities. The men had to wait for two to three hours after asking before they were allowed to leave the pits to relieve themselves and sometimes were able to remove their blindfolds for the purpose. A few of them were told to relieve themselves inside the pit, behind a small mount of sand. They stated that it was culturally too difficult for the women to seek permission to relieve themselves and they did not ask.

AD/01 states that some tanks were inside the pit with at least one tank positioned at the eastern end. While the people were held there, the tank facing inland each day sporadically fired on the houses along the road opposite the site.

AD/01B and AD/01C recounted that on 8 January, the women and children were released and told to go to Jabaliyah. The men were transferred to military barracks near the northern border, identified as the Izokim barracks. At the Izokim barracks, the men were detained in pits similar to but smaller than those in al-Kaklouk. They continued to be exposed to the cold temperature, rain and the constant sound of tank movement overhead. The witnesses have described to the Mission the experience of continued and prolonged exposure to the sound of this tank movement as disorienting and creating feelings of futility, isolation, helplessness and abject terror.

The men were held handcuffed and in their underwear in the Izokim barracks overnight. They were questioned intermittently, mostly on details and locations of Qassam rockets, the tunnels and the whereabouts of Hamas parliamentarians. According to statements made to the Mission, they were beaten during the interrogation and threatened with death and being run over by tanks. The Mission notes that the nature and types of questions asked remained the same throughout the interrogations in various detention facilities.

On 9 January, the men were taken to a prison in Israel, indentified by one witness as the Negev prison, where they remained until 12 January. They were detained in one section of the prison, alternating between being held in isolation and in shared cells, and were subjected to harsh interrogation, often by two people dressed in civilian clothes. Interrogation focused on the identification of Hamas tunnels and arms as well as the whereabouts of Gilad Shalit.

AD/01B and AD/01C recounted that they were shackled to a chair with plastic strips and interrogated several times, with AD/01B stating that he was made to strip naked during an interrogation. He was kept in solitary confinement where a soldier would come intermittently during the day, and slam the cell door open and shut, exposing him to extremely cold temperatures. AD/01C stated that during the first interrogation he was verbally threatened and in the subsequent two he was blindfolded and beaten. He was made to stand up and face the wall, following which his face was smashed against the wall several times before he was severely beaten (kicked and punched) on his back and buttocks.

Requests for clothing were denied. During the interrogation the detainees were informed that they were "illegal combatants" and that they had no protection under the Geneva Conventions. They had limited access to food, water and sanitation. Their morning meal was a bottle-cap-sized piece of bread with a drop of marmalade. The evening meal, if provided, consisted of rotting sardines and cheese on mouldy bread.

AD/01C described the experience of being detained, stripped and shackled as one of abandonment, desperation, suffocation and isolation. He continues to experience discomfort where he was beaten and is unable to sit and sleep comfortably.

AD/01C stated that while [he was] in Negev prison an additional group arrived. They were kept separately in the second section. The exact number of detainees in the second group is unknown, although AD/01C indicated to the Mission that the second group was smaller.

On 12 January, nine people including the witnesses were blindfolded, handcuffed and transported to the Erez border. AD/01 described to the Mission how they were subjected to harsh interrogation at Erez and made to strip completely. Several hours later they were told to run into Gaza, to look straight ahead and not to look back.

AD/01 states that all 65 detainees from the original group taken from al-Atatra to Israel were eventually released. Some members of his family were detained afterwards, but not in the original group of 65. At the time of writing, three of these remain incarcerated in various detention facilities of the Israel Prison Service. An unknown number remain in prison facing charges of being illegal combatants and members of al-Qassam Brigades. The first hearing was scheduled to be held in August in Israel (exact date not known).

[Removed: section B (paragraphs 1127–1142)]

C. AD/03

AD/03 is a resident of al-Salam neighbourhood, east of Jabaliyah and close to the eastern border with Israel. His arrest and detention were preceded by aerial attacks and a ground invasion in his neighbourhood. His house was struck several times, over a period of five days, by projectiles fired from F-16 aircraft. The attacks continued throughout the night when most people were asleep. As a result of the continued attacks, he sought refuge in a relative's house nearby.

AD/03 stated that, although the area could be considered as a frontline where armed groups had been present, the neighbourhood could not reasonably have been perceived as a military threat by the time the Israeli armed forces arrived on the ground. There was no resistance going on in the neighbourhood when it was targeted. If the intent of the attacks was to destroy alleged command centres, positions or weapons caches of Hamas, he felt that those positions would have been destroyed in the first few attacks on the neighbourhood given the intensity of the shelling.

On 8 January, at around 11.30 A.M., the house where AD/03 was seeking refuge was struck by a missile so he decided to return to his own house. He described how Israeli soldiers fired at them, including women and children carrying white flags, when they tried to leave his cousin's house. His father's wife sustained a bullet injury to her leg. Thirty minutes later, around noon, the Israeli armed forces ordered all residents to evacuate their homes and come out in the street. The men were separated from the women and children, and told to line up against a wall, lift their shirts and strip to their underwear. They remained stripped and lined up against the wall for approximately 15 minutes. The men, women and children were then told to walk down the street.

AD/03 recounted that the street was blocked with large piles of heavy rubble and debris of bulldozed buildings, which provided a difficult obstacle for several people, including children and elderly people. They walked 200–250 metres before arriving at a house. Two hours later the women and children were told to go to Jabaliyah. Shortly afterwards, AD/03, his brother, cousin and an unknown man were taken to another room, where they were forced to lie on the ground. They were then blindfolded and their hands were tied behind their backs with plastic strips. They were interrogated individually for several hours. Later that evening, they were made to walk about 100 metres eastward to another house. They were detained overnight in a room, together with three others, who identified themselves as residents of Abd Rabbo. They had no access to food, water or toilets. The next morning, on 9 January, their blindfolds were removed and all seven were interrogated, individually, by one soldier.

AD/03 stated that the house was being used as a military base and sniper position. On the second day of detention the Israeli soldiers began to use some detainees as human shields. By then the detainees had been without food and sleep for a day. They had been subjected to what AD/03 described as psychological torture. There were constant death threats and insults. To carry out house searches with human shields the Israeli soldiers took off AD/03's blindfold but he remained handcuffed.

He was forced to walk in front of the soldiers and told that, if he saw someone in the house but failed to tell them, he would be killed. He was instructed to search each room in each house, cupboard by cupboard. After one house was completed he was taken to another house with a gun pressed against his head and told to carry out the same procedure there. He was punched, slapped and insulted throughout the process.

AD/03 indicated that he was forced to do this twice while the group was being held in this house for eight days. Others were also required to do the same thing. On the first occasion he was forced to carry out searches in three houses and on the second in four. AD/03 estimates that these searches took between one hour and one hour and a half. At no point did he come across any explosive devices or armed group members.

AD/03 stated that, at the end of every search, the houses were vandalized by the Israeli soldiers, who broke doors, windows, kitchenware and furniture, for instance.

At the end of the day he was taken back to the house, where he and six others continued to be detained for 8 days, until 16 January. They had limited access to food and water and were often denied access to toilets. They were told that their ordeal would continue indefinitely. One soldier reportedly told them that the soldiers were "following instructions issued by the chain of command."

For the first time the detainees were asked for proof of identity. AD/03 said that their identification documents were thoroughly inspected. Had they revealed anything in relation to militant activities, he believed they would have been killed.

[AD/03 was detained for another 11 days, including in Ktziot prison in Israel, till his release on 27 January.]

[Removed: remainder of section C (paragraphs 1152–1163)]

D. FACTUAL FINDINGS

The Mission found the witnesses credible and reliable, taking into account their demeanour and the consistency of their statements. At least one of them was still suffering considerable anguish because of the treatment he had endured at the hands of the Israeli soldiers and other officials. The Mission notes that there are several common features to these incidents that disclose a pattern of behaviour on the part of the Israeli soldiers, indicating that the treatment meted out to the persons deposing before the Mission were not isolated incidents. The facts available to the Mission indicate that:

- All [of the] locations were near the border with Israel;
- Before the arrival of ground troops, all three had been under aerial or ground attack. The soldiers on the ground were in complete control of the area at the time of their encounter with the civilians;
- There was no combat activity by the persons reporting, nor any likelihood of such activity being under way in the area or nearby at the time that the soldiers started the operation against civilians in the three locations. None of the civilians was armed or posed any apparent threat to the soldiers. In two of the incidents they were holding white flags as a sign of their non-combatant status;
- It is clear in two of the incidents that none of those detained had been asked for their names by the soldiers for several days. This establishes that there was no definite suspicion against them that they were combatants or otherwise engaged in hostile activities;
- In all cases a number of persons were herded together and detained in open spaces for several hours at a time and exposed to extreme weather conditions;
- The soldiers deliberately subjected civilians, including women and children, to cruel, inhuman and degrading treatment throughout their ordeal in order to terrorize, intimidate and humiliate them. The men were made to strip, sometimes naked, at different stages of their detention. All the men were handcuffed in a most painful manner and blindfolded, increasing their sense of fear and helplessness;
- Men, women and children were held close to artillery and tank positions, where constant shelling and firing was taking place, thus not only exposing them to danger but increasing their fear and terror. This was deliberate, as is apparent from the fact that the sandpits to which they were taken were specially prepared and surrounded by barbed wire;
- During their detention in the Gaza Strip, whether in the open or in houses, the detainees were subjected to beatings and other physical abuse that amounts to torture. This continued systematically throughout their detention;
- Civilians were used as human shields by the Israeli armed forces on more

than one occasion in one of the three incidents. Taking account of other incidents in which the Mission has found this to have happened, it would not be difficult to conclude that this was a practice repeatedly adopted by the Israeli armed forces during the military operation in Gaza;

- Many civilians were transferred across the border to Israel and detained in open spaces as well as in prisons;
- The methods of interrogation amounted not only to torture in some of the cases but also to physical and moral coercion of civilians to obtain information;
- These persons were subjected to torture, maltreatment and foul conditions in the prisons. They were deprived of food and water for several hours at a time and any food they did receive was inadequate and inedible;
- While in detention in Israel they were denied due process.

[Removed: section E (paragraphs 1165–1176)]

CHAPTER XVI.

OBJECTIVES AND STRATEGY OF ISRAEL'S MILITARY OPERATIONS IN GAZA

This chapter addresses the objectives and the strategy underlying the Israeli military operations in Gaza.

A. PLANNING

The question of whether incidents involving the Israeli armed forces that occurred between 27 December 2008 and 18 January 2009 are likely to be the result of error, the activities of rogue elements or a deliberate policy or planning depends on a number of factors, including the degree and level of planning involved, the degree of discretion field commanders have in operations, the technical sophistication and specification of weaponry, and the degree of control commanders have over their subordinates.

The Government of Israel has refused to cooperate with the Mission. The Mission has therefore been unable to interview high-level members of the Israeli armed forces. It has, nevertheless, reviewed a significant amount of commentary and conducted a number of interviews on planning and discipline, including with persons who have been connected with the planning of Israeli military operations in the recent past. The Mission has also analysed the views expressed by Israeli officials in official statements, official activities and articles, and considered comments by former senior soldiers and politicians.

1. The context

Before considering the issue of planning there is an important issue that has to be borne in mind about the context of Israeli operations in Gaza. The land mass of Gaza covers 360 square kilometres of land. Israel had a physical presence on the ground for almost 40 years with a significant military force until 2005. Israel's extensive and intimate knowledge of the realities of Gaza present a considerable advantage in terms of planning military operations. The Mission has seen grid maps in possession of the Israeli armed forces, for example, that show the identification by number of blocks of houses throughout Gaza City.

In addition to such detailed background knowledge, it is also clear that the Israeli armed forces were able to access the telephone networks to contact a significant number of users in the course of their operations.

Since the departure of its ground forces from Gaza in 2005, Israel has maintained almost total control over land access and total control over air and sea access. This has also included the ability to maintain a monitoring capacity in Gaza, by a variety of surveillance and electronic means, including UAVs. In short, Israel's intelligence gathering capacity in Gaza since its ground forces withdrew has remained extremely effective.

[Removed: section 2 (paragraphs 1183–1184)]

3. The means at the disposal of the Israeli armed forces

The Israeli armed forces are, in technological terms, among the most advanced in the world. Not only do they possess the most advanced hardware in many respects, they are also a market leader in the production of some of the most advanced pieces of technology available, including UAVs. They have a very significant capacity for precision strikes by a variety of methods, including aerial and ground launches. Moreover, some new targeting systems may have been employed in Gaza.

Taking into account all of the foregoing factors, the Mission, therefore, concludes that Israel had the means necessary to plan the December–January military operations in detail. Given both the means at Israel's disposal and the apparent degree of training, including training in international humanitarian law, and legal advice received, the Mission considers it highly unlikely that actions were taken, at least in the aerial phase of the operations, that had not been the subject of planning and deliberation. In relation to the land-air phase, ground commanders would have had some discretion to decide on the specific tactics used to attack or respond to attacks. The same degree of planning and premeditation would therefore not be present. However, the Mission deduces from a review of many elements, including some soldiers' statements at seminars in Tel Aviv and to Breaking the Silence, that what occurred on the ground reflected guidance that had been provided to soldiers in training and briefing exercises.

The Mission notes that it has found only one example where the Israeli authorities have acknowledged that an error had occurred. This was in relation to the deaths of 22 members of the al-Daya family in Zeytoun. The Government of Israel explained that its armed forces had intended to strike the house next door, but that errors were made in the planning of the operation. The Mission expresses elsewhere its concerns about this explanation. However, since it appears to be the only incident that has elicited an admission of error by the Israeli authorities, the Mission takes the view that the Government of Israel does not consider the other strikes brought to its attention to be the result of similar or other errors.

In relation to air strikes, the Mission notes the statement issued in Hebrew posted on the website of the Israeli armed forces on 23 March 2009:

> Official data gathered by the Air Force concluded that 99 per cent of the firing that was carried out hit targets accurately. It also concluded that over 80 per cent of the bombs and missiles used by the Air Force are defined as accurate and their use reduces innocent casualties significantly. . . .

The Mission understands this to mean that in over 80 per cent of its attacks the Air Force deployed weapons considered to be accurate by definition—what are known colloquially as precision weapons as a result of guidance technology. In the other 20 per cent of attacks, therefore, it apparently used unguided bombs. According to the Israeli armed forces, the fact that these 20 per cent were unguided did not diminish their accuracy in hitting their targets, but may have caused greater damage than those caused by precision or "accurate" weapons.

These represent extremely important findings by the Israeli Air Force. It means that what was struck was meant to be struck. It should also be borne in mind that the beginning of the ground phase of the operation on 3 January did not mean the end of the use of the Israeli Air Force. The statement indicates:

> During the days prior to the operation "Cast Lead," every brigade was provided with an escorting UAV squadron that would participate in action with it during the operation. Teams from the squadrons arrived at the armour and infantry corps, personally met the soldiers they were about to join and assisted in planning the infantry manoeuvres. The UAV squadrons had representatives in the command headquarters and officers in locations of actual combat who assisted in communication between the UAVs—operated by only two people, who are in Israeli territory—and the forces on the ground. The assistance of UAVs sometimes reached a ratio of one UAV to a regiment and, during extreme cases, even one UAV to a team.

Taking into account the ability to plan, the means to execute plans with the most developed technology available, the indication that almost no errors occurred and the determination by investigating authorities thus far that no violations occurred, the Mission finds that the incidents and patterns of events that are considered in this report have resulted from deliberate planning and policy decisions throughout the chain of command, down to the standard operating procedures and instructions given to the troops on the ground.

B. THE DEVELOPMENT OF STRATEGIC OBJECTIVES IN ISRAELI MILITARY THINKING

Israel's operations in the Occupied Palestinian Territory have had certain consistent features. In particular, the destruction of buildings, including houses, has been a recurrent tactical theme. The specific means Israel has adopted to meet its military objectives in the Occupied Palestinian Territory and in Lebanon have repeatedly been censured by the United Nations Security Council, especially its attacks on houses. The military operations from 27 December to 18 January did not occur in a vacuum, either in terms of proximate causes in relation to the Hamas/Israeli dynamics or in relation to the development of Israeli military thinking about how best to describe the nature of its military objectives.

A review of the available information reveals that, while many of the tactics remain the same, the reframing of the strategic goals has resulted in a qualitative shift from relatively focused operations to massive and deliberate destruction.

In its operations in southern Lebanon in 2006, there emerged from Israeli military thinking a concept known as the Dahiya doctrine, as a result of the approach taken to the Beirut neighbourhood of that name. Major General Gadi Eisenkot, the Israeli Northern Command chief, expressed the premise of the doctrine:

> What happened in the Dahiya quarter of Beirut in 2006 will happen in every village from which Israel is fired on. . . . We will apply disproportionate force on it and cause great damage and destruction there. From our standpoint, these are not civilian villages, they are military bases. . . . This is not a recommendation. This is a plan. And it has been approved.

After the war in southern Lebanon in 2006, a number of senior former military figures appeared to develop the thinking that underlay the strategy set out by Gen. Eisenkot. In particular Major General (Ret.) Giora Eiland has argued that, in the event of another war with Hezbollah, the target must not be the defeat of Hezbollah but "the elimination of the Lebanese military, the destruction of the national infrastructure and intense suffering among the population. . . . Serious damage to the Republic of Lebanon, the destruction of homes and infrastructure, and the suffering of hundreds of thousands of people are consequences that can influence Hizbollah's behaviour more than anything else."

These thoughts, published in October 2008 were preceded by one month by the reflections of Col. (Ret.) Gabriel Siboni:

> With an outbreak of hostilities, the IDF will need to act immediately, decisively, and with force that is disproportionate to the enemy's actions and the threat it poses. Such a response aims at inflicting damage and meting out punishment to an extent that will demand long and expensive reconstruction processes. The strike must be carried out as quickly as possible, and must prioritize damaging assets over seeking out each and every launcher. Punishment must be aimed at decision makers and the power elite. . . . In Lebanon, attacks should both aim at Hizbollah's military capabilities and should target economic interests and the centres of civilian power that support the organization. Moreover, the closer the relationship between Hizbollah and the Lebanese Government, the more the elements of the Lebanese State infrastructure should be targeted. Such a response will create a lasting memory among . . . Lebanese decision makers, thereby increasing Israeli deterrence and reducing the likelihood of hostilities

against Israel for an extended period. At the same time, it will force Syria, Hizbollah, and Lebanon to commit to lengthy and resource-intensive reconstruction programmes. . . .

This approach is applicable to the Gaza Strip as well. There, the IDF will be required to strike hard at Hamas and to refrain from the cat and mouse games of searching for Qassam rocket launchers. The IDF should not be expected to stop the rocket and missile fire against the Israeli home front through attacks on the launchers themselves, but by means of imposing a ceasefire on the enemy.

General Eisenkot used the language quoted above while he was in active service in a senior command position and clarified that this was not a theoretical idea but an approved plan. Major General Eiland, though retired, was a man of considerable seniority. Colonel Siboni, while less senior than the other two, was nonetheless an experienced officer writing on his field of expertise in a publication regarded as serious.

The Mission does not have to consider whether Israeli military officials were directly influenced by these writings. It is able to conclude from a review of the facts on the ground that it witnessed for itself that what is prescribed as the best strategy appears to have been precisely what was put into practice.

C. OFFICIAL ISRAELI STATEMENTS ON THE OBJECTIVES OF THE MILITARY OPERATIONS IN GAZA

The Mission is aware of the official statements on the goals of the military operations:

The Operation was limited to what the IDF believed necessary to accomplish its objectives: to stop the bombardment of Israeli civilians by destroying and damaging the mortar and rocket launching apparatus and its supporting infrastructure, and to improve the safety and security of Southern Israel and its residents by reducing the ability of Hamas and other terrorist organizations in Gaza to carry out future attacks.

The Israeli Government states that this expression of its objectives is no broader than those expressed by NATO in 1998 during its campaign in the Federal Republic of Yugoslavia.

The Mission makes no comment on the legality or otherwise of NATO actions there.

D. THE STRATEGY TO ACHIEVE THE OBJECTIVES

The issue that is of special concern to the Mission is the conceptualization of the "supporting infrastructure." The notion is indicated quite clearly in General Eisenkot's statements in 2006 and reinforced by the reflections cited by non-serving but well-informed military thinkers.

On 6 January 2009, during the military operations in Gaza, Deputy Prime Minister Eli Yishai stated: "It [should be] possible to destroy Gaza, so they will understand not to mess with us." He added that "it is a great opportunity to demolish thousands of houses of all the terrorists, so they will think twice before they launch rockets." "I hope the operation will come to an end with great achievements and with the complete destruction of terrorism and Hamas. In my opinion, they should be razed to the ground, so thousands of houses, tunnels and industries will be demolished." He added that "residents of the South are strengthening us, so the operation will continue until a total destruction of Hamas [is achieved]."

On 2 February 2009, after the end of the military operations, Eli Yishai went on: "Even if the rockets fall in an open air or to the sea, we should hit their infrastruc-ture, and destroy 100 homes for every rocket fired."

On 13 January 2009, Israel's Foreign Minister, Tzipi Livni, was quoted as saying:

> We have proven to Hamas that we have changed the equation. Israel is not
> a country upon which you fire missiles and it does not respond. It is a coun-
> try that when you fire on its citizens it responds by going wild—and this is
> a good thing.

It is in the context of comments such as these that the massive destruction of busi-nesses, agricultural land, chicken farms and residential houses has to be under-stood. In particular, the Mission notes the large-scale destruction that occurred in the days leading up to the end of the operations. During the withdrawal phase it appears that possibly thousands of homes were destroyed. The Mission has referred elsewhere in this report to the "day after" doctrine, as explained in the testimonies

of Israeli soldiers, which can fit in with the general approach of massively disproportionate destruction without much difficulty.

The concept of what constituted the supporting infrastructure has to be understood
not only in the context of the military operations of December and January, but in
the tightening of the restrictions of access to goods and people into and out of
Gaza, especially since Hamas took power. The Mission does not accept that these
restrictions can be characterized as primarily an attempt to limit the flow of materials to armed groups. The expected impact, and the Mission believes primary purpose, was to bring about a situation in which the civilian population would find
life so intolerable that they would leave (if that were possible) or turn Hamas out
of office, as well as to collectively punish the civilian population.

The Israeli Government has stated:

> While Hamas operates ministries and is in charge of a variety of adminis-
> trative and traditionally governmental functions in the Gaza Strip, it still re-
> mains a terrorist organization. Many of the ostensibly civilian elements of
> its regime are in reality active components of its terrorist and military efforts.
> Indeed, Hamas does not separate its civilian and military activities in the
> manner in which a legitimate government might. Instead, Hamas uses ap-
> paratuses under its control, including quasi-governmental institutions, to
> promote its terrorist activity.

The framing of the military objectives Israel sought to strike is thus very wide indeed. There is, in particular, a lack of clarity about the concept of promoting "terrorist activity": Since Israel claims there is no real division between civilian and
military activities and it considers Hamas to be a terrorist organization, it would
appear that anyone who supports Hamas in any way may be considered as promoting its terrorist activity. Hamas was the clear winner of the latest elections in
Gaza. It is not far-fetched for the Mission to consider that Israel regards very large
sections of the Gazan civilian population as part of the "supporting infrastructure."

The indiscriminate and disproportionate impact of the restrictions on the movement of goods and people indicates that, from as early as some point in 2007, Israel
had already determined its view about what constitutes attacking the supporting
infrastructure, and it appears to encompass effectively the population of Gaza.

A statement of objectives that explicitly admits the intentional targeting of civilian objects as part of the Israeli strategy is attributed to the Deputy Chief of Staff, Maj. Gen. Dan Harel. While the Israeli military operations in Gaza were under way, Maj. Gen. Harel was reported as saying, in a meeting with local authorities in southern Israel:

> This operation is different from previous ones. We have set a high goal which we are aiming for. We are hitting not only terrorists and launchers, but also the whole Hamas government and all its wings. . . . We are hitting government buildings, production factories, security wings and more. We are demanding governmental responsibility from Hamas and are not making distinctions between the various wings. After this operation there will not be one Hamas building left standing in Gaza, and we plan to change the rules of the game.

E. CONCLUSIONS

The Israeli military conception of what was necessary in a future war with Hamas seems to have been developed from at least the time of the 2006 conflict in southern Lebanon. It finds its origin in a military doctrine that views disproportionate destruction and creating maximum disruption in the lives of many people as a legitimate means to achieve military and political goals.

Through its overly broad framing of the "supporting infrastructure," the Israeli armed forces have sought to construct a scope for their activities that, in the Mission's view, was designed to have inevitably dire consequences for the noncombatants in Gaza.

Statements by political and military leaders prior to and during the military operations in Gaza leave little doubt that disproportionate destruction and violence against civilians were part of a deliberate policy.

To the extent to which statements such as that of Mr. Yishai on 2 February 2009 indicate that the destruction of civilian objects, homes in that case, would be justified as a response to rocket attacks ("destroy 100 homes for every rocket fired"), the Mission is of the view that reprisals against civilians in armed hostilities are contrary to international humanitarian law. Even if such actions could be considered a lawful reprisal, they do not meet the stringent conditions imposed, in particular they are disproportionate, and violate fundamental human rights and obligations of a humanitarian character. One party's targeting of civilians or civilian areas can never justify the opposing party's targeting of civilians and civilian objects, such as homes, public and religious buildings, or schools.

CHAPTER XVII.

THE IMPACT OF THE BLOCKADE AND OF THE MILITARY OPERATIONS ON THE PEOPLE OF GAZA AND THEIR HUMAN RIGHTS

[Removed: two quotations that serve as epigraphs to this section]

During its visits to the Occupied Palestinian Territory, and its meetings and hearings in Gaza, Amman, Geneva and other places, the Mission saw for itself and received reports and testimonies about the negative effects that the severe restrictions on the movement of goods and people from and to the Gaza Strip had caused to the full enjoyment of a range of social, economic and civil rights by women, men and children. These reports and testimonies come from a variety of sources, including businesspeople, industry owners, ordinary residents, public officials and NGOs in the Occupied Palestinian Territory and abroad.

People in Gaza, as in other parts of the Occupied Palestinian Territory, have been living under foreign occupation for decades and enduring the restrictions and other effects of the policies implemented by the occupying Power. While the start of the blockade and the most recent military operations have undoubtedly added to those restrictions and scarcities, people in Gaza have not been living in what can be called a "normal" situation for a long time.

The restrictions imposed by Israel on the imports to and exports from the Gaza Strip through the border crossings as well as the naval and airspace blockade have had a severe impact on the availability and accessibility of a whole range of goods and services necessary for the people of Gaza to enjoy their human rights. Their already eroded ability to access and buy basic goods was compounded by the effects of the four-week Israeli military campaign, which further restricted access to those essential items and destroyed goods, land, facilities and infrastructure vital for the enjoyment of their fundamental rights. In conjunction, the blockade and the military hostilities have created a situation in which most people are destitute. Women and children have been particularly affected. The current situation has been described as a crisis of human dignity.

A. THE ECONOMY, LIVELIHOODS AND EMPLOYMENT

The Mission received information about the state of the economy, employment and family livelihoods in the Gaza Strip. Before the December–January military operations, the Gaza economy was already in dire straits, with few business sectors able to operate at full capacity. The blockade restricted or denied entry to a range of items and energy necessary for the economy to function. These included fuel and industrial diesel for the Gaza power plant to produce enough electricity for factories and businesses to function and for agricultural activities to continue on a regular basis. The net result was a stalled economy, with many businesses, factories and farms either closed or operating at reduced capacity.

Electricity was purchased directly from Israel (51 per cent) and Egypt (7 per cent), while the Gaza power plant produced only 34 per cent, leaving an 8 per cent electricity deficit. Following additional cuts by Israel in the supply of industrial fuel, the Gaza power plant further reduced its output. The shortage of fuel caused the plant to malfunction, while the lack of spare parts and maintenance is likely to damage the plant in the long term. According to OCHA, the electricity shortfall in the Gaza Strip was 41 per cent by 15 December 2008. Cooking gas was also restricted although less drastically.

Raw materials, equipment, spare parts and other inputs necessary for industrial and agricultural activity were not allowed into the Gaza Strip either.

The consequences for day-to-day life were considerable. Some areas of the Gaza Strip were left without electricity for several hours a week, many households, especially those in buildings that depend on the use of water pumps, had access to water only a few hours a week. Intermittent electricity supply damaged medical equipment in hospitals and doctors' practices, and generally disrupted civilian life. The operation of sewage treatment facilities was also reduced and increased quantities of untreated sewage were dumped into the sea, causing public health risks and pollution, which in turn affected fishing.

Several companies closed or cut back their operations, laying off employees, who consequently lost their livelihoods. Information provided to the Mission covering June 2007 to July 2008 showed that 98 per cent of industries were temporarily shut down and five establishments were relocated to the West Bank and Jordan. Around 16,000 workers were laid off. The ban on all exports caused losses for the agricultural sector estimated at US$30 million up until July 2008 and 40,000 jobs lost. Similarly, the construction sector endured severe losses resulting from the halt in development projects and other construction projects owing to the absence of construction materials. Some 42,000 workers were reported to have lost their jobs as a result. Those who were laid off searched for employment in other sectors, such as agriculture, or joined the ranks of those who live on food assistance from the United Nations and aid agencies.

As a result of the closure of the crossings to the transit of people, many families also lost the financial support they had from relatives, usually the male head of the family, who used to work abroad, either in Israel or in neighbouring Arab countries. In its submission to the Mission, UNCTAD stated that 15.4 per cent of Gaza's labour force was employed in Israel by 2000. In his presentation to the Mission, the economist Shir Hever explained that by 2009 no one from Gaza could find work in Israel. Even Palestinian workers from the West Bank mostly work in industrial zones in settlements rather than in Israel.

By December 2008 the destructive impact of the blockade on the local economy had doubled unemployment levels. While in 2007 79 per cent of households lived below the official poverty line (US$4 per capita/day) and some 70 per cent below the deep poverty line (US$3 per capita/day), these figures were expected to increase by the end of 2008—even before the Israeli military operations. The Mission received information from organizations explaining how the agricultural sector had traditionally absorbed unemployed workers from other sectors, but in the circumstances imposed by the blockade, without fertilizers, pesticides, machinery, spare parts and, crucially, without access to markets, it could no longer fulfil the role of shock absorber. In its submission to the Mission, UNCTAD noted that when the industrial and agricultural sectors lost their capacity to provide jobs, public administration and services absorbed up to 54 per cent of Gaza's labour force (up from 37 per cent in 1999). UNCTAD concluded:

The ultimate impact of this momentum is the systematic erosion of the Palestinian productive base to deprive them from the ability to produce and feed themselves, and turn them into poor consumers of essential goods imported mainly from Israel and financed mainly by donors.

The military operations destroyed a substantial part of the Gaza Strip's economic infrastructure and its capacity to support decent livelihoods for families. Many factories and businesses were directly targeted and destroyed or damaged. Poverty, unemployment and food insecurity increased dramatically.

Information provided to the Mission showed that some 700 private (industry and trade) businesses were damaged or destroyed during the military operations, with direct losses totalling approximately US$140 million. The industrial sector appeared the most affected, as it suffered 61 per cent of those losses, in particular in the sub-sectors of construction and food. Because of the extent and gravity of the destruction inflicted on the industrial sector, businesspeople and industrialists who spoke to the Mission stated their belief that Israel had as one of its military objectives the destruction of local industrial capacity so as to harm the prospects for an economic recovery in the Gaza Strip.

The severe restrictions on the availability of banknotes imposed by Israel caused serious disruptions in economic transactions and affected the ability of the public sector and the nongovernmental sector to carry out operations such as contracting or procuring goods and services.

The agricultural sector, including crop farming, fisheries, livestock farming and poultry farming, suffered direct losses worth some US$170 million. Indirect losses have still to be definitively calculated. One business organization estimates that 60 per cent of all agricultural land had been destroyed, 40 per cent directly during the military operations. Moreover, 17 per cent of all orchards, 8.3 per cent of livestock, 2.6 per cent of poultry, 18.1 per cent of hatcheries, 25.6 per cent of beehives, 9.2 per cent of open fields and 13 per cent of groundwater wells were destroyed. Agriculture had already lost a third of its capacity since the start of the second intifada and the frequent Israeli incursions, according to NGO estimates used by UNDP-Gaza. Parts of the land were reportedly contaminated by unexploded munitions and chemical weapons residues (e.g. white phosphorous) and would need to be tested and cleared before agricultural activity could resume. Some 250 agricultural wells were reportedly destroyed or severely damaged.

Fishing that provided direct employment to some 3,000 people was also affected by the blockade and the military operations. Several boats and some fishermen were directly hit. The Mission met representatives of fishermen's associations and a fisherman testified at the public hearings in Gaza. One fisherman interviewed by the Mission explained that he had previously owned a fishing boat, mainly to fish sardines. It was hit by shelling as it was moored beside the civil defence buildings that were hit by air strikes on 27 December. Half of it was destroyed. Another small boat was also destroyed, as were the nets. The family house was also destroyed and he had been out of work since the beginning of the military operations in December. However, his fishing activities had already been affected before the operations, when the Government of Israel had imposed a limit of six nautical miles for fishing, and then further reduced it to only three.

The continuation of the blockade does not permit the reconstruction of the economic infrastructure that was destroyed. Not only do construction materials continue to be banned but the provision of energy is also still insufficient and irregular. Local purchasing capacity being shattered, there is not enough market demand for many products.

Exports also continue to be prohibited, with the exception of some truckloads of flowers that crossed the borders between January and March 2009. Without external markets, local production of all kinds has no prospect and so employment and livelihoods will remain precarious and diminished. A strawberry farmer and the Head of the Association of Strawberry Farmers based in Beit Lahia explained that before the military operations he used to export up to 2,000 tons of strawberries to Europe. Hundreds of dunums of land were destroyed during the operations as well as some 300 greenhouses and 2,000 acres of citrus trees. As a result, they had lost the European market for their products.

B. FOOD AND NUTRITION

The availability of food in the Gaza Strip is determined by the amount imported through the crossings and that which is locally produced. The Mission received credible information indicating that during the months preceding the military operations both sources of food suffered from the severe restrictions imposed by Israel.

The closing of the Karni grain conveyor belt, the only mechanism for importing wheat, during part of December, resulted in the depletion of wheat stocks, forcing the six mills in the Gaza Strip to close down or reduce operations. The el-Bader Flour Mill appeared to be the only one that kept working as its owners had kept a good stock of grain, but it was later bombed and destroyed (see chap. XIII). However, about one third of the previous number of truckloads of wheat continued entering through the Kerem Shalom crossing. The blockade was tightened following the confrontations of November 2008, further restricting United Nations food assistance. On 18 December, UNRWA was compelled to halt its food distribution programme to thousands of families because its stocks were depleted. It also had to downsize its cash-for-work programmes as it ran out of banknotes.

By December 2008 food insecurity was on the rise. Food security is the capacity of each individual to have access to sufficient and adequate food at all times. The Mission received information indicating that rising food insecurity was the result of falling income levels, eroded livelihoods and higher food prices. Some food items were also unavailable in the local markets. Consequently, the average Gazan household was spending two thirds of its income on food. People had to reduce the quantity and the quality of food they ate, shifting a diet based on low-cost and high-energy cereals, sugar and oil.

Changes in diet patterns are likely to prejudice the long-term health and nutrition of the population. According to the WHO office in Gaza, there are indications of chronic micronutrient deficiencies among the population, in particular among children. Among the most worrying indicators is the high prevalence of stunting among 6- to 16-year-old children (7.2 per cent), while the prevalence of thinness among that group was 3.4 per cent for 2008 (the WHO standard is 5 per cent). Levels of anaemia are alarming: 66 per cent on average among 9- to 12-month-old babies (the rate being higher for girls [69 per cent]). On average, 35 per cent of pregnant women suffer from anaemia.

During the military operations the availability and quality of fresh food dropped: Local production was suspended during the fighting and local produce was spoilt. Mr. Muhammad Husein al-Atar, Mayor of al-Atatra, told the Mission how agricultural land in his neighbourhood was razed. The area is close to the Israeli border and 95 per cent of the work is farming-related. Israeli military incursions had been happening since 2000 accompanied by destruction and bulldozing. As a result, 50,000 acres of land had not a single tree left standing and between 10 and 15 farmers had been killed every year during the last nine years. During the December–January military operations the area was bombed from the air, land and sea. He had personally lost three (industrial) refrigerators, each capable of holding 600 tons of vegetables, for instance. His sister's chicken farms were also destroyed, including some 70,000 chickens (see chap. XIII).

The destruction of land and greenhouses has an impact on the availability of fresh food in the Gaza Strip and, consequently, on the total supply of micronutrients to the population. Satellite imagery commissioned by the Mission shows that for the whole Gaza Strip an estimated 187 greenhouse complexes were either destroyed or severely damaged, representing approximately 30.2 hectares. Of all the destroyed greenhouses 68.6 per cent were in the Gaza and Gaza North Governorates, and 85.4 per cent were destroyed or damaged during the last week of the military operations. Satellite imagery also gives strong indications that tanks and/or heavy vehicles were likely to have been responsible for most of the damage.

[Removed: remainder of section B (paragraphs 1240–1241)]

C. HOUSING

Figures about the overall damage to residential housing vary according to the source and time of the measurement as well as the methodology. The human rights NGO Al Mezan reports that a total of 11,135 homes were partially or fully destroyed. According to the human rights NGO Al Dameer-Gaza, 2,011 civilian and cultural premises were destroyed, of which 1,404 were houses that were completely demolished and 453 were partially destroyed or damaged. A UNDP survey immediately after the end of military operations reported 3,354 houses completely destroyed and 11,112 partially damaged. The destruction was more serious in the north, where 65 per cent of houses were completely destroyed. As a result of the destruction, more than 600 tons of rubble had to be removed, with the consequent costs and potential impact on the environment and public health. Information provided to the Mission showed that much of the construction in Gaza contained important amounts of asbestos, the particles of which had been or could be released into the air at the time of destruction or removal. The refugee population was concentrated in the north and the destruction of residential housing appeared to have particularly affected them.

The destruction or damage of their homes forced many people to flee and find shelter with relatives or agencies providing assistance, such as UNRWA. At the height of the military operations UNRWA was providing shelter to 50,896 displaced persons in 50 shelters. This number was estimated to be a fraction of those who had become homeless, most of whom found temporary shelter with relatives. The Mission was informed that this situation created extreme hardship for people who had to share already deteriorated and limited housing, sanitary and water facilities. It saw for itself people who were still living in tents some six months after the end of the operations.

[Removed: remainder of section C (paragraphs 1244–1245)]

D. WATER AND SANITATION

The Mission received submissions, testimonies and information about the effects of the blockade and of the military operations on the supply of and access to water and sanitation facilities by the population of the Gaza Strip. During the months preceding the military operations the water and sanitation sectors were already under severe strain. The lack of construction materials, pipes and spare parts had prevented the building of additional infrastructure and the proper maintenance of existing facilities. Desalinization plants and works to preserve the aquifer had to be postponed. By December 2008, OCHA reported that the degradation of the system "is posing a major public health hazard." Frequent power outages, fuel shortages and a lack of spare parts for electricity generators had also affected the functioning of the water and sanitation systems.

By December 2008, it was reported that some 80 per cent of Gaza's water wells were only partially functioning while the others were not functioning at all. This situation had already affected the population's access to water: Over half of the residents of Gaza City had access to running water [only a] few hours a week, with those living in houses and buildings using water pumps spending many hours trying to get water by other means. Of the water supplied in Gaza 80 per cent did not meet WHO standards for drinking water owing to, among other factors, the shortage of chlorine to purify the water. Important health risks were consequently likely to arise. Other health hazards were expected to arise from the practice of discharging untreated or partially treated wastewater into the sea. More than 70 million litres a day were discharged into the sea, creating significant environmental damage and health risks for human beings and marine life.

As with other sectors, the military operations worsened the situation in the water and sanitation sector. Services and infrastructure already partially paralysed or in serious need of maintenance suffered further destruction or damage. The Gaza wastewater treatment plant was hit sometime between 3 and 10 January and one of its lagoons was severely damaged (see chap. XIII). Sewage pipes leading to the plant and others in different parts of the city were hit or damaged. Up to 11 water wells that supplied water for human consumption were hit and 3 completely destroyed. Thousands of metres of water and sewage pipes/networks were destroyed or damaged and around 5,700 rooftop water tanks destroyed and some 2,900 damaged.

By the end of January only 70 per cent of Gaza's water wells were working, either fully or partially, i.e. 10 per cent less than before the hostilities. At the height of the military operations some 500,000 Palestinians did not have access to running water at all, whereas the rest received water for few hours a week. Sanitation and water facilities in public shelters were overwhelmed, and raw sewage ran through fields and streets in some areas. The water authorities' reparations team were prevented from going to the sites to carry out urgent repairs and had to wait in most cases until Israeli troops had withdrawn. All urgent repairs were done on a provisional basis given the lack or shortage of construction materials and equipment. The Mission witnessed how precarious those repairs could be when it saw one sewage pipe in the vicinity of the Gaza wastewater treatment plant explode during a site visit.

E. ENVIRONMENT

The Mission has received comments and concerns from non-governmental organizations and concerned individuals in Gaza relating to threatened environmental damage by reason of munitions or debris from munitions. These concerns relate to the fear that hazardous material might have remained or will remain in the soil and water of parts of the Gaza Strip for indefinite periods of time and could enter the food chain or otherwise be hazardous to life.

The Mission was unable to further investigate these concerns, but is aware of an environmental impact study being undertaken by the United Nations Environmental Programme (UNEP) in the Gaza Strip. Preliminary results from UNEP indicate that the environment in the Gaza Strip has been seriously impacted by the Israeli military operations of December–January. In particular, the groundwater in Gaza shows high nitrate levels exceeding WHO ceilings, putting infants at risk of nitrate poisoning.

F. PHYSICAL AND MENTAL HEALTH

The capacity of the health sector in the Gaza Strip was already diminished by the blockade when the Israeli offensive started. While hospitals and clinics continued operating, the quality of their service and its accessibility were eroded. The insufficient and erratic supply of electricity caused equipment to malfunction even when the staff had recourse to generators. Power cuts and water impurities damaged equipment and created additional health hazards. The lack of maintenance and spare parts that were blocked at the crossings further compounded the situation. In addition, the lack of construction materials and inputs hampered the development of additional facilities and needed infrastructure.

Reported confrontation between the Palestinian Authority in Ramallah and the Gaza authorities also affected the quantity and quality of the service provided. The Ministry of Health in Ramallah had been responsible for the supply of medicines to Gaza since September 2008, but it was reported that few trucks with medicines actually reached the Gaza Strip after that time, resulting in serious availability problems for some 20 per cent of essential medicines. The referral of patients needing specialized treatment abroad (e.g. in Israel, Jordan and Egypt) was also affected by the blockade established in 2007. Before that date only some 9 per cent of patients intending to cross the border were rejected or their permits delayed, but that proportion had reached some 22 per cent by September 2008.

The beleaguered health sector was subjected to severe strain when the military operations started on 28 December. Hospitals and health centres of the Ministry of Health worked on an emergency basis under extremely difficult conditions and with limited resources. They nevertheless responded effectively to the crisis. Urgent medical interventions to treat critical injuries were performed under severe circumstances. Of the 5,380 injured people reported by the Ministry, 40 per cent were admitted to the main hospitals, but because of the policy of discharging patients as soon as feasible to free up beds and staff, there were concerns that some injuries (e.g. burns and acute surgical conditions) might have led to complications as follow-up care may have been inadequate. Some injuries will result in permanent disability (see also section G below).

Medical facilities and personnel were targeted during the fighting. Seventeen health personnel were killed and 26 injured. In total, 29 ambulances were damaged or destroyed by bombs or crushed by armoured vehicles, while 48 per cent of Gaza's 122 health facilities were either directly or indirectly hit by shelling. Medical relief and rescue were in many cases also intentionally hindered.

[Removed: paragraphs 1256–1257]

WHO also cited the preliminary results from UNEP initial sampling in Gaza, which showed that "much of the rubble is contaminated with asbestos; damage to the waste treatment system had contaminated the aquifer; the health waste handling system had completely broken down, with such waste going into domestic waste. The results on heavy metal contamination are so far inconclusive." The Mission also investigated and confirmed allegations about the use of weapons whose potential long-term impact on individual victims' health raises concern. They include allegations of the use of weapons containing chemical pollutants such as tungsten and white phosphorus (see also chapter XII).

Conditions under Israeli occupation prior to 2005, together with poverty and the difficulties caused by the blockade, had already made a deep impact on the mental health of the local population. The three weeks of intense bombardment and military ground action added new, serious psychological traumas, especially noticeable in children. According to Dr. Iyad al-Sarraj of the Gaza Community Mental Health Programme, over 20 per cent of Palestinian children in Gaza suffer from post-traumatic stress disorders, the symptoms of which "will appear over the days, months, years, or decades to come."

One particular characteristic of the conflict, namely that the population could not flee the conflict areas as can be done in many conflicts, and had no shelters or safe places in which to hide or protect themselves, reinforced feelings of being trapped, defenceless and vulnerable to more attacks with a sense of inevitability. Many of those who met the Mission stated that they felt terrorized.

According to Dr. Ahmad Abu Tawahina, psychosomatic disorders have a particularly serious impact on Palestinian society, where social stigma is often associated with mental suffering. In general, this makes it difficult for people to express psychological problems. This condition is frequently experienced in the form of recurrent psychosomatic symptoms, such as migraines, pains in joints and muscles, general fatigue and the inability to do even normal daily activities. Most of these patients are referred not to mental health practitioners but to general physicians, who prescribe drugs to alleviate the symptoms and not the causes. This in turn has given rise to a serious problem of drug dependency.

The sense of security that comes from living in a supportive and safe environment had already been eroded over the years by constant attacks and military confrontation, but was further undermined by the direct experience and/or witnessing of violence against relatives. The widespread destruction, the displacement, the inability to find a safe place anywhere, together with the direct exposure to life-threatening events, will continue to have a serious impact on the population. The general state of the inhabitants of the Gaza Strip was described as a form of alienation.

Many of the mental health problems are the result of years of conflict, living in poverty, scarcity and instability in the area and will probably continue until the root causes are eliminated. People, in particular children, live or grow up in a society under occupation, with constant episodes of violence and no sense of security or normalcy.

The situation is compounded by the relative scarcity of qualified professionals and inadequate facilities. The Gaza Community Mental Health Programme has only about 40 members of staff specialized in mental health, including physicians, social researchers, nurses, as well as psychologists. According to Dr. al-Sarraj, this number is not sufficient to cover even the needs of Gaza City district, whereas for the entire population of the Gaza Strip a team of 300 specialists would be necessary.

Over the past two decades, the Gaza Community Mental Health Programme and others have worked to build resilience in people. They told the Mission that the recent military operations had wiped out their achievements. People suffering severe loss also detach themselves from reality, in a phenomenon called "numbness." According to Dr. Tawahina, the general feeling among most people in Gaza is that they have been completely abandoned by the international community. This feeling of abandonment in turn increases their frustration, creating additional pain, and leads eventually to more violence and extremism. The Gaza Community Mental Health Programme studied children's attitudes towards violence and found that, as a result of this situation, and especially when children had lost their parents and with them the associated protection and sense of security, they tended to look at "martyrs" and members of armed groups as adult role models instead.

TESTIMONY 9

Dr. Ahmad Abu Tawahina

Executive Director of the Gaza Community Mental Health Programme, explaining the psychological impact of the Gaza war on the people of Gaza

The Gaza Strip after the last war became a place that is not safe for life. The last statistics by the Gaza Community Mental Health Programme immediately after the last war established that about 25 per cent of the inhabitants of Gaza want to migrate out of the Gaza Strip. This percentage is relevant to another percentage in these statistics that show that 98.8 per cent of the population did not feel that Gaza is a safe place to live. The Gaza Strip—we used to say in the past that it's a large prison. However I believe that this prison has become too tight and constrained for its people. Freedom of movement is restricted. People cannot go for treatment. University students cannot go to study abroad and we can only imagine how this will influence in the long term the psychological state of people. This matter led to many, many psychological disorders, the treatment of which and the rehabilitation of the victims will need a very long time. . . .

A study conducted by the United Nations Development Fund for Women (UNIFEM) revealed that men also showed more symptoms of psychological trauma after the December–January military operations. Based on specialists' reports, the Mission is of the view that this could in part be due to the additional stress that men face as heads of families in a male-dominated society when they are unable to fulfill their role as main breadwinners or to provide protection and security to their children, wives and other family members.

[Removed: paragraph 1267]

G. EDUCATION

The Mission received information about the state of the education sector in the Gaza Strip. UNRWA operates one of the largest school systems in the Middle East and has been the main provider of basic education to Palestine refugees for nearly five decades. The Mission was greatly impressed by its activities and achievements. UNRWA runs 221 schools, while the Government runs 383. UNRWA schools are also a vehicle for health-monitoring and food/nutritional programmes. That Palestinians have high levels of education is largely the result of that work. By the same token, the Mission was shocked to learn how badly educational facilities and activities in the Gaza Strip have been affected as a result of the blockade and the recent military operations.

Information and testimonies received by the Mission showed that the education system was affected in several ways by the restrictions imposed by the blockade. The lack of construction materials had halted all new construction. Repairs to the educational infrastructure also had to be postponed. Around 88 per cent of UNRWA schools and 82 per cent of Government schools operated on a shift system to cope with the demand. The lack of educational material and equipment hampered the ability to maintain teaching standards. This situation was causing a decline in attendance and performance at governmental schools.

The ban on the movement of people through the crossings affected not only university students planning to study or already undertaking studies abroad but also the possibilities for academics and scholars to travel abroad on academic exchanges. Between July and September 2008 only 70 students managed to leave the Gaza Strip via Erez but hundreds saw their aspirations to study abroad truncated.

The military operations destroyed or damaged at least 280 schools and kindergartens. Six of them were located in northern Gaza, affecting some 9,000 pupils, who had to be relocated. According to the Ministry of Education and Higher Education, 164 pupils and 12 teachers were killed during the military operations. Another 454 pupils and five teachers were injured. At UNRWA schools, 86 children and three teachers were killed, and 402 children and 14 teachers injured. During the military operations, 44 UNRWA schools were used as emergency shelters to cope with the more than 50,000 displaced individuals.

Schools were generally closed for the duration of the hostilities, disrupting the study programme. After the ceasefire it was unclear how many students and teachers returned to schools but that number was reported to reach up to 90 per cent in UNRWA schools. Children and teachers reported situations of anxiety and trauma as a result of the extreme violence to which they had been exposed and the loss of relatives or friends. The Mission heard that the start of the military operations with air strikes at a time when schools were functioning exposed children to a heightened risk and filled them with fear and panic. Schools and the roads towards them occasionally remained unsafe because of the presence of explosive remnants of war. Two Palestinian children were killed by those explosives in Zeytoun shortly after the ceasefire was declared. The Mission heard reports that some children were injured by white phosphorous on their way to school.

The Mission saw the destruction caused to the American School. It also saw the destruction caused at the Islamic University and in other university buildings that were destroyed or damaged. These were civilian, educational buildings and the Mission did not find any information about their use as a military facility or their contribution to a military effort that might have made them a legitimate target in the eyes of the Israeli armed forces.

The Mission was also informed of indoctrination programmes allegedly introduced by the Gaza authorities, and of a process of ideological and political polarization. Such programmes have a high potential for imposing models of education at odds with human rights values and with a culture of peace and tolerance. In this regard, the Mission believes that efforts to incorporate human rights in the curricula should be encouraged by the relevant authorities.

H. IMPACT ON WOMEN AND CHILDREN

The attention of the Mission was drawn to the particular manner in which children and women had been affected by the blockade policies and the military operations. In its report, WHO took figures from PCHR: Out of 1,417 persons killed, 313 were children and 116 women. It also takes figures from the Israeli armed forces that showed that 1,166 were killed, of whom 49 were women and 89 were under 16. Among the 5,380 injured, 1,872 were children and 800 women. The Mission directly investigated many incidents in which women and children had been killed as a result of deliberate or indiscriminate attacks by the Israeli armed forces. WHO also reported that among the many injured people who crossed the Rafah border and were accepted for medical treatment in Egypt during the second week of the military operations there were 10 children showing a single bullet injury to the head and one with two.

The Mission held interviews with a number of women and representatives of women's organizations and heard the testimony of Mariam Zaqout of the Culture and Free Thought Association. It heard that the blockade and the military operations had aggravated poverty, which particularly affected women, who must find food and other essentials for their families. Women were often the sole breadwinners (for instance, if male family members had died or been injured as a result of conflict or violence, or were imprisoned) but jobs were hard to come by. Over 300 women had been widowed as a result of the military operations and had become dependent on food and income assistance. In addition, women bore a greater social burden, having to deal with daily life made harsher by the crisis and, at the same

TESTIMONY 10

Abir Mohammed Hajji

Mother and widow describing the death of her husband during the Israeli ground offensive in Zeytoun, January 5, 2009

On the morning of January 5, it was a Monday at about 1:30 A.M., we were woken up by a very loud explosion which shook the house, shattered the windowpanes. I and my husband were sleeping on the floor to get refuge from the shooting. So we crawled to the sitting room. I tried to get some blankets and some mattresses for my kids. . . . [I looked] for my mobile phone to use it as a lamp. After that I heard an explosion inside the house. When I heard the explosion I heard my children screaming and shouting for their father but their father did not answer them back. I ran towards them. It was pitch black. I didn't see anything. I tried to probe myself around until I reached them. I called, "Mohammed . . . my husband," but he did not answer me. I tried to find my way through using my mobile lamp. I saw that he was lying behind my daughter. My daughter told me that her arm was warm but her arm was covered with blood. . . . I tried to pull him towards me but I found out that his ear, his eyes were damaged. He was bleeding from his ear and eye.

So I shouted at my brother-in-law in the neighboring house and I called him to come to the house to see what happened. I ran to the door. I opened the door but I didn't know that the Israeli soldiers were outside the house. . . .

My brother-in-law came into the house, hugged his brother and he told me that his brother died, and then he joined us in the room where we time, provide security and care for injured family members and children, their own and others who have lost their parents. These responsibilities sometimes compelled them to conceal their own sufferings, so their concerns remained unaddressed.

In the same interviews, the participants stated that women were particularly affected by the destruction of homes and the invasion of privacy. Having to live in tents without privacy or appropriate sanitary facilities added to their hardship. Moreover, the military operations had strained relations among family members.

Testimony 10 (*continued*)

were gathered. My son asked his uncle to shut the door but as soon as he shut the door the Israeli soldier broke into the door, shooting the door down. I was carrying my 3-year-old daughter and I waved my daughter to the Israelis telling them that I have kids with me. But the soldiers shouted at Nasser, my brother-in-law, and the Israeli soldiers asked him if he was Hamas. So my brother-in-law told the soldiers that he was neither Hamas nor Fatah and that there were no members of either Hamas or Fatah in the area. But the Israeli soldiers said, "No, no you are Hamas," and the Israeli soldiers were laughing aloud although they saw the corpse of my husband and that made them laugh.

So they asked my brother-in-law to strip and then asked him to pull his brother to another room. The soldiers carried all the mattresses and blankets and threw them on my husband's body. The Israeli soldiers came to our room and pointed their laser pointed guns at us. We were filled with panic and fear. We had never seen soldiers acting so atrociously and appallingly. They took us to another room inside the house and asked us to all sit down inside that room but there were glass panes everywhere, glass pieces everywhere. But that did not prevent them from taking us to that room. They asked my brother-in-law to wipe my husband's blood with a bucket of water and we heard them dig into the tiles in the house. . . .

Postscript: Shortly after her husband's death, Hajji and her daughters were forced to evacuate and begin a days-long search for safety, from one relative's house to another. During this odyssey, Israeli soldiers shot and wounded Hajji and killed her three-year-old daughter. They had been waving white flags. Hajji, who was two months pregnant at the time, later suffered a miscarriage.

Psychological pressures on men and women, together with financial difficulties, led to family disputes, family violence and divorce. There were frequent disputes between widows and their in-laws regarding child custody and inheritance. Widows were also under increased pressure to get married again to be able to sustain themselves. Consequently, there was an increase in women seeking legal aid, as legal problems tended to become aggravated because of shortcomings in the law and fewer safeguards for the rights of women.

The particular manner in which the conflict affected women was dramatically illustrated for the Mission by the testimony of a woman of the al-Samouni family (see chap. XI). She had three children and was pregnant when her family and her house came under attack. She commented on how the children were scared and crying. She was distressed when recounting how her 10-month-old baby, whom she was carrying in her arms, was hungry but she did not have anything to give him to eat, and how she tried to feed him by chewing on a piece of bread, the only food available, and giving it to him. She also managed to get half a cup of water from an ill-functioning tap. There were other babies and older children. She and her sister exposed themselves to danger by going out to search for food for them. Her husband, mother and sister were killed but she managed to survive. Her other son was wounded in the back, and she carried both out of the house.

Many women felt helpless and embarrassed at not being able to protect and care for their children. Others felt frustrated, invaded in their personal space and powerless when their houses and possessions were destroyed or vandalized. Those feelings contributed to their psychological suffering.

A UNFPA study conducted immediately after the December–January military operations reported a 40 per cent increase in miscarriages admitted to maternity wards, a 50 per cent increase in neonatal deaths, a rise in obstetric complications and anecdotal evidence of deaths or health complications because pregnant women were unable to reach hospital to deliver their babies. Women interviewed in the context of another UNFPA study expressed extreme fears for themselves and their loved ones. Associated symptoms included anxiety, panic attacks, feelings of insecurity, disturbed sleep and eating patterns, depression, sadness and fear of sudden death.

Adults and children showed signs of profound depression, while children suffered from insomnia and bed-wetting. Numerous testimonies received by the Mission highlight the presence of children in situations where houses were searched or occupied with force by Israeli soldiers, and when killings occurred. The Mission heard the testimony of a mother whose children, aged 3 to 16, had witnessed the killing of their father in their own house. With Israeli soldiers forcefully questioning their mother and uncle and vandalizing their house, the children asked their mother whether they would be killed as well. Their mother felt the only comfort she could give them was to tell them to say the Shehada, the prayer recited in the face of death. Children were present in improvised shelters on United Nations premises, enduring the trauma of displacement as well as feelings of fear from the military attacks and of deep insecurity from having been attacked in their own homes or in a shelter that was expected to be safe. During its visits, the Mission saw many children living with their families in the ruins of their homes and in makeshift accommodation. The trauma for children having witnessed violence and often the killing of their own family members will no doubt be long-lasting. Mrs. Massouda Sobhia al-Samouni told the Mission that her son was still traumatized. He kept placing coins in his mouth and when she told him it was dangerous and he might die if he did so, he replied that he wanted to join his father.

Some 30 per cent of children screened at UNRWA schools had mental health problems, while some 10 per cent of children had lost relatives or friends or lost their homes and possessions. WHO estimated that some 30,000 children would need continued psychological support and warned of the potential for many to grow up with aggressive attitudes and hatred.

I. PERSONS WITH DISABILITIES

Information provided to the Mission showed that many of those who were injured during the Israeli military operations sustained permanent disabilities owing to the severity of their injuries and/or the lack of adequate and timely medical attention and rehabilitation. Gaza hospitals reportedly had to discharge patients too early so as to handle incoming emergencies. Other cases resulted in amputations or disfigurement. About 30 per cent of patients were expected to have long-term disabilities.

WHO reported that by mid-April 2009 the number of people with different types of permanent disability (e.g. brain injuries, amputations, spinal injuries, hearing deficiencies, mental health problems) as a result of the military operations was not yet known. It reported speculations that there might be some 1,000 amputees; but information provided by the WHO office in Gaza and based on estimates by Handicap International indicated that around 200 persons underwent amputations.

While the exact number of people who will suffer permanent disabilities is still unknown, the Mission understands that many persons who sustained traumatic injuries during the conflict still face the risk of permanent disability owing to complications and inadequate follow-up and physical rehabilitation.

The Mission also heard moving accounts of families with disabled relatives whose disability had slowed their evacuation from a dangerous area or who lived with a constant fear that, in an emergency, their families would have to leave them behind because it would be too difficult to evacuate them.

One testimony concerned a person whose electric wheelchair was lost after his house was targeted and destroyed. Since the residents were given very short notice of the impending attack, the wheelchair could not be salvaged and the person had to be taken to safety on a plastic chair carried by four people.

The Mission also heard a testimony concerning a pregnant woman who was instructed by an Israeli soldier to evacuate her home with her children, but to leave behind a mentally disabled child, which she refused to do.

Even in the relative safety of shelters, people with disabilities continued to be exposed to additional hardship, as these shelters were not equipped for their special needs. The Mission heard of the case of a person with a hearing disability who was sheltering in an UNRWA school, but was unable to communicate in sign language or understand what was happening and experienced sheer fear.

[Removed: remainder of section I (paragraphs 1290–1291)]

[Removed: sections J and K (paragraphs 1292–1335)]

CHAPTER XVIII.

THE CONTINUING DETENTION OF ISRAELI SOLDIER GILAD SHALIT

The Mission notes the continued detention of Gilad Shalit, a member of the Israeli armed forces, captured in 2006 by Palestinian armed groups during a cross-border operation. In reaction to the capture, the Israeli Government ordered a number of incursions to attack important infrastructure in the Gaza Strip as well as Palestinian Authority offices. This was followed by the arrest of eight Palestinian Government ministers and 26 members of the Palestinian Legislative Council by the Israeli security forces.

Israeli Government officials have repeatedly stated that the easing of the blockade on the Gaza Strip (see chaps. V and XVII) is linked to the release of Gilad Shalit. In February 2009, it appeared that the Israeli Government had dropped its demand for Palestinian militants to release Gilad Shalit before it would end the blockade. However, the then Deputy Prime Minister stated shortly after that "Israel is facing a serious humanitarian crisis, and it is called Gilad Shalit, and . . . until he is returned home, not only will we not allow more cargo to reach the residents of Gaza, we will even diminish it." Israel's then Prime Minister also stated that "we will not reopen the border crossings [into Gaza] and assist Hamas so long as Gilad Shalit is in their brutal prison." According to the CBS News Channel, this position was reiterated by the current Israeli Prime Minister in July 2009.

In October 2008, a Hamas spokesman stated that "the Shalit case is dependent on prisoners swap. . . . He will never be released if the Israeli occupation does not release Palestinian prisoners whom Hamas wants free. . . . "

The Mission is aware that negotiations, through intermediaries, continue with regard to the exchange of prisoners between the Israeli Government and Hamas representatives.

The Mission asked the Gaza authorities to confirm the status of Gilad Shalit. In their reply, which the Mission considered to be unsatisfactory, the Gaza authorities denied being involved in any way with the capture and detention of Gilad Shalit and stated that they are not in possession of any information regarding his current status.

During its investigations in the Gaza Strip, the Mission heard testimonies indicating that during the military operations of December 2008–January 2009, Israeli soldiers questioned captured Palestinians about the whereabouts of Gilad Shalit (see chap. XV).

Gilad Shalit's father, Noam Shalit, appeared before the Mission at the public hearing held in Geneva on 6 July 2009. He informed the Mission of his extreme concern about the condition of his son, who has not been able to communicate with his family and has not been allowed to receive ICRC visits. Mr. Shalit expressed concern about the health and psychological status of his son after more than three years of captivity and appealed for his release.

[Removed: "Legal findings and conclusions" (paragraphs 1343–1344)]

CHAPTER XIX.

INTERNAL VIOLENCE AND TARGETING OF FATAH AFFILIATES BY SECURITY SERVICES UNDER THE CONTROL OF THE GAZA AUTHORITIES

The Mission has received reports and allegations of violations committed in Gaza by the security services in the period under inquiry. It has heard some of those allegations first-hand and investigated them by comparing the accounts it received with reports of domestic and international human rights organizations.

From the beginning of 2006, when Hamas won the majority of seats in the Palestinian Legislative Council, violence between competing Palestinian political groups in the Gaza Strip escalated. Armed clashes periodically erupted between the security forces affiliated with the two main political groups—Fatah and Hamas—and culminated in June 2007, when Hamas seized control of the Palestinian Authority's civil and security institutions of the Gaza Strip.

During the six months preceding the Israeli military operations in Gaza of December 2008–January 2009, reports of deaths in suspicious circumstances and abuses by the security services reporting to the Gaza authorities continued to be documented by domestic monitoring mechanisms, including by the Independent Commission for Human Rights (ICHR).

Between June and December 2008, ICHR received 45 complaints from citizens alleging that they were subjected to torture while being detained or interrogated.

All these complaints were lodged against the Ministry of Interior, the police, the military intelligence, the general intelligence and the internal security services of the Gaza authorities, as well as al-Qassam Brigades.

During the same period, ICHR received about 250 complaints from citizens that security agencies (namely the internal security and the police) detained them without respecting legally prescribed procedures. In particular, ICHR reported that no arrest warrants from the competent authorities were presented to detainees and that the security services searched civilian houses without having obtained the relevant search warrants. ICHR reported that family visits to detainees were denied, especially in the al-Sarayah and al-Mashtal detention and interrogation centres of the internal security agency. In addition, detainees were not brought before the judicial authorities within the legally prescribed period. According to ICHR, the security services also continued to detain citizens with arrest warrants issued by the military justice authority.

Many leaders of the Fatah movement as well as the Governors of Khan Yunis and Gaza were at the time of drafting this report still in detention at the al-Mashtal detention and interrogation centre.

In the course of its investigations in Gaza, the Mission obtained information from international and domestic organizations and from individuals in Gaza about violence against political opponents by the security services that report to the Gaza authorities. The Israeli attacks, including the aerial strikes targeting police stations and the main prison in Gaza City (see chap. VII), created chaos, making it impossible to independently verify initial reports about violations by the security services. Towards the end of the military operations, however, domestic human rights organizations started to verify such allegations, including by analysing information from hospitals that they had received bodies of persons who had apparently not been killed in the Israeli attacks.

According to both domestic and international human rights organizations, members of the security services and unidentified gunmen killed between 29 and 32 Gaza residents between the beginning of the Israeli military operations and 27 February. Among these, between 17 and 22 detainees, who had been at al-Sarayah detention facility on 28 December and had fled following an Israeli aerial attack, were killed in seemingly extrajudicial or summary executions, some of them while seeking medical assistance in hospitals.

Not all those killed after escaping detention were Fatah affiliates, detained for political reasons, or charged with collaborating with the enemy. Some of the escapees had been convicted of serious crimes, such as drug-dealing or murder, and had been sentenced to death. Regardless of the intended scope of the Israeli attack on the prison, the effect was to create a chaotic situation that, according to some domestic observers, was exploited by some elements in the security services.

During the course of its work in Gaza, the Mission heard first-hand accounts of violations against Fatah affiliates committed during the period of the Israeli military operations. Some of the witnesses who were interviewed by the Mission were severely distressed and asked that their identity not be disclosed for fear of retaliation. The Mission questioned the witnesses and found them to be credible. The following cases are among those reported to the Mission and are based on information it gathered from a variety of sources.

One of the individuals killed following their escape from the damaged al-Sarayah prison was a Fatah affiliate who had been arrested and detained long before the Israeli military operations in Gaza. For about two weeks his family made several unsuccessful enquiries with different security services to discover his whereabouts. After finally tracing him, the family was able to visit him in the detention facility run by the internal security and saw that he was in poor health as the likely result of torture and inadequate detention conditions. He was reportedly not able to speak freely while in detention.

He was still in al-Sarayah prison on 28 December 2008, when it was hit during an Israeli aerial bombardment. His dead body was later found with signs of bullet wounds at al-Shifa hospital in Gaza City. The family was told that he had been shot dead by unknown persons. Independent sources consulted by the Mission seem to indicate that the victim had fled from al-Sarayah detention facility after the aerial attack and had been wounded in the attack itself or shot by the prison staff trying to prevent detainees from escaping.

The Mission received a number of reports of violent attacks against individuals affiliated with Fatah by armed men who broke into their homes. In one incident, a group of persons claiming to be police officers knocked at the door of a family residence in Gaza City. The family was confronted by a group of 7 to 10 men wearing civilian clothes, most of them masked. They took one member of the family outside. When they brought him back roughly half an hour later, he appeared to have been beaten violently with metal pipes. He died of his injuries about a month later.

In another incident reported to the Mission, a group of 10 to 12 masked men wearing military uniforms broke into the residence of an individual who used to work for the preventive security under the Palestinian Authority before the Hamas takeover. When the family tried to resist attempts to capture him, the masked men started shooting indiscriminately, killing one member of the family and injuring 11 others. After the shooting, the masked men fled. According to the information provided to the Mission, when the injured were transferred to al-Shifa hospital, members of the security services there prevented medical staff from providing assistance.

The Mission was informed that—although serious—this was only one of many incidents in which this family had been targeted by Hamas operatives. One year earlier, a member of the family had been abducted and shot in the legs.

The Mission was also informed of an incident in which a group of armed, masked men broke into the house of a Fatah supporter in Gaza City, abducted him and took him to a nearby location, where he was tortured and shot in the leg. He was reportedly left unconscious and rescued by neighbours. The ordeal reportedly lasted about one hour. The same individual had previously been arrested by members of the security services and kept in detention for a month and a half. He was released only after signing a pledge not to participate in Fatah political celebrations or occasions.

The Mission was informed that, in another incident, three armed, masked men wearing symbols of al-Qassam Brigades broke into the residence in Gaza City of an individual who is a Fatah supporter and on the payroll of a Fatah-controlled institution. The men started beating everyone inside, including a child, and were screaming insults. All the males were then reportedly made to go outside—where other masked men were waiting—and were beaten with metal bars and with rifle butts. After this, the masked men took one of the men to a nearby location, where they again beat him very violently. While he was being beaten, the masked men reportedly kept insulting him, accusing him of collaborating with Israel and calling him a traitor. In response to a question by the Mission, a witness stated that he had the feeling that there was a clear chain of command among the group of masked men. Shortly before meeting the Mission, the same individual had been summoned by the internal security in Gaza along with other Fatah affiliates and kept for four hours at an internal security detention centre in Gaza City before being released.

Similarly, a group of people who were identified as belonging to the internal security stormed the residence of an individual in Gaza City and beat members of the family. The group was composed of masked men who left only after shooting him in the leg. The victim was allegedly prevented by members of the security services from getting treatment at al-Shifa hospital for his injuries. He had previously been arrested and detained by members of the security services. During his detention, he was allegedly subjected to different forms of torture, including beatings, *shabah* [a torture method in which the prisoner is tightly shackled for long periods], electric shocks and sleep deprivation. His captors did not reportedly question him or levy specific charges against him. Finally, towards the end of his detention, he was formally accused of "having contacts with the Ramallah government." He was reportedly arrested again after the end of the conflict by members of the security services and again subjected to torture.

The Mission was also informed of the case of another Fatah affiliate who had been summoned by the internal security in Gaza and detained on the basis of evidence provided by another member of his family who accused him of collaborating with Israel. Additional abuses allegedly committed by the security services include the confiscation of property from the families of Fatah affiliates, as well as additional cases of torture while in detention in facilities that they operate.

The Mission was informed that the movement of many Fatah members was restricted during Israel's military operations in Gaza and that many were put under house arrest very early on and threatened with "action" should they disobey. Hundreds of cases in which house arrest was imposed without any kind of due process were reported to domestic human rights organizations during this period. Some individuals received a written order from the police or the internal security (the Mission has a sample of these orders), or a verbal order from the members of al-Qassam Brigades or the internal security. In some cases, those issuing these orders would not identify themselves. The Mission was informed of one case in which an individual put under house arrest in this way was allegedly shot dead by the security services when he and other members of his family were evacuated from their home owing to the presence of the Israeli armed forces.

The Gaza authorities denied that any arrests had taken place in Gaza between 27 December 2008 and 18 January 2009 owing to the insecurity created by the Israeli military operations. They stated that arrests were made only after the end of these operations and only in relation to criminal acts, "security prevention and to restore public order."

A. FACTUAL FINDINGS

The Mission finds that the statements provided to it in relation to abuses committed by the Gaza authorities' security services are credible and has no reason to doubt their veracity.

As for violent attacks against individuals either in their homes or after being taken from their homes, this finding is reinforced by a number of factors. The pattern of armed, and sometimes uniformed, masked men breaking into houses is described in almost all incidents reported to the Mission. Also, in most cases those abducted from their homes or otherwise detained were reportedly not accused of offences related to specific incidents but, rather, targeted because of their political affiliation. When charges were laid, these were always linked to suspected political activities contrary to the perceived interest of the Gaza authorities. Some of the accounts also indicate that elements of hierarchical control were present within the groups of armed, masked men executing the attacks. The testimonies of witnesses and the reports provided by international and domestic human rights organizations bear striking similarities and indicate that these attacks were not randomly executed, but constituted part of a pattern of organized violence directed mainly against Fatah affiliates and supporters.

In relation to the allegations that between 27 December 2008 and 18 January 2009 more than 20 persons suspected of collaborating with Israel were killed or maimed by being shot in the leg or otherwise severely injured, the Gaza authorities stated that their investigations found these incidents to be the result of family feuds "or otherwise they were individual acts motivated by personal revenge." In addition, they stated that "the Government, through its competent agencies, opened investigations into these events immediately after the war, and submitted charges before the competent Courts." According to PCHR, however, on 2 February 2009 a spokesperson for the Gaza authorities stated that "the Government makes distinctions between abuses of law and the actions of the Palestinian resistance during the war, regarding the execution of some collaborators who are involved in collaborating with the [Israeli] occupation." The statement seems to express support for a number of acts of violence that occurred in the chaotic atmosphere created by the military operations.

[Removed: section B (paragraphs 1369–1372)]

The West Bank, Including East Jerusalem

As explained above in chapter I, the Mission believes that the reference in its mandate to violations "in the context" of the military operations in Gaza required it to go beyond the violations that occurred in and around Gaza. It also believes that violations within its mandate in terms of time, objectives and targets include those that are linked to the December 2008–January 2009 military operations, and include restrictions on human rights and fundamental freedoms related to the strategies and actions of Israel in the context of its military operations.

Developments in Gaza and the West Bank are closely interrelated; in the Mission's view, an analysis of both is necessary to reach an informed understanding of and to report on issues within the Mission's mandate. On the one hand, the events in Gaza have consequences in the West Bank; on the other, pre-existing problems in the West Bank have been exacerbated by the Gaza military operations.

In its examination of the West Bank with respect to actions taken by Israel, the Mission focused on four key aspects in their linkage to the Israeli military operations in Gaza: (a) the sharp increase in the use of force by Israeli security forces, including the military, in the West Bank; (b) the tightening and entrenchment of the system of movement and access restrictions; (c) the issue of Palestinian detainees and especially the increase in child detainees during and after the military operations; and (d) the Gaza corollary of the detention of Hamas members of the Palestinian Legislative Council. While the treatment by the Gaza authorities of those opposing its policies is discussed in chapter XIX, similar issues with regard to the conduct of the Palestinian Authority in the West Bank also called for investigation. Linkages with the Israeli operation in Gaza are elaborated in the respective chapters.

[Removed: Methodology (paragraphs 1376–1380)]

CHAPTER XX.

TREATMENT OF PALESTINIANS IN THE WEST BANK BY ISRAELI SECURITY FORCES, INCLUDING USE OF EXCESSIVE OR LETHAL FORCE DURING DEMONSTRATIONS

The information gathered by the Mission indicates an ongoing pattern of ill treatment and use of force by the Israeli security forces against Palestinians in the West Bank, including East Jerusalem. Ill treatment and low levels of force are reported being common in encounters at checkpoints between Palestinians and the Israeli security forces (army, police and border police), while a greater, sometimes lethal, degree of force has been used during demonstrations, incursions and search and arrest operations. With heavily armed Israeli military forces present throughout the West Bank, the possibility of violence always exists. As a witness reported to the Mission, "the use of force is part of the system of control of the occupation, where a key element is fear, which can only be sustained by the constant threat and the periodic act of violence."

Violence against Palestinians in the West Bank does not only come from the security forces. The Israeli military operations in Gaza commenced when the West Bank was experiencing some of the worst acts of settler violence in several years.

Witnesses and experts informed the Mission of a sharp increase in the use of force by the Israeli security forces against Palestinians in the West Bank from the commencement of the Israeli operations in Gaza. A number of protesters were killed and scores were injured by Israeli forces during Palestinian demonstrations following the beginning of the [conflict]; the degree of violence employed in the West Bank during the operations in Gaza has been sustained since 18 January. Reports from non-governmental organizations confirm this information.

A. SETTLER VIOLENCE IN THE WEST BANK IN THE PERIOD PRECEDING THE ISRAELI MILITARY OPERATIONS IN GAZA

In early December 2008, Israeli settlers in the city of Hebron rioted and perpetrated acts of violence against the local Palestinian population. Although Israel, as the occupying power, has the responsibility to maintain public order and safety in the occupied territory, the Israeli police did not intervene to protect Palestinians. Settler violence is a regular occurrence, targeting primarily Palestinian civilians and their property but also, on occasion, Israeli soldiers. According to the Office for the Coordination of Humanitarian Affairs, "a root cause of the phenomenon is Israel's decade-long policy of facilitating and encouraging the settling of its citizens inside occupied Palestinian territory, defined as transfer of population and prohibited by international humanitarian law." Israeli media attribute the increase in settler violence to the settler movement, which became increasingly radicalized after the Gaza Disengagement in August 2005.

[Removed: paragraphs 1385–1387]

The use of force against Gaza solidarity demonstations in the West Bank during the Israeli operations in Gaza

There was a significant increase in the use of force by Israeli security forces during demonstrations in the West Bank after the start of the Israeli operations in Gaza. The degree of force used against protests during the previous year had already been high, including during protests against the Wall in places such as Jayyous, al-Ma'sara, Bi'lin and Ni'lin. The villages where demonstrations are regularly held have lost or stand to lose much of their land to Israeli settlements and the Wall. A vibrant grass-roots, non-violent resistance movement has evolved that has attracted support from Israeli and international activists. New tactics and weapons used by the Israeli security forces aimed at suppressing the popular movement have resulted in deaths and injuries. For example, in July 2008, Israeli border police killed two children, Ahmad Musa, aged 10, and Yusef Amera, aged 17, both of whom were shot in the head.

Another cause of concern for the Mission were further allegations of the use of unnecessary, lethal force by Israeli security forces. At the public hearing in Geneva of 6 July 2009, two witnesses, Mohamed Srour and Jonathan Pollak, described the fatal shooting, on 28 December 2008, of two young men from the village of Ni'lin during a protest against the Israeli operations in Gaza. Mr. Srour was himself shot in the leg during the same protest.

At the hearing on 6 July, Mr. Srour stated that as a result of this war, many people all around the West Bank, but also in his village Ni'lin, wanted to demonstrate and express their solidarity with the people of Gaza. The demonstration included important participation of people from the different solidarity movements, from Israel as well [as] the international community. The two witnesses spoke of the atmosphere that they had encountered in the confrontation with the soldiers and border police, which was markedly different from the situation before the operations in Gaza. Mr. Pollak stated:

> The atmosphere of the incident, and during and after the start of the war generally was that all checks and balances had been removed. The soldiers were saying things related to the Gaza war, taunting things like, "It's a shame we're not in Gaza killing Arabs." There seemed to be an enthusiasm to confront and the amount of live ammunition used shows this. The behaviour of the soldiers has escalated immensely—not that in the past the army was so gentle.

According to the witnesses, the main demonstration had ended when the army and border police used tear gas and stun grenades to disperse the crowd. The next sequence of events took place on the edge of the village, at a considerable distance from the site of the construction of the Wall. The two young men killed were part of a small group of demonstrators, some of whom had thrown stones at the soldiers. In video footage, four or five soldiers appeared to be casually walking around and not seemingly threatened. No tear gas was used at that stage. Dozens of rounds of live ammunition were fired in the direction of the group of young men, hitting three of them within minutes of each other. Mohamed Khawaja was shot in the forehead; Arafat Khawaja, who had turned to run away, was shot in the back, and Mohamed Srour was shot in the leg. Subsequently an ambulance was prevented from reaching the victims, who had to be carried some distance and were eventually put onto a pick-up truck, at which the army fired tear gas. Arafat Khawaja was pronounced dead on arrival at the hospital and Mohamed Khawaja passed away a few days later.

Two Palestinians were killed during other protests against the military operations in Gaza. On 4 January, Mufid Walwel was shot dead during a demonstration near Qalqilya, where the Wall is to be built. In Hebron, on 16 January, Mus'ab Da'na died after being shot in the head. According to an NGO report, the Israeli border police are believed to have been responsible for both incidents.

The Mission has asked the Government of Israel to explain the increased use of live ammunitions during demonstrations in the West Bank, but has received no reply.

B. THE INCREASED LEVEL OF FORCE SINCE THE END OF THE OPERATIONS IN GAZA

Since the end of the December–January military operations in Gaza, the increased level of force has reportedly continued against demonstrators and in other situations. The Mission heard from an eye witness how, on 13 March 2009, United States citizen Tristan Anderson was hit, while participating in an anti-Wall demonstration in Ni'lin, with a high velocity tear gas canister in the forehead. According to the witness, Mr. Anderson was taking pictures of Israeli soldiers and border police attacking the demonstrators. A high velocity long-range tear gas canister was used at short range, crushing his forehead. As he lay on the ground, the border police, who would have been able to see him falling down and lying on the ground, continued to shoot tear gas in his direction. Video footage received by the Mission showed Palestinian paramedics in bright-orange uniforms putting Mr. Anderson's body onto a stretcher, a tear gas canister landing directly beside them and a large cloud of gas developing. According to the witness, Israeli forces delayed Mr. Anderson's transfer from the Palestinian ambulance to an Israeli ambulance at the checkpoint before entering Israel. At 1 August 2009, Mr. Anderson remains in a critical condition in an Israeli hospital.

On 17 April 2009, in Bi'lin, Bassem Abu Rahma was killed by a high velocity tear gas canister which was shot at his chest from a distance of 30 to 40 metres. The killing, which took place during a peaceful demonstration against the Wall, was filmed. The footage shows Mr. Abu Rahma standing on a small hill, clearly visible and not armed or otherwise posing a threat.

Eye witnesses reported to the Mission that they felt that it had become almost a sport for snipers, who now routinely enter villages and occupy roofs of buildings, to aim at protesters in a manner that is inappropriate in the context of crowd control, with apparent disregard for the lives or limbs of the persons they hit.

On 5 June 2009, five people were shot by snipers in a demonstration in Ni'lin, of whom one, Aqel Srour, was killed, and another, a 15-year-old boy, was shot in the abdomen and will be permanently disabled. Al-Haq described the shooting of Srour, who according to Al-Haq had run to assist the boy who was shot in the abdomen, as a case of "wilful killing."

The weapons used by the security forces are also a cause for concern. Many of the injuries to protesters during anti-Wall demonstrations in recent months (in Ni'lin, Bi'lin, Jayyous, Bitunya and Budrus) and the death of Aqel Srour and that of a 14-year-old who was killed in Hebron in February were reportedly inflicted by a .22 caliber Ruger rifle. B'Tselem has protested against the use of this weapon as a means of crowd control on the grounds that it is potentially lethal. In its response to B'Tselem's letter of 26 February, the Israeli Judge Advocate General wrote that "the open-fire regulations applying to the .22 ammunition are comparable, in general, to the open-fire rules applying to 'ordinary' ammunition" and that "following your letter, we directed that the forces again be instructed with respect to the binding Open-Fire Regulations that apply to use of the Ruger rifle." However, from the nature of the killing of Aqel Srour and the injuries sustained by protesters in the months following the Judge Advocate General's response, it is clear that the use of the Ruger rifle has not been tempered.

The Israeli armed forces' open-fire regulations for the West Bank provide that different rules apply in situations where Israeli citizens are present, as compared to situations where there are only Palestinians present. For example, they provide for the use of live ammunitions under certain conditions, in the case of violent "disturbances" near the Wall or in the nearby area. Where Israelis participate, however, the use of live ammunitions is forbidden. Similarly different provisions are found with regard to the use of warning shots and rubber bullets. Witnesses indicated to the Mission, however, that the army no longer distinguishes between Palestinians and their Israeli and international supporters, and uses a greater degree of force against all.

The Mission asked the Government of Israel about the differences in open-fire regulations applied in the Occupied Palestinian Territory in situations in which Israeli citizens are present as opposed to situations where none are present, but has received no reply.

In a recent court hearing, Colonel Virob, an Israeli Brigade Commander in the West Bank, defended the routine use of force in achieving the goals of the occupation. According to the Association for Civil Rights in Israel, when Colonel Virob was asked about using physical force during an investigation against people who are not suspects, he stated that "using violence and aggression to prevent the situation from escalating and the need to use even more violence is not only allowed but sometimes imperative . . . , giving a blow, a push, in a situation even with people who are not involved in an operational situation, if it can advance the mission, is certainly possible." He added that "the way you use violence should also be appropriate . . . , a slap, sometimes a hit to the back of the neck or the chest, in cases that there is friction, a reaction from the Palestinian side, sometimes a knee jab or strangulation to calm someone down is reasonable."

The Mission considers with concern reports of gratuitous abuse by Israeli soldiers. It heard testimonies in a video footage shown on Israeli television that described a search and detain operation by the Kfir Brigade in the West Bank village of Haris. Hundreds of troops had participated in a nocturnal raid on a village aimed at finding boys who were thought to have thrown stones at settlers' cars some days previously. On 9 June 2009, *The Independent* reported on the operation, quoting soldiers of the Kfir Brigade involved. One was quoted as saying he saw many soldiers "just knee [Palestinians] because it's boring, because you stand there ten hours, you're not doing anything, so they beat people up." A second soldier described a "fanatical atmosphere" during the search operations. "We would go into a house and turn the whole thing upside down," he recalled, but no weapons were found. "They confiscated kitchen knives." The first soldier stated that numerous soldiers were involved. "There were a lot of reservists that participated, and they totally had a celebration on the Palestinians: curses, humiliation, pulling hair and ears, kicks, slaps. These things were the norm." He described the beating of a child:

> The soldiers who took [detainees] to the toilet just exploded [over] them with beatings; cursed them with no reason. When they took one Arab to the toilet so that he could urinate, one of them gave him a slap that brought him to the ground. He had been handcuffed from behind with a nylon restraint and blindfolded. He wasn't insolent, he didn't do anything to get on anyone's nerves . . . [it was] just because he's an Arab. He was something like 15 years old.

He stated that the incidents in the toilet were the "extreme" and added that the beatings did not draw blood. They were "dry beatings, but it's still a beating."

Video footage uploaded to the internet by Israeli border police, and filed under "comedy," offers an insight into how wanton abuse is perceived by members of the security forces themselves. The Mission has received reports of other, similar occurrences, giving rise to the concern that an increased level of force and dehumanization have become normalized in the practice of security forces.

C. THE ROLE OF IMPUNITY

Several witnesses told the Mission that, during the operations in Gaza, the sense in the West Bank was one of a "free for all," where any behavior was permitted for Israeli forces. An even greater use of force than that used in the West Bank could be attributed to a change in atmosphere or attitude towards the "other" during time of war. There are indications that this shift in attitude was also apparent during the war in Lebanon in 2006. The concept of what is considered "normal" and "acceptable" conduct risks shifting to even higher levels, if those in positions of responsibility do not respond appropriately. In the face of the recent increase in violence by the Israeli security forces in the West Bank, B'Tselem stated that condemnations by Ministers and other officials

> remain solely declarative. Security forces, meanwhile, misusing their power, continue to abuse and beat Palestinians, among them, minors . . . . If a message is sent to security forces, it is that even if the establishment does not accept acts of violence, it will not take measures against those who commit them. The effect of such a message is that the lives and dignity of Palestinians are meaningless and that security forces can continue, pursuant to the function they serve, to abuse, humiliate, and beat Palestinians with whom they come into contact.

In the past, every case in which a Palestinian not participating in hostilities was killed was subject to criminal investigation. This policy changed in 2000. Criminal investigations are now the exception; these cases are now simply discussed in an "operational debriefing" by the military itself. In 2003, the Association for Civil Rights in Israel and B'Tselem filed a petition to reverse this policy change, demanding that every civilian death be independently investigated. The petition included demands for investigations into individual deaths as well as the principal question relating to the overall policy. The former were dismissed, while the principal question is still pending.

Yesh Din reports that over 90 per cent of investigations into settler violence are closed without an "indictment being filed." B'Tselem reported in June 2009 that the charges against [Ze'ev] Braude, the Hebron settler who was filmed shooting and injuring three Palestinians in December 2009, would be dropped, as the court had ordered that "secret evidence" against him be disclosed, and the potential public harm of this disclosure would outweigh the harm done by a person, documented as having committed a violent crime, being released back into society.

In July 2009, an Israeli activist who had been shot in the head in 2006 by the Israeli border police was awarded compensation for his injury in an out-of-court settlement. To date, the commander who ordered the shooting has not been subject to criminal investigation.

On 7 July 2008, Ashraf Abu-Rahma was shot at short range while blindfolded and handcuffed. The incident was filmed and widely broadcast. When the Israeli Military Advocate General charged the officer who ordered the shooting with "conduct unbecoming," Israeli international law professor Orna Ben-Naftali stated that "the decision [was] indicative of a policy of tolerance towards violence against non-violent civilian protests against the construction of the Separation Wall." She added that "the implication of such a policy is twofold: first, it might transform 'conduct unbecoming'—which as a matter of law is a war crime—into a crime against humanity; second, it may well be construed as an invitation to the international community to intervene through the exercise of universal jurisdiction."

D. LEGAL ANALYSIS AND CONCLUSIONS

[Removed: paragraph 1410]

[Removed: section 1 (paragraphs 1411–1418)]

2. Actions by Israel with regard to Gaza solidarity demonstrations

[Removed: paragraphs 1419–1428]

Conclusions

The dispersal by Israeli security forces of demonstrations in the West Bank is prima facie in violation of the rights to freedom of expression and to peaceful assembly. Insofar as the protesters were protesting against the violation of human rights in Gaza, the activities of the security forces in dispersing demonstrations ran counter to the provisions of the Declaration on Human Rights Defenders.

Regardless of whether the facts indicate that the above-mentioned rights could be permissibly limited under the terms of the International Covenant on Civil and Political Rights, the methods and means of dispersal are questionable. The use of force described to the Mission against peaceful demonstrations is clearly prohibited in such situations, in particular the lethal use of tear gas canisters against demonstrators, of live ammunition (including .22 ammunition), and of snipers. It should be emphasized that the norms relating to the use of force by law enforcement officers, outlined above, continue to apply even when the demonstrations are no longer peaceful, such as when stones are thrown, such as in the case of the Ni'lin demonstration of 28 December. The situation described by the witnesses to the killings in Ni'lin suggests that firearms were used when there was no threat to the life of the Israeli security forces or others under their protection. According to the witnesses, both the deceased were shot in the upper body and one of them in the back.

On the basis of the facts obtained, the Mission finds that the use of firearms resulting in the death of demonstrators constitutes a violation of article 6 of the International Covenant on Civil and Political Rights as an arbitrary deprivation of life. Reports that Israeli security forces delayed the provision of medical aid to the injured in at least two demonstrations also suggest that violations occurred under the Fourth Geneva Convention and Principle 5 of the Basic Principles on the Use of Force and Firearms by Law Enforcement Officials.

[Removed: remainder of section 2 (paragraphs 1432–1434)]

[Removed: sections 3 and 4 (paragraphs 1435–1436)]

5. Conclusions

The Mission is alarmed at both the reported increase in settler violence over the past year and the failure of the Israeli security forces to prevent settler attacks against Palestinian civilians and their property.

The Mission is also gravely concerned at the increased use of force, including the use of lethal force, in response to demonstrations, and at the generalized violence of security forces against Palestinians living under occupation in the West Bank. Of particular concern is the apparent and systematic lack of accountability for acts of violence committed by Israeli security forces against Palestinian civilians.

While the filming of incidents has led to the exposure of particular grave incidents of violence, the Mission is also concerned about violence that may have occurred out of sight and gone unreported.

In the opinion of the Mission, a line has been crossed; what is fallaciously considered acceptable "wartime behaviour" has become the norm. Public support for a more hard-line attitude towards Palestinians generally, lack of public censure and lack of accountability all combine to increase the already critical level of violence against the protected population.

CHAPTER XXI.

DETENTION OF PALESTINIANS IN
ISRAELI PRISONS

According to estimates, as at 1 June 2009 there were approximately 8,100 Palestinian "political prisoners" in detention in Israel, including 60 women and around 390 children. Most of these detainees are charged or convicted by the Israeli military court system that operates for Palestinians in the West Bank. The most common convictions are for stone-throwing. Being a "member of an illegal organization" is another common charge. All but one of the Israeli prisons holding Palestinians from the Occupied Palestinian Territory are located inside Israel.

As at June 2009, of all the Palestinians held by Israel for reasons related to the occupation, 512 were held without charge or trial, of whom 12 were held under the Israeli Unlawful Combatants Law and 500 as "administrative detainees."

The military courts system has been specifically set up by Israel to deal with Palestinians from the Occupied Palestinian Territory, while Israeli citizens living or otherwise present in the West Bank, if arrested, are dealt with under the Israeli civilian legal system. The Palestinian Authority is not allowed to arrest or detain Israeli citizens.

It is estimated that during the past 43 years of occupation, approximately 700,000 Palestinian men, women and children have been detained under Israeli military orders. Israel argues that these detentions are necessary on grounds of security.

Due process rights for Palestinians in the Israeli military court system are severely limited. Military Order No. 378, which is the main source regulating detention and trial, allows for a Palestinian detainee from the Occupied Palestinian Territory, including children as young as 12, to be held for up to eight days before being brought before a military judge (Israeli detainees must be brought before a judge within 48 hours). Moreover, Palestinian detainees can be held for up to 90 days without access to a lawyer (compared to 48 hours for Israeli detainees). Palestinian detainees can be held for up to 188 days before being charged (an Israeli detainee must be charged within 30 days).

Accusations of torture and other ill-treatment during arrest, interrogation and detention are common, while the court system is criticized for the use of coerced evidence. It is also alleged that complaints about the ill-treatment of detainees rarely lead to investigations or to prosecution, let alone conviction. The Israeli military court system treats Palestinian children as adults from the age of 16. Israeli citizens, however, are considered adults only from the age of 18.

Palestinian prisoners are reportedly held in substandard detention facilities (for example, Ktziot prison houses prisoners in tents) with very limited access to health care and education. Detention inside Israel also means that many detainees do not receive family visits, as their relatives are prohibited from entering Israel (see chap. XXII).

During the Israeli military operations in Gaza, scores of Gazans were detained by the Israeli armed forces. A portion of those were taken to prisons inside Israel, where some remain at the time of writing. This is discussed in chapter XV.

A. ISSUES LINKED TO ISRAEL'S DECEMBER–JANUARY MILITARY OPERATIONS IN GAZA

1. Differential treatment of Gaza prisoners

After its disengagement from Gaza in August 2005, Israel ceased to apply its military orders to Gaza and began to prosecute Gaza detainees under domestic criminal law. In June 2006, the Knesset passed a law which alters existing Israeli criminal law due process guarantees by, for example, allowing a detainee to be held incommunicado for 21 days (after an initial appearance before a judge within 96 hours).

The Law does not discriminate. However, in practice, it is applied only to Palestinian suspects, whether Palestinians from the Occupied Palestinian Territory or Palestinian citizens of Israel. According to estimates submitted to the Knesset's

Constitution, Law and Justice Committee by the head of the investigations unit of the General Security Services concerning the applicability of the Law, "over 90 per cent of detainees (to whom this Law was applied) were from the Gaza Strip, but there were cases of detainees who are not from the Gaza Strip such as East Jerusalem and the Arab-Israeli . . . who are Israeli civilians."

The Law was extended in January 2008. In January 2009 a petition submitted to the Israeli High Court of Justice by ACRI, PCATI and Adalah was heard. The Court criticized many aspects of the Law, but the Government argued that it had secret materials that explained why such a law was necessary. In March 2009, the Court decided, on the basis of the secret evidence provided by the State, that the restrictions imposed by the Law were legal and proportionate. In protest against the Court's use of secret evidence to determine the constitutionality of the Law, the human rights organizations withdrew their petition.

(a) Unlawful Combatants Law

The Israeli Internment of Unlawful Combatants Law 2002 provides for the indefinite detention of "foreign" nationals. It offers a lower level of protection than the Law described above. In addition, it provides for a lower burden of proof and a higher threshold for judicial review. In its submission to the Committee against Torture, the United Against Torture coalition of NGOs concludes that "an examination of its provisions suggests that the goal behind the law is to allow Israel to hold suspects as hostages who can be used as bargaining chips in future negotiations."

According to this Law [the Israeli Internment of Unlawful Combatants Law 2002], a person is designated an "unlawful combatant" by the Chief of General Staff. The definition the Law gives to the concept of "unlawful combatant" is:

> a person who has participated either directly or indirectly in hostile acts against the State of Israel or is a member of a force perpetrating hostile acts against the State of Israel, where the conditions prescribed in article 4 of the Third Geneva Convention of 12th August 1949 with respect to prisoners-of-war and granting prisoner-of-war status in international humanitarian law, do not apply to him (art. 2).

The amendments made to the Law in July 2008, which included lengthening the time detainees can be held before they must be brought before a judge and before they must be allowed access to a lawyer, were challenged and upheld on appeal. Israel's Court of Criminal Appeals considered the Law constitutional and consistent with international humanitarian law.

Detention under this Law does not require admission of guilt or the existence of evidence acceptable as part of fair trial standards. According to Al Mezan, "this law essentially licenses the military to hold individuals arbitrarily and indefinitely, on the basis of assumed rather than proven guilt that they are conducting direct or indirect activities that could harm the security of Israel or are affiliated to groups working to harm the security of Israel."

(b) Gaza and the ICRC Family Visits Programme

On 6 June 2007, the Israeli authorities suspended the ICRC Family Visits Programme in the Gaza Strip, effectively barring all means of communication between Gazan prisoners and the outside world. Before the new arrests of Gazan residents during Israel's latest offensive in the Gaza Strip (see chapter XV), the ban affected approximately 900 prisoners and their families. In June 2009, ICRC called for the ban to be lifted.

According to Addameer, the timing of the decision to ban family visits coincided with factional fighting in the Gaza Strip which was followed by Hamas's seizing of control, a party which Israel does not recognize and defines as a "terrorist" organization. Therefore, the decision to suspend the programme appears to be a form of collective punishment intended to coerce Palestinians to respond to Israel's demands in terms of Palestinian leadership. On 17 June 2008, Adalah filed a petition on behalf of Gazan prisoners' families, Al Mezan and the Association for the Palestinian Prisoners, challenging the legality of the ban on visits. At the time of writing, this petition remained pending. In October 2008, the Government of Israel submitted arguments to the Supreme Court to suggest that the State is not obliged to permit families from Gaza to visit their relatives incarcerated in Israeli prisons.

In addition, during the December–January military operations in Gaza, Adalah filed a petition demanding that Gazan prisoners should be allowed to use the telephone to contact family members. Not allowing this, Adalah argues, violates detainees' right to dignity and their right to family life, and "transforms their imprisonment to a humiliating and degrading experience that contradicts international norms and conventions, in particular the Universal Declaration of Human Rights." According to Adalah, the Prison Authority replied that they allowed each detainee to use the telephone once. Some prisoners confirmed to Adalah that they had been allowed to use the telephone, but others said that they were not allowed to do so on the grounds that they did not present a certificate proving that a close relative had passed away during the offensive.

2. Increase in children from the West Bank arrested and detained during or after the military operations in Gaza

The Mission received information that during the Israeli military operations in Gaza the numbers of children from the West Bank detained by Israel increased. According to Defence for Children International–Palestine Section, the figures for January and February were 389 and 423, compared with 327 and 307 the previous year and a monthly average of 319 in 2008. Many of these children were reportedly arrested on the street and/or during demonstrations. Defence for Children International also found that their average age changed: for the 12–15 age range, the percentage is usually 23; in January–February 2009, it was 36. In January–March, it represented 69 children in the Israeli military courts. As of 20 June 2009, eight of these children were released without charge, while among the 61 charged, 47 were sentenced and 14 are still awaiting trial.

Defence for Children International also found that there was a change in the percentages of children charged with particular offences in the first three months of 2009: in 2008, 27 per cent of children had been charged with throwing stones, as opposed to 61 per cent in the period covered by the report. "During OCL, the army didn't want to lose control of the West Bank, so they came down like a tonne of bricks on demonstrations." It concludes "The fact that many of these children were younger than the average child detainee and the fact that the majority were charged with minor offences suggest that this increase is the result of children's participation in a high number of demonstrations in the West Bank during Operation Cast Lead, and the increased use of force, including mass arrest, by Israeli authorities to suppress and discourage these protests."

Number of Palestinian children in Israeli detention at the end of each month (2008)

YEAR/ MONTH	JAN	FEB	MAR	APR	MAY	JUN	JUL	AUG	SEP	OCT	NOV	DEC
2008	327	307	325	327	337	323	324	293	304	297	327	342
2009	389	423	420	391	346	355	—	—	—	—	—	—

Note: These figures are not cumulative.

One of the cases recorded by Defence for Children International is summarized as follows:

> Ahmad Q.: 15-year-old boy arrested on 1 January 2009 and accused of throwing stones. On 1 January 2009, Ahmad was protesting against the war in Gaza near Qalandiya checkpoint. He was arrested by soldiers and dragged 100 metres to a jeep. He was slapped and kicked, had his hands tied with plastic cords and he was blindfolded. He was transferred to Atarot for interrogation, made to sit outside in the cold until 4 A.M., transferred to Ofer prison, and then to prisons inside Israel. He was charged with throwing stones and sentenced to four and a half months in prison and fined NIS 1,000.

The Israeli operations in Gaza caused a wave of demonstrations that did not end with the operations. Child detentions continued to be high in February and March, with the high percentage of children charged with stone-throwing indicating that they were detained during demonstrations. Defence for Children International reports two incidents of mass arrests of children after demonstrations in January and March 2009, including one in the village of Haris, where the Israeli armed forces entered the village at around midnight and rounded up about 90 children, detaining them in a school for almost a day, before finally arresting four of them.

[Removed: remainder of paragraph 1462]

On 6 March 2009, the President of Defence for Children International wrote to the Israeli Minister of Justice, Daniel Friedmann, seeking an explanation for the sharp increase in the number of Palestinian children being detained by Israel and notified the United Nations Committee on the Rights of the Child of these developments. At the time of writing, there had been no response.

In its report on Israel's detention of Palestinian children, Defence for Children International concluded that the abuse of Palestinian children by Israeli authorities is systematic and institutionalized.

In a statement issued in support of this report, UNICEF, WHO, OHCHR and local and international child protection agencies (together the 1612 Working Group on Grave Violations against Children) stated that "Israeli military courts violate many basic fair trial rights according to international humanitarian and human rights law. . . . For example, in almost all cases, the primary evidence used to convict children is a confession obtained through coercive interrogations carried out in the absence of a lawyer. The most common charge made against children was stone-throwing (about 27 per cent), which carries a maximum sentence of 20 years. . . . With the potential for harsh sentences, approximately 95 per cent of cases end in the child pleading guilty, whether the offence was committed or not."

A former Israeli military commander told the BBC that Palestinian youngsters are routinely ill-treated by Israeli soldiers while in custody. The BBC website item included a video of a young Palestinian boy being arrested at night. Col. Efrati, who had left the army five months previously, said: "I never arrested anyone younger than nine or 10, but 14, 13, 11 for me, they're still kids. But they're arrested like adults. Every soldier who was in the Occupied Territories can tell you the same story. The first months after I left the army I dreamed about kids all the time. Jewish kids. Arab kids. Screaming." He added, "Maybe [the kid is] blindfolded for him not to see the base and how we're working. . . . But I believe maybe we put the blindfold because we don't want to see his eyes. You don't want him to look at us—you know, beg us to stop, or cry in front of us. It's a lot easier if we don't see his eyes."

3. Members of the Palestinian Legislative Council

In September 2005, i.e. some months before the Palestinian Legislative Council elections, the Israeli military conducted a two-day arrest campaign in which 450 persons affiliated with the political parties Hamas and Islamic Jihad were detained. These individuals had been involved in either, or both, the municipal elections or the Council elections. Most were kept in administrative detention and many were released just before or after the Palestinian Legislative Council elections on 25 January 2006. Some candidates were elected while in detention. A number of those released were subsequently rearrested.

Hamas had taken part in municipal elections in 2005 and in Council elections in mid-2005. While Hamas is considered an unlawful organization by Israel, its candidates participated under a list named "Change and Reform Bloc," underlining the main election pledge of reforming the system. Not all candidates and elected persons on that list were members of Hamas; some independent candidates joined the list, including a number of Palestinian Christians.

Israel had not banned the Change and Reform Bloc from participating in the elections, which were supported by the international community. Reportedly, Israel had agreed [to] the list of proposed candidates for the elections with the Palestinian Authority and facilitated voting on the day. However, the mass arrests in September 2005 hampered campaigning and organization, and candidates of all parties were banned by Israel from campaigning in Jerusalem. The Mission met Dr. Mustafa Barghouti, a member of the Council for the Palestinian National Initiative, who reported being arrested and beaten while attempting to campaign for the elections in Jerusalem.

Nevertheless, the "Change and Reform" list won the elections, gaining 74 seats out of 132, which is said to have come as a surprise to all involved. The tenth Government was inaugurated on 20 March 2006 and included a number of non-Hamas ministers.

As referred to in [chapter XVIII], on 24 June 2006, an Israeli soldier, Gilad Shalit, was captured by Palestinian armed groups based in Gaza. The Government of Israel held the Palestinian Authority fully responsible for his capture "with all this implies." It made it clear that it would "take all necessary actions" to bring about his release and that "no person or organization will have immunity at this time." On 29 June, the Israeli armed forces arrested some 65 members of the Palestinian Legislative Council, mayors and ministers. Most were Hamas members. They were taken from their homes during the night. Interviewees described situations where up to 20 jeeps surrounded a Council member's home or where their homes were ransacked, and computers and papers taken.

According to Mr. Fadi Qawasme, lawyer to most of the detained Council members, the members detained on 29 June were prevented from having access to lawyers for a week, during which time they were interrogated. Some refused to cooperate; others openly admitted that they were members of Change and Reform. Some were released; others were kept in detention and charged with "membership of a terrorist organization," or held under administrative detention orders. The prosecution requested that all should be remanded in custody pending trial, a period which took two years. Mr. Qawasme protested against the charges on the grounds that members of the Council should have immunity from prosecution and that they did not recognize the jurisdiction of the court (those arrested should have come under the jurisdiction of the Palestinian Authority according to the Oslo Accords), and argued that Israel had accepted the participation of Change and Reform in the elections.

Also according to Mr. Qawasme, the Court initially accepted the arguments and proposed releasing all on bail. The prosecution appealed and rejected the lawyer's arguments, claiming that Israel had not allowed Hamas to participate in the elections, and that "Change and Reform" was in fact Hamas. In February 2007, a year after the election, Israel declared "Change and Reform" a prohibited organization. All were held for at least two years and some were convicted of "membership of Change and Reform," or "standing in election on behalf of Change and Reform." The minimum sentence given to the Council members was 42 months, with longer sentences for higher-ranking members.

(a) Arrest, interrogation and detention conditions

The Mission interviewed three members of the Palestinian Legislative Council who were detained by Israel. Dr. Mariam Saleh related how, on the night of her arrest, around 20–25 military jeeps surrounded her house and masked men entered the house by force. Having locked Dr. Saleh and her family on the balcony, they ransacked the house before putting her in a military jeep. They drove her to her office, which they entered by force and from which they took her computer hard disc and many papers. She was then taken to al-Maskobiya (an interrogation centre in Jerusalem), where she was held for a month. She reported being interrogated for three-day stretches from 8 A.M. to 5 A.M. the next morning. Dr. Saleh further reported that her son and husband were brought to the interrogation centre in order to pressure her into confessing that she was a member of Hamas.

The interviewees related that, as most members were in their fifties or sixties, detention was hard to cope with and a particularly humiliating experience. They spoke of a lack of access to medical assistance and proper medication, of ailments worsening because of the dire detention conditions, of a lack of adequate food, and of specific dietary adjustment, for a diabetic patient for instance. They further spoke of humiliation by prison guards (who initially found it amusing to have, for example, a minister as prisoner), of attempts to gain confessions by collaborators, of the use of stress positions and of sleep deprivation. They further reported extremely difficult transport conditions, being enclosed in a car with a dog, for example, or being shackled hands and feet inside a bus for 12 hours at a time with no water or access to a toilet. The trips from prison to court and back could take many days, with the bus stopping at a number of different prisons on the way, picking up and dropping off passengers, and the detainees being tied up and crammed for lengthy periods despite some being elderly and in poor health. One interviewee reported having spent altogether about 350 days, "almost a year," on such multi-day trips.

Interviewees reported extremely limited family visits, with one being told his mother was not considered "immediate family" and not being allowed a visit from her for three years.

The former detainees interviewed by the Mission feared rearrest, at times had been rearrested, on the same charges, and reported trying to minimize their travel and public appearances. One interviewee reported that, during his last detention, he had been given a two-year suspended sentence, which would take him past any prospective election date. He added that, in any case, no one could stand in these elections for Hamas or Change and Reform, since doing so had become punishable and subject to three years' imprisonment. All interviewees also reported family and friends receiving threats and being harassed by Palestinian Authority security forces.

According to B'Tselem, Israeli officials have made public statements relating the arrests of the Council members to political goals:

> [I]n an interview with [Associated Press] a few hours after the first wave of arrests, on 29 June 2006, Major-General Yair Naveh, OC Central Command, said that the decision to arrest senior Palestinian officials was made by the political echelon and that they would be released upon the release of Gilad Shalit. In an interview with the army radio station on 24 May 2007, the day that the second wave of arrests took place, the then Defense Minister, Amir Peretz, stated that "the arrest of those heads of Hamas is to show the military organizations that we demand that the firing stop."

The Inter-Parliamentary Union has recently adopted a number of resolutions protesting against the arrest and detention of the Palestinian parliamentarians, including those from the Change and Reform Bloc. It notes that the Council members were sentenced to much longer periods in detention than persons convicted of military action and that "clearly, the intention was to keep them in prison for the rest of their parliamentary term." It "considers that the rearrest of four Change and Reform parliamentarians following the failure of the negotiations regarding the release of Gilad Shalit and the simultaneous restrictions of the rights of political prisoners suggests that Israel is in fact holding the [Palestinian Legislative Council] members concerned as hostages."

(b) Associated measures

In May 2006, the Israeli Minister of Interior at the time, Roni Bar-On, decided to revoke the permanent residency status (i.e. the right to reside in Jerusalem under Israeli law) of four Council members (including the then Minister of Jerusalem Affairs). The letter received stated "Pursuant to [the Law of Entry into Israel], you are deemed to be a resident in the State of Israel. You are obliged to pay allegiance to the State of Israel. Nonetheless, your actions prove otherwise and indicate that your allegiance is paid to the Palestinian Authority." The members petitioned the Israeli High Court, while ACRI and Adalah submitted an amicus curiae brief, arguing that the Jerusalemites' reduction to permanent resident status of the city after it was annexed by Israel could not be removed. The human rights organizations argued that the residency status of the members was cancelled because the Government of Israel did not welcome the election result. The petition was filed at the Israeli High Court of Justice contesting the status removal or de facto exile, in 2006, but it is still pending. Potentially, a ruling that Jerusalem residency can be revoked on the basis of a lack of loyalty to Israel could have extremely far-reaching consequences for the Palestinian residents of occupied East Jerusalem. Until now Israeli law has allowed the revocation of Jerusalem residency rights only of Palestinians who are unable to prove that their "centre of life" is in Jerusalem.

(c) Recent developments

In January 2009, during the Israeli operation in Gaza, the Israeli armed forces once again arrested a number of Hamas leaders on 1 and 9 January 2009.

Addameer comments "the timing of the waves of arrests indicates that the arrests were intended to put pressure on the Palestinian people and its leadership." Interviewees have indicated that the arrest campaigns effectively work as deterrence. They report having family members, colleagues and employees arrested by both Israel and the Palestinian Authority.

In March, two Council members and former detainees interviewed by the Mission reported that a group of detainees associated with Hamas were given mobile telephones and asked to meet as a group and to intervene in the negotiations surrounding the release of Gilad Shalit. According to the interviewees, detainees were gathered from different prisons for this meeting in Ktziot prison in the Negev. Some detainees were brought out of solitary confinement for this purpose, while solitary confinement is normally imposed because allowing these specific detainees to meet and speak with others is considered a security risk. On this occasion, the group of senior Hamas detainees (Council members and other leaders) were asked to call other Hamas leaders in Gaza and Damascus to influence the negotiations over Gilad Shalit and the prisoner exchange. However, they decided not to cooperate, stating that they were not free to confer or negotiate from detention.

According to Addameer, a few hours after Hamas declared an end to the negotiations for the release of Gilad Shalit, the Israeli armed forces conducted a series of raids into the West Bank towns of Nablus, Ramallah, Hebron and Bethlehem, and arrested four Council members, the former Deputy Prime Minister of the 10th Government, a university professor and a Hamas leader. For PCHR these arrests "could be acts of pressure exerted by Israel on the Hamas leadership in order to resolve the case of captured Israeli soldier Gilad Shalit, and conclude the prisoner exchange." Ms. Sahar Francis of Addameer commented:

> It is unthinkable that the Israeli Government first engages in a political process and negotiations with Hamas, and then kidnaps 10 political leaders associated with the movement and uses them as bargaining chips. This is not only a form of collective punishment, which in itself is a violation of international humanitarian law, but also a politically counterproductive move.

(d) The downgrading of Hamas prisoners' detention conditions

On 18 March 2009, the Israeli Justice Minister, Daniel Friedmann, established a committee to "work to reduce privileges afforded Hamas and Islamic Jihad security prisoners." He reportedly announced in the media that the downgrade was intended "to match [these prisoners'] conditions of incarceration to those of Gilad Shalit." The Mission interviewed two former Hamas detainees who confirmed that from the end of March they had stopped receiving newspapers and books and had their "recreation" time reduced to 3 hours per day. According to HaMoked, the decision to create the committee "establishes the use of a large group of prisoners as 'bargaining chips' until the resolution of a matter to which they have no connection and which they cannot influence." According to Addameer, "on 29 March the Israeli Government accepted recommendations presented by a special Ministerial Committee aiming at downgrading detention conditions of prisoners identified with Hamas and Islamic Jihad."

(e) Effect of the detention of the Palestinian Legislative Council's members: disabling the legislative and enabling the executive

The detention of the Council's members has meant that it has been unable to function for three years and no laws have been passed. According to ICHR, it has not been able to exercise its oversight function over the Government's administrative and financial performance, "whether through the questioning, granting/withholding confidence, or holding the Government accountable, or inquiry of finding the facts in cases of grave violations of Palestinian human rights during 2008."

Conversely, the executive authority in the West Bank has played a major role in legislative policymaking—where the Government has referred a number of laws to the President, and the President issued 11 decisions with the power of law in 2008. The Palestinian Basic Law provides that a caretaker government may, in exceptional circumstances which cannot be postponed, issue decisions with the power of law; however, these must be submitted to the Council at the first available session and be approved or cease to have power of law. ICHR argues that some of the laws issued by the President of the Palestinian Authority represent a retreat from the legal guarantees for the protection of fundamental rights and freedoms of Palestinian citizens.

B. LEGAL ANALYSIS AND CONCLUSIONS

[Removed: paragraph 1488]

[Removed: sections 1 through 4 (paragraphs 1489–1502)]

5. Conclusions

The Mission is concerned about the detention of children and adults on political grounds, in poor conditions and outside the occupied territory in violation of international humanitarian law. The Mission notes the very high number of Palestinians who have been detained since the beginning of the occupation (amounting to 40 per cent of the adult male population of the Occupied Palestinian Territory) according to a practice that appears to aim at exercising control, humiliating, instilling fear, deterring political activity and serving political interests.

The Mission is equally concerned by the reports of coercion and torture during interrogations, trials based on coerced confessions or secret evidence, and the reportedly systematic and institutionalized ill-treatment in prisons.

The Mission is particularly alarmed at the arrest and detention of hundreds of young children, and the rise in child detention during and following the Israeli military operations in Gaza. The ill-treatment of children and adults described to the Mission is disturbing in its seemingly deliberate cruelty.

The legal instruments allowing for the indefinite detention of "unlawful combatants," as well as enshrining the deficient due process regimes, the differential treatment of Palestinian and Israeli prisoners (including the differential definition of a "child"), and the exemptions de facto allowing for harsher interrogation techniques raise concerns about the legal system being a part of this practice, rendering it deliberate and systematic.

The Mission notes with concern the arrest and lengthy detention of democratically elected Palestinian parliamentarians, which appears to be a deliberate act to interrupt the democratic functioning and self-governance of Palestinians.

CHAPTER XXII.

ISRAELI VIOLATIONS OF THE RIGHT TO FREE MOVEMENT AND ACCESS

In the West Bank, Israel has imposed a system of interlocking measures, only some of which are physical barriers that restrict the movement and access of Palestinians within the West Bank. This includes movement between Jerusalem and the rest of the West Bank, between the West Bank and Israel, between the West Bank and Gaza and between the West Bank and the outside world and vice versa.

Movement is restricted by physical obstacles, such as roadblocks, checkpoints and the Wall, but also by administrative measures, such as identity cards, permits, assigned residence, laws on family reunification and policies on the right to enter from abroad and the right of return for refugees. The restriction on the ability to move freely, without obstacle or delay, or without another person's authorization, is often perceived as a humiliating experience.

Restrictions include denial access, mainly to Jerusalem for all Palestinians except those who are designated by Israel as Jerusalem residents, citizens of Israel and special permit holders. Special permits are rarely granted.

Palestinians are denied access to areas expropriated for the building of the Wall and its infrastructure, for use by settlements, buffer zones, military bases and military training zones, and the roads built to connect these places. Many of the roads are "Israeli only" and forbidden for Palestinian use. An example of an "Israeli only" road is Road 443, between Tel Aviv and Jerusalem, which passes through the West Bank. Once a major Palestinian traffic artery serving 33 villages, this stretch of the road has now been turned into a highway that Palestinians are forbidden to use. A number of tunnels have been built under the road to enable access, but movement is still extremely restricted for the villagers.

Movement between Gaza and the West Bank for Palestinians is virtually impossible.

Generally speaking, Israelis can and do travel freely around the West Bank, with the exception of the main Palestinian cities, which are off-limits to Israelis, according to Israeli law.

The Mission has reviewed claims that foreign passport holders, whether or not of Palestinian origin, can be and are regularly denied entry to the West Bank by Israeli border authorities. According to a report of June 2009 received by the Mission, in the first six months of 2009, the number of entry denial cases reported increased relative to the last quarter of 2008, "raising concerns that Israel is again escalating its policy of arbitrary entry denial." Recent reports criticize the new "Palestinian Authority only" visas issued by Israel to foreign citizens. These practices severely limit the ability of international humanitarian workers and human rights defenders to carry out their activities.

A. MOVEMENT RESTRICTIONS AFFECTING THE MISSION'S WORK

At the public hearing in Geneva on 6 July 2009, Mr. Shawan Jabarin of Al-Haq reported that tens of thousands of Palestinians today are subject to a travel ban imposed by Israel, preventing them from travelling abroad. Mr. Jabarin, whom the Mission heard in Geneva by way of videoconference, had been subject to such a travel ban since he became the director of Al-Haq, the West Bank's oldest human rights organization. Mr. Jabarin challenged his travel ban in the Israeli High Court after he was prevented from travelling to the Netherlands to receive a human rights prize, but the ban was upheld on the basis of "secret evidence." Mr. Jabarin believed that the ban was imposed as punishment. On 3 July 2009, the Mission also spoke with Khalida Jarrar, a member of the Palestinian Legislative Council for the Palestinian Liberation Front Party, by telephone conference, as she too was unable to travel out of the West Bank because of an Israeli-imposed travel ban. Ms. Jarrar, who prior to her election to the Palestinian Legislative Council in 2006 directed the prisoners' rights organization Addameer, told the Mission that she had not been allowed to travel out of the West Bank since attending the Human Rights Defenders Summit in Paris in 1998.

[. . .] [T]he Palestinian Minister for Justice, Dr. Ali Khashan, was unable to leave the West Bank to meet the Mission in Amman, Jordan; he had been prevented from crossing the border.

B. MOVEMENT AND ACCESS AND THE ISRAELI MILITARY OPERATIONS IN GAZA

The Mission received reports that, during the Israeli offensive in Gaza, movement restrictions in the West Bank were tightened. For several days, Israel imposed a "closure" on the West Bank, a restrictive measure in addition to those already in place. Given that it is an ad hoc measure, people cannot plan their movements around it.

It was also reported to the Mission that, during and following the operations in Gaza, Israel tightened its hold on the West Bank through more expropriation, an increase in house demolitions, demolition orders and permits granted for homes built in settlements, and increased exploitation of the West Bank's natural resources. Various policies and decisions implemented in the first six months of 2009 relating to settlements, and Jerusalem's demography, affected the access and movement of Palestinians, while increasing the overall control by Israel over the West Bank.

Following the operations in Gaza, the Mission received reports that Israel had amended the regulations determining the ability of persons with a Gaza identity card to move to the West Bank, and vice versa, further entrenching the separation between the people of the West Bank and Gaza.

[Removed: section C (paragraphs 1520–1523)]

D. NEW MEASURES TO FORMALIZE THE SEPARATION OF GAZA AND THE WEST BANK

The Mission received reports about measures that further formalize the separation of Gaza and the West Bank. Following HaMoked's petition to the High Court, a new Israeli Ministry of Defense procedure has been revealed detailing the very strict conditions under which a resident of the Gaza Strip may change her or his residency to that of the West Bank. The procedure of 8 March 2009 states:

> Against the backdrop of the security/political situation in the Gaza Strip it has been decided on State level to limit the movement of residents between the Gaza Strip and the Judea and Samaria area to the necessary minimum, so that for all practical purposes entry of residents of Gaza into the Judea and Samaria areas shall only be allowed in the most exceptional humanitarian cases. . . . [T]he Deputy Minister of Defence . . . established that in every case involving the settlement of Gaza residents in the Judea and Samaria Area one should adopt the most restrictive policy, which is derived a fortiori from the general policy of restricting movement between the two Areas. The Deputy Minister clarified that a family relationship, in and of itself, does not qualify as a humanitarian reason that would justify settlement by Gaza residents in the Judea and Samaria Area.

In the terms of the procedure, as reviewed by the Mission, one of the situations envisaged by the regulations, is where

> [a] minor resident of Gaza who is under 16 years old, where one of his parents, who was a resident of Gaza, passed away and the other parent is a resident of the Judea and Samaria Area and there is no other family relative who is a resident of Gaza who is able to take the minor under his wings. In the event that it is necessary, the nature and scope of the existing relationship with the parent who is a resident of the Judea and Samaria Area shall be examined in relation to the degree, nature and scope of the relationship with other family relatives in Gaza (para. 10 B).

Furthermore, according to paragraph 15 of the procedure, a successful application is subject to periodic renewal and a seven-year "naturalization" period, after which there is an examination "as to whether to grant a permit of settlement in the Judea and Samaria Area and a change of the registered address in the copy of the file of the Palestinian population registry, which is in the possession of the Israeli side."

In the reports reviewed by the Mission, HaMoked and Gisha call this regulation an additional measure in a deliberate Israeli policy to deepen the separation between the West Bank and Gaza "in the pursuance by Israel of political goals at the expense of the civilian population, in blatant violation of international humanitarian law."

It also "undermines the possibility of a two state solution" and "contradicts a long list of Israeli undertakings to conduct negotiations for the establishment of an independent, viable Palestinian State, including an explicit commitment in the Oslo Accords to preserve the status of the West Bank and Gaza Strip as a 'single territorial unit.'"

[Removed: section E (paragraphs 1528–1534)]

F. JERUSALEM: ACCELERATING THE "SILENT TRANSFER"

In May 2009, the *New York Times* reported that the Office [of the] Israeli Prime Minister of Israel and the Israeli-defined Jerusalem municipality, in cooperation with the Jerusalem Development Authority and settler organizations, were implementing an eight-year "confidential" plan to create a string of nine parks, pathways and sites, incorporating new or existing settlements in and around East Jerusalem. The NGO Peace Now concluded that "the completion of the Israeli plan will change dramatically the map of East Jerusalem and might prevent a permanent status agreement and a compromise in Jerusalem."

In a report reviewed by the Mission, the Association for Civil Rights in Israel stated that, in Jerusalem, "discrimination in planning and building, expropriation of lands, and minimal investment in physical infrastructure and government and municipal services—these are concrete expressions of an Israeli policy designed to secure a Jewish majority in Jerusalem and push Palestinian residents outside the city's borders."

In a report of April 2009, addressing "the failure of the Israeli authorities to provide adequate planning for Palestinian neighborhoods," the Office for the Coordination of Humanitarian affairs states that "some 60,000 Palestinians in East Jerusalem . . . are at risk of having their homes demolished by the Israeli authorities. This is a conservative estimate and the actual number may be much higher."

[Removed: section G (paragraphs 1538–1539)]

H. CONNECTING THE DOTS

According to reports reviewed by the Mission, aside from the settlements themselves, much new infrastructure is being built to service the settlements, including roads, rail and tram lines, tunnels and waste dumps. Notable examples of these are the Jerusalem ring road (eastern section), a four-lane highway which will connect Israeli settlements in East Jerusalem and run through Palestinian neighborhoods, requiring the confiscation of many dunums of Palestinian land and demolitions of homes and businesses; and the Jerusalem light rail project and train line between Tel Aviv and Jerusalem, part of which will run through the West Bank.

Observers have noted that Israeli control over the movement and access of the West Bank Palestinians is necessary to maintain control over the West Bank's land and natural resources. Easing Palestinian access on alternative roads and the removal of some checkpoints would allow Israel to offer "transportational" rather than territorial contiguity. At the same time, full Israeli access through the separate road system and full control over the border allow for a level of continuous population control. The increased movement and access limitations recently implemented by Israel in the West Bank would seem to share with the military operations of December 2008–January 2009 Israel's objective of "getting rid of Gaza in order to consolidate its permanent hold on the West Bank."

[Removed: section I (paragraphs 1542–1549)]

CHAPTER XXIII.

INTERNAL VIOLENCE, TARGETING OF HAMAS SUPPORTERS AND RESTRICTIONS ON FREEDOM OF ASSEMBLY AND EXPRESSION BY THE PALESTINIAN AUTHORITY

The Mission has received allegations of violations relevant to its mandate committed by the Palestinian Authority in the period under inquiry. These include violations related to the treatment of (suspected) Hamas affiliates by the Preventive Security Service, the Military Intelligence and the General Intelligence, such as their unlawful arrest and detention, and ill-treatment of political opponents while in detention. Other allegations are the arbitrary closure of charities and associations affiliated with Hamas and other Islamic groups or the revocation and non-renewal of their licences, the forcible replacement of board members of Islamic schools and other institutions and the dismissal of Hamas-affiliated teachers.

There have also been allegations of the use of excessive force and the suppression by Palestinian security services of demonstrations, particularly those in support of the population of Gaza during the Israeli military operations. On these occasions the Palestinian Authority's security services allegedly arrested many individuals and prevented the media from covering the events, at times breaking cameras or erasing footage. The Mission also received allegations of harassment by Palestinian security services of journalists who expressed critical views of the Palestinian Authority.

The Mission noted the reluctance of some of the residents of the West Bank it approached to speak openly about these issues. A number of individuals expressed concern that there might be repercussions if they did so.

The Mission also received reports that highlight the lack of parliamentary oversight over acts and decisions by the executive. As noted in chapter [XXI], the arrest and detention by Israel of several members of the Palestinian Legislative Council has effectively curtailed such parliamentary oversight. The executive has passed decrees and regulations to enable it to continue its day-to-day operations. Palestinian human rights organizations have argued that this has resulted in the use of the security apparatus to suppress political opposition and of military courts to ignore any judicial challenge to arbitrary detention on political grounds.

The Mission asked the Palestinian Authority for information about the above allegations; however, its reply does not address these issues.

[Removed: sections A through D (paragraphs 1555–1583)]

E. CONCLUSIONS

From the information available to it, the Mission finds that there are features of the repressive measures against actual or perceived Hamas affiliates and supporters in the West Bank that would constitute violations of international law. Furthermore, in efforts to minimize the power and influence of Hamas, the protection and the promotion of human rights have generally been eroded. The Mission notes that these measures and their objectives are relevant to the context within which the Israeli offensive in Gaza was launched, as analysed in chapter II.

The Mission is concerned that, by failing to take action to put an end to the practices described above, the Palestinian executive and judicial authorities are contributing to the further deterioration of the fundamental rights and freedoms of Palestinians, the rule of law and the independence of the judiciary.

It appears from the information the Mission received that the Palestinian Authority's actions against political opponents in the West Bank started in January 2006, intensified between 27 December 2008 and 18 January 2009, and is continuing until today.

The Mission considers detentions on political grounds legally unacceptable for several reasons: The arrest and indefinite detention (without trial) by security services and under the military judiciary system are in violation of Palestinian law and international human rights law; and the arrests and detentions are apparently based on political affiliation, which would violate the right not to be arbitrarily detained, the right to a fair trial, and the right not to be discriminated against on the basis of one's political opinion, which are both part of customary international law. Moreover, the reports of torture and other forms of ill-treatment during arrest and detention, and the reports of deaths in detention, raise further concerns and warrant proper investigation and accountability.

[Removed: remainder of section E (paragraphs 1588–1589)]

PART THREE

ISRAEL

The Mission, in examining, as required by its mandate, alleged violations occurring in the context of the Israeli military operations conducted in Gaza from 27 December 2008 to 18 January 2009, whether before, during or after, also considered allegations of violations against Israeli citizens and residents. The Mission focused on two areas that it considered particularly relevant: (a) the launching of rockets and mortars from the Gaza Strip into southern Israel by Palestinian armed groups, and their effects on the civilian population; (b) the action taken by the Government of Israel to repress dissent among its citizens and residents vis-à-vis its military operations in Gaza, and to limit independent and critical reporting on it by human rights organizations and media.

[Removed: paragraphs 1591–1593]

CHAPTER XXIV.

THE IMPACT ON CIVILIANS OF ROCKET AND MORTAR ATTACKS BY PALESTINIAN ARMED GROUPS ON SOUTHERN ISRAEL

The Mission conducted telephone interviews with people either living in or working with communities in southern Israel. Five residents of southern Israel appeared at the public hearings in Geneva on 6 July 2009 while three representatives of the Israel Trauma Center for Victims of Terror and War (NATAL) appeared via videolink from Tel Aviv. The issue of rocket and mortar attacks on Israel was also covered in interviews conducted in Gaza in May and June 2009 and in communications with the Gaza authorities.

The Mission was unable to conduct on-site investigations owing to the decision of the Government of Israel not to cooperate with the Mission.

The Mission addressed questions to the Government of Israel regarding individuals who have been affected by rocket and other fire from the Gaza Strip. The request of information included data about any psychological, social and economic harm caused by the rocket and mortar shells that have been launched into Israel. The Mission did not receive any reply to its questions.

Since April 2001, Palestinian armed groups have launched more than 8,000 rockets and mortars from Gaza into southern Israel. Communities such as Sderot, the surrounding kibbutzim and some of the unrecognized villages in the Negev have been in range since that time. During the Israeli military operations in Gaza in December 2008 and January 2009, the range of the rockets and mortars increased significantly to nearly 40 kilometres from the Gaza border, encompassing the Israeli towns of Yavne 30 kilometres to the north and Beersheba 28 kilometres to the south-east.

Since the rocket and mortar fire does not often hit populated areas, and because of the precautions taken by the Government of Israel, the rockets and mortars have caused relatively few fatalities and physical injuries among the residents of southern Israel. Property damage, while by no means insignificant, has not been extensive. More widespread, however, has been the psychological trauma and the feeling

TESTIMONY 11

Dr. Mirela Siderer

Israeli gynecologist, describing her injury in a Grad missile attack on an Ashkelon mall, May 2008

I'm 53 years old. I was born in Romania. I studied medicine in Romania. That's where I met my husband and I came to Israel to be with him. He too is a physician. I arrived in Israel in 1984. I live in Ashkelon in Israel. I am in gynecology. I am known in my city by many patients. I have many patients and I have many women patients from Gaza who would come to me before the Intifada, they would come to me for treatment.

My life was quiet, was calm, more or less. You know, like anywhere in the world with the usual day-to-day issues of ordinary life that everyone confronts. I raised two children. You can see the pictures of my family, my two children. I have a family that is beautiful, wonderful, very supportive. . . .

This whole quiet life that I had was altered in a split second, in a moment, when one day in May 2008 in the evening without any alert, without any prior warning a rocket landed in the clinic where I was working. I must say that at that time it was a very tense time. There were many rockets landing in the area, but for some reason I continued to work because I knew that and I felt I was secure in my clinic. I knew that I'm in a hospital, in a clinic, and places like that, in infirmaries where people are being treated, nothing's going to happen. It's a protected place. And yet it happened.

Within a split second the place was utterly demolished. The clinic is situated at the upper story of one of the shopping malls in Ashkelon and I found myself under the debris. For a few seconds I lost consciousness, but then very quickly I became conscious again. I understood what was happening at that moment and I saw blood, a lot of blood coming out of my left arm, but I couldn't do anything to stop the bleeding.

of insecurity that living under rocket fire has caused, and continues to cause, to people living in the affected towns and villages, as well as the erosion of the economic, social and cultural life of these communities.

Every death and injury is not only a tragedy but a matter of utmost concern to the Mission. The Mission wishes to emphasize that the issues of concern, and indeed the consequences of any attack affecting civilians, cannot be reduced to a recitation of statistics, nor should they be.

Testimony 11 (*continued*)

In the room with me was a patient and I was concerned all the time to talk to her to tell her not to fall asleep and to remain awake until someone comes to save us. The patient, too, was critically wounded. She got to the hospital with her abdomen open and her intestines exposed.

Instinctively I looked for my mobile phone and I called my husband who is also a physician and I told him that I had been very badly injured and that he should come to save me. My worst injury was in the face. I felt like a ball of fire spinning inside my face. All of my teeth flew out. At the moment I have false teeth.

But the rescue team came and took me and quickly transferred me to a hospital.... From that moment on my life changed radically. I heard that in that event there were over 100 people wounded in the shopping mall. Just people who were shoppers; various types of injuries.

Since then I've undergone six operations; five plastic operations and one in the mouth for my teeth. I'm waiting to finish that whole implant procedure. I have a piece of shrapnel almost 4 centimeters lodged on the left side of my back very close to the spine, but at the moment it cannot be removed. Perhaps it will never be removed so long as it doesn't cause other complications. I have to go for more operations, including as I said the teeth implantations. I hope that makes me look better. It's very difficult for me to endure the way I look and it also impairs my breathing. I apologize.

But of course the worst is my psychological state. What was my sin? What was my crime? I'm a Jewish physician working in Ashkelon. I studied medicine to help people. I didn't care if they were from Gaza, from anywhere in the world, from Israel, wherever. What was my crime? What did I do wrong? Why did I wind up in this situation? I just want to mention that I'm just an ordinary citizen.

A. SUMMARY OF ROCKET AND MORTAR FIRE FROM 18 JUNE 2008 TO 31 JULY 2009

1. 18 June 2008–26 December 2008

According to Israeli sources, 230 rockets and 298 mortars were fired against Israel between 18 June and 26 December 2008; 227 rockets and 285 mortars struck territory inside the State of Israel. Media reports indicate that areas struck by rockets included the Western Negev, Sderot and Ashkelon. This includes the 157 rockets and 203 mortars that were fired during the ceasefire, which ended officially on 18 December 2008.

The Mission notes that 92 per cent (212) of the rockets and 93 per cent (279) of the mortars fired between 18 June and 26 December 2008 were fired after 5 November 2008.

While there were no fatalities inside Israel, two young Palestinian girls, aged 5 and 12 years, were killed when a rocket fell short, landing in northern Gaza on 26 December 2008.

Media reports indicated that, during this period, six Israelis and one foreign worker were wounded as a result of rockets landing in built-up areas in southern Israel. Where rockets did not land in open space, property damage was sustained. As is discussed below, an unknown number of people in southern Israel were treated for shock following the sounding of the early warning system and the subsequent rocket strikes.

2. 27 December 2008–18 January 2009

According to the Israeli authorities, armed groups in Gaza fired approximately 570 rockets and 205 mortars into Israel during the 22 days of the military operations in Gaza. On their websites, the al-Qassam Brigades and Islamic Jihad claimed to have fired over 800 rockets into Israel during this time.

During the Israeli military operations in Gaza, the range of rocket and mortar fire increased dramatically, reaching towns such as Beersheba 28 kilometres to the south-east and Ashdod 24 kilometres to the north of the Gaza Strip. Rockets continued to fall in areas such as Sderot, the Eshkol Regional Council and the surrounding kibbutzim, which had experienced rocket strikes since 2001. A total of 90 rockets struck Sderot during the 22 days of military operations in Gaza.

During the period of the operations, three civilian fatalities and one military fatality were recorded in Israel resulting from the rocket and mortar strikes launched from Gaza. According to Magen David Adom, 918 people were injured (17 critically injured, 62 medium injuries and 829 slightly injured) in this time period. There were also 1,595 people inside Israel treated for stress-related injuries.

3. 19 January 2009–31 July 2009

According to the Israeli authorities, more than 100 rockets and 65 mortars were fired into Israel after 19 January 2009. No fatalities resulted from these rocket and mortar strikes. The Mission was unable to obtain any official statistics of civilians physically injured by rockets and mortars during this time. On 1 February 2009, one Israeli civilian was slightly wounded when mortar shells, fired from Gaza, exploded in the Sha'ar Hanegev region.

The majority of the rockets and mortars were fired prior to 15 March 2009. On 12 March 2009, the Ministry of the Interior of the Gaza authorities stated that rockets were being "fired at the wrong time" and that the Gaza authorities were investigating those responsible. On 20 April 2009, a member of Hamas called on other armed groups to stop firing rockets "in the interests of the Palestinian people." On 19 July 2009, *Xinhua News* reported that Hamas had arrested two members of Islamic Jihad firing mortars at Israeli forces.

In July 2009, Hamas declared that it was entering a period of "cultural resistance," stating that it was suspending its use of rockets and shifting its focus to winning support at home and abroad through cultural initiatives and public relations.

B. RELEVANT PALESTINIAN ARMED GROUPS

The Palestinian armed factions operating in the Gaza Strip and claiming responsibility for the majority of the rocket and mortar launchings are the Izz al-Din al-Qassam Brigades, the al-Aqsa Martyrs' Brigades and Islamic Jihad. A brief description of each group is given below.

The "al-Qassam Brigades" are the armed wing of the Hamas political movement. According to a June 2007 report of Human Rights Watch, the al-Qassam Brigades initiated the manufacture of rockets, now generically known as "Qassams," inside the Gaza Strip. According to figures given on the al-Qassam Brigades website, the group launched 335 Qassam rockets, 211 Grad rockets and 397 mortars into Israel during the Israeli military operations in Gaza.

The al-Aqsa Martyrs' Brigades were organized during the second intifada and claim affiliation with Fatah. This group too has claimed responsibility for rocket and mortar fire on Israel following the Egyptian brokered ceasefire (tahdiya), which started on 18 June 2008.

Islamic Jihad wields considerably less political power than either Hamas or Fatah. Its military wing is known as Sarayah al-Quds and the group calls the rockets it manufactures inside Gaza "al-Quds." Islamic Jihad has made numerous claims of responsibility for the launching of rockets into Israel, including the first spate of rocket fire after 18 June 2008.

On its website, the Abu Ali Mustafa Brigades, the military wing of the Popular Front for the Liberation of Palestine also claimed responsibility for launching 177 rocket attacks and 115 mortars on several towns and villages inside Israel from 27 December 2008 to 18 January 2009.

The al-Naser Salah ad-Din Brigades, the military wing of the Popular Resistance Committee, has stated that it too has launched rockets into Israel. The Committee is a coalition of different armed factions who oppose what they perceive as the Palestinian Authority and Fatah's conciliatory approach to Israel.

C. TYPE OF ROCKETS AND MORTARS HELD BY THE PALESTINIAN ARMED GROUPS

There is little independent confirmation of the types of weaponry held by Palestinian armed groups or the number of weapons that may be stockpiled. According to an Amnesty International report, of February 2009, the arsenals held by armed groups in the Gaza Strip include: al-Qassam (or al-Quds), 122 mm Grad and 220 Fadjr-3 rockets as well as the al-Battar, the Banna 1 and Banna 2 anti-armour rockets.

1. al-Qassams

There are thought to be at least three generations of Qassam rockets: (a) the Qassam 1, developed in 2001, with a range of 4.5 kilometres and an explosive load of 0.5 kilograms; (b) the Qassam 2, developed in 2002, with a range of 8–9.5 kilometres and an explosive load of 5–9 kilograms; and (c) the Qassam 3, developed in 2005, with a range of 10 kilometres and an explosive load of 20 kilograms.

The rockets manufactured in the Gaza Strip are fashioned from rudimentary materials, such as hollow metal pipes. They are relatively unsophisticated weapons and lack a guidance system, and so cannot be aimed at specific targets. Jane's Terrorism and Security Monitor has described them as "inaccurate, short-range and rarely lethal." Even so, Qassam rockets have inflicted both fatalities and injuries to residents of southern Israel.

2. 122 mm Grad rocket

122 mm Grad rocket is a Russian-designed missile with a range of approximately 20 to 25 kilometres. Given the higher level of technological sophistication and the fact that it is manufactured with material not easily (if at all) available in Gaza, it is likely that they are not made in Gaza.

While most 122 mm Grad rockets have a range of about 20 kilometres, some have landed 40 kilometres inside Israel. Global Security has concluded, on the basis of photographs, that the rockets that struck open space near Yavne and Bnei Darom on 28 December 2008 were Chinese-manufactured 122 mm WeiShei-1E rockets, which can travel distances of 20 to 40 kilometres.

3. 220 mm Fadjr-3 rocket

The 220 mm Fadjr-3 rocket is Iranian designed and is also thought to be smuggled into Gaza.

4. Anti-armour rockets

Palestinian armed groups are also alleged to possess Chinese-designed rockets that have been smuggled into Gaza. According to Jane's Defence Weekly, Hamas is also in possession of several home-made anti-armour rockets, including the al-Battar, the Banna 1 and the Banna 2.

5. Mortars

Mortars are short-range weapons that are generally more accurate than rockets manufactured inside the Gaza Strip. Mortars have rudimentary aiming systems, in which the coordinates of previous strikes can be used to better target subsequent launches. Most mortars have a range of 2 kilometres; according to the Jaffa Centre for Strategic Studies, however, the Palestinian Sariya-1 is a 240 mm mortar with 15 kilometre range.

D. ROCKET AND MORTAR ATTACKS BY THE PALESTINIAN ARMED GROUPS ON ISRAEL

The Mission is providing a brief history of rocket and mortar attacks, as it is relevant to an understanding of the breadth and depth of the psychological trauma suffered by residents of communities closest to the border, such as Sderot, that have been in range since 2001.

The first recorded rocket launch took place on 16 April 2001. On 10 February 2002, the first rocket struck territory inside Israel, when a Qassam 2 rocket fired from Gaza landed in a field six kilometres from the border, near Kibbutz Sa'ad, in the Negev. The first recorded strike of a rocket from Gaza on an Israeli city was on 5 March 2002, when two rockets struck Sderot.

According to statistics compiled by the Intelligence and Terrorism Information Centre at the Israel Heritage & Commemoration Center, an organization with links to the Government of Israel, 3,455 rockets and 3,742 mortar shells were fired into Israel from Gaza from 16 April 2001 to 18 June 2008.

The first civilian casualties from rocket fire were recorded on 28 June 2004 in Sderot, when Afik Zahavi (4 years old) and Mordehai Yosefof (49 years old) were killed by a Qassam rocket. Afik's mother, Ruthie Zahavi (28 years old), was critically injured and nine others were wounded. Hamas claimed responsibility.

From 28 June 2004, when the first fatalities from rocket fire were recorded, to 17 June 2008, 21 Israeli citizens, including two Palestinian citizens of Israel, two Palestinians and one foreign worker, were killed inside Israel as a result of rocket attacks and mortar fire. In addition, a Palestinian was killed in Gaza when a rocket landed short of the border, and 20 Palestinians were killed when a vehicle transporting rockets exploded in Jabaliyah refugee camp. Eleven of those killed inside Israel were killed in Sderot, a town of just over 20,000 people situated just over a kilometre from the Gaza Strip border.

E. STATEMENTS BY PALESTINIAN ARMED GROUPS CONCERNING THEIR LAUNCHING OF ROCKETS INTO ISRAEL

The al-Qassam Brigades, al-Aqsa Brigades, Islamic Jihad and Popular Resistance Committee all claimed responsibility for rocket and mortar attacks during the time period under review by the Mission. Palestinian armed groups generally justify these attacks as a legitimate form of resistance to Israeli occupation and as acts of self-defence and reprisals for Israeli attacks.

On 5 January 2009, Hamas member Mahmoud Zahar was quoted as saying that "the Israeli enemy . . . shelled everyone in Gaza. They shelled children and hospitals and mosques, and in doing so, they gave us legitimacy to strike them in the same way."

On 6 January 2009, during the Israeli military operations in Gaza, Khaled Mashal, Chairman of the Hamas Political Bureau, wrote in an open letter that the demand to stop the Palestinian resistance was "absurd . . . our modest home-made rockets are our cry of protest to the world." Hamas, in a press release published on 28 December 2008, declared:

> We appeal to all factions of the Palestinian resistance and its military arm, especially the Brigades of the Martyr Izz el-Din al-Qassam to declare a state of general alert . . . and take upon themselves the responsibility to protect the Palestinian people, by striking with all the strength it has the Zionist enemy, its military barracks and colonies, and by using all forms of resistance . . . including the martyrdom operations and striking the Zionist depths. . . .

A spokesperson for the Popular Front for the Liberation of Palestine stated two days before the end of the operations in Gaza that "the rockets are both practical and a symbolic representation of our resistance to the occupier."

On 25 May 2009, the Gaza authorities denied that they were preventing rocket attacks on Israel. A spokesman stated "we don't make such [a] decision without agreeing with all the resistance factions in a national consensus. . . . The factions have the right to respond to any Zionist crime using any sort of resistance and there is no lull with the [Israeli] occupation."

F. STATEMENTS BY THE GAZA AUTHORITIES TO THE MISSION

In a meeting with the Mission on 1 June 2008, the Gaza authorities stated that they had taken the initiative to spare civilian lives when they renounced suicide attacks in April 2006. At the same meeting, a Government spokesperson stated that the resistance factions did not aim their rockets at civilians but rather at IDF artillery and other positions from which attacks against Gaza were launched.

In response to questions by the Mission, on 29 July 2009, the Gaza authorities stated that they had "nothing to do, directly or indirectly, with al-Qassam or other resistance factions" and stated that they were able to exercise a degree of persuasion over the armed factions in relation to proposed ceasefires. While noting that the weaponry used by the armed factions was not accurate, the Gaza authorities discouraged the targeting of civilians.

Despite various attempts, the Mission was unable to contact members of armed factions operating within the Gaza Strip.

G. PRECAUTIONARY MEASURES IN EFFECT IN SOUTHERN ISRAEL

1. The *Tseva Adom* early warning system

The *Tseva Adom* (or 'Red Colour') is an early warning radar system installed by the Israeli armed forces in towns in southern Israel. It was installed in Sderot in 2002 and in different areas of Ashkelon in 2005 and 2006.

When the early warning system detects the signature of a rocket launch originating in Gaza, it automatically activates the public broadcast warning system in nearby Israeli communities and military bases. A two-tone electronic audio alert is broadcast twice, followed by a recorded female voice intoning the words "*Tseva Adom.*" The entire programme is repeated until all rockets have hit and launches are no longer detected. During the public hearings held in Geneva on 6 July 2009, Noam Bedein of the Sderot Media Center screened footage of the sounding of the early warning system in Sderot and its effect on the community, for the benefit of the Mission.

In Sderot, the system gives residents a warning of approximately 15 seconds before an incoming missile strikes. The further residents are from the Gaza Strip, the longer the warning period. Residents of Ashkelon interviewed by the Mission estimated that the system gives them a 20-second warning, while residents of the more northern city of Ashdod or of the town of Beersheba in the Negev estimate that the system gives them a warning of approximately 40 to 45 seconds.

It should be noted that the *Tseva Adom* system is not 100 per cent effective; according to Noam Bedein, the system failed to detect a rocket that struck Sderot on 21 May 2007, killing one and wounding two others. Moreover, the system may also give false alerts, a fact which led authorities in Ashkelon to switch off the system in May 2008. Consequently, no warning was given when a rocket struck a shopping centre on 14 May 2008, seriously injuring three people (including Dr. [Mirela] Siderer, who appeared before the Mission at the public hearings held in Geneva on 6 July 2009).

The sounding of the *Tseva Adom* system and the knowledge that it does not provide a guaranteed forewarning of a rocket strike, have, according to organizations providing mental health services, also had a profound, adverse psychological effect on the communities living within the range of rocket and mortar fire. This issue is discussed in detail below.

[Removed: section 2 (paragraphs 1642–1646)]

H. IMPACT OF ROCKET AND MORTAR FIRE ON COMMUNITIES IN SOUTHERN ISRAEL

The Mission notes that the impact on communities is greater than the numbers of fatalities and injuries actually sustained. The Mission also notes the information in the Government of Israel paper of July 2009, in which an article from *The Guardian* article was cited, stating that as at July 2009, 92 per cent of Sderot residents had seen or heard a rocket impact, 56 per cent had had shrapnel fall on their homes and 65 per cent knew someone who had been injured.

1. Fatalities

Between 18 June 2008 and 31 July 2009, there were four fatalities in Israel as a consequence of rocket and mortar fire from Gaza, of which there were three civilian and one military casualties.

On 27 December 2008, Beber Vaknin, 58 years of age, of Netivot was killed when a rocket fired from Gaza hit an apartment building in Netivot.

On 29 December 2008, Hani al-Mahdi, 27 years of age, of Aroar, a Bedouin settlement in the Negev, was killed when a Grad-type missile fired from Gaza exploded at a construction site in Ashkelon. On the same day, in a separate incident, Irit Sheetrit, 39 years of age, was killed and several wounded when a Grad rocket exploded in the centre of Ashdod. The al-Qassam Brigades claimed responsibility for the attack.

On 29 December 2008, a member of the military, Warrant Officer Lutfi Nasraladin, 38 years of age, of the Druze town of Daliat el-Carmel, was killed by a mortar attack on a military base near Nahal Oz.

2. Physical injuries

According to Magen David Adom, during the period of the Israeli military operations in Gaza, a total of 918 civilians were wounded by rocket attacks. This figure includes 27 critically wounded, 62 moderately wounded and 829 slightly wounded. From 19 January to 19 March 2009, 10 people physically injured from rocket fire were treated by MDA.

3. Psychological trauma/ mental health

In interviews with both residents of southern Israel and the organizations dealing with mental health issues, the issue of psychological trauma suffered by adults and children living in the zone of rocket fire was repeatedly raised. While news articles sometimes report on people being treated for shock following a rocket strike, both individuals and organizations have voiced a real frustration with the lack of focus on what they termed the "invisible damage" caused by rockets. According to MDA, 1,596 people were treated by health facilities in Israel between 27 December 2008 and 18 January 2009. From 19 January to 2 August 2009, 549 people from Sderot alone were treated for stress-related injuries.

A study of October 2007, commissioned by NATAL, on the impact of the ongoing traumatic stress conditions on Sderot found that 28.4 per cent of adults and between 72 and 94 per cent of children in Sderot reported signs indicative of post-traumatic stress disorder. The study also found that children under the age of 12 years showed a high frequency of reported symptoms including fear, avoidance, behavioural problems, problems at school, somatic problems, regression and difficulty in sleeping.

In a submission to the Mission, Dr. Rony Berger, a clinical psychologist and Director of Community Services, described a January 2009 visit to a family in Ofakim, a town 12–15 kilometres from the Gaza border, in the following terms:

> The family was referred to the Community Staff for treatment by the father, who works at one of the factories in the south. He said that his house had "turned into a madhouse," and that the level of stress was so high that "you could cut the air with a knife." . . . When I reached the family home in

Ofakim, I found a house full of children (12 children, aged one year to 22 years). It was a large house, and full of life; perhaps more accurately— frantic. I arrived exactly as the siren was sounding, and I saw a range of anxiety-related responses, some of which were certainly extreme. The mother was screaming at the top of her voice, her sister turned completely white, the younger children cried, the eldest daughter (22) froze and had difficulty moving towards the secure room, while her younger brother (14) seemed almost catatonic. The father, who had called me, moved towards the reinforced room slowly and apathetically, as he turned towards me, pointing towards his family members, and said: "You see what I have to deal with every day." His daughter urged him, screaming, to move faster, but it seemed that the louder she shouted, the slower he moved towards the reinforced room. They started arguing very loudly, while all the rest of the family joined into the fray.

Dalia Yosef of the Sderot Resiliency Center stated that the Center's 18 therapists provided counselling to over 300 people in Sderot during the military operations in Gaza and noted that trauma symptoms were particularly noticeable in children. Ms. Yosef stated that trauma was triggered not only by the rocket strikes but also by the sounding of the early warning system alerts, even where no rocket strike subsequently occurred.

The observations made by the organizations dealing with treating trauma were borne out in the descriptions of daily life made in the interviews held with residents in the affected communities. The Community Manager of Kibbutz Gevim, near Sderot, stated that 60 per cent of children in the kibbutz were in touch with psychological services. A resident of Beersheba described how she was unable to sleep in her apartment because of panic attacks and how she now lived with relatives.

In a telephone interview on 29 July 2009, Avirama Golan, a journalist for *Haaretz* who lived in Sderot from April 2008 to May 2009, commented on the psychological impact of living under rocket fire:

> You get used to it in a sense but it changes your perception of the world, of the way that the world functions. Your sense of what is normal becomes skewed. You cannot be sure of anything. All the authorities that children have—their mother, their father—they don't count. Nothing can keep you safe.

[Removed: sections 4 and 5 (paragraphs 1659–1669)]

6. Impact on the economic and social life of communities

In the interviews conducted by the Mission, it was clear that the impact on communities that had only recently come under the effect of rocket and mortar fire was different to that on those that had been living in that situation for the past five to eight years.

In towns such as Ashdod, Yavne and Beersheba, which experienced rocket strikes for the first time during the military operations in Gaza, there was temporary displacement of some of its residents, who chose to move northwards out of the range of fire for the duration of the operations. In these towns, brief disruption to the economic and social life of the communities was experienced.

In towns closer to the Gaza border, such as Sderot, the recent rocket fire has merely consolidated an exodus started in the previous years. In an interview with the Mission, Eli Moyal, former mayor of Sderot, stated:

> Over 15 per cent of the people living in Sderot have left, moved away permanently. Mainly it was the people who could afford to move and it meant that a lot of business closed down—almost half the businesses that existed in 2001 have closed down. It also meant that the municipality was losing its tax base and it made it much more difficult to supply the services that we are supposed to. This includes kindergartens and other educational services.

Stewart Ganulin, on behalf of Hope for Sderot, a non-profit organization which assists, financially and practically, those injured by rocket fire and families who have lost a member, stated to the Mission on 8 July 2009 that the organization alone was helping 576 people from 133 families of the 3,000 families on welfare in Sderot.

The kibbutzim surrounding Sderot have also been particularly affected because tourists from abroad and other parts of Israel no longer come to stay there. Yeela Ranan, interviewed on 9 July 2009, stated that house prices in Sderot had fallen by 50 per cent. Both residents of Sderot and the surrounding kibbutzim commented on the downturn in their livelihood resulting from living in a community under rocket and mortar fire.

7. The unrecognized Palestinian Arab Bedouin villages of the Negev

The unrecognized villages in the Negev are Palestinian Arab Bedouin villages that are not recognized by Israel and have been subjected to demolitions by the Israeli authorities. They are not marked on any commercial maps and are ineligible for municipal services such as connection to the electricity grid, water mains or for garbage collection. According to the Director of the Regional Council for the Un-recognized Villages, Atwa Abu Fraih, in an interview on 30 July 2009, approximately 90,000 people live in these villages, including 17,000 school children.

According to Physicians for Human Rights–Israel, these villages are in range of rocket fire but have no early warning system, nor have any shelters been built to protect the residents who live there. As much was confirmed by the Director of the Regional Council of Unrecognized Villages, Atwa Abu Fraih, who told the Mission that most of the structures in the villages were made of zinc, including all the schools, and that none of the unrecognized villages had any shelters from rocket or mortar fire. He also pointed out that none of the unrecognized villages was equipped with the early warning alarm system though seven recognized villages were. Unrecognized villages close to either recognized villages with an early warning system or Jewish Israeli towns could hear the alarms. He stated, however, that the early warning system was of little use if there were no shelters. The Director of the Regional Council stated that, if a rocket landed in the unrecognized villages, the consequences would be "disastrous."

While no fatalities or injuries have been recorded in these communities, Physicians for Human Rights–Israel has confirmed that a number of the residents of these villages have been referred for psychological treatment in the aftermath of rocket and mortar strikes.

8. Recognized Palestinian towns and villages in southern Israel

Where the towns and villages predominantly populated by Palestinian citizens of Israel are recognized (and consequently eligible for municipal services such as electricity), they still lack the public shelters commonly found in towns and villages populated predominantly by Israel's Jewish citizens.

Rahat is located 24 kilometres from Gaza and has a population of 45,000 residents. It has no public shelters and few houses have secure rooms. On 30 January 2009, a rocket exploded approximately half a mile from Rahat. The Government of Israel, in a report in the *Associated Press*, stated that it was conducting a public information campaign in Arabic in the broadcast and print media; according to residents, however, this was of little use if public shelters were not made available.

In its recent paper, "The Operation in Gaza: Factual and Legal Aspects," the Government of Israel stated that the "Israeli authorities took a variety of measures to protect its citizens and to reduce the risk to civilians, with special attention being

TESTIMONY 12

Dr. Alan Marcus

Director of strategic planning for the city of Ashkelon, on the early warning system for rocket attacks in southern Israel

We had about 12 seconds in Ashkelon, which is not—we had almost no time to do anything. It's now up to 20 seconds, but at the end of the war what the Palestinians started to do . . . they started shooting like artillery shells. In other words they would lower the angle and it would fly horizontal and we were getting buildings being hit direct into the sides of the buildings causing terrific damage and also shortened the amount of time that the sensors could pick up the warning. So it reduced actually the amount of time that people had, and, of course, you don't have much time even in 20 seconds to go to any place. I mean if you're driving the car and you hear, you pull over to the side and get out of the car and go on the ground.

We had one incident, for example, at near the end of the war, where a mother . . . [who] lived in a single-family-home community took her children in the car and they were going out. They heard the alarm so she couldn't run back in the house, but they ran out of the car and they ran to a neighbor's within the 20 seconds and it hit a house next door. Again, into the wall—and the grad missiles—I don't know if you're familiar, but they're filled with ball bearings and these ball bearings become extremely hot and if they penetrate a hole like that through a house, then they catch on to a sofa, the sofa bursts into flames.

And what happened was afterwards when they got back to the car, the entire car was shredded with the ball bearings. So again, a miracle happened and these people happened to evacuate. They took the 20 seconds; enough to save their lives.

given to sensitive facilities, such as educational institutions and hospitals. These efforts included the establishment of public shelters and fortifications of public institutions, as well as the instruction of the population in risk how to act in times of emergency."

The Mission is concerned about the disparity in treatment of Jewish and Palestinian citizens by the Government of Israel in the installation of early warning systems and provision of public shelters and fortified schools between its Jewish and Palestinian citizens. This is particularly noticeable in the case of the unrecognized villages, some of which are within the now increased zone of rocket fire, and which have no means of protection from rocket and mortar attacks.

[Removed: sections I and J (paragraphs 1682–1691)]

CHAPTER XXV.

REPRESSION OF DISSENT IN ISRAEL, RIGHT TO ACCESS TO INFORMATION AND TREATMENT OF HUMAN RIGHTS DEFENDERS

[Removed: paragraphs 1692–1696]

A. PROTESTS INSIDE ISRAEL

1. General

While the majority of Jewish citizens in Israel supported military action in Gaza, demonstrations and vigils were held across Israel—daily in some areas—against the military operations. As might be expected, smaller protests took place on weekdays, while larger ones were held on the weekends. Protests took place in numerous towns and villages across Israel, the most important being: the demonstration of 150,000 people in Sakhnin, the largest demonstration of Palestinian Israelis since 1948; a 100,000-strong protest in Baqa al-Gharbiyah in the "Triangle"; a demonstration of 15,000 people in Naqab; a protest by more than 10,000 people in Tel Aviv and protests of a similar size in Haifa. Protests were also witnessed in southern localities, including Beersheba and Ararah. Daily protests took place not only in towns and villages populated mainly by Palestinian citizens of Israel but also in Haifa and Tel Aviv.

According to information received by the Mission, the protests against the Israeli military operations in Gaza were, in the main, attended by Palestinian Israelis, even though protests usually also included Jewish Israelis. In Tel Aviv, Jewish Israelis reportedly made up 30 to 40 per cent of the larger weekend demonstrations. The Mission took note of reports that in areas where mainly Jewish Israelis resided, such as Tel Aviv and Beersheba, counter-protests were sometimes organized or spontaneously formed. While there were verbal confrontations between the two groups of protesters, physical violence was rare.

2. Police conduct

According to information received by the Mission, in areas of northern Israel populated mainly by Israel's Palestinian citizens (such as Sakhnin, Nazareth and Baqa al-Gharbiyah), the police did not enter the town during the protests but remained on the outskirts. This decision was apparently taken in coordination with town authorities, on the agreed view that the protests would be more orderly if the police remained out of sight.

In Tel Aviv and Haifa, the police tended to be visible to protesters. With a few exceptions (see below) police interference was limited. In Haifa, smaller demonstrations were attended by almost as many police officers as protesters, and the number of cameras being used by the police to record the protest had an intimidating effect. Police blocked off streets around the demonstrations in both cities, with the consequence that protests took place in near-deserted areas; one protester remarked that "it was as though we were demonstrating to ourselves." While the media had free access, the Mission's attention was drawn to the fact that there was little coverage of the protests by the international or Israeli media.

In the south, in towns populated by Palestinian Israelis, police action mirrored that taken in the north, remaining on the outskirts of the town while the protests continued inside. There were reports, however, of significant difficulties for protesters in obtaining permits, even where the protests were being staged in areas outside the military zone, in effect in the areas around Gaza. This compared unfavourably with reports from Tel Aviv and Haifa, where police generally allowed protests, regardless of whether permits had been obtained.

In areas in the south populated by Jewish Israelis, such as Beersheba, police maintained a presence near the demonstrators and were apparently less tolerant of the protests against the military operations in Gaza than their colleagues policing protests in the north. One protester stated that this was because dissent in the south was an embarrassment to Israel, which claimed that the military operations in Gaza were motivated by the need to defend southern Israel. It should be noted, however, that there were significant episodes of counter-protest in Beersheba, which had come under rocket fire during the operations in Gaza.

3. Arrests of protesters

According to statistics that Adalah obtained from the police, 715 protesters were arrested inside Israel. This number included 277 people arrested in Jerusalem. Unfortunately, the statistics make no distinction between East and West Jerusalem.

The Mission notes that, given the large number of people involved in the demonstrations, which it estimates to be in the hundreds of thousands, relatively few arrests were made. It was, however, struck by reports that no arrests seem to have been made of people participating in counter-demonstrations supporting the military operations in the Gaza Strip.

According to the police statistics obtained by Adalah, 34 per cent of those arrested were under the age of 18. Of those charged with an offence, the majority were charged with "attacking police officers," "unlawful assembly" and "disturbing public order." While Adalah noted that only in a few cases were those arrested charged with "endangering life on a public road," the Mezan Center for Human Rights in Nazareth noted that a large number of those arrested in the northern areas mainly populated by Palestinian Israelis had been charged with that offence.

4. Physical violence against protesters

The Mission received several submissions about the beating of protesters by the police. These incidents appeared to have been a disproportionate response by the police when they believed that the protesters were not complying or not complying fast enough with their orders and, in some instances, where protesters were themselves breaking the law (for example, by throwing stones at the police).

[Removed: remainder of section 4 (paragraphs 1707–1709)]

[Removed: section 5 (paragraphs 1710–1711)]

B. JUDICIAL RESPONSES FOLLOWING THE ARRESTS OF PROTESTERS

1. Detention pending trial

In his public testimony before the Mission, Shir Hever of the Alternative Information Center highlighted a worrying new trend in the way that arrests of protestors were dealt with in the Israeli legal system. In many cases, the Prosecutor requests that the Court order that the protester be detained pending conviction or release and these submissions are generally accepted by the courts. According to Hever, detention pending trial is usually reserved for defendants thought to be dangerous, not for people arrested during protests. This has resulted in protesters being detained for weeks and months at a time.

Hassan Tabaja stated that those arrested often faced "super-charged" indictments, where the most serious possible charge had been selected by the Prosecution. For example, for protesting on a road, instead of being charged with disturbing the peace or an illegal gathering, people were sometimes charged with "endangering life on a public road," a charge that carries a sentence of 20 years. The severity of the charge greatly increases the chance of being detained pending trial.

On 12 January 2009, the Israeli Supreme Court decided that, given the ongoing military operations in Gaza, it could not allow certain persons to be released on bail. This decision was subsequently followed by those of the lower courts, where petitions demanding the release of individuals arrested in connection with the demonstrations were refused.

It is clear from statistics obtained by Adalah from the Israeli police that, of all the protesters arrested, it was the Palestinian Israelis who were disproportionately held in detention pending trial. For example, of the 60 people arrested in the Northern District of Israel (mainly populated by Palestinian Israelis), all were detained pending trial; in Tel Aviv, of the 27 people arrested, none were detained pending trial. According to the Mezan Center for Human Rights in Nazareth, there are still people being detained pending trial following their arrest at the protests against the military operations in Gaza.

[Removed: section 2 (paragraphs 1716–1718)]

C. THE INTERROGATION OF POLITICAL ACTIVISTS BY THE GENERAL SECURITY SERVICES

During the Israeli military operations in Gaza, members of Arab political parties and activists in various non-governmental organizations were invited in for interrogation by the General Security Services, commonly known as the Shabak.

According to Adalah, the Shabak incorrectly informed those invited that they were required by law to come. Ameer Makhoul, the Director of Ittijah and Chairperson of the Popular Committee for the Protection of Political Freedoms, declined the invitation to the interrogation because he was not legally required to do so. He stated that, shortly afterwards, police officers arrived at his office and took him to the interview.

Mr. Makhoul was taken to the Shabak headquarters in Tel Aviv, where he was kept for four hours, during which time he was questioned about the people he knew and their whereabouts. On refusing to answer, he was told that, if he continued his political activities, he would be sent to prison and that, if he wished to go to Gaza, arrangements could be made to send him there. During his interview, it became apparent that the Shabak was aware of his address, and the car he drove, and referred to a speech that he had made in Haifa on 29 December 2008.

The Mission received reports of 20 prominent activists and political figures within the Palestinian community being called in for interrogation by the Shabak and being questioned about their political activities. It has also received reports of younger political activists having been taken for interview and asked to collaborate with the Israeli authorities. In the case of student activists, the offer of collaboration was accompanied by the threat of arrest or of future difficulties in continuing their studies.

According to those interviewed, the summoning and indeed taking of activists for interrogation by the Shabak created a climate of intimidation against dissent in Israel. Many activists appear to have been "invited" for interview following their attendance at protests against the military operations in Gaza, and their presence at protests was noted by those interviewing them.

[Removed: section D (paragraphs 1724–1732)]

E. THE ACCESS OF THE MEDIA AND HUMAN RIGHTS MONITORS TO GAZA PRIOR TO, DURING AND AFTER THE MILITARY OPERATIONS

The decision by Israel to deny access to the media and international human rights monitors to Gaza during—and indeed prior—to the start of its military operations in Gaza on 27 December 2008, created a storm of protest from the international media and human rights NGOs. Some human rights organizations, including Human Rights Watch and B'Tselem, are still denied access to Gaza to this day.

The Mission notes that, during the military operations in Gaza, there were a number of Palestinian human rights organizations conducting independent monitoring of international human rights and international humanitarian law. As noted elsewhere in the present report, the Mission found the work of these organizations to be of a very high professional standard and one that deserved recognition given the extremely difficult circumstances under which they usually operated, particularly during the Israeli military operations. The Mission is of the view that the presence of international human rights monitors would have been of great assistance in not only investigating and reporting but also in the publicizing of events on the ground.

1. Media

Israeli military authorities stopped allowing foreign journalists into the Gaza Strip, without prior notification to media organizations, on 5 November 2008 when hostilities escalated. Israeli citizens, including journalists, have been barred from entering the Gaza Strip since the abduction in 2006 of Gilad Shalit, on security grounds. One journalist, Amira Hass, has been arrested on two occasions, in December 2008 and in May 2009, for being in Gaza illegally.

After the closure, on 5 November 2008, of the Gaza Strip to journalists (among other groups, including human rights monitors), there was international and domestic protest; the ban was lifted briefly on 4 December 2008, but reinstated the following day. At the start of the military operations in Gaza, Israeli defence officials indicated that there would be a complete ban on access of the media to Gaza for the duration of the operations. On 27 December 2008, the day military operations started, the Israeli authorities imposed a closed military zone inside Gaza and through a 2-kilometre strip around its perimeter.

On 19 November 2008, the heads of many international news organizations, including the BBC, CNN and Reuters, protested against the ban on media access to Gaza in a letter to the then President Ehud Olmert. On 24 November 2008, the Foreign Press Association petitioned the Supreme Court to rule on the legality of such a ban.

In an open letter, dated 29 December 2008, the Foreign Press Association stated that the denial of media access to Gaza was

> an unprecedented restriction of press freedom. As a result, the world's media is unable to accurately report on events inside Gaza at this critical time. . . .

Despite our protests, the Israeli authorities have refused to let journalists in. . . . Never before have journalists been prevented from doing their work in this way. We believe it is vital that journalists be allowed to find out for themselves what is going on in Gaza. Israel controls access to Gaza. Israel must allow professional journalists access to this important story.

On 31 December 2008, the Supreme Court ruled on the Association's petition, ordering the Government of Israel to grant 12 journalists entry into Gaza each time the Erez crossing opened. On 2 January 2009, the Court amended its order to state that eight journalists, rather than 12, should be admitted whenever the Erez crossing opened.

On 8 January 2009, the Israeli authorities briefly gave the BBC and two Israeli channels access to accompany Israeli forces into Gaza. On 22 January 2009, access was granted to eight journalists to accompany Israeli forces into Gaza. The media and non-governmental organizations continued to complain about the lack of independent, unfettered access to Gaza.

On the same day, the United Nations Chief of Communications and Public Information called on the Government of Israel to ensure immediate access to the international media to Gaza, stressing the need for "full and independent" coverage of events.

On 23 January 2009, five days after its unilateral ceasefire, Israel removed all restrictions put in place in early November 2008 and the media was given free access to Gaza.

On 25 January 2009, the Supreme Court of Israel issued its final ruling, overturning the blanket ban and stating that reporters should have access to Gaza "unless the security situation changes drastically in such a way that the Erez crossing has to be closed completely for security reasons, and we assume that this will happen only in dire circumstances of concrete danger."

There have been various explanations from the Government of Israel. A spokesman from the Embassy of Israel in London, speaking to *Press Gazette*, stated, "Gaza is a war zone and so it is very difficult to allow people who are not soldiers in. Their presence might endanger both themselves and our operations there."

The Director of Press Office of the Government of Israel, Daniel Seaman, stated, "Any journalist who enters Gaza becomes a fig leaf and front for the Hamas terror organization, and I see no reason why we should help that." He was later quoted in the Associated Press as saying [that] foreign journalists were "unprofessional" and took "questionable reports at face value without checking."

[Removed: paragraph 1745]

The media ban coupled with the comments made by the Director of the Government's Press Office have raised concerns, aired in the media, that the ban was aimed at controlling the narrative of the conflict for political reasons.

2. International human rights monitors

The denial of access to Gaza had an impact not only on the media but also international human rights monitors, who required access to report violations and, like journalists, make events in Gaza known to the public. The Mission also notes that the presence of international human rights monitors is likely to have a deterrent effect, dissuading parties to a conflict from engaging in violations of international law.

On 31 December 2008, Amnesty International issued a statement calling for Israel to allow "humanitarian workers and observers" immediate access to Gaza.

Human Rights Watch requested permission from the Israel military authorities to enter Gaza on 5 January 2009. The request was rejected on 9 February 2009 on the grounds that Human Rights Watch was not registered with the Ministry of Social Affairs. Human Rights Watch asked for clarification, given that it had never heard of such a requirement, even though it had received permission to enter Gaza on previous occasions, and was unsure of the basis in Israeli law or regulation for such a requirement. To date, Human Rights Watch has yet to receive a response from the Israeli authorities. At 2 August 2009, it had still not been granted permission by the Israeli authorities to enter Gaza to conduct investigations.

On 20 January 2009, B'Tselem requested permission from the Israel military authorities for its fieldwork director to enter Gaza; the application was rejected on 29 January 2009. In a news update dated 19 January 2009, Amnesty International stated that it had made numerous applications to the Israeli authorities to enter Gaza, but had received no response.

To date, Amnesty International, Human Rights Watch and B'Tselem have been denied access to Gaza to collect data for their independent investigations into allegations of war crimes committed by both the Israeli forces and Palestinian armed groups.

[Removed: section F (paragraphs 1752–1772)]

[Removed: Part Four (paragraphs 1773–1873)]

PART FIVE

CONCLUSIONS AND RECOMMENDATIONS

CHAPTER XXX.

CONCLUSIONS

A. CONCLUDING OBSERVATIONS

An objective assessment of the events it investigated and their causes and context is crucial for the success of any effort to achieve justice for victims of violations and peace and security in the region, and as such is in the interest of all concerned and affected by this situation, including the parties to the continuing hostilities. It is in this spirit, and with full appreciation of the complexity of its task, that the Mission received and implemented its mandate.

The international community as well as Israel, and, to the extent determined by their authority and means, Palestinian authorities, have the responsibility to protect victims of violations and ensure that they do not continue to suffer the scourge of war or the oppression and humiliations of occupation or indiscriminate rocket attacks. People of Palestine have the right to freely determine their own political and economic system, including the right to resist forcible deprivation of their right to self-determination and the right to live, in peace and freedom, in their own State. The people of Israel have the right to live in peace and security. Both peoples are entitled to justice in accordance with international law.

In carrying out its mandate, the Mission had regard, as its only guides, for general international law, international human rights and humanitarian law, and the obligations they place on States, the obligations they place on non-State actors and, above all, the rights and entitlements they bestow on individuals. This in no way implies equating the position of Israel as the occupying Power with that of the occupied Palestinian population or entities representing it. The differences with regard to the power and capacity to inflict harm or to protect, including by securing justice when violations occur, are obvious and a comparison is neither possible nor necessary. What requires equal attention and effort, however, is the protection of all victims in accordance with international law.

B. THE ISRAELI MILITARY OPERATIONS IN GAZA: RELEVANCE TO AND LINKS WITH ISRAEL'S POLICIES VIS-À-VIS THE OCCUPIED PALESTINIAN TERRITORY

The Mission is of the view that Israel's military operation in Gaza between 27 December 2008 and 18 January 2009 and its impact cannot be understood or assessed in isolation from developments prior and subsequent to it. The operation fits into a continuum of policies aimed at pursuing Israel's political objectives with regard to Gaza and the Occupied Palestinian Territory as a whole. Many such policies are based on or result in violations of international human rights and humanitarian law. Military objectives as stated by the Government of Israel do not explain the facts ascertained by the Mission, nor are they congruous with the patterns identified by the Mission during the investigation.

The continuum is evident most immediately with the policy of blockade that preceded the operations and that in the Mission's view amounts to collective punishment intentionally inflicted by the Government of Israel on the people of the Gaza Strip. When the operations began, the Gaza Strip had been under a severe regime of closures and restrictions on the movement of people, goods and services for almost three years. This included basic necessities of life, such as food and medical supplies, and products required for the conduct of daily life, such as fuel, electricity, school items, and repair and construction material. These measures were imposed by Israel purportedly to isolate and weaken Hamas after its electoral victory in view of the perceived continuing threat to Israel's security that it represented. Their effect was compounded by the withholding of financial and other assistance by some donors on similar grounds. Adding hardship to the already difficult situation in the Gaza Strip, the effects of the prolonged blockade did not spare any aspect of the life of Gazans. Prior to the military operation, the Gaza economy had been depleted, the health sector beleaguered, the population had been made dependent on humanitarian assistance for survival and the conduct of daily life. Men, women and children were psychologically suffering from long-standing poverty, insecurity and violence, and enforced confinement in a heavily overcrowded territory. The dignity of the people of Gaza had been severely eroded. This was the situation in the Gaza Strip when the Israeli armed forces launched their offensive in December 2008. The military operations and the manner in which they were conducted considerably exacerbated the aforementioned effects of the blockade. The result, in a very short time, was unprecedented long-term damage both to the people and to their development and recovery prospects.

An analysis of the modalities and impact of the December–January military operations also sets them, in the Mission's view, in a continuum with a number of other pre-existing Israeli policies with regard to the Occupied Palestinian Territory. The progressive isolation and separation of the Gaza Strip from the West Bank, a policy that began much earlier and which was consolidated in particular with the imposition of tight closures, restrictions on movement and eventually the blockade, are among the most apparent. Several measures adopted by Israel in the West Bank during and following the military operations in Gaza also further deepen Israel's control over the West Bank, including East Jerusalem, and point to a convergence of objectives with the Gaza military operations. Such measures include increased land expropriation, house demolitions, demolition orders and permits to build homes in settlements, greater and more formalized access and movement restrictions on Palestinians, new and stricter procedures for residents of the Gaza Strip to change their residency to the West Bank. Systematic efforts to hinder and control Palestinian self-determined democratic processes, not least through the detention of elected political representatives and members of Government and the punishment of the Gaza population for its perceived support for Hamas, culminated in the attacks on government buildings during the Gaza offensive, most prominently the Palestinian Legislative Council. The cumulative impact of these policies and actions make prospects for political and economic integration between Gaza and the West Bank more remote.

C. NATURE, OBJECTIVES AND TARGETS OF THE ISRAELI MILITARY OPERATIONS IN GAZA

Both Palestinians and Israelis whom the Mission met repeatedly stressed that the military operations carried out by Israel in Gaza from 27 December 2008 until 18 January 2009 were qualitatively different from any previous military action by Israel in the Occupied Palestinian Territory. Despite the hard conditions that have long been prevailing in the Gaza Strip, victims and long-time observers stated that the operations were unprecedented in their severity and that their consequences would be long-lasting.

When the Mission conducted its first visit to the Gaza Strip in early June 2009, almost five months had passed since the end of the Israeli military operations. The devastating effects of the operations on the population were, however, unequivocally manifest. In addition to the visible destruction of houses, factories, wells, schools, hospitals, police stations and other public buildings, the sight of families, including the elderly and children, still living amid the rubble of their former dwellings—no reconstruction possible due to the continuing blockade—was evidence of the protracted impact of the operations on the living conditions of the Gaza population. Reports of the trauma suffered during the attacks, the stress due to the uncertainty about the future, the hardship of life and the fear of further attacks pointed to less tangible but not less real long-term effects.

Women were affected in significant ways. Their situation must be given specific attention in any effort to address the consequences of the blockade, of the continuing occupation and of the latest Israeli military operations.

The Gaza military operations were, according to the Israeli Government, thoroughly and extensively planned. While the Israeli Government has sought to portray its operations as essentially a response to rocket attacks in the exercise of its right to self-defence, the Mission considers the plan to have been directed, at least in part, at a different target: the people of Gaza as a whole.

In this respect, the operations were in furtherance of an overall policy aimed at punishing the Gaza population for its resilience and for its apparent support for Hamas, and possibly with the intent of forcing a change in such support. The Mission considers this position to be firmly based in fact, bearing in mind what it saw and heard on the ground, what it read in the accounts of soldiers who served in the campaign, and what it heard and read from current and former military officers and political leaders whom the Mission considers to be representative of the thinking that informed the policy and strategy of the military operations.

The Mission recognizes that the principal focus in the aftermath of military operations will often be on the people who have been killed—more than 1,400 in just three weeks. This is rightly so. Part of the functions of reports such as this is to attempt, albeit in a very small way, to restore the dignity of those whose rights have been violated in the most fundamental way of all—the arbitrary deprivation of life. It is important that the international community asserts formally and unequivocally that such violence to the most basic fundamental rights and freedoms of individuals should not be overlooked and should be condemned.

In this respect, the Mission recognizes that not all deaths constitute violations of international humanitarian law. The principle of proportionality acknowledges that, under certain strict conditions, actions resulting in the loss of civilian life may not be unlawful. What makes the application and assessment of proportionality difficult in respect of many of the events investigated by the Mission is that deeds by the Israeli armed forces and words of military and political leaders prior to and during the operations indicate that, as a whole, they were premised on a deliberate policy of disproportionate force aimed not at the enemy but at the "supporting infrastructure." In practice, this appears to have meant the civilian population.

The timing of the first Israeli attack, at 11.30 A.M. on a weekday, when children were returning from school and the streets of Gaza were crowded with people going about their daily business, appears to have been calculated to create the greatest disruption and widespread panic among the civilian population. The treatment of many civilians detained or even killed while trying to surrender is one manifestation of the way in which the effective rules of engagement, standard operating procedures and instructions to the troops on the ground appear to have been framed in order to create an environment in which due regard for civilian lives and basic human dignity was replaced with disregard for basic international humanitarian law and human rights norms.

The Mission recognizes fully that the Israeli armed forces, like any army attempting to act within the parameters of international law, must avoid taking undue risks with their soldiers' lives, but neither can they transfer that risk onto the lives of civilian men, women and children. The fundamental principles of distinction and proportionality apply on the battlefield, whether that battlefield is a built-up urban area or an open field.

The repeated failure to distinguish between combatants and civilians appears to the Mission to have been the result of deliberate guidance issued to soldiers, as described by some of them, and not the result of occasional lapses.

The Mission recognizes that some of those killed were combatants directly engaged in hostilities against Israel, but many were not. The outcome and the modalities of the operations indicate, in the Mission's view, that they were only partially aimed at killing leaders and members of Hamas, al-Qassam Brigades and other

TESTIMONY 13

Sameh al-Sawafeary

Owner of egg production farm in the al-Samouni area,
describing the forced evacuation of his neighborhood

The Red Cross asked us to wave white flags and to leave the house. So we waved white flags, we left the house altogether, the al-Sawafeary family, the al-Juha family, the Mughrabi family and the other family. But as we were walking, the Israeli army opened fire on us. Ibrahim Mu'een Juha, who is a 15-year-old young man, received a bullet in his chest and fell on the ground. We carried him—that was on Monday. We carried him. His mother . . . asked Abu Nabil al-Mughrabi to give her some needle and thread and some eau de cologne. She wanted to stitch her son up. He was still alive.

Abu Nabil brought a needle and a thread but she ran out of thread. She asked him for more threads. She sterilized the needle with the eau de cologne and stitched her son up. She was extremely happy. She thought that she saved her son's life. That was about 3:00 P.M. . . . But at 11:00 P.M. the young man died.

armed groups. They were also to a large degree aimed at destroying or incapacitating civilian property and the means of subsistence of the civilian population.

It is clear from evidence gathered by the Mission that the destruction of food supply installations, water sanitation systems, concrete factories and residential houses was the result of a deliberate and systematic policy by the Israeli armed forces. It was not carried out because those objects presented a military threat or opportunity, but to make the daily process of living, and dignified living, more difficult for the civilian population.

Allied to the systematic destruction of the economic capacity of the Gaza Strip, there appears also to have been an assault on the dignity of the people. This was seen not only in the use of human shields and unlawful detentions, sometimes in unacceptable conditions, but also in the vandalizing of houses when occupied and the way in which people were treated when their houses were entered. The graffiti on the walls, the obscenities and often racist slogans, all constituted an overall image of humiliation and dehumanization of the Palestinian population.

The operations were carefully planned in all their phases. Legal opinions and advice were given throughout the planning stages and at certain operational levels during the campaign. There were almost no mistakes made according to the Government of Israel. It is in these circumstances that the Mission concludes that what occurred in just over three weeks at the end of 2008 and the beginning of 2009 was a deliberately disproportionate attack designed to punish, humiliate and terrorize a civilian population, radically diminish its local economic capacity both to work and to provide for itself, and to force upon it an ever increasing sense of dependency and vulnerability.

The Mission has noted with concern public statements by Israeli officials, including senior military officials, to the effect that the use of disproportionate force, attacks on civilian population and the destruction of civilian property are legitimate means to achieve Israel's military and political objectives. The Mission believes that such statements not only undermine the entire regime of international law, they are inconsistent with the spirit of the Charter of the United Nations and, therefore, deserve to be categorically denounced.

Whatever violations of international humanitarian and human rights law may have been committed, the systematic and deliberate nature of the activities described in this report leave the Mission in no doubt that responsibility lies in the first place with those who designed, planned, ordered and oversaw the operations.

D. OCCUPATION, RESILIENCE AND CIVIL SOCIETY

The accounts of more severe violence during the recent military operations did not obscure the fact that the concept of "normalcy" in the Gaza Strip has long been redefined owing to the protracted situation of abuse and lack of protection deriving from the decades-long occupation.

As the Mission focused on investigating and analysing the specific matters within its mandate, Israel's continuing occupation of the Gaza Strip and the West Bank emerged as the fundamental factor underlying violations of international humanitarian and human rights law against the protected population and undermining prospects for development and peace. Israel's failure to acknowledge and exercise its responsibilities as the occupying Power further exacerbated the effects of occupation on the Palestinian people, and continue to do so. Furthermore, the harsh and unlawful practices of occupation, far from quelling resistance, breed it, including its violent manifestations. The Mission is of the view that ending occupation is a prerequisite for the return of a dignified life for Palestinians, as well as development and a peaceful solution to the conflict.

The Mission was struck by the resilience and dignity shown by people in the face of dire circumstances. UNRWA Director of Operations, John Ging, relayed to the Mission the answer of a Gaza teacher during a discussion after the end of the Israeli military operations about strengthening human rights education in schools. Rather than expressing scepticism at the relevance of teaching human rights in a context of renewed denial of rights, the teacher unhesitantly supported the resumption of human rights education: "This is a war of values, and we are not going to lose it."

The assiduous work of Palestinian non-governmental and civil society organizations in providing support to the population in such extreme circumstances, and in giving voice to the suffering and expectations of victims of violations, deserves to be fully acknowledged. Their role in helping to sustain the resilience and dignity of the population cannot be overstated. The Mission heard many accounts of NGO workers, doctors, ambulance drivers, journalists, human rights monitors, who, at the height of the military operations, risked their lives to be of service to people in need. They frequently relayed the anxiety of having to choose between remaining close to their own families and continuing to work to assist others in need, thereby often being cut off from news about the safety or whereabouts of family members. The Mission wishes to pay tribute to the courage and work of the numerous individuals who so contributed to alleviating the suffering of the population and to report on the events in Gaza.

E. ROCKET AND MORTAR ATTACKS IN ISRAEL

Palestinian armed groups have launched thousands of rockets and mortars into Israel since April 2001. These have succeeded in causing terror within Israel's civilian population, as evidenced by the high rates of psychological trauma within the affected communities. The attacks have also led to an erosion of the social, cultural and economic lives of the communities in southern Israel, and have affected the rights to education of the tens of thousands of children and young adults who attend classes in the affected areas.

Between 27 December 2008 and 18 January 2009, these attacks left four people dead and hundreds injured. That there have not been more casualties is due to a combination of luck and measures taken by the Israeli Government, including the fortification of public buildings, the construction of shelters and, in times of escalated hostilities, the closure of schools.

The Mission notes, with concern, that Israel has not provided the same level of protection from rockets and mortars to affected Palestinian citizens as it has to Jewish citizens. In particular, it has failed to provide public shelters or fortification of schools, for example, to the Palestinian communities living in the unrecognized villages and some of the recognized villages. It ought to go without saying that the thousands of Palestinian Israelis—including a significant number of children—who live within the range of rocket fire deserve the same protection as the Israeli Government provides to its Jewish citizens.

F. DISSENTING VOICES IN ISRAEL

While the Israeli military offensive in Gaza was widely supported by the Israeli public, there were also dissenting voices, which expressed themselves through demonstrations, protests, as well as public reporting on Israel's conduct. The Mission is of the view that actions of the Israeli Government during and following the military operations in the Gaza Strip, including interrogation of political activists, repression of criticism and sources of potential criticism of Israeli military actions, in particular NGOs, have contributed significantly to a political climate in which dissent with the Government and its actions in the Occupied Palestinian Territory is not tolerated. The denial of media access to Gaza and the continuing denial of access to human rights monitors are, in the Mission's view, an attempt both to remove the Government's actions in the Occupied Palestinian Territory from public scrutiny and to impede investigations and reporting of the conduct of the parties to the conflict in the Gaza Strip.

In this context of increased intolerance for dissenting opinions in Israel, the Mission wishes to acknowledge the difficult work of NGOs in Israel, which courageously continue to express criticism of Government action that violates international human rights and humanitarian law. The work of these organizations is essential not only to ensure independent information to the Israeli and international public but also to encourage a facts-based debate about these issues within Israeli society.

G. THE IMPACT OF DEHUMANIZATION

As in many conflicts, one of the features of the Palestinian-Israeli conflict is the dehumanization of the other, and of victims in particular. Palestinian psychiatrist Dr. Iyad al-Sarraj explained the cycle of aggression and victimization through which "the Palestinian in the eyes of the Israeli soldier is not an equal human being. Sometimes . . . even becomes a demon . . . ." This "culture of demonization and dehumanization" adds to a state of paranoia. "Paranoia has two sides, the side of victimization, I am a victim of this world, the whole world is against me and on the other side, I am superior to this world and I can oppress it. This leads to what is called the arrogance of power." As Palestinians, "we look in general to the Israelis as demons and that we can hate them, that what we do is a reaction, and we say that the Israelis can only understand the language of power. The same thing that we say about the Israelis they say about us, that we only understand the language of violence or force. There we see the arrogance of power and [the Israeli] uses it without thinking of humanity at all. In my view we are seeing not only a state of war but also a state that is cultural and psychological and I hope, I wish that the Israelis would start, and there are many, many Jews in the world and in Israel that look into themselves, have an insight that would make them alleviate the fear that they have, because there's a state of fear in Israel, in spite of all the power, and that they would start to walk on the road of dealing with the consequences of their own victimization and to start dealing with the Palestinian as a human being, a full human being who's equal in rights with the Israeli and also the other way around, the Palestinian must deal with himself, must respect himself and respect his own differences in order to be able to stand before the Israeli also as a full human being with equal rights and obligations. This is the real road for justice and for peace."

Israeli college teacher Ofer Shinar offered a similar analysis: "Israeli society's problem is that, because of the conflict, Israeli society feels itself to be a victim and to a large extent that's justified and it's very difficult for Israeli society to move and to feel that it can also see the other side and to understand that the other side is also a victim. This I think is the greatest tragedy of the conflict and it's terribly difficult to overcome it. . . . I think that the initiative that you've taken in listening to . . . people . . . is very important. The message that you're giving Israeli society is absolutely unambiguous that you are impartial, that you should be able to see that the feeling of being a victim is something that characterizes both sides. What requires you to take this responsibility is the fact that you have to understand how difficult it is to get this message through to Israeli society, how closed the Israeli society is, how difficult it is for Israeli society to understand that the other side is not just the party which is infringing our own human rights, but how they are having their human rights infringed, how they are suffering as well."

The Mission, in fulfilling its mandate to investigate alleged violations of international law that occurred in the context of the December 2008–January 2009 military operations in Gaza, spoke predominantly to those most affected by the most recent events in a conflict that has spanned decades. As may be expected, the Mission found societies scarred by living in conflict, with significant psychological trauma stemming from a life that may rightly seem to those living in more peaceful countries to be unbearable.

Both the Palestinians and the Israelis are legitimately angered at the lives that they are forced to lead. For the Palestinians, the anger about individual events—the civilian casualties, injuries and destruction in Gaza following from military attacks, the blockade, the continued construction of the Wall outside of the 1967 borders— feed into an underlying anger about the continuing Israeli occupation, its daily humiliations and their as-yet-unfulfilled right to self-determination. For the Israelis, the public statements of Palestinian armed groups celebrating rocket and mortar attacks on civilians strengthen a deep-rooted concern that negotiation will yield little and that their nation remains under existential threat from which only it can protect its people. In this way, both the Israelis and the Palestinians share a secret fear—for some, a belief—that each has no intention of accepting the other's right to a country of their own. This anger and fear are unfortunately ably represented by many politicians.

Some Israelis pointed out to the Mission that policies of the Israeli Government relating to the isolation of the Gaza Strip and the tighter restrictions on the movement of Palestinians within the Occupied Palestinian Territory, and between the Occupied Palestinian Territory and Israel, have contributed to increasing the distance between Palestinians and Israelis, reducing the opportunities to interact other than in situations of control and coercion such as checkpoints and military posts.

In this context, the Mission was encouraged by reports of exchange and cooperation between Palestinians and Israelis, for example with regard to mental health
specialists working with Palestinians from Gaza and southern Israel's communities, and with regard to cooperation between Magen David Adom and the Palestinian Red Crescent Society, especially in the West Bank, as they fulfil a shared
commitment to providing humanitarian assistance to the communities in which
they work, regardless of the ethnicity of the patient who lies before them.

H. THE INTRA-PALESTINIAN SITUATION

The division and violence between Fatah and Hamas, which culminated in the establishment of parallel governance entities and structures in the Gaza Strip and
the West Bank, is having adverse consequences for the human rights of the Palestinian population in both areas, as well as contributing to erode the rule of law in
the Occupied Palestinian Territory in addition to the threats already linked to foreign occupation. Even with the narrow focus of the Mission on violations relevant
to the context of the December–January military operations, the diminishing protections for Palestinians are evident from the cases of arbitrary deprivation of life,
arbitrary detention of political activists or sympathizers, limitations on freedom
of expression and association, and abuses by security forces. The situation is compounded by the ever reducing role of the judiciary in ensuring the rule of law and
legal remedies for violations. A resolution of the internal divisions based on the
free will and decisions of Palestinians and without external interference would
strengthen the ability of Palestinian authorities and institutions to protect the rights
of the people under their responsibility.

I. THE NEED FOR PROTECTION AND THE ROLE
OF THE INTERNATIONAL COMMUNITY

International law sets obligations on States not only to respect but also to ensure
respect for international humanitarian law. The International Court of Justice stated
in its Advisory Opinion on the *Legal Consequences of the Construction of a Wall
in the Occupied Palestinian Territory* that "all States parties to the Fourth Geneva
Convention relative to the Protection of Civilian Persons in Time of War of 12
August 1949 have in addition the obligation, while respecting the United Nations
Charter and international law, to ensure compliance by Israel with international
humanitarian law as embodied in that Convention."

The 2005 World Summit Outcome document recognized that the international community, through the United Nations, also has the responsibility to use appropriate diplomatic, humanitarian and other peaceful means, in accordance with Chapters VI and VIII of the Charter, to help protect populations from, inter alia, war crimes and crimes against humanity. The document stressed that the Members of the United Nations are prepared to take collective action, in a timely and decisive manner, through the Security Council, in accordance with the Charter, including Chapter VII, should peaceful means be inadequate and national authorities are manifestly failing to protect their populations from genocide, war crimes, ethnic cleansing and crimes against humanity. In 2009, the Secretary-General, in his report on implementing the responsibility to protect, noted that the enumeration of these crimes did not "detract in any way from the much broader range of obligations existing under international humanitarian law, international human rights law, refugee law and international criminal law."

After decades of sustained conflict, the level of threat to which both Palestinians and Israelis are subjected has not abated, but if anything increased with continued escalations of violence, death and suffering for the civilian population, of which the December–January military operations in Gaza are only the most recent occurrence. Israel is therefore also failing to protect its own citizens by refusing to acknowledge the futility of resorting to violent means and military power.

Israeli incursions and military actions in the Gaza Strip did not stop after the end of the military operations of December–January.

The Security Council has placed the protection of civilian populations on its agenda as a regular item, recognizing it as a matter falling within its responsibility. The Mission notes that the international community has been largely silent and has to date failed to act to ensure the protection of the civilian population in the Gaza Strip and generally the Occupied Palestinian Territory. Suffice it to notice the lack of adequate reaction to the blockade and its consequences, to the Gaza military operations and, in their aftermath, to the continuing obstacles to reconstruction. The Mission also considers that the isolation of the Gaza authorities and the sanctions against the Gaza Strip have had a negative impact on the protection of the population. Immediate action to enable reconstruction in Gaza is no doubt required. However, it also needs to be accompanied by a firmer and principled stance by the international community on violations of international humanitarian and human rights law and long-delayed action to end them. Protection of civilian populations requires respect for international law and accountability for violations. When the international community does not live up to its own legal standards, the threat to the international rule of law is obvious and potentially far-reaching in its consequences.

The Mission acknowledges and emphasizes the impressive and essential role played by the staff of the numerous United Nations agencies and bodies working to assist the population of the Occupied Palestinian Territory in all aspects of daily life. An additional disturbing feature of the December–January military operations was the disregard in several incidents, some of which are documented in this report, for the inviolability of United Nations premises, facilities and staff. It ought to go without saying that attacks on the United Nations are unacceptable and undermine its ability to fulfil its protection and assistance role vis-à-vis a population that so badly needs it.

J. SUMMARY OF LEGAL FINDINGS

Detailed legal findings by the Mission are included in each of the chapters of the report where specific facts and events are analysed. The following is a summary of those findings.

1. Actions by Israel in Gaza in the context of the military operations of 27 December 2008 to 18 January 2009
(a) Precautions in launching attacks

The Mission finds that in a number of cases Israel failed to take feasible precautions required by customary law reflected in article 57 (2) (a) (ii) of Additional Protocol I to avoid or minimize incidental loss of civilian life, injury to civilians and damage to civilian objects. The firing of white phosphorous shells over the UNRWA compound in Gaza City is one of such cases in which precautions were not taken in the choice of weapons and methods in the attack, and these facts were compounded by reckless disregard for the consequences. The intentional strike at al-Quds hospital using high-explosive artillery shells and white phosphorous in and around the hospital also violated articles 18 and 19 of the Fourth Geneva Convention. With regard to the attack against al-Wafa hospital, the Mission found a violation of the same provisions, as well as a violation of the customary law prohibition against attacks which may be expected to cause excessive damage to civilians and civilian objects.

The Mission finds that the different kinds of warnings issued by Israel in Gaza cannot be considered as sufficiently effective in the circumstances to comply with customary law as reflected in Additional Protocol I, article 57 (2) (c). While some of the leaflet warnings were specific in nature, the Mission does not consider that general messages telling people to leave wherever they were and go to city centres, in the particular circumstances of the military campaign, meet the threshold of effectiveness. Firing missiles into or on top of buildings as a "warning" is essentially a dangerous practice and a form of attack rather than a warning.

(b) Incidents involving the killing of civilians

The Mission found numerous instances of deliberate attacks on civilians and civilian objects (individuals, whole families, houses, mosques) in violation of the fundamental international humanitarian law principle of distinction, resulting in deaths and serious injuries. In these cases the Mission found that the protected status of civilians was not respected and the attacks were intentional, in clear violation of customary law reflected in article 51 (2) and 75 of Additional Protocol I, article 27 of the Fourth Geneva Convention and articles 6 and 7 of the International Covenant on Civil and Political Rights. In some cases the Mission additionally concluded that the attack was also launched with the intention of spreading terror among the civilian population. Moreover, in several of the incidents investigated, the Israeli armed forces not only did not use their best efforts to permit humanitarian organizations access to the wounded and medical relief, as required by customary international law reflected in article 10 (2) of Additional Protocol I, but they arbitrarily withheld such access.

With regard to one incident investigated, involving the death of at least 35 Palestinians, the Mission finds that the Israeli armed forces launched an attack which a reasonable commander would have expected to cause excessive loss of civilian life in relation to the military advantage sought, in violation of customary international humanitarian law as reflected in Additional Protocol I, articles 57 (2) (a) (ii) and (iii). The Mission finds a violation of the right to life (ICCPR, article 6) of the civilians killed in this incident.

The Mission also concludes that Israel, by deliberately attacking police stations and killing large numbers of policemen (99 in the incidents investigated by the Mission) during the first minutes of the military operations, failed to respect the principle of proportionality between the military advantage anticipated by killing some policemen who might have been members of Palestinian armed groups and the loss of civilian life (the majority of policemen and members of the public present in the police stations or nearby during the attack). Therefore, these were disproportionate attacks in violation of customary international law. The Mission finds a violation of the right to life (ICCPR, article 6) of the policemen killed in these attacks who were not members of Palestinian armed groups.

(c) Certain weapons used by the Israeli armed forces

In relation to the weapons used by the Israeli armed forces during military operations, the Mission accepts that white phosphorous, flechettes and heavy metal (such as tungsten) are not currently proscribed under international law. Their use is, however, restricted or even prohibited in certain circumstances by virtue of the principles of proportionality and precautions necessary in the attack. Flechettes, as an area weapon, are particularly unsuitable for use in urban settings, while, in the Mission's view, the use of white phosphorous as an obscurant at least should be banned because of the number and variety of hazards that attach to the use of such a pyrophoric chemical.

(d) Treatment of Palestinians in the hands of the Israeli armed forces

(i) Use of human shields

The Mission investigated several incidents in which the Israeli armed forces used local Palestinian residents to enter houses which might be booby-trapped or harbour enemy combatants (this practice, known in the West Bank as "neighbour procedure," was called "Johnnie procedure" during the military operations in Gaza). The Mission found that the practice constitutes the use of human shields prohibited by international humanitarian law. It further constitutes a violation of the right to life, protected in article 6 of ICCPR, and of the prohibition against cruel and inhuman treatment in its article 7.

The questioning of Palestinian civilians under threat of death or injury to extract information about Hamas and Palestinian combatants and tunnels constitutes a violation of article 31 of the Fourth Geneva Convention, which prohibits physical or moral coercion against protected persons.

(ii) Detention

The Mission found that the Israeli armed forces in Gaza rounded up and detained large groups of persons protected under the Fourth Geneva Convention. The Mission finds that their detention cannot be justified either as detention of "unlawful combatants" or as internment of civilians for imperative reasons of security. The

Mission considers that the severe beatings, constant humiliating and degrading treatment and detention in foul conditions allegedly suffered by individuals in the Gaza Strip under the control of the Israeli armed forces and in detention in Israel constitute a failure to treat protected persons humanely in violation of article 27 of the Fourth Geneva Convention, as well as violations of articles 7 and 10 of the International Covenant on Civil and Political Rights regarding torture and the treatment of persons in detention, and of its article 14 with regard to due process guarantees. The treatment of women during detention was contrary to the special respect for women required under customary law as reflected in the article 76 of Additional Protocol I. The Mission finds that the rounding-up of large groups of civilians and their prolonged detention under the circumstances described in this report constitute a collective penalty on those persons in violation of article 33 of the Fourth Geneva Convention and article 50 of the Hague Regulations. Such treatment amounts to measures of intimidation or terror prohibited by article 33 of the Fourth Geneva Convention.

(e) Destruction of property

The Mission finds that the attacks against the Palestinian Legislative Council building and the main prison in Gaza constituted deliberate attacks on civilian objects in violation of the rule of customary international humanitarian law whereby attacks must be strictly limited to military objectives.

The Mission also finds that the Israeli armed forces unlawfully and wantonly attacked and destroyed without military necessity a number of food production or food-processing objects and facilities (including mills, land and greenhouses), drinking-water installations, farms and animals in violation of the principle of distinction. From the facts ascertained by it, the Mission finds that this destruction was carried out with the purpose of denying sustenance to the civilian population, in violation of customary law reflected in article 54 (2) of the First Additional Protocol. The Mission further concludes that the Israeli armed forces carried out widespread destruction of private residential houses, water wells and water tanks unlawfully and wantonly.

In addition to being violations of international humanitarian law, these extensive wanton acts of destruction amount to violations of Israel's duties to respect the right to an adequate standard of living of the people in the Gaza Strip, which includes the rights to food, water and housing, as well as the right to the highest attainable standard of health, protected under articles 11 and 12 of the International Covenant on Economic, Social and Cultural Rights.

(f) Impact of the blockade and the
military operations on the Gaza population

The Mission concludes that the blockade policies implemented by Israel against the Gaza Strip, in particular the closure of or restrictions imposed on border crossings in the immediate period before the military operations, subjected the local population to extreme hardship and deprivations that amounted to a violation of Israel's obligations as an occupying Power under the Fourth Geneva Convention. These measures led to a severe deterioration and regression in the levels of real-

TESTIMONY 14

Rashad Mohammed Hamada

General Director of Rashad Mohammed and Brothers Holdings,
describing the destruction of el-Bader Flour Mill

One week or ten days before the start of the war, all the other flour mills in Gaza no longer had any wheat, and the concentration of flour for the whole need of the Gaza Strip was only from our factory, from el-Bader Flour Mill. And we coordinated with the bakeries to distribute wheat only to bakeries, not to houses, not to households, because the flour, when given to the bakeries, every particular quantity or bag of wheat can cover for 20 families, when given to a bakery. However, when the bag itself is sold to a household, then it is only sufficient for one household. . . .

On the 27th of December the war was waged. We continued working for four, five days. During the war, the mill was working 24 hours a day and we had also been working 24 hours a day one month prior to this date, we were working around the clock.

We received a recorded message by telephone on a landline asking us to evacuate the mill. This call came from Israel. That was a Wednesday [December 31]. . . . We evacuated the factory of all workers, a total evacuation and waited until the next day. The factory was not hit. We went back to work for 24 hours, another 24 hours. We worked until Saturday or Sunday. So, this was about eight, nine days after the beginning of the war.

We received another message, I do not remember—the workers told me that it was Sunday, maybe, or Monday [January 5]. We were told to evacuate the factory. The factory was evacuated. . . .

ization of economic and social rights of Palestinians in the Gaza Strip and weakened its social and economic fabric, leaving health, education, sanitation and other essential services in a very vulnerable position to cope with the immediate effects of the military operations.

The Mission finds that, despite the information circulated by Israel about the humanitarian relief schemes in place during the military operations, Israel has essentially violated its obligation to allow free passage of all consignments of medical

Testimony 14 (*continued*)

On the dawn of the 10th of January, we received a call from the guard telling us that the factory was targeted by air with a missile and that it had caught fire. After 15 minutes, he called us again and told us that there are tanks approaching the area and that the factory was targeted with tank fire. We immediately informed the ICRC and the Civil Defense in order to put out the fire in the mill. At 11:00 A.M., we were told by the Civil Defense that the fire had been put out and that the guard had been evacuated from the surface area of the factory.

What happened at the mill is a total destruction, a total destruction of the whole production line of the factory. Because this factory in fact, is vertical, the equipment is set vertically. There are six floors. The production line was destroyed from the sixth floor to the ground floor. . . . This led to the following.

Firstly, this flour mill today is no longer operational at all. Secondly, the wheat that was to be brought in from the Israeli companies could not come through, could not be received at the mill, and the workers and employees who used to work for this factory are now unemployed. We also have a worse catastrophe. Our losses in this mill are 2.5 million American dollars. In addition to the loss of income from the day of the strike until this very day, as I said, there is also another problem because we lost what is more precious than the treasures of the world—our son, my nephew and the son of my partner and my brother-in-law, Dr. Mahir Hamada, who has six children. He fell from the fifth floor to the ground and that was during his going through to check on the results of the events on the 19th of February 2009. . . .

From what we could see on the ground and from what we had in Gaza, this flour mill was the only flour mill for the past ten years providing for the needs of the Gaza Strip in wheat. It is well known everywhere in Gaza. And in Israel, they know that el-Bader Flour Mill—know that the strategic reserve of flour for the Strip was there.

and hospital objects, food and clothing that were needed to meet the urgent humanitarian needs of the civilian population in the context of the military operations, which is in violation of article 23 of the Fourth Geneva Convention.

In addition to the above general findings, the Mission also considers that Israel has violated its specific obligations under the Convention on the Rights of the Child and the Convention on the Elimination of All Forms of Discrimination against Women, including the rights to peace and security, free movement, livelihood and health.

The Mission concludes that the conditions resulting from deliberate actions of the Israeli armed forces and the declared policies of the Government with regard to the Gaza Strip before, during and after the military operation cumulatively indicate the intention to inflict collective punishment on the people of the Gaza Strip. The Mission, therefore, finds a violation of the provisions of article 33 of the Fourth Geneva Convention.

(g) Grave breaches of the Geneva Conventions and acts raising individual criminal responsibility under international criminal law

From the facts gathered, the Mission found that the following grave breaches of the Fourth Geneva Convention were committed by the Israeli armed forces in Gaza: wilful killing, torture or inhuman treatment, willfully causing great suffering or serious injury to body or health, and extensive destruction of property, not justified by military necessity and carried out unlawfully and wantonly. As grave breaches these acts give rise to individual criminal responsibility. The Mission notes that the use of human shields also constitutes a war crime under the Rome Statute of the International Criminal Court.

The Mission further considers that the series of acts that deprive Palestinians in the Gaza Strip of their means of subsistence, employment, housing and water, that deny their freedom of movement and their right to leave and enter their own country, that limit their rights to access a court of law and an effective remedy, could lead a competent court to find that the crime of persecution, a crime against humanity, has been committed.

2. Actions by Israel in the West Bank in the context of the military operations in Gaza from 27 December 2008 to 18 January 2009

(a) Treatment of Palestinians in the West Bank by Israeli security forces, including use of excessive or lethal force during demonstrations

With regard to acts of violence by settlers against Palestinians, the Mission concludes that Israel has failed to fulfil its international obligations to protect the Palestinians from violence by private individuals under both international human rights law and international humanitarian law. In some instances security forces acquiesced to the acts of violence in violation of the prohibition against cruel, inhuman or degrading treatment. When this acquiescence occurs only in respect of violence against Palestinians by settlers and not vice versa, it would amount to discrimination on the basis of national origin, prohibited under ICCPR.

Israel also violated a series of human rights by unlawfully repressing peaceful public demonstrations and using excessive force against demonstrators. The use of firearms, including live ammunitions, and the use of snipers resulting in the death of demonstrators are a violation of article 6 of ICCPR as an arbitrary deprivation of life and, in the circumstances examined by the Mission, appear to indicate an intention or at least a recklessness towards causing harm to civilians which may amount to wilful killing.

Excessive use of force that resulted in injury rather than death constitutes violations of a number of standards, including articles 7 and 9 of ICCPR. These violations are compounded by the seemingly discriminatory "open-fire regulations" for security forces dealing with demonstrations, based on the presence of persons with a particular nationality, violating the principle of non-discrimination in ICCPR (art. 2) as well as under article 27 of the Fourth Geneva Convention.

The Mission finds that Israel failed to investigate, and when appropriate prosecute, acts by its agents or by third parties involving serious violations of international humanitarian law and human rights law.

The Mission was alarmed at the reported increase in settler violence in the past year and the failure of the Israeli security forces to prevent settlers' attacks against Palestinian civilians and their property. These are accompanied by a series of violations by Israeli forces or acquiesced by them, including the removal of residential status from Palestinians, which could eventually lead to a situation of virtual deportation and entail additional violations of other rights.

(b) Detention of Palestinians by Israel

The Mission analysed information it received on the detention of Palestinians in Israeli prisons during or in the context of the military operations of December 2008–January 2009 and found those practices generally inconsistent with human rights and international humanitarian law. The military court system to which Palestinians from the Occupied Palestinian Territory are subjected deprives them of due process guarantees in keeping with international law.

The Mission finds that the detention of members of the Palestinian Legislative Council by Israel violates the right not to be arbitrarily detained, as protected by article 9 of ICCPR. Insofar as it is based on political affiliation and prevents those members from participating in the conduct of public affairs, it is also in violation of its articles 25 recognizing the right to take part in public affairs and 26, which provides for the right to equal protection under the law. Insofar as their detention is unrelated to their individual behaviour, it constitutes collective punishment, prohibited by article 33 of the Fourth Geneva Convention. Information on the detention of large numbers of children and their treatment by Israeli security forces point to violations of their rights under ICCPR and the Convention on the Rights of the Child.

(c) Violations of the right to free movement and access

The Mission finds that the extensive restrictions imposed by Israel on the movement and access of Palestinians in the West Bank are disproportionate to any legitimate objective served and in violation of article 27 of the Fourth Geneva Convention and article 12 of ICCPR, guaranteeing freedom of movement.

Where checkpoints become a site of humiliation of the protected population by military or civilian operators, this may entail a violation of the customary law rule reflected in article 75 (2) (b) of Additional Protocol I.

The continued construction of settlements in occupied territory constitutes a violation of article 49 of the Fourth Geneva Convention. The extensive destruction and appropriation of property, including land confiscation and house demolitions in the West Bank, including East Jerusalem, not justified by military necessity and carried out unlawfully and wantonly, amounts to a grave breach under article 147 of the Fourth Geneva Convention.

Insofar as movement and access restrictions, the settlements and their infrastructure, demographic policies vis-à-vis Jerusalem and "Area C" of the West Bank, as well as the separation of Gaza from the West Bank, prevent a viable, contiguous and sovereign Palestinian State from arising, they are in violation of the *jus cogens* right to self-determination.

3. Actions by Israel in Israel

In relation to alleged violations within Israel, the Mission concludes that, although there does not appear to be a policy in this respect, there were occasions when reportedly the authorities placed obstacles in the way of protesters seeking to exercise their right to peaceful assembly and freedom of speech to criticize Israel's military actions in the Gaza Strip. These rights are protected by the International Covenant on Civil and Political Rights. Instances of physical violence against protesters and other humiliations, not rising to the level of physical violence, of the protesters by the police violated Israel's obligations under article 10 of the Covenant. The Mission is also concerned about activists being compelled to attend interviews with the General Security Services (*Shabak*), which reportedly creates an atmosphere intolerant of dissent within Israel. Hostile retaliatory actions against civil society organizations by the Government of Israel for criticisms of the Israeli authorities and for exposing alleged violations of international human rights law and international humanitarian law during the military operations are inconsistent with the Declaration on the Right and Responsibility of Individuals, Groups and Organs of Society to Promote and Protect Universally Recognized Human Rights and Fundamental Freedoms.

The Mission finds that the imposition of a near blanket exclusion of the media and human rights monitors from Gaza since 5 November 2008 and throughout the operations is inconsistent with Israel's obligations with regard to the right to access to information.

4. Actions by Palestinian armed groups

In relation to the firing of rockets and mortars into southern Israel by Palestinian armed groups operating in the Gaza Strip, the Mission finds that the Palestinian armed groups fail to distinguish between military targets and the civilian population and civilian objects in southern Israel. The launching of rockets and mortars which cannot be aimed with sufficient precision at military targets breaches the fundamental principle of distinction. Where there is no intended military target and the rockets and mortars are launched into civilian areas, they constitute a deliberate attack against the civilian population. These actions would constitute war crimes and may amount to crimes against humanity.

The Mission concludes that the rocket and mortar attacks, launched by Palestinian armed groups operating from Gaza, have caused terror in the affected communities of southern Israel. The attacks have caused loss of life and physical and mental injury to civilians as well as damaging private houses, religious buildings and property, and eroded the economic and cultural life of the affected communities and severely affected the economic and social rights of the population.

With regard to the continuing detention of Israeli soldier Gilad Shalit, the Mission finds that, as a soldier who belongs to the Israeli armed forces and who was captured during an enemy incursion into Israel, Gilad Shalit meets the requirements for prisoner-of-war status under the Third Geneva Convention and should be protected, treated humanely and be allowed external communication as appropriate according to that Convention.

The Mission also examined whether the Palestinian armed groups complied with their obligations under international humanitarian law to take constant care to minimize the risk of harm to the civilian population in Gaza among whom the hostilities were being conducted. The conduct of hostilities in built-up areas does not, of itself, constitute a violation of international law. However, launching attacks—whether of rockets and mortars at the population of southern Israel or at the Israeli armed forces inside Gaza—close to civilian or protected buildings constitutes a failure to take all feasible precautions. In cases where this occurred, the Palestinian armed groups would have unnecessarily exposed the civilian population of Gaza to the inherent dangers of the military operations taking place around them. The Mission found no evidence to suggest that Palestinian armed groups either directed civilians to areas where attacks were being launched or that they forced civilians to remain within the vicinity of the attacks. The Mission also found no evidence that members of Palestinian armed groups engaged in combat in civilian dress. Although in the one incident of an Israeli attack on a mosque it investigated the Mission found that there was no indication that that mosque was used for military purposes or to shield military activities, the Mission cannot exclude that this might have occurred in other cases.

5. Actions by responsible Palestinian authorities

Although the Gaza authorities deny any control over armed groups and responsibility for their acts, in the Mission's view, if they failed to take the necessary measures to prevent the Palestinian armed groups from endangering the civilian population, the Gaza authorities would bear responsibility for the damage arising to the civilians living in Gaza.

The Mission finds that security services under the control of the Gaza authorities carried out extrajudicial executions, arbitrary arrests, detentions and ill-treatment of people, in particular political opponents, which constitute serious violations of the human rights to life, to liberty and security of the person, to freedom from torture or cruel, inhuman or degrading treatment or punishment, to be protected against arbitrary arrest and detention, to a fair and impartial legal proceeding, and to freedom of opinion and expression, including freedom to hold opinions without interference.

The Mission also concludes that the Palestinian Authority's actions against political opponents in the West Bank, which started in January 2006 and intensified during the period between 27 December 2008 and 18 January 2009, constitute violations of human rights and of the Palestinians' own Basic Law. Detentions on political grounds violate the rights to liberty and security of person, the right to a fair trial and the right not to be discriminated against on the basis of one's political opinion, which are all part of customary international law. Reports of torture and other forms of ill-treatment during arrest and detention and of death in detention require prompt investigation and accountability.

K. THE NEED FOR ACCOUNTABILITY

The Mission was struck by the repeated comment of Palestinian victims, human rights defenders, civil society interlocutors and officials that they hoped that this would be the last investigative mission of its kind, because action for justice would follow from it. It was struck, as well, by the comment that every time a report is published and no action follows, this "emboldens Israel and her conviction of being untouchable." To deny modes of accountability reinforces impunity, and tarnishes the credibility of the United Nations and of the international community. The Mission believes these comments ought to be at the forefront in the consideration by Member States and United Nations bodies of its findings and recommendations and action consequent upon them.

The Mission is firmly convinced that justice and respect for the rule of law are the indispensable basis for peace. The prolonged situation of impunity has created a justice crisis in the Occupied Palestinian Territory that warrants action.

After reviewing Israel's system of investigation and prosecution of serious violations of human rights and humanitarian law, in particular of suspected war crimes and crimes against humanity, the Mission found major structural flaws that, in its view, make the system inconsistent with international standards. With military "operational debriefings" at the core of the system, there is no effective and impartial investigation mechanism and victims of such alleged violations are deprived of any effective or prompt remedy. Furthermore, such investigations, being internal to the Israeli military authority, do not comply with international standards of independence and impartiality. The Mission believes that the few investigations conducted by the Israeli authorities on alleged serious violations of international human rights and humanitarian law and, in particular, alleged war crimes, in the context of the military operations in Gaza between 27 December 2008 and 18 January 2009, are affected by the defects in the system, have been unduly delayed despite the gravity of the allegations, and, therefore, lack the required credibility and conformity with international standards. The Mission is concerned that investigations of relatively less serious violations that the Government of Israel claims to be investigating have also been unduly protracted.

The Mission noted the pattern of delays, inaction or otherwise unsatisfactory handling by Israeli authorities of investigations, prosecutions and convictions of military personnel and settlers for violence and offences against Palestinians, including in the West Bank, as well as their discriminatory outcome. Additionally, the current constitutional and legal framework in Israel provides very few possibilities, if any, for Palestinians to seek compensation and reparations.

In the light of the information it reviewed and its analysis, the Mission concludes that there are serious doubts about the willingness of Israel to carry out genuine investigations in an impartial, independent, prompt and effective way as required by international law. The Mission is also of the view that the system presents inherently discriminatory features that make the pursuit of justice for Palestinian victims extremely difficult.

With regard to allegations of violations of international humanitarian law falling within the jurisdiction of responsible Palestinian authorities in Gaza, the Mission finds that these allegations have not been investigated.

The Mission notes that the responsibility to investigate violations of international human rights and humanitarian law, prosecute if appropriate and try perpetrators belongs in the first place to domestic authorities and institutions. This is a legal obligation incumbent on States and State-like entities. However, where domestic authorities are unable or unwilling to comply with this obligation, international justice mechanisms must be activated to prevent impunity.

The Mission believes that, in the circumstances, there is little potential for accountability for serious violations of international humanitarian and human rights law through domestic institutions in Israel and even less in Gaza. The Mission is of the view that long-standing impunity has been a key factor in the perpetuation of violence in the region and in the reoccurrence of violations, as well as in the erosion of confidence among Palestinians and many Israelis concerning prospects for justice and a peaceful solution to the conflict.

The Mission considers that several of the violations referred to in this report amount to grave breaches of the Fourth Geneva Convention. It notes that there is a duty imposed by the Geneva Conventions on all high contracting parties to search for and bring before their courts those responsible for the alleged violations.

The Mission considers that the serious violations of international humanitarian law recounted in this report fall within the subject-matter jurisdiction of the International Criminal Court. The Mission notes that the United Nations Security Council has long recognized the impact of the situation in the Middle East, including the Palestinian question, on international peace and security, and that it regularly considers and reviews this situation. The Mission is persuaded that, in the light of the long-standing nature of the conflict, the frequent and consistent allegations of violations of international humanitarian law against all parties, the apparent increase in intensity of such violations in the recent military operations, and the regrettable possibility of a return to further violence, meaningful and practical steps to end impunity for such violations would offer an effective way to deter such violations recurring in the future. The Mission is of the view that the prosecution of persons responsible for serious violations of international humanitarian law would contribute to ending such violations, to the protection of civilians and to the restoration and maintenance of peace.

CHAPTER XXXI.

RECOMMENDATIONS

The Mission makes the following recommendations related to:

(a)   Accountability for serious violations of international humanitarian law;

(b)   Reparations;

(c)   Serious violations of human rights law;

(d)   The blockade and reconstruction;

(e)   The use of weapons and military procedures;

(f)   The protection of human rights organizations and defenders;

(g)   Follow-up to the Mission's recommendations.

To the Human Rights Council,

(a)   The Mission recommends that the United Nations Human Rights Council should endorse the recommendations contained in this report, take appropriate action to implement them as recommended by the Mission and through other means as it may deem appropriate, and continue to review their implementation in future sessions;

(b)   In view of the gravity of the violations of international human rights and humanitarian law and possible war crimes and crimes against humanity that it has reported, the Mission recommends that the United Nations Human Rights Council should request the United Nations Secretary-General to bring this report to the attention of the United Nations Security Council under Article 99 of the Charter of the United Nations so that the Security Council may consider action according to the Mission's relevant recommendations below;

(c)   The Mission further recommends that the United Nations Human Rights Council should formally submit this report to the Prosecutor of the International Criminal Court;

(d)   The Mission recommends that the Human Rights Council should submit this report to the General Assembly with a request that it should be considered;

(e)   The Mission recommends that the Human Rights Council should bring the Mission's recommendations to the attention of the relevant United Nations human rights treaty bodies so that they may include review of progress in their implementation, as may be relevant to their mandate and procedures, in their periodic review of compliance by Israel with its human rights obligations. The Mission further recommends that the Human Rights Council should consider review of progress as part of its universal periodic review process.

To the United Nations Security Council,

(a)   The Mission recommends that the Security Council should require the Government of Israel, under Article 40 of the Charter of the United Nations:

  (i)   To take all appropriate steps, within a period of three months, to launch appropriate investigations that are independent and in conformity with international standards, into the serious violations of international humanitarian and international human rights law reported by the Mission and any other serious allegations that might come to its attention;

  (ii)   To inform the Security Council, within a further period of three months, of actions taken, or in process of being taken, by the Government of Israel to inquire into, investigate and prosecute such serious violations;

(b)   The Mission further recommends that the Security Council should at the same time establish an independent committee of experts in international humanitarian and human rights law to monitor and report on any domestic legal or other proceedings undertaken by the Government of Israel in relation to the aforesaid investigations. Such committee of experts should report at the end of the six-month period to the Security Council on its assessment of relevant domestic proceedings initiated by the Government of Israel, including their progress, effectiveness and genuineness, so that the Security Council may assess whether appropriate action to ensure justice for victims and accountability for perpetrators has been or is being taken at the domestic level. The Security Council should request the committee to report to it at determined intervals, as may be necessary. The committee should be appropriately supported by the Office of the United Nations High Commissioner for Human Rights;

(c)   The Mission recommends that, upon receipt of the committee's report, the Security Council should consider the situation and, in the absence of good-faith investigations that are independent and in conformity with international standards having been undertaken or being under way within six months of the date of its resolution under Article 40 by the appropriate authorities of the State of Israel, again acting under Chapter VII of the Charter of the United Nations, refer the situation in Gaza to the Prosecutor of the International Criminal Court pursuant to article 13 (b) of the Rome Statute;

(d)   The Mission recommends that the Security Council should require the independent committee of experts referred to in subparagraph (b) to monitor and report on any domestic legal or other proceedings undertaken by the relevant authorities in the Gaza Strip in relation to the aforesaid investigations. The committee should report at the end of the six-month period to the Security Council on its assessment of relevant domestic proceedings initiated by the relevant authorities in Gaza, including their progress, effectiveness and genuineness, so that the Security Council may assess whether appropriate action to ensure justice for victims and accountability for perpetrators has been taken or is being taken at the domestic level. The Security Council should request the committee to report to it at determined intervals, as may be necessary;

(e)   The Mission recommends that, upon receipt of the committee's report, the Security Council should consider the situation and, in the absence of good-faith investigations that are independent and in conformity with international standards having been undertaken or being under way within six months of the date of its resolution under Article 40 by the appropriate authorities in Gaza, acting under Chapter VII of the Charter of the United Nations, refer the situation in Gaza to the Prosecutor of the International Criminal Court pursuant to article 13 (b) of the Rome Statute;

(f)   The Mission recommends that lack of cooperation by the Government of Israel or the Gaza authorities with the work of the committee should be regarded by the Security Council to be obstruction of the work of the committee.

To the Prosecutor of the International Criminal Court, with reference to the declaration under article 12 (3) received by the Office of the Prosecutor of the International Criminal Court from the Government of Palestine, the Mission considers that accountability for victims and the interests of peace and justice in the region require that the Prosecutor should make the required legal determination as expeditiously as possible.

To the General Assembly,

(a)   The Mission recommends that the General Assembly should request the Security Council to report to it on measures taken with regard to ensuring accountability for serious violations of international humanitarian law and human rights in relation to the facts in this report and any other relevant facts in the context of the military operations in Gaza, including the implementation of the Mission's recommendations. The General Assembly may remain [apprised] of the matter until it is satisfied that appropriate action is taken at the domestic or international level in order to ensure justice for victims and accountability for perpetrators. The General Assembly may consider whether additional action within its powers is required in the interests of justice, including under its resolution 377 (V) on uniting for peace;

(b)   The Mission recommends that the General Assembly should establish an escrow fund to be used to pay adequate compensation to Palestinians who have suffered loss and damage as a result of unlawful acts attributable to Israel during the December–January military operation and actions in connection with it, and that the Government of Israel should pay the required amounts into such fund. The Mission further recommends that the General Assembly should ask the Office of the United Nations High Commissioner for Human Rights to provide expert advice on the appropriate modalities to establish the escrow fund;

(c)   The Mission recommends that the General Assembly should ask the Government of Switzerland to convene a conference of the high contracting parties to the Fourth Geneva Convention of 1949 on measures to enforce the Convention in the Occupied Palestinian Territory and to ensure its respect in accordance with its article 1;

(d)   The Mission recommends that the General Assembly should promote an urgent discussion on the future legality of the use of certain munitions referred to in this report, and in particular white phosphorous, flechettes and heavy metal such as tungsten. In such discussion the General Assembly should draw, inter alia, on the expertise of the International Committee of the Red Cross (ICRC). The Mission further recommends that the Government of Israel should undertake a moratorium on the use of such weapons in the light of the human suffering and damage they have caused in the Gaza Strip.

To the State of Israel,

(a)   The Mission recommends that Israel should immediately cease the border closures and restrictions on passage through border crossings with the Gaza Strip and allow the passage of goods necessary and sufficient to meet the needs of the population, for the recovery and reconstruction of housing and essential services, and for the resumption of meaningful economic activity in the Gaza Strip;

(b)   The Mission recommends that Israel should cease the restrictions on access to the sea for fishing purposes imposed on the Gaza Strip and allow such fishing activities within the 20 nautical miles as provided for in the Oslo Accords. It further recommends that Israel should allow the resumption of agricultural activity within the Gaza Strip, including within areas in the vicinity of the borders with Israel;

(c)   Israel should initiate a review of the rules of engagement, standard operating procedures, open-fire regulations and other guidance for military and security personnel. The Mission recommends that Israel should avail itself of the expertise of the International Committee of the Red Cross, the Office of the United Nations High Commissioner for Human Rights and other relevant bodies, and Israeli experts, civil society organizations with the relevant expertise and specialization, in order to ensure compliance in this respect with international humanitarian law and international human rights law. In particular such rules of engagement should ensure that the principles of proportionality, distinction, precaution and non-discrimination are effectively integrated in all such guidance and in any oral briefings provided to officers, soldiers and security forces, so as to avoid the recurrence of Palestinian civilian deaths, destruction and affronts on human dignity in violation of international law;

(d)   The Mission recommends that Israel should allow freedom of movement for Palestinians within the Occupied Palestinian Territory—within the West Bank, including East Jerusalem, between the Gaza Strip and the West Bank, and between the Occupied Palestinian Territory and the outside world—in accordance with international human rights standards and international commitments entered into by Israel and the representatives of the Palestinian people. The Mission further recommends that Israel should forthwith lift travel bans currently placed on Palestinians by reason of their human rights or political activities;

(e)   The Mission recommends that Israel should release Palestinians who are detained in Israeli prisons in connection with the occupation. The release of children should be an utmost priority. The Mission further recommends that Israel should cease the discriminatory treatment of Palestinian detainees. Family visits for prisoners from Gaza should resume;

(f)   The Mission recommends that Israel should forthwith cease interference with national political processes in the Occupied Palestinian Territory, and as a first step release all members of the Palestinian Legislative Council currently in detention and allow all members of the Council to move between Gaza and the West Bank so that it may resume functioning;

(g)   The Mission recommends that the Government of Israel should cease actions aimed at limiting the expression of criticism by civil society and members of the public concerning Israel's policies and conduct during the military operations in the Gaza Strip. The Mission also recommends that Israel should set up an independent inquiry to assess whether the treatment by Israeli judicial authorities of Palestinian and Jewish Israelis expressing dissent in connection with the offensive was discriminatory, in terms of both charges and detention pending trial. The results of the inquiry should be made public and, subject to the findings, appropriate remedial action should be taken;

(h)   The Mission recommends that the Government of Israel should refrain from any action of reprisal against Palestinian and Israeli individuals and organizations that have cooperated with the United Nations Fact-Finding Mission on the Gaza Conflict, in particular individuals who have appeared at the public hearings held by the Mission in Gaza and Geneva and expressed criticism of actions by Israel;

(i)   The Mission recommends that Israel should reiterate its commitment to respecting the inviolability of United Nations premises and personnel and that it should undertake all appropriate measures to ensure that there is no repetition of violations in the future. It further recommends that reparation to the United Nations should be provided fully and without further delay by Israel, and that the General Assembly should consider this matter.

To Palestinian armed groups,

(a)   The Mission recommends that Palestinian armed groups should undertake forthwith to respect international humanitarian law, in particular by renouncing attacks on Israeli civilians and civilian objects, and take all feasible precautionary measures to avoid harm to Palestinian civilians during hostilities;

(b)   The Mission recommends that Palestinian armed groups who hold Israeli soldier Gilad Shalit in detention should release him on humanitarian grounds. Pending such release they should recognize his status as prisoner of war, treat him as such, and allow him ICRC visits.

To responsible Palestinian authorities,

(a)   The Mission recommends that the Palestinian Authority should issue clear instructions to security forces under its command to abide by human rights norms as enshrined in the Palestinian Basic Law and international instruments, ensure prompt and independent investigation of all allegations of serious human rights violations by security forces under its control, and end resort to military justice to deal with cases involving civilians;

(b)   The Mission recommends that the Palestinian Authority and the Gaza authorities should release without delay all political detainees currently in their power and refrain from further arrests on political grounds and in violation of international human rights law;

(c)   The Mission recommends that the Palestinian Authority and the Gaza authorities should continue to enable the free and independent operation of Palestinian non-governmental organizations, including human rights organizations, and of the Independent Commission for Human Rights.

To the international community,

(a)   The Mission recommends that the States parties to the Geneva Conventions of 1949 should start criminal investigations in national courts, using universal jurisdiction, where there is sufficient evidence of the commission of grave breaches of the Geneva Conventions of 1949. Where so warranted following investigation, alleged perpetrators should be arrested and prosecuted in accordance with internationally recognized standards of justice;

(b)   International aid providers should step up financial and technical assistance for organizations providing psychological support and mental health services to the Palestinian population;

(c)   In view of their crucial function, the Mission recommends that donor countries/ assistance providers should continue to support the work of Palestinian and Israeli human rights organizations in documenting and publicly reporting on violations of human rights and international humanitarian law, and advising relevant authorities on their compliance with international law;

(d)   The Mission recommends that States involved in peace negotiations between Israel and representatives of the Palestinian people, especially the Quartet, should ensure that respect for the rule of law, international law and human rights assumes a central role in internationally sponsored peace initiatives;

(e)   In view of the allegations and reports about long-term environmental damage that may have been created by certain munitions or debris from munitions, the Mission recommends that a programme of environmental monitoring should take place under the auspices of the United Nations, for as long as deemed necessary. The programme should include the Gaza Strip and areas within southern Israel close to impact sites. The environmental monitoring programme should be in accordance with the recommendations of an independent body, and samples and analyses should be analysed by one or more independent expert institutions. Such recommendations, at least at the outset, should include measurement mechanisms which address the fears of the population of Gaza and southern Israel at this time and should at a minimum be in a position to determine the presences of heavy metals of all varieties, white phosphorous, tungsten micro-shrapnel and granules and such other chemicals as may be revealed by the investigation.

To the international community and responsible Palestinian authorities,

(a) The Mission recommends that appropriate mechanisms should be established to ensure that the funds pledged by international donors for reconstruction activities in the Gaza Strip are smoothly and efficiently disbursed, and urgently put to use for the benefit of the population of Gaza;

(b) In view of the consequences of the military operations, the Mission recommends that responsible Palestinian authorities as well as international aid providers should pay special attention to the needs of persons with disabilities. In addition, the Mission recommends that medical follow-up should be ensured by relevant international and Palestinian structures with regard to patients who suffered amputations or were otherwise injured by munitions, the nature of which has not been clarified, in order to monitor any possible long-term impact on their health. Financial and technical assistance should be provided to ensure adequate medical follow-up to Palestinian patients.

To the international community, Israel and Palestinian authorities,

(a) The Mission recommends that Israel and representatives of the Palestinian people, and international actors involved in the peace process, should involve Israeli and Palestinian civil society in devising sustainable peace agreements based on respect for international law. The participation of women should be ensured in accordance with Security Council resolution 1325 (2000);

(b) The Mission recommends that attention should be given to the position of women and steps be taken to ensure their access to compensation, legal assistance and economic security.

To the United Nations Secretary-General, the Mission recommends that the Secretary-General should develop a policy to integrate human rights in peace initiatives in which the United Nations is involved, especially the Quartet, and requests the United Nations High Commissioner for Human Rights to provide the expertise required to implement this recommendation.

To the Office of the United Nations High Commissioner for Human Rights,

(a)   The Mission recommends that the Office of the United Nations High Commissioner for Human Rights should monitor the situation of persons who have co-operated with the United Nations Fact-Finding Mission on the Gaza Conflict and periodically update the Human Rights Council through its public reports and in other ways as it may deem appropriate;

(b)   The Mission recommends that the Office of the High Commissioner for Human Rights should give attention to the Mission's recommendations in its periodic reporting on the Occupied Palestinian Territory to the Human Rights Council.

Khaled Abd Rabbo

*Thirty-year-old father of three, describing the death of his
two young daughters in Izbat Abd Rabbo, January 7, 2009*

On the 7th of January at 12:50 P.M., the Israeli army bulldozed our garden and the Israeli tanks were positioned in front of our house. They started yelling at us through the speakers and asked us to leave the house.

So I came out along with my wife and my three children: Suad, 8 years old, Samar, 4 years old, and Amal, 3 years old, and my mother, 60 years old. We were all holding white flags. The Israeli army was stationed right across from our house. So we stood by our entrance and were holding flags, white flags. The tanks were seven meters away from our house. . . . They did not say anything to us. There were two soldiers sitting on top of the tank. One of them was eating chips. The other one was eating chocolate. We were looking at them like, you know, what are we supposed to do, where should we go. . . .

We were surprised because there was all of a sudden a third soldier coming out of the tank and they starting shooting at the children with no reason, no reason, with no explanation, no pretext. My daughter, 3 years old, her stomach was hit and her intestines were coming out. So really I was amazed at how could a soldier be firing at my daughter? So I carried my daughter, 3 years old. She could hardly breathe. Like I said, her stomach was wounded. My other daughter was also wounded in her chest. So I took both of them, Samar and Amal, inside the house. My wife and my mother and my other daughter Suad were still outside. All of a sudden my wife joined me carrying Suad. . . . Her chest was wounded by many bullets. My mother, 60 years old, she was carrying the white flag and she was wounded on her forearm and also in her stomach. So we were all inside the house and we started calling the ICRC, the ambulances, anybody to come and rescue us but nobody came and all of a sudden we heard an ambulance but all of a sudden nothing, silence. But later, we saw that the Israeli soldiers asked the ambulance drivers to come out of the car, to undress, and they bulldozed the ambulance with the tank. . . .

My daughter, Amal, 3 years old, she was dying and at the end of the day she did die. My other daughter, 8 years old, like I said, her chest was riddled with bullets. She passed away. My other daughter, Samar, her back was riddled with bullets. Her back was open. She was not breathing through her nose but through her lungs and she was telling me, "Dad, help, help," and I couldn't do anything. She was thirsty. I was afraid if I gave her any water something would happen. I didn't know what to do. My mother, 60 years old, was also dying. I was helpless. I didn't know what to do for my children. There was my daughter dying in front of me. So I carried her and left the house even if I had to die myself because I couldn't take it anymore. So I carried my daughter and left the house again so that the soldier, he might just as well kill my daughter and kill me myself because I couldn't take it anymore. I couldn't let my children die in front of me.

PART II

The Legacy of the Goldstone Report

1

The Right to Live in Dignity

Raji Sourani

The reality of Israel's offensive on the Gaza Strip is hard to convey; its brutality and horror almost defy belief.

In twenty-three days 1,419 Palestinians were killed.

The overwhelming majority of the dead—1,167 or 82 percent—were civilians, the so-called protected persons of international humanitarian law.

A further 5,300 Palestinians were injured, of whom approximately 2,400 were women and children.

Public and private infrastructure throughout the Gaza Strip was extensively, and deliberately, targeted and destroyed: 2,114 houses were completely destroyed and a further 3,242 rendered uninhabitable, displacing 51,842 individuals; 16,000 additional homes suffered moderate damage; and 6,855 dunums[1] of agricultural land were razed. The direct losses inflicted on the economic sector alone amounted to more than US$300 million.

This was the single most brutal Israeli offensive in the history of the Gaza Strip. On 27 December 2008, 334 Palestinians were killed (321 of them were protected persons: civilians and civilian police forces); this will be remembered as the single bloodiest day in over forty-two years of belligerent occupation. In the apparent implementation of the Dahiya doctrine,[2] Israeli forces deliberately targeted civilians and civilian objects. The Palestinian Centre for Human Rights (PCHR), a nongovernmental organization with headquarters in Gaza City dedicated to protecting human rights, promoting the rule of law, and upholding democratic principles in the Occupied Palestinian Territory, has documented numerous cases in which civilians were shot, or targeted, in circumstances in which there could be no doubt about their status—findings that have been confirmed by other national and international organizations. Israel sought to make life in the Gaza Strip unbearable, to fundamentally erode or remove the necessities of normal life, and thus to deter any future acts of resistance.

As noted by the Report of the United Nations Fact-Finding Mission on the Gaza Conflict, also known as the Goldstone Report:

> It is clear from evidence gathered by the Mission that the destruction of food supply installations, water sanitation systems, concrete factories and residential houses was the result of a deliberate and systematic policy by the Israeli armed forces. It was not carried out because those objects presented a military threat or opportunity, but to make the daily process of living, and dignified living, more difficult for the civilian population. [para. 1891]

For Palestinians, the Goldstone Report represents an acknowledgement of their suffering and of the systematic nature of Israel's illegal actions, not only during the 2008–2009 attacks but also in the months and years leading up to it. An internationally respected jurist was saying to the international community what had been known in the Occupied Palestinian Territory for years but had never been brought up so sharply on the international level.

The fact-finding mission and numerous other national and international organizations found that during the 2008–2009 attacks, Israeli forces systematically violated the laws of war. Documented violations include, but are by no means limited to, grave breaches of the Geneva Conventions such as wilful killing and the extensive destruction of property not justified by military necessity, and war crimes such as intentionally directing attacks against the civilian population, intentionally directing attacks against civilian objects, intentionally directing attacks against United Nations installations, intentionally launching indiscriminate attacks, and the use of human shields.

However, although the scale of the offensive was unprecedented—and few will forget the sight of white phosphorous raining down over Gaza City—it must be emphasized that these crimes have been a consistent feature of Israel's long-standing occupation policy. The offensive on the Gaza Strip was not an anomaly; it was the carefully thought-out and planned manifestation of decades-old, officially sanctioned, and Supreme Court–approved Israeli policy.

When the offensive began at 11:25 A.M. on 27 December 2008, the 1.5 million inhabitants of the Gaza Strip had already been subjected to over a year and a half of Israeli-imposed isolation. In June 2007, following the Hamas takeover, Israel sealed Gaza's borders, closing them to the movement of people—including medical patients—as well as goods. In explicit violation of its international legal obligations, in particular Article 33 of the Fourth Geneva Convention, the State of Israel sought to collectively punish the civilian population of Gaza.

By 27 December, the illegal closure of the Gaza Strip had resulted in the emergence of a man-made, and completely preventable, humanitarian crisis. Hospitals were on the verge of shutting down completely due to a lack of electricity, and patients had to be turned away; food shortages were commonplace; and blackouts and water shortages (along with the contamination that resulted) were widespread.

Today, almost a year and a half after the end of the offensive, the closure is still resolutely in place. Unemployment and poverty rates are among the highest in the world, 85 percent of the population are dependent on food aid, and patients continue to suffer and die as they are denied access to essential treatment unavailable in the Gaza Strip.

The closure regime also prohibits the entry of necessary reconstruction materials. Effectively, the Gaza Strip remains as it was on 18 January 2009. In a daily visual reminder of the offensive's horror, destroyed or semi-destroyed buildings continue to scar the skyline. Unable to rebuild or repair, 20,000 individuals remain homeless. There is not even the concrete with which to construct gravestones.

This is the reality of life in the Gaza Strip. Under the continuing closure, the attainment of fundamental human rights is an impossibility. The right to live in simple human dignity is callously disregarded both by the Occupying Power, Israel, and by an international community that is complicit in the ongoing closure, the siege of the Gaza Strip.

As a human rights organization, we have been reduced to demanding food, medicine, and concrete. We have been reduced to demanding the right to survive, the right to exist.

The reason we have been forced to advocate for such basic humanitarian needs is clear. Looking back over forty-two years of occupation, we find that Israeli policy has been characterized both by systematic violations of international law and by total impunity for these violations. At PCHR we firmly believe that these two characteristics are interrelated and interdependent.

It is a self-evident truth that if the law is to be protected, then it must be enforced. History has shown us, time and again, that as long as individuals are granted impunity, they will continue to violate the law. It is innocent civilians, the "protected persons" of international humanitarian law, who are forced to suffer the horrific consequences.

Not once has Israel been held to account in any meaningful way for its illegal acts. Not once have the State of Israel or senior Israeli officials been investigated or prosecuted in accordance with the demands of international law. Instead, Israel is rewarded with preferential aid and trade agreements, such as the United States' bilateral aid and the European Union–Israel Association Agreement. The result is Israel's continued and escalating violation of international law—as evidenced by the offensive on the Gaza Strip and the ongoing annexation of East Jerusalem—and the continued suffering of innocent Palestinian civilians; since the outbreak of the second intifada in September 2000 alone, 6,566 Palestinians have been killed (4,339 civilians) and at least 20,000 injured.

It is this reality that makes the Report of the United Nations Fact-Finding Mission on the Gaza Conflict so significant. For us, as a Palestinian human rights organization, the overwhelming importance of the Goldstone Report lies not in its findings[3] but in its recommendations, and in particular in their emphasis on accountability.

The report acknowledged that the "prolonged situation of impunity has created a justice crisis in the Occupied Palestinian Territory that warrants action" and, equally, that to "deny modes of accountability reinforces impunity, and tarnishes the credibility of the United Nations and of the international community."

To this end, the Mission made specific, practicable recommendations, accompanied by a timeline for their implementation. These recommendations are cited elsewhere in this book and thus will not be listed in full here; however, their focus on criminal accountability must be emphasized.

The Goldstone Report recommended "that the Security Council should require the Government of Israel, under Article 40 of the Charter of the United Nations:

> (i) To take all appropriate steps, within a period of three months, to launch appropriate investigations that are independent and in conformity with international standards, into the serious violations of international humanitarian and international human rights law reported by the Mission and any other serious allegations that might come to its attention; [para. 1969]

If, after a period of six months, good-faith investigations were not conducted or begun in accordance with international legal standards, the Goldstone Report requested that the Security Council "acting under Chapter VII of the Charter of the United Nations, refer the situation in Gaza to the Prosecutor of the International Criminal Court pursuant to article 13 (b) of the Rome Statute." A similar demand was made of the responsible Palestinian authorities.

These recommendations are appropriate and timely. In light of the subsequent controversy over the report, it must be emphasized that the obligation to investigate in such situations is part of customary international law. The Goldstone Report merely highlighted and reiterated this pressing legal obligation. Additionally, it is a long-standing principle of international law that, if those states with a more traditional jurisdictional connection[4] fail to properly investigate heinous "crimes that shock the conscience of humanity," the international community should investigate and prosecute those responsible for them. This legal principle of universal jurisdiction serves as one of the bases for the International Criminal Court.

However, universal jurisdiction also allows individual states, acting as de facto agents of the international community, to conduct investigations and prosecutions into the commission of international crimes.[5] Indeed, this is a legal obligation, arising from, inter alia, Article 146 of the Fourth Geneva Convention. Realizing the pressing importance of accountability, the Mission also recommended "that the States parties to the Geneva Conventions of 1949 should start criminal investigations in national courts, using universal jurisdiction, where there is sufficient evidence of the commission of grave breaches of the Geneva Conventions of 1949. Where so warranted following investigation, alleged perpetrators should be arrested and prosecuted in accordance with internationally recognized standards of justice." [para. 1975(a)]

The Goldstone Report set a deadline for this process. If credible domestic investigations were not forthcoming six months after the submission of the report, recourse must be had to mechanisms of international justice.

This deadline has now passed.

On 26 February 2010, the UN General Assembly voted to grant Israel and the Palestinians a further five months to conduct investigations. This resolution was later endorsed, on 25 March 2010, by the UN Human Rights Council.

PCHR has extensive experience working within both the Israeli and Palestinian systems, and we have closely monitored all investigations conducted so far. Our research and practical involvement have led us to conclude that genuine investigations and prosecutions are impossible within the current Israeli military and judicial systems.[6] In the language of the International Criminal Court, Israel has proved itself unwilling to genuinely carry out investigations and prosecutions. Likewise, the Palestinian authorities are unable to conduct investigations in accordance with international standards.[7]

Given Israel's unwillingness and the Palestinians' inability to conduct genuine investigations, granting both sides a further five months will likely have little or no positive impact. As noted by the Inter-American Court of Human Rights in *Del*

Caracazo v. Venezuela, investigations that persist for a long time, without those responsible for gross human rights violations being identified or punished, constitute "a situation of serious impunity and . . . a breach of the State's duty." By consistently and unjustifiably deferring resort to mechanisms of international justice, the United Nations risks contributing to, and indeed perpetuating, an already pervasive culture of impunity.

The conflict in Israel and Palestine is one of the most visible in the world, and it receives significant political and media attention. The actions of all parties involved in this arena, whether the UN, the EU, or individual members of the international community, have implications that reverberate throughout the world.

It is imperative that the rule of international law be returned to the forefront of international relations. The law grants explicit—and necessary—protections to civilian populations, and imposes specific rights and obligations on all states. Yet, if the law is to be relevant, if it is to prove capable of protecting innocent civilians, then it must be respected and enforced. I offer the reminder that international law is the product of states; it was written and codified by states. These are obligations that states themselves have agreed to be bound by.

Ultimately, impunity results in a complete disregard for the rule of international law. This outcome is evident in the illegal closure of the Gaza Strip, and in the methods and means of warfare utilized by Israel during last year's offensive on the Gaza Strip. More recently it has been illustrated by Israel's complete disregard for international law in the planning and execution of the attack on the *Mavi Marmara*, one of six boats seeking to bring humanitarian supplies to Gaza. During the early hours of Monday, 31 May 2010, Israeli commandos attacked the boats in international waters, killing 9 civilians and injuring many more. The nature of this act demonstrates how little regard the Israeli government has for its obligations under international law and how confident it is that its actions—no matter how egregious—will have no serious consequences in the international arena.

This crime is the inevitable consequence of systematic impunity. There must finally be accountability for Israel's crimes; otherwise, the international community risks setting yet another precedent showing that Israel will be allowed to act as a state above the law. Equally, and as a matter of urgency, the illegal closure of the Gaza Strip must be lifted in order to end the socioeconomic strangulation of the 1.5 million Palestinians living in the Gaza Strip.

I would argue that if the UN Security Council had acted on the Goldstone Report, if the international community had fulfilled its obligation to enforce international humanitarian law, if the rule of law had been respected, it is almost certain that the unjustifiable bloodshed in the Mediterranean could have been prevented. Had Israel been held accountable for its systematic disregard of Palestinian civilians' dignity and human rights—instead of being rewarded for its violations of international human rights and humanitarian law—it surely would not have dared to violently attack, kill, and injure foreign civilians on a peaceful mission in international waters. Ultimately, the root cause of the crime lies in the continued Israeli occupation and the denial of Palestinians' legitimate right to self-determination.

So far, in the absence of the rule of law, Palestinians have been consigned to the rule of the jungle. They have been denied their basic and inviolable rights, including, perhaps most significantly with respect to this discussion, the right to the equal protection of the law and the right to an effective judicial remedy.

This situation whereby individuals suspected of committing international crimes are granted impunity, free to commit further crimes, cannot be allowed to continue. Nor can human rights and international law continue to be disregarded in the name of "political momentum" or an elusive "peace process." Human rights are rights arising from an individual's humanity; they are not ideals but minimum standards. They are not open for political trading, barter, or negotiation. They are our rights.

International law and human rights are not inimical to peace: They are its central components. Indeed, the consequences of disregarding international law and human rights in the name of politics can be seen in the failure of the Oslo process and the resultant reality in the Occupied Palestinian Territory.

All we ask is that the rule of law be applied, and upheld, equally.

The Goldstone Report concluded "that what happened in just over three weeks at the end of 2008 and the beginning of 2009 was a deliberately disproportionate attack designed to punish, humiliate and terrorize a civilian population, radically diminish its local economic capacity both to work and to provide for itself, and to force upon it an ever increasing sense of dependency and vulnerability."

Without accountability, without enforcement of the rule of law, how can anyone in Gaza ever feel safe again? How can we guarantee that what happened here over twenty-three days in late December 2008 and early January 2009 will not be repeated?

NOTES

1. One dunum is equivalent to about one-quarter of an acre, or 10,764 square feet.

2. Named after the Dahiya quarter of Beirut, a Hezbollah stronghold decimated by Israeli forces in the 2006 Lebanon war, this doctrine is predicated on the removal of the distinction between civilians/civilian objects and legitimate military targets. It entails the

use of disproportionate force to punish and deter civilians from supporting resistance activities.

3. This is not intended to underplay the significance of the findings themselves. Having the previous findings of human rights organizations confirmed by a mission led by a prominent jurist such as Justice Goldstone not only had a significant positive impact in terms of perception but also brought these findings to a much wider audience. Moreover, the Mission had access to information, such as satellite imagery, unavailable to other organizations.

4. Traditionally, jurisdiction can be exercised in the following circumstances: if the accused is a national of the state (nationality), if the alleged crimes occurred on the forum state's territory (territoriality), to protect a state's interests (the protective principle), or if the alleged criminal action harmed a national of the state (the passive personality principle).

5. International crimes include, inter alia, grave breaches of the Geneva Conventions, genocide, crimes against humanity, and torture.

6. For more information, see Palestinian Centre for Human Rights, *Genuinely Unwilling: Israel's Investigations into Violations of International Law Including Crimes Committed During the Offensive on the Gaza Strip, 27 December 2008–18 January 2009*, February 2010.

7. See, Palestinian Centre for Human Rights, *PCHR Expresses Grave Concern Regarding Credibility of Investigations Carried Out in Response to Recommendations of the Goldstone Report*, 5 February 2010, Ref. 06/2010.

2

International Law and the Goldstone Report

Jules Lobel

The Goldstone Report concludes that the Israeli government and the Hamas government in Gaza committed serious violations of widely accepted principles of international law during and before the Gaza war. This chapter will explicate what those basic principles of international law are and why the Goldstone Report found that they had been violated.

The overwhelming thrust of the Goldstone Report is that Israel attacked the civilian population during the Gaza war, including destroying the basic means of sustaining life (from clean water wells to poultry farms), and that these attacks violate two central bodies of international law: international humanitarian law and international human rights law. In violating these two bodies of law, Israel may have committed war crimes and crimes against humanity. The report also criticizes the Hamas government's violations of these basic principles of international law and points out that it, too, may have committed such crimes.

The Goldstone Report's conclusions are neither new nor surprising, and echo those reached by numerous other human rights investigations into the Gaza war. However, they are nonetheless significant since the allegations of war crimes, set forth in a well-documented report by respected international jurists on behalf of a major international body, come with the rare (if remote) possibility of consequences for the perpetrators. Moreover, in drawing a clear connection between Israel's sense of impunity and the historical lack of accountability for its treatment of the Palestinian civilian population, and in invoking the well-established

337

principles of international law, the Goldstone Report's authors have made a powerful bid to hold Israel to the same international standards as have been applied to
other countries.

INTERNATIONAL HUMANITARIAN LAW, HUMAN RIGHTS LAW, AND WAR CRIMES

The Goldstone Report is part of a modern tradition of international efforts to enforce criminal responsibility for war crimes committed during hostilities. The
Nuremburg and Tokyo Tribunals after World War II in which Nazi and Japanese
leaders were prosecuted for war crimes and crimes against humanity were landmark achievements. The Cold War and the resulting deadlock in the United Nations Security Council stymied the development of international criminal tribunals
to enforce accountability for war crimes, and it was not until the breakup of the
former Yugoslavia in the early 1990s that the international community again established an international tribunal to punish atrocities. The tribunal for the former
Yugoslavia was followed by similar tribunals in Rwanda and Sierra Leone (and
Richard Goldstone served as chief prosecutor in the Yugoslavia and Rwanda tribunals). An international tribunal that was set up in Lebanon in 2007 following the
murder of the former prime minister, Rafic Hariri, is still proceeding. Most important, and directly relevant to the Goldstone Mission, over one hundred nations—
albeit neither the United States or Israel—have now ratified the International
Criminal Court, which is a permanent court having jurisdiction over genocide, war
crimes, and crimes against humanity.

These efforts to bring accountability have drawn on two bodies of law: international humanitarian law and human rights law.

International humanitarian law (IHL) is a branch of international law that gov-
erns the conduct of governments or non-state entities during warfare, especially
with respect to civilians. By contrast, international human rights law (IHRL) pro-
tects the fundamental and inalienable rights that a state must give its citizens and
aliens who are under its power during both peacetime and wartime. When the president of the Human Rights Council established the United Nations Fact-Finding
Mission on the Gaza Conflict in April 2009, he charged the Mission with investigating "all violations of international human rights law and international humanitarian law that might have been committed at any time in the context of the
military operations that were conducted in Gaza during the period from 27 December 2008 to 18 January 2009, whether before, during or after."

IHL can be found in treaties ratified by governments, such as the pre–World
War I Hague Regulations, the four post–World War II Geneva Conventions and

the Additional Protocols to the Geneva Conventions, and treaties outlawing particular weapons. In addition to treaties, IHL is found in customary international norms that are universally recognized by governments as binding legal norms. These customary norms are binding even where a government has not ratified a particular treaty; for example, neither Israel nor the United States has ratified the Additional Protocols to the Geneva Conventions, although both have ratified the four Geneva Conventions.

There are two basic, universally recognized IHL principles of both customary and treaty law. The first is what is known as the principle of distinction: that armed forces must distinguish between civilian and military targets and cannot deliberately attack civilians or civilian targets.

The second principle is that of proportionality: that in conducting warfare, military forces may not engage in attacks that will cause a loss of civilian life or property that is excessive or disproportionate to the military gain or advantage to be gained by the attack. The classic example of a disproportionate attack is bombarding a whole town and killing hundreds because one sniper is holed up in a building.

Various other principles flow out of these two, such as the prohibition on collective punishment, which bars retaliation against a civilian population; the requirement that armies take precautionary measures and plan attacks so as to minimize civilian casualties; specific prohibitions on indiscriminate weapons such as chemical weapons; and protections for civilians in occupied territories. The Goldstone Report found that these principles were violated by Israel and that some were violated by Hamas during and before the Gaza war.

Crimes against humanity and human rights law are concepts that are closely related to international humanitarian law and that apply not only during wartime but also in non-warfare situations. Human rights treaties prohibit governments from engaging in activities such as torturing their citizens or aliens whether in peacetime or during a war. Crimes against humanity constitute serious crimes such as murder, torture, rape, or persecution committed either by state or non-state actors, whether in peacetime or wartime, but only where the acts are committed as part of a widespread or systematic attack directed against a civilian population. War crimes are grave breaches of the Geneva Conventions or other serious violations of IHL committed during international or non-international warfare.

DISTINCTION AND PROPORTION

As noted, at the heart of international humanitarian law are two principles: the requirement of a warring party to distinguish between civilian and military targets, and the requirement to attack military targets with proportionate force. Israel was found to have violated both principles during the Gaza conflict.

The overriding finding of the Goldstone Report is that Israel deliberately targeted civilians through everything from attacking medical facilities to polluting the water. The report accepts the Israeli position that war was a just response to Palestinian attacks but says that Israel was required to distinguish between combatants and civilians; as long as people are not actively engaged in hostilities, they are protected persons. Among the civilian targets it enumerates are the Legislative Council building, the prison, police stations (which normally are considered civilian rather than military targets), residential houses, a mosque during evening prayers, and civilians walking in the street. "[T]he repeated failure to distinguish between combatants and civilians appears to have been the result of deliberate guidance issued to soldiers, as described by some of them, and not the result of occasional lapses," the report concludes.[1] The Goldstone Mission was particularly struck by the shelling of the al-Maqadmah mosque on January 3, 2009, because even if Hamas used some mosques to shelter fighters or store weapons (and the Mission found that this was not the case with respect to the al-Maqadmah mosque), there was no reason to attack the mosque during evening prayers when the Mission determined that there were hundreds of people in the mosque, 15 of whom were killed and another 40 wounded.

The attack on the mosque touches on the second principle, proportionality. During Operation Cast Lead, the Mission found that Israel had violated this principle on numerous occasions. Even assuming that some Hamas fighters fought among the population in certain civilian areas, as Israel claimed, the Goldstone Report's authors concluded that attacks on hospitals, UN buildings, police stations, wells, schools, and other structures caused disproportionate and excessive casualties to civilians in relation to the claimed military advantage.

In particular, the report describes an incident on January 6, 2009, in which the Israeli army used mortars to attack a civilian area near a UN school in the Jabaliyah refugee camp at which 1,300 Palestinians had sought refuge. At least 35 Palestinians were killed, and the Mission concluded that it was an excessive, disproportionate attack.[2] Moreover, the Mission determined that the Israelis attacked hospitals and UN buildings without taking proper precautions to ensure that civilians were not killed, and that whatever warnings the Israelis gave were inadequate and ineffective.

The Goldstone Report also criticizes the use of white phosphorus, which causes severe and sometimes untreatable burns. White phosphorus is a weapon that is not as yet prohibited by international law, and Israel claimed that it used the substance in populated areas only as a smoke projectile. However, the report found that despite the general legality of white phosphorus, "the Israeli armed forces were systematically reckless in determining to use white phosphorous in built-up areas and in particular in and around areas of particular importance to civilian health and safety [hospitals]."[3]

The use of white phosphorus was thus one example of "a deliberate policy of disproportionate force aimed not at the enemy but at the 'supporting infrastructure'"—which, in practice, the report concludes, meant the civilian population.[4] As Richard Goldstone himself explained in a later interview, in the context of proportionality, "the government of Israel has not provided any explanation for the bombing of food factories, egg-producing chicken farms and what was the sole flour factory in Gaza. It has not explained why it destroyed or severely damaged thousands of homes. And it has not explained why the bombing on the first day of the military operations of densely populated civilian areas was timed for the busiest time on a weekday when the streets were full of people going about their business."[5]

COLLECTIVE PUNISHMENT

The Goldstone Report's findings on collective punishment are among its most important conclusions. Article 33 of the Fourth Geneva Convention prohibits "collective penalties" against a civilian population. The prohibition on collective punishment derived from the world's experience during World War II when the Nazis often punished a whole town for the acts of a few, leading the world community to conclude that collective punishment constitutes a war crime. In its commentary to the Geneva Conventions, the International Committee of the Red Cross points out that Article 33 prohibits "intimidatory measures to terrorize the population," which "strike at guilty and innocent alike" and "are opposed to all principles based on humanity and justice." Collective punishment is generally recognized as a war crime.

The report concludes that the Israeli conduct of the Gaza war was "part of an overall policy aimed at punishing the Gaza population for its resilience and for its apparent support for Hamas."[6] It found that Israel's military operations had "devastating effects"[7] on the civilian population, and Goldstone said later that he was "shocked" at the number of buildings destroyed.[8] Moreover, the destruction was not accidental or incidental to the Israeli action.

"It is clear from the evidence gathered by the Mission that the destruction of food supply installations, water sanitation systems, concrete factories and residential houses was the result of a deliberate and systematic policy by the Israeli armed forces. It was not carried out because those objects presented a military threat or opportunity, but to make the daily process of living, and dignified living, more difficult for the civilian population."[9] According to the report, "Israel, rather than fighting the Palestinian armed groups operating in Gaza in a targeted way, has chosen to punish the whole Gaza Strip and the population in it with economic, political and military sanctions," an action that clearly constitutes collective punishment as prohibited by Article 33 of the Geneva Convention.[10]

The report also found that the blockade of Gaza constituted collective punishment of civilians as well as a breach of Israel's obligations as an occupying power under Article 55 of the Fourth Geneva Convention to ensure that civilians have access to basic necessities of life such as food and medical supplies.[11] While Israel claims that its withdrawal from Gaza means that it no longer occupies Gaza, the world community rejects that position, as did the Goldstone Report, because the absolute control that Israel maintains over Gaza's airspace, borders, and seacoast renders it effectively still an occupying power (a reality reflected in Israel's May 2010 raid on the humanitarian flotilla headed for Gaza in international waters). Israel's military operations in Gaza thus had to be viewed as part of a continuum that greatly exacerbated the three years of the blockade, denying the civilian population of Gaza access to the "basic necessities of life" as punishment for their support of Hamas.[12] Israel claims that the blockade was a lawful economic sanction similar to economic sanctions imposed by governments and the international community against states supporting terrorism or otherwise violating international law; however, the extreme nature of the blockade, Israel's military and physical control over access into Gaza, and its duties as an occupying power to protect the civilian population led the Mission to conclude that the blockade constituted not a lawful regime of economic sanctions but, rather, collective punishment of an occupied civilian population.

THE USE OF CIVILIANS AS HUMAN SHIELDS

The Goldstone Report found that both sides used civilians as human shields for military activity, though its conclusions were more tentative when it came to Palestinian activities. It criticized the Israeli use of the "Johnnie procedure" in which Israeli soldiers detained Palestinian civilians and then forced them at gunpoint to precede Israeli soldiers during house searches. These actions terrorized and traumatized the Palestinians who were used in this manner and are a violation of Article 28 of the Geneva Conventions, customary IHL, and human rights treaties. While the Israeli government's rules of engagement prohibit using civilians as human shields, and Israel denies that its forces did so in Gaza, Israeli soldiers stated that the practice was carried out with commanders' knowledge and/or approval despite the army's formal ban.[13]

INTERNATIONAL CRIMINAL PROSECUTION

The need to ensure accountability for serious violations of international law led the Goldstone Report's authors to recommend potential prosecutions of Israeli or Hamas officials alleged to have committed war crimes. There are two main devices under international law for doing so.

First, the report recommends possible referral of the allegations to the International Criminal Court (ICC), which has jurisdiction to prosecute war crimes and crimes against humanity. Israel is not a party to the Court, but one important method of initiating a prosecution before the Court that has been undertaken in the past is for the United Nations Security Council to refer a case to the Court prosecutor. Specifically, the report recommends that the Security Council accord Israel and Hamas six months to conduct or at least initiate independent investigations, in conformity with international standards, into the serious violations of international humanitarian and human rights law reported by the Goldstone Mission and, if Israel does not do so, to refer the situation to the prosecutor of the ICC.

Second, the report recommends that under the principle of universal jurisdiction, nations that are parties to the Geneva Conventions initiate criminal investigations in their national courts in cases where there is sufficient evidence that an Israeli official (or, implicitly, a Palestinian official) has committed grave breaches of the Conventions. The universal-jurisdiction principle permits nations to prosecute persons who commit crimes universally recognized as heinous under international law, such as torture, piracy, slave trading, genocide, and war crimes, even if the persons prosecuted are not nationals of that country and did not commit the crime in that nation's territory, under the theory that the crime is of universal concern to the entire world community. The principle of universal jurisdiction is controversial, but it is nonetheless well recognized in international law. It was utilized by Israel to seize former Nazi official Adolph Eichmann in Argentina in 1960 and then prosecute him for war crimes in Israel and by the British House of Lords to support the extradition of former Chilean president Augusto Pinochet in 2000. The Geneva Conventions specifically require all state parties to the Conventions to investigate and prosecute those responsible for committing grave breaches of the Conventions.

THE IMPACT AND LEGACY OF
THE GOLDSTONE REPORT

The Goldstone Report follows in a recent tradition of detailed fact-finding missions that investigate conflicts that have drawn global concern. In this sense the report does not single out Israel. Rather, it demonstrates the importance of prosecuting war crimes, no matter where they occur, as a way of solidifying the growing body of international law that will help to curtail such actions in the future.

The report emphasizes the importance of enforcing international law, given the tormented history of Israel and Palestine. "[L]ong-standing impunity has been a key factor in the perpetuation of violence in the region and in the reoccurrence of violations,"[14] the report says, and this lack of accountability undermines the prospect of peace between Israelis and Palestinians. The report notes that Hamas had not investigated its alleged violations and that the Israeli system of investigation contained "major structural flaws" that rendered its investigations "inconsistent with international standards."[15] The Mission expressed "serious doubts about the willingness of Israel to carry out genuine investigations in an impartial, independent, prompt and effective way as required by international law"[16] and therefore required the Security Council oversight referred to above.[17]

The Goldstone Report's main legacy and impact lie in its effort to create accountability among the actors in one of the longest ongoing conflicts since World War II. By publishing detailed factual and legal findings, it has the potential to undermine the legitimacy accorded Israel's repressive actions and its continuing occupation of Palestinian lands. Most critical is the Mission's focus on the need to break the legal impunity that Israel has long been granted.

As of this writing, in July 2010, the report's chief recommendations have not been acted upon. The U.S. government has, of course, blocked the report's recommendation that the Security Council require Israel to conduct an independent investigation and, if Israel fails to do so, to refer the situation to the ICC prosecutor. Israel and its supporters have denounced the report and sought to negate any impact it might have. As this chapter went to press, Israel announced indictments of a number of officers and soldiers in four incidents during the Gaza conflict, including charges related to a human-shield case as well as a manslaughter charge against a sniper who killed a mother and daughter in a group of women waving white flags. Israel also said it would investigate the al-Maqadmah mosque attack. But this response falls far short. Israel has not done what the United Nations Human Rights Council and long-standing principles of international law require— conduct an independent, transparent investigation into the allegations of the Goldstone Report. Instead it has relied on a non-public, internal military investigation, which predictably recommended a few indictments of specific incidents without investigating the overall policy that, as determined by the Goldstone Mission, targeted the civilian population.

The report's call for Israel to be held responsible for its actions must be taken up by NGOs and civic organizations around the world, particularly in the United States, whose funding and support of Israel's military actions and occupation permit it to act with impunity. At a minimum, the report and Goldstone's own call for Israel to conduct an independent investigation of the allegations or face prosecution must not be allowed to die, and the U.S. government and Congress should be pressured to condition military and economic support to Israel on such an independent Israeli investigation. The view expressed in the Goldstone Report—that without accountability there can be no real peace in the Middle East—is a vital contribution to the movement to end the Israeli occupation.

NOTES

1. Goldstone Report, para. 1889.

2. Ibid., para. 1922.

3. Ibid., para. 890.

4. Ibid., para. 1886.

5. Richard Goldstone, "Who's Being Unfair?" *The Jerusalem Post*, September 22, 2009.

6. Goldstone Report, para. 1884.

7. Ibid., para. 1881.

8. Interview with Michael Lerner, Tikkun, October 2, 2009, http://www.tikkun.org/article.php/20091002111513371.

9. Goldstone Report, para. 1891.

10. Ibid., paras. 1330–1331.

11. Ibid., paras. 1878, 1331.

12. Ibid., para. 1878.

13. Goldstone Report, para. 1093 (fn. 535) and, generally, paras. 1056–1106.

14. Ibid., para. 1964.

15. Ibid., para. 1959.

16. Ibid., para. 1961.

17. Ibid., para. 1963.

3

The Goldstone Illusion

Moshe Halbertal

I.

In 2000, I was asked by the Israel Defense Forces to join a group of philosophers, lawyers, and generals for the purpose of drafting the army's ethics code. Since then, I have been deeply involved in the analysis of the moral issues that Israel faces in its war on terrorism. I have spent many hours in discussions with soldiers and officers in order to better grasp the dilemmas that they tackle in the field, and in an attempt to help facilitate the internalization of the code of ethics in war. It was no wonder that, when the Goldstone Report on the Gaza war was published, I was keen to read it, with some hope of getting a perspective on Israeli successes or failures in this effort to comprehend war, and to fight it, morally. Unlike many who responded to the report, in praise or in blame, I gave this immensely long document a careful reading.

Let us begin with a sense of the moral stakes. Since the early 1990s, the nature of the military conflict facing Israel has been dramatically shifting. What was mainly a clash between states and armies has turned into a clash between a state and paramilitary terror organizations, Hamas in the south and Hezbollah in the north. This new form of struggle is now called "asymmetrical war." It is defined by an attempt on the part of those groups to erase two basic features of war: the front and the uniform. Hamas militants fight without military uniforms, in ordinary and undistinguishing civilian garb, taking shelter among their own civilian population; and they attack Israeli civilians wherever they are, intentionally and indiscriminately. During the Gaza operation, for example, some Hamas militants embedded in the civilian population did not carry weapons while moving from one position to another. Arms and ammunition had been pre-positioned for them and stored in different houses.

In addressing this vexing issue, the Goldstone Report uses a rather strange formulation: "While reports reviewed by the Mission credibly indicate that members of the Palestinian armed groups were not always dressed in a way that distinguished them from the civilians, the Mission found no evidence that Palestinian combatants mingled with the civilian population with the intention of shielding themselves from the attack." The reader of such a sentence might well wonder what its author means. Did Hamas militants not wear their uniforms because they were inconveniently at the laundry? What other reasons for wearing civilian clothes could they have had, if not for deliberately sheltering themselves among the civilians?

As for the new "front" in asymmetrical warfare, we read in another passage, which is typical of the report's overall biased tone, that, "[o]n the basis of the information it gathered, the Mission finds that there are indications that Palestinian armed groups launched rockets from urban areas. The Mission has not been able to obtain any direct evidence that this was done with the specific intent of shielding the rocket launchers from counterstrikes by the Israeli armed forces." What reason could there possibly be for launching rockets from urban centers, if not shielding those rockets from counterattack? And what is the moral distinction that is purportedly being established here?

By disguising themselves as civilians and by attacking civilians with no uniforms and with no front, these paramilitary terrorist organizations attempt nothing less than to erase the distinction between combatants and noncombatants on both sides of the struggle. Suicide bombers exploded themselves on buses and in restaurants in Tel Aviv, Jerusalem, Haifa, Dimona, Eilat, and many other places. Qassam rockets and Katyushas were fired randomly at various Israeli civilian centers, as far as their range allowed. So the war had no defined place and was waged by unidentified murderers. It justifiably felt like a change in the very nature of warfare. The goal of this momentous transformation was to create a war of all against all and everywhere. It aimed at shifting the Israeli population from a healthy sense of cautious fear attached to a particular place—a border, a security zone—to a generalized panic that has no location. Everywhere and everyone is now regarded as dangerous. This is not paranoia. It has a basis in a new reality, and is the outcome of a new strategic paradigm.

Faced with this unprecedented and deeply perplexing situation, two extreme positions have emerged in Israel. The radical left claims that, since such a struggle necessarily involves the killing of innocent civilians, there is no justifiable way of fighting it. Soldiers ought to refuse to engage in such a war, and the government has only one option, which is to end the occupation. This view is wrong, since Israel has the right and the obligation to protect its citizens, and without providing real security, it will fail also to achieve peace and to put an end to the occupation. The radical right claims that, since Hamas and Hezbollah initiated the targeting of Israeli civilians, and since they take refuge among their own civilians, the responsibility for harming Palestinian civilians during Israel's attempt to defend itself falls upon the Palestinians exclusively. This approach is also wrong. The killing of our civilians does not justify the killing of their civilians. Civilians do not lose their right to life when they are used as shields by Hamas and Hezbollah. In fighting the militants, Israel must do as much as it possibly can do to avoid and minimize harm to civilian life and property.

The aim of the IDF ethics code is to strike a coherent and morally plausible position that provides Israel with the effective tools to protect its citizens and win the war while also setting the proper moral limits that have to be met while legitimately securing its citizens. In debating the code, I heard many times that it imposes constraints upon Israeli action that would limit the capacity of the army to win the battle and to provide security. In fact, the moral constraints and the strategic goals are mutually reinforcing. Radical groups such as Hamas start their struggle with little support from their population, which tends to be more moderate. They increase their base of support cynically, by murdering Israeli civilians and thereby goading Israel into an overreaction (this is not to deny, of course, that Israel can choose not to overreact) in a way that ends up causing suffering to the Palestinian civilians among whom the militants take shelter. The death and the suffering of the civilian Palestinian population, in the short run, is a part of the Hamas strategy, since it increases the sympathy of the population with the movement's aims. An Israeli overreaction also leads to the shattering of Israel's moral legitimacy in its own struggle. In a democratic society with a citizen's army, any erosion of the ethical foundation of its soldiers and its citizens is of immense political and strategic consequence.

And so, Israel's goal in its struggle with Hamas and Hezbollah is to reverse their attempt to strengthen themselves politically by means of their morally bankrupt strategy. Rather than being drawn into a war of all against all and everywhere, Israel has sought to isolate the militants from their environment: to mark them and "clothe" them with a uniform, and to force them to a definite front. The moral restraints in this case are of great strategic value. I am convinced, for this reason, that targeted killing, especially of the militants' leadership, is an effective and legitimate endeavor. It is for this same reason that I believe that Israel's siege of Gaza, and its harsh effect upon general civilian life, is morally problematic and strategically counterproductive.

II.

In accordance with the just-war tradition in Western history and philosophy, three principles are articulated in the IDF code concerning moral behavior in war. The first is the principle of necessity. It requires that force be used solely for the purposes of accomplishing the mission. If, for example, a soldier has to break down the door of a home in order to search for a suspected terrorist, he has no right to smash the TV set on his way in: Such gratuitous use of force has no relation to the mission. This is a straightforward principle, professionally and morally, though its implementation might be complicated if the mission is not well-articulated or if there are serious arguments about what kind of force is necessary to accomplish a given mission. In ordinary war, the collapse of the enemy's army is a more or less clear event; but in an asymmetrical war, victory is never final—the mission seems not so much to end as to shift; and so it may be difficult to apply the necessity principle.

The second principle articulated in the code is the principle of distinction. It is an absolute prohibition on the intentional targeting of noncombatants. The intentional killing of innocent civilians is prohibited even in cases where such a policy might be effective in stopping terrorism. At the height of the violence in 2002, some suggested that the only deterrence against suicide bombers who wish to die anyway is the killing of their families. But such a policy is blatantly murderous, and it is prohibited. An Israeli soldier is prohibited from intentionally targeting noncombatants, and, in the event that he is given such an order, he must refuse it. He is obligated to engage in fighting only those who threaten his fellow soldiers and civilians.

The implementation of the principle of distinction is also very difficult in an asymmetrical war. Since the enemy does not appear in uniform and there is no specified zone that can be described as the battlefield, the question of who is a combatant becomes crucial. In the process of identifying combatants, a whole causal chain must be established and marked as a legitimate target. This "food chain" of terrorism is made up of people whose intentional actions, one after the other, will end up threatening Israeli civilians or soldiers. This chain includes the one who plans the attack, the one who recruits the bomber, the one who prepares the bomb, the driver of the car that transports the bomber to his or her target, and so on. It is clear that such an attempt gives rise to difficult cases, and even the most scrupulous effort will leave some room for doubt. What about the financer of the bombing, for example?

It is also clear that applying the international law of war to this new battlefield is fraught with problems. Consider a painful issue that comes up in the Goldstone Report—the matter of the Gaza police force. In the first minutes of the war, Israel targeted Hamas police, killing dozens. There is no question that, in an ordinary war, a police force that is dedicated to keeping the civilian peace is not a military target. The report therefore blames Israel for an intentional targeting of noncombatants. But such a charge is only valid concerning a war against a state with a clear and defined military institution, one that therefore practices a clear division of labor between the police and the army. What happens in semi-states that do not have an institutionalized army, whose armed forces are a militia loyal to the movement or party that seized power? In such situations, the police force might be just a way of putting combatants on the payroll of the state, while basically assigning them clear military roles. Israeli intelligence claims that it has clear proof that this was the case in Gaza. This is certainly something that Israel will have to clarify. But it is clear to me that Goldstone's accusation that targeting of the police forces automatically constitutes an attack on noncombatants represents a gross misunderstanding of the nature of such a conflict.

The third principle, the most difficult of all, is the principle of proportionality, or the principle of avoidance. Its subject is the situation in which, while targeting combatants, it is foreseeable that noncombatants will be killed collaterally. In such a case, a proportionality test has to be enacted, according to which the foreseeable collateral death of civilians will be proportionate to the military advantage that will be achieved by eliminating the target. If an enemy sniper is situated on a roof, and 60 civilians live under the roof, and the only way to kill the sniper is to bomb the roof, which is to say, bomb the house, such bombing is prohibited. The military advantage in eliminating the sniper is disproportionate to the probable cost of civilian life.

In discussing the proportionality constraint, there emerges a natural pressure to provide an exact criterion for measuring the proper ratio between collateral deaths and military advantage. I must admit that I do not know the formula for such a precise calculation, and I do not believe that a clear-cut numerical rule can be established. Different people have different intuitions about strategic value and moral cost. And yet, the Israeli army has traditions and precedents that can be relied upon. In 2002, for example, Israel bombed the Gazan home of Salah Shehadeh, who was one of the main Hamas operatives responsible for the deaths of many Israeli civilians. Fourteen innocent people were killed along with Shehadeh. The Israeli chief of staff, Moshe Yaalon, claimed that the collateral deaths were not only unintentional, they were not even foreseeable. The innocent people who were killed lived in shacks in the backyard of the building, which, in aerial photographs, looked like storage units. Yaalon claimed that, had Israel known about this collateral harm, it would not have bombed Shehadeh's hiding place. It had already aborted such an operation a few times because of concern with foreseeable civilian death. I believe that such care is right. It is better to err on the side of over-cautiousness concerning collateral damage.

Besides the difficulties that are raised by the proportionality test, there is a far greater and more momentous issue at stake in the principle of avoidance. The IDF code states that soldiers have to do their utmost to avoid the harming of civilians. This principle states that it is not enough not to intend to kill civilians while attacking legitimate targets. A deliberate effort has to be made not to harm them. If such an active, positive effort to avoid civilian harm is not taken, in what serious way can the claim be made that the foreseeable death was unintended? After all, the death occurred, and could have been expected to occur. So the proper ammunition has to be chosen to minimize innocent deaths; and, if another opportunity is expected to arise for eliminating the target, the operation must be aborted or delayed. Civilians have to be warned ahead of time to move from the area of operation if this is possible, and units have to be well aware that they must operate with caution, even after warning has been given, since not all civilians are quick to move. A leaflet dropped from the sky warning of an attack does not matter to the people— the sick, the old, the poor—who are not immediately mobile.

In line with such principles, the Israeli Air Force developed the following tactic. Since Hamas hides its headquarters and ammunition storage facilities inside civilian residential areas, the Israeli army calls the residents' telephones or cell phones, asking them to move immediately out of the house because an attack is imminent. But Hamas, in reaction to such calls, brings the innocent residents up to the roof, so as to protect the target from an attack, knowing that, as a rule, the Israeli army films the target with an unmanned drone and will avoid attacking the civilians on the roof. In response to this tactic, Israel developed a missile that hits the roof without causing any actual harm in order to show the seriousness of its intention. The procedure, called "roof-knocking," causes the civilians to move away before the deadly attack.

It is rather a strange point in the Goldstone Report that this practice, which goes a long way to protect civilians, is actually criticized. Concerning such a practice, the report states that, "if this was meant as a warning shot, it has to be deemed reckless in the extreme." The truth is that this is an admirable and costly effort to avoid civilian collateral harm. As is true with many of its criticisms, the report does not state what the alternative should be. What should Israel do in such a case? Attack the house without calling on its residents to move, or attack it while they are gathered on the roof? Or maybe avoid attacks altogether, allowing the enemy to take effective shelter among civilians?

In the deliberations about the Israeli army's code of military conduct, a crucial question emerged in connection with the requirement that efforts be made to avoid harming civilians. For such efforts surely must include the expectation that soldiers assume some risk to their own lives in order to avoid causing the deaths of civilians. As far as I know, such an expectation is not demanded in international law—but it is demanded in Israel's military code, and this has always been its tradition. In Operation Defensive Shield in 2002, for example, Israeli army units faced a tough battle in the Jenin refugee camp. The army refused to opt for the easy military solution—aerial bombardment of the camp—because it would have resulted in many civilian deaths, and it elected instead to engage in house-to-house combat, losing 23 soldiers in the battle. This norm of taking risks with soldiers' lives in order to avoid civilian deaths came under criticism in Israel, but I believe that it is right. Innocent civilian lives are important enough to obligate such risks. And, if commanders are told that they do not have to assume such risk, then they will shoot at any suspicious person, which will result in widespread killing.

Yet the application of such norms in battle raises difficult moral quandaries. One of them comes up in the Goldstone Report. When the operation started, Hamas militants mostly avoided face-to-face battles with Israeli soldiers. They withdrew into the civilian heartland and fired mortar rockets from within their own population, targeting Israeli units. Mortar locations can be detected by radar, but the crew can move the mortar to a new location in a few minutes, and then fire from there. It is therefore impossible to target these mortars and their crews with a helicopter or in any other way that would provide a direct visual of the target and use accurate ammunition: Such means simply take too much time to deploy. The only option is to fire back with mortars that can be quickly and accurately directed at the coordinates of the mortars on the other side.

The problem with such a tactic is that such mortars are of 120 millimeter caliber and the radius of their hit is 50 meters. This means that collateral damage to civilians might occur while hitting the legitimate target. Of course, the commanding officer can choose not to fire back and put his soldiers at risk from the next rounds of mortar shots. It is important also to note that, when returning fire, the commanding officer cannot know whether there are civilians in that radius and how many of them are there. In "fog of war" conditions, and under pressure to react, such information is not available.

The Goldstone Report claims that the shooting of mortars caused disproportionate collateral harm, which is, of course, an empirical matter; but it is important to understand that this can be known only after the fact. So what to do? My own view is that, if the fire that the unit is taking is not accurate, and if the commander can move his own unit to another location, he should do so rather than fire back and endanger civilians. But this is a very difficult choice, and sometimes this choice might not be available. It is wrong to give the commanding officer a blank check to shoot anytime his soldiers are at probable risk—but he must be given the means of protecting them as well. The Goldstone Report is very critical about the firing of the Israeli mortars, but it does not take seriously into account the problems that such a situation imposes.

It is my impression that the Israeli army in Gaza did not provide clear guidance on the matter of whether soldiers have to assume risk. Some units took risks in the Gaza Strip in order to avoid the collateral killing of civilians, while some units accepted the policy of no risk to soldiers. This does not amount to a war crime, but it is a wrong policy. It also might be a cause of unnecessary civilian deaths: It could inspire a reason for a misguided order to shoot whoever crosses a certain line on the map in proximity to an Israeli unit. Given the fact that anyone in the battle zone could be a militant, and that warnings were given, such an order might make sense—and yet, the order should refer to someone who seems to pose a threat rather than to anyone who crosses the line, since fear and confusion might cause innocent civilians to move too close to the line and even to cross it.

These are not simple issues. They are also not political issues. They are the occasions of deep moral struggle, because they are matters of life and death. If you are looking for an understanding of these issues, or for guidance about them, in the Goldstone Report, you will not find it.

III.

In discussing the code of ethical conduct with Israeli officers, many times I encounter the following complaint: "Do you want to say that, before I open fire, I have to go through all these moral dilemmas and calculations? It will be completely paralyzing. Nobody can fight a war in such a straitjacket!" My answer to them is that the whole point of training is about performing well under pressure without succumbing to paralysis. This is the case with battlefields that have nothing to do with moral concerns. Do I attack from the right or from the left? How do I respond to this new tactic, or to that? And so on. This is why moral considerations have to be an essential part of military training. If there is no time for moral reflection in battle, then moral reflection must be accomplished before battle, and drilled into the soldiers who will have to answer for their actions after battle.

Besides the great difficulty of adjusting the norms of warfare—the principles of necessity, distinction, proportionality, and avoidance—to a non-traditional battle-field without uniforms and without a front, there is still another pedagogical chal-lenge. In a traditional war, the difficult moral choices are made by the political elites and the high command, such as whether to bomb Dresden or to destroy Hi-roshima. But in this new kind of micro-war, every soldier is a kind of commanding officer, a full moral and strategic agent. Every soldier must decide whether the in-dividual standing before him in jeans and sneakers is a combatant or not. What sorts of risks must a soldier assume in order to avoid killing civilians while targeting a seeming combatant? The challenge is to make these rules part of the inner world of each soldier, and this takes more than just formulating the norms and the rules properly. It is for this reason that I looked to the Goldstone Report to learn whether these norms were in fact applied, and in what way Israeli soldiers did or did not succeed in internalizing and acting upon them.

The commission that wrote the report could have performed a great service if it had concentrated on gathering the testimonies from Gaza and assessing them critically, while acknowledging (as it failed to do) that they are partial and incom-plete. This would have forced Israel to investigate various matters, provide answers, and take appropriate measures. (I do not imagine Hamas engaging in such an in-vestigation of its own crimes. This is yet another asymmetry.) But instead the com-mission opted to add to its findings three unnecessary elements: the context of the history that led to the war; its assessment of Israel's strategic goals; and long sections on Israel's occupation of the West Bank. Why should a committee with a mandate to inquire into the operation in Gaza deal with the Israeli-Palestinian conflict at large?

The honest reader of these sections cannot avoid the impression that their ob-jective is to prepare a general indictment of Israel as a predatory state that is geared toward violating human rights all the time. It will naturally follow from such a premise that the Gaza operation was yet another instance of Israel's general wicked behavior. These long sections are the weakest, the most biased, and the most out-rageous in this long document. They are nothing if not political. In Goldstone's ac-count of the history that led to the war, for example, Hamas is basically described as a legitimate party that had the bad luck to clash with Israel. The bloody history of the movement—which, since the beginning of the Oslo Accords, was determined to do everything in its power, including the massacre of civilians, to defeat the peace process—is not mentioned.

The Israeli reader who actually experienced the events at the time remembers vividly that Hamas terrorists murdered Israeli men, women, and children all over Israel while a peace process was underway. Hamas was doing all this in accordance with its religious ideology, which is committed to the destruction of Israel and is fueled by Iranian military and financial support. In the supposed context that the report analyzes, there is no mention of Hamas's role and its ideology as reflected in its extraordinary charter, which calls for the destruction of Israel and the genocidal killing of Jews. In its attempt to stop Hamas's vicious attacks on Israel's citizens, Israel built a long fence—an obstacle to prevent a suicide bomber in Kalkilya from rolling out of bed and driving to the heart of Kfar Saba and Netanya in five or ten minutes. (The distances between life and death are really that short.) The Goldstone Report mentions the fence, of course—but as a great violation of human rights, as motivated sheerly by predatory desires.

Hamas was responsible in many ways for torpedoing the next opportunity for ending Israel's occupation. After the collapse of the Oslo agreement, Ariel Sharon, then the prime minister, decided to withdraw unilaterally from Gaza, in the belief that there was no reliable partner on the Palestinian side and that Israel had to start putting an end to its control of the Palestinian population. Ehud Olmert, Sharon's successor, was elected on a platform that committed him to unilateral withdrawals from the West Bank. But the implementation of this policy of continued Israeli withdrawal was cut short by the unrelenting shelling of Israeli cities and villages from recently vacated Gaza. Such ongoing attacks made Israelis rightly concerned that an evacuation of the West Bank would expose Israel's population centers to such attacks, and the possibility of unilateral evacuation from the West Bank collapsed.

In the last ten years, Israel has withdrawn unilaterally from south Lebanon and Gaza. In both cases, the vacuum was filled by militant Islamic movements religiously committed to the destruction of Israel. Anyone who supports a peaceful two-state solution must ponder the role of Hamas in destroying such a prospect—and yet, quite astonishingly, nothing of this is mentioned in the Goldstone Report. It also avoids mentioning the legitimate concern of Israel about the ongoing rearmament of Hamas in Gaza, which supplies them with more lethal long-range missiles to wreak destruction on Israeli population centers. The commission should not have dealt with the context leading to the war; it should have concentrated on its mandate, which concerned only the Gaza operation. By setting its findings about the Gaza war in a greatly distorted description of the larger historical context, it makes it difficult for Israelis—even of the left, where I include myself—to take its findings seriously.

Then there is the report's conclusion concerning Israel's larger aims in the Gaza war. It claims that Israel's objective in Gaza was a direct and intentional attack on civilian infrastructure and lives: "In reviewing the above incidents the Mission found in every case that the Israeli armed forces had carried out direct intentional strikes against civilians." In another statement, intentional destruction of property and attacks against civilians are lumped together: "Statements by political and military leaders prior to and during the military operations in Gaza leave little doubt that disproportionate destruction and violence against civilians were part of a deliberate policy." Now, there is a huge moral difference between the accusation that Israel did not do enough to minimize collateral civilian death and the claim that Israel targeted civilians intentionally. It might well be that Israel should have done more than it did to minimize collateral deaths—it is a harsh enough claim, and it deserves a thorough examination. But the claim that Israel intentionally targeted civilians as a policy of war is false and slanderous.

There are different accounts of the numbers of civilian deaths in Gaza, and of the ratio between civilian and militant deaths. B'Tselem, the reliable Israeli human rights organization, carefully examined names and lists of people who were killed and came up with the following ratio: Out of the 1,387 people killed in Gaza, for every militant that was killed, three civilians were killed. This ratio—1:3—holds if you include the police force among the civilians; but if you consider the police force as combatants, the ratio comes out to 2:3. There are 1.5 million people in Gaza and around 10,000 Hamas militants, so the ratio of militants to civilians is 1:150. If Israel targeted civilians intentionally, how on earth did it reduce such a ratio to 1:3 or 2:3?

The commission never asks that question, or an even more obvious one. In operating under such conditions—Gaza is an extremely densely populated area—is such a ratio a sign of reckless shooting and targeting? One way to think about this is to compare it with what other civilized armies achieve in the same sort of warfare. I do not have the exact numbers of the ratio of civilian to militant deaths in NATO's war in Afghanistan, but I doubt that it has achieved such a ratio. Is it ten civilians to one combatant, or maybe 20 civilians to one combatant? From various accounts in the press, it certainly seems worse. The number of collateral deaths that are reported concerning the campaign to kill Baitullah Mehsud, one of the main Pakistani militant operatives, is also alarming: In 16 missile strikes in the various failed attempts at killing him, and in the one that eventually killed him (at his father-in-law's house, in the company of his family), between 207 and 321 people were killed. If such were the numbers in Israel in a case of targeted killing, its press and even its public opinion would have been in an uproar.

Besides the 500 civilians who were killed in the bombing of Serbia, how many militants were killed? The inaccurate high-altitude bombings in Serbia, carried out in a manner so as to protect NATO pilots, caused mainly civilian deaths. What would have been the ratio of deaths if NATO forces were fighting not in faraway Afghanistan, but while protecting European citizens from ongoing shelling next to its borders? And there are still more chilling comparisons. If accurate numbers were available from the wars by Russia in Chechnya, the ratio would have been far more devastating to the civilian population. Needless to say, the behavior of the Russian army in Chechnya should hardly serve as a standard for moral scrupulousness—but I cannot avoid adducing this example after reading that Russia voted in the United Nations for the adoption of the UN report on Gaza. (The other human rights luminaries who voted for the Goldstone Report include China and Pakistan.) So what would be a justified proportionality? The Goldstone Report never says. But we may safely conclude that, if the legal and moral standard is current European and American behavior in war, then Israel has done pretty well.

IV.

So a good deal of the outrage that has greeted the Goldstone Report is perfectly justified. And yet its sections devoted to the Gaza war do make claims and cite testimonies that no honest Israeli can ignore. They demand a thorough investigation, and I will enumerate them in their order of severity.

The worst testimonies are of civilian deaths, some of which sound like cold-blooded murders. In the report, such cases amount to a few individual incidents, and they call for criminal investigation of particular soldiers. Was there indeed a killing at close range of a mother and her three daughters carrying white flags? Then there are a few cases of alleged civilian deaths that are the result of the reckless use of firepower. The most disturbing of them is the testimony about the Al-Samouni neighborhood in Gaza City, in which 21 members of a family were killed in an attack on a house. The place and the names are given in the report, and Israel will have to provide answers. Was it a mistake? Were some of the family members Hamas fighters? Did someone shoot at the soldiers from the house? Or was this an act of unjustified homicide?

The testimonies in the Goldstone Report are Palestinian testimonies. They were collected in Gaza, where the watchful eye of Hamas authorities always looms, rendering them vulnerable and partial. Israel chose not to cooperate with the commission, and so the Israeli version of events is not here. It was a mistake on Israel's part not to participate in the inquiry—though, after reading the report, I am more sympathetic to Israel's reluctance. This commission that describes its mission as fact-finding treats the missing Israeli testimonies as if they are Israel's problem, rather than a methodological and empirical shortcoming in the report itself. Whatever one thinks about Israel's refusal to cooperate, the Goldstone Report is still only 452 pages of mostly Palestinian testimony, and this grave limitation must be acknowledged.

Yet the allegations have now been made, and Israeli answers must be given. The next issue that Israel will have to deal with is the use of what the report calls "human shields," which seems to have been an Israeli practice on some occasions. In justifying such a practice, Israeli commanders claim that they forced Palestinian civilians to go to certain homes to warn other civilians before attacking the houses. This might be justified, but the testimonies sound different. They sound as if Israeli soldiers were using civilians to gather information. After attacking a certain building, a civilian was allegedly forced to go and check whether the Hamas militants were dead or not. This is a troubling testimony. Was this done, or not? If it was done, then it is in violation of Israel's own Supreme Court ruling on the matter of human shields.

Other testimonies pertain to the destruction of civilian property. One of the most disturbing is the report of the flattening with bulldozers of the chicken farm at Zeytoun, in which 31,000 chickens were killed. Such destruction, like other reported destructions of agricultural and industrial facilities, does not seem to serve any purpose. The accusation concerning the destruction of civilian property pertains as well to the large-scale destruction of homes. According to the commission, aerial photographs show that, of the total number of homes that were destroyed in two of the hardest-hit neighborhoods, about half were destroyed in the last three days of the operation. If so, then such destruction cannot be justified as in the heat of the battle. It was done to leave a brutal scar as proof of the Israeli presence, as immoral and illegal instruments of deterrence. If this were the case, then reparations should be made to the families whose homes were destroyed.

Next in order of severity comes the bombing of civilian infrastructure. According to the report, the Israeli Air Force bombed the flour mill, the water wells, and the sewage pipes in Gaza. It is possible that the flour mill was strategically located and was used as a perch for snipers or as a launching facility for Qassam rockets fired in the war. This would be the only justification for such a bombing. Israel should now provide its version of these events. If indeed these facilities were attacked as part of a premeditated policy, then this was wrong, and Israel should say so.

I do not see much substance in the complaint against Israel's bombing of the Hamas parliament and other offices while they were empty. A persuasive case can be made that an organization such as Hamas does not have a division of labor between its military and civilian functions. The report's long section on the attack on the prison in Gaza also seems to me a mistaken accusation. The commission notes that only one guard was killed in the bombing, but it blames Israel for endangering the prisoners in attacking a target that has no military use. It did not occur to the commission that Israel attacked the prison to allow Fatah prisoners to escape harsh treatment at the hands of Hamas. (The commission is well-aware that this was the population of the prison.) Some of them did escape, and some were subsequently shot by Hamas militants.

The Goldstone Report as a whole is a terrible document. It is biased and unfair. It offers no help in sorting out the real issues. What methods can Israel—and other countries in similar situations—legitimately apply in the defense of their citizens? To create standards of morality in war that leave a state without the means of legitimate self-protection is politically foolish and morally problematic; but real answers to these real problems cannot be found in the Goldstone Report. What should Israel do when Hezbollah's more lethal and accurate missiles strike the center of Tel Aviv, causing hundreds of civilian deaths? It is a well-known fact that these missiles are in Hezbollah's possession, and, when they are fired, it will be from populated villages in Lebanon.

It is important, for this reason, that Israel respond to the UN report by clarifying the principles that it operated upon in Gaza, thus exposing the limits and the prejudices of the report. A mere denunciation of the report will not suffice. Israel must establish an independent investigation into the concrete allegations that the report makes. By clearing up these issues, by refuting what can be refuted, and by admitting wrongs when wrongs were done, Israel can establish the legitimacy of its self-defense in the next round, as well as honestly deal with its own failures.

4

The Attacks on the Goldstone Report

Jerome Slater

The Israeli-Palestinian conflict is unique: It is hard to think of any other issue in international politics or U.S. foreign policy in which intelligent and generally well-informed people simply refuse to acknowledge crucial, long-established, and irrefutable facts, let alone confront their unmistakable implications. Perhaps the most serious and shocking case in point is the reaction to the investigation and report of the Goldstone Mission, the most detailed and thoroughly documented report on the Israeli attack on Gaza in 2008–2009.

The Goldstone Report has been so relentlessly and bitterly attacked in Israel and the United States that it has become toxic: It was immediately rejected by the Obama administration, and even critics of Israeli policies, such as the leaders of J Street and Americans for Peace Now, have gone out of their way to dissociate themselves from its main findings. In a particularly revealing example of the Do Not Touch Goldstone syndrome, in an acclaimed article in the *New York Review of Books*,[1] Peter Beinart essentially recanted his previously uncritical support of Israel, pointing especially to the findings of Amnesty International, Human Rights Watch, and seven Israeli human rights groups—but not the Goldstone Report.

Readers of this book are surely familiar with the overall findings and conclusions of the Goldstone Mission's 452-page, extraordinarily detailed, and fully sourced report. But a brief summary may be helpful. The Mission estimated that between 1,300 and 1,400 Palestinians were killed in the Israeli attack; it accepted the general assessment of various Israeli and international human rights groups that at least half were civilians, up to 40 percent of whom were women and children. Most of these casualties (as well as the other destruction) were not "collateral damage," the Mission found, but, rather, the consequence of "systematically reckless" and indiscriminate attacks in densely populated areas of Gaza. It concluded that a number of public statements by political and military leaders prior to the attack and Israel's actual behavior during the attack left "little doubt that disproportionate destruction and violence were part of a deliberate policy."

Beyond the direct killings—and leading to outcomes that, in some respects, were even worse—the Israelis intentionally targeted the Gazan economy and the civilian infrastructure and institutions, the very "foundations of civilian life," as the Mission put it. And these infrastructure attacks were preceded by the Israeli blockade or siege of Gaza—interspersed with outright military attacks—that began after Hamas's victory in the Gaza parliamentary elections in early 2006.

The Israeli blockade and military attacks intensified after the complete Hamas takeover of Gaza in June 2007. Then, the Goldstone Report continues, in the course of the 2008–2009 conflict, Israel deliberately engaged in extensive and "wanton" attacks that destroyed private homes, schools, hospitals and ambulances, government institutions and police stations, electrical generation plants, power lines, industrial facilities, fuel depots, sewage plants, water storage tanks, and various food production systems, including orchards, greenhouses, and fishing boats—all "for the specific purpose of denying them for their sustenance to the population of Gaza." These actions, the Mission concluded, "amounted to collective punishment intentionally inflicted by Israel on the people of Gaza."

Taken together, the Mission stated, these Israeli actions, "designed to humiliate and terrorize a civilian population," were "war crimes" under established international law, and "could lead a competent court to find that . . . a crime against humanity has been committed."

THE CRITIQUE OF GOLDSTONE

There is now an extensive literature attacking the Goldstone Report.[2] The major criticisms are the following.

Just Purpose: Self-Defense and "The War on Terrorism"

Alan Dershowitz angrily defends Israel against what he alleges is the real message of the Goldstone Report: that "the Israeli military action in Gaza was motivated not by the defense of its citizens but rather by desire to murder Palestinian civilians." On the contrary, he and other leading critics argue, the Israeli attack on Gaza fully met the just-war requirement of just purpose, for it was a legitimate and necessary act of self-defense, a last resort to stop the Hamas and Islamic Jihad terrorist attacks on Israel. After all, Dershowitz argues, Israel had unilaterally withdrawn from Gaza in 2005, only to be met with unrelenting shelling of Israeli cities and villages, which torpedoed Israel's efforts to promote a peace settlement with the Palestinian people as a whole. Moreover, the argument continues, a political settlement with Hamas is impossible because its goal is the destruction of Israel.

This criticism of the report touches on a broader claim. The Israeli government and many critics, including Dershowitz, contend that by failing to comprehend the nature of modern "asymmetrical warfare," the report undermines the ability of the West to defend itself against Islamic terrorism. In such warfare, the argument goes, the terrorists "use the civilian population as human shields" by refusing to wear uniforms, hiding among the civilians, firing weapons deliberately placed in densely populated areas, and the like. In such circumstances some civilians are bound to be unintentionally killed, but that is the responsibility of Hamas and other terrorists, not of Israel and other Western states.

Just Methods

The Goldstone Mission's conclusion that Israel intentionally targeted civilians was "false and slanderous," the critics charge. Their rebuttal is this:

- The Israeli army is "the most moral army in the world" (the familiar hubristic claim of Israelis, recently echoed by Ehud Barak in his furious rejection of the Goldstone Report), and its military code contains far-reaching prohibitions against attacks on civilians.
- Attacks on property are not the same as attacks on civilians; the two should be sharply distinguished rather than "lumped together," as Moshe Halbertal (an Israeli political philosopher) claims was done by the Goldstone Report. While Israel did attack some civilian property, Halbertal and a few other critics reluctantly concede, it did so to a far lesser degree and with greater military justification than charged by the Mission.
- If Israel had really deliberately killed civilians—or, in Dershowitz's words, intended to "kill as many civilians as possible"—it would have killed far more, and the ratio of civilians-to-activists killed would have been far worse. In a much-cited argument, Halbertal (whose overall attack on the Goldstone Report is the most influential and widely quoted one) calculated this ratio and concluded that fewer than two civilians were killed for every Palestinian combatant—a far better ratio, he asserted, than that of the United States and its allies in Kosovo and Afghanistan, where three or four and sometimes even

ten civilians have been killed for every combatant or terrorist killed in bombing attacks.

The conclusion of the critics is that Israel is the victim of double standards: Only the Jewish state gets charged with war crimes, despite a far better record of avoiding civilian casualties than that of the United States and its various allies in recent conflicts.

THE CRITICISM EVALUATED

Just Cause?

The consensus liberal criticism of the Israeli attack on Gaza is that while Israel's methods were "disproportionate," it had every right to defend itself against Hamas attacks on its territory and population. The Goldstone Mission essentially accepted this assessment, perhaps in the hope that conceding that Israel had the "right" of self-defense would somewhat defuse the firestorm that predictably followed the publication of its report. If so, it did not succeed, and in fact its concession to the wrong-headed consensus has done a great deal of damage to public understanding of the true depths of Israeli war crimes.

The argument of Israel and its defenders is that Hamas attacks following Israel's withdrawal from Gaza left Israel no alternative but to respond with the economic blockade of Gaza and, when that proved to be insufficient, with military force. For several reasons, the argument is wholly unpersuasive.

First, there is a wealth of evidence—much of it from candid statements of high Israeli officials—that the real purpose of the 2005 withdrawal of Jewish settlements in Gaza was to consolidate Israel's continued occupation and ever-expanding settlements in the much more important West Bank and East Jerusalem areas. Accordingly, this limited "withdrawal" did not end the right of Palestinian resistance, for it hardly met the need and the right of the Palestinian people as a whole for a viable and independent state of their own. The Palestinians living in Gaza are not a separate nation from those living in the West Bank and East Jerusalem; to state otherwise is the equivalent of claiming that if in the 1770s the British had withdrawn from New Jersey but continued to occupy the remaining colonies, the residents of New Jersey would no longer have the right to take up arms in support of American independence.

Second, in any case there was no true Israeli "withdrawal," even from Gaza. Israel retained control over its borders, coastline, and airspace; refused to allow Gaza a functioning airport or seaport; continued to control Gaza's electricity, water, and telecommunications networks; and launched a number of military attacks. As the Goldstone Mission put it: Gaza continued to be "effectively occupied" by Israel, and was so regarded by the international community.

Third, Israel had no legitimate recourse to the argument that it used force as a "last resort," for it had refused to negotiate with Hamas to see if an acceptable political settlement could be reached, even though Hamas repeatedly indicated it was amenable to a "truce" that could last ten years or more, and that in all likelihood would become a de facto if not formal settlement of the conflict.

Fourth, on several occasions Israel unilaterally violated ceasefires with Hamas that had ended the organization's attacks on Israeli towns, especially the six-month truce agreed to by both sides in June 2008. Although Israel continued its siege of Gaza, including over food supplies, medicines, fuel, and repair parts for water and sewage systems, Hamas did not retaliate.[3] However, in early November Israel attacked a Gazan tunnel, killing six Hamas men. Following that attack, Hamas fired rockets into southern Israel but announced it would be prepared to renew the truce if Israel agreed to ease its siege. A few weeks later Israel launched its all-out attack on Gaza.

It is true that the Hamas rocket attacks aimed at Israeli towns constituted terrorism, and were considered by the Goldstone Mission to constitute war crimes. Nonetheless, Hamas had a claim to mitigation that was not available to Israel, for Palestinian attacks on Israeli civilians have been primarily a consequence of over forty years of continued Israeli occupation and increasingly cruel repression of the Palestinian people.

Therefore, the argument that Israel had a last-resort right to use force in "self-defense" is entirely unpersuasive, for its obvious alternative was to end the occupation and negotiate a settlement with the Palestinian leadership, including Hamas. Put differently, there can be no right of self-defense when illegitimate and violent repression engenders resistance—and that holds true even when the form of resistance, terrorism, is itself morally wrong. In that light, the Israeli attack was a war crime in and of itself—the crime of aggression—even if its methods of warfare did not also constitute war crimes.

Just Methods?
The "Most Moral Army in the World"?

Whatever the official code of the Israeli armed forces, prior to the attack on Gaza top Israeli military and political officials publicly and repeatedly announced a revised military doctrine that, in the Goldstone Mission's words, "explicitly admits the intentional targeting of civilian targets as part of the Israeli strategy." Subsequent statements by high Israeli officials during the attack, many of which were not even included in the Mission's summary, leave no doubt that (in the Mission's words), Israel regarded "attacks on civilian population and destruction of civilian property [as] legitimate means to achieve [its] military and political objectives."

While it is true that Israel issued warnings to many civilians to leave their homes prior to air attacks, the best response is a letter sent to Halbertal by eight of his former Israeli graduate students, most of them now teaching political philosophy at Israeli universities. They wrote that Halbertal's argument misses the point: "[T]he warning was useless since the residents had nowhere safe to flee to. . . . But in any event merely warning the civilians did not excuse the IDF from adhering to the principle of distinction. A non-combatant does not lose his status because he has not fled his house."[4]

Attacks on Property Are Not the Same as Attacks on People?

In light of the nature of the Israeli attack, the distinction between attacks on people and attacks on "property"—better described as "civilian infrastructure"—is largely meaningless. When homes, medical facilities, electrical systems, sewage treatment facilities, farms and orchards, fishing boats, roads and bridges, and so on are attacked, people suffer and die, even though it takes a little longer than when they are bombed. Indeed, the same holds true for the Israeli blockade, which even in the absence of direct military attacks has been deliberately intended to cause great civilian suffering. No one knows how many premature deaths will result from the blockade and military attacks, but it is certain to be high.

Finally, for the sake of argument let us assume that the distinction between attacks on infrastructure and attacks on people is significant. Was the Israeli attack intended to *directly* kill many civilians—although obviously not "as many as possible"? Without quite saying so explicitly, the Goldstone Mission comes close, concluding that the "deliberately disproportionate" attacks were in furtherance of a policy that was designed to "punish, humiliate, and terrorize a civilian population."

Let us lean over backward to give Israel the benefit of the doubt. So far as I am aware there is no current proof that intentionally killing civilians was part of Israel's strategy in the 2008–2009 attack on Gaza as a matter of state policy; for instance, no one has discovered internal statements by a high-level Israeli political or military leader saying that civilians should be targeted and killed.

That said, the history of Israel's attacks not only on crucial civilian infrastructures but on civilians justifies the suspicion that it did the same in Gaza.

Let me be more specific on this important point. One of the most frequent criticisms of the Goldstone Mission is that it exceeded its mandate, thereby demonstrating bias, because it included a brief discussion of the devastating Israeli attack on Lebanon in 2006. On the contrary, however, there can be no full understanding of the nature and purpose of Israeli policies without including the relevant historical context. Indeed, if anything the Mission *understated* that context: Throughout the course of the Arab-Israeli conflict, Israel has repeatedly engaged in indiscriminate and sometimes even clearly deliberate attacks, not only against the Palestinians but also against Jordanian, Egyptian, and Lebanese civilians. It has done so in order to "enhance its deterrence" (the preferred Israeli euphemism): that is, to intimidate civilians, or punish them for their supposed or actual support of Israel's enemies, and especially to induce them to turn against their own governments or militant organizations.[5]

"Human Shields" and "Asymmetrical Warfare"?

The Goldstone Mission found no evidence to support the widespread charge by Israelis and their supporters that most of the civilian deaths and property damage were a consequence of a deliberate Hamas "human shields" strategy. In its recent 110-page report, Human Rights Watch did find evidence that Hamas "used civilian structures to engage Israeli forces and to store arms." However, HRW did not find that this evidence explained the disproportionate civilian death toll and property destruction. Indeed, it was careful to point out that its conclusion that Israel's "wanton destruction" of civilian infrastructure could be prosecuted as war crimes was based *solely* on detailed case studies showing that Israel continued its "extensive destruction of homes, factories, farms and greenhouses [even though] the fighting had ended prior to Israeli attacks . . . [and] Israeli forces were in control."[6] In short, the "human shields" justification was not available to Israel in such cases.

As for the broader argument about the problems posed to Israel and the West by the supposedly new methods of "asymmetrical warfare," the term is merely the current jargon for age-old guerrilla warfare, in which poorly armed insurgents rise up against much more powerful state armies. Guerrillas, by definition, do not make themselves easy targets. But there's a reason why defenders of Israeli methods prefer the new terminology: It implies that the "asymmetries" somehow give Hamas an unfair advantage. Zeev Sternhell, one of Israel's leading political philosophers, has challenged those who seek to change the rules: "What is it that Israel wants? Permission to fearlessly attack defenseless population centers with planes, tanks and artillery?"[7]

Finally, one would think that indiscriminate and devastating attacks on innocent civilians, their economy, and their crucial institutions would "create more terrorists than it kills," as the unlovely phrase has it, thus undermining rather than facilitating a "war on terrorism."

"Death Ratios" and "Double Standards"?

As noted, the critics argue that if Israel had really deliberately intended to kill civilians, it would have killed far more, and the ratio of civilian to "terrorist" (combatant) deaths would have been far worse. However, neither the Goldstone Mission nor anyone else accused Israel of killing as many civilians as it could. Rather, the charge is that Israel intended to inflict *substantial* civilian destruction, in part to punish Hamas and Palestinian civilians for attacks on Israel, in part to intimidate and deter future acts of Palestinian resistance, and in part to induce the Gazan population to turn against Hamas.

The double-standards charge—Israeli actions were not as bad as those of the United States *et al.* in Serbia or Afghanistan—is no more convincing. In the first place, the argument is a moral non sequitur: You are not absolved from war crimes even if it is true that your crimes were not as bad as someone else's. Secondly, unlike Israel's purposes in Gaza, no one has suggested that the allies deliberately killed civilians, and still less that they sought to colonize and repress the peoples of Serbia and Afghanistan; rather, they had a legitimate just-war argument: humanitarian intervention in Kosovo and, in light of Al Qaeda's presence in Afghanistan, self-defense in Afghanistan.

In Iraq, Afghanistan, and now Pakistan, the killing of civilians clearly undermines the war effort, as openly acknowledged by top U.S. military leaders, who have taken a number of steps intended to minimize them, including those—such as restrictions on the use of air power—that result in greater U.S. casualties. Perhaps even more should be done to minimize civilian destruction. Even so, the contrast with Israeli behavior is stark: The Israeli military has made it clear that it intends to continue its announced strategy of minimizing its own casualties through the massive use of firepower regardless of the consequences for "enemy" civilians. Indeed, there have been reports that influential Israeli strategists believe that in "the next round . . . the only way to be successful is to take much harsher action."[8]

Put differently, in Afghanistan the U.S. generals have acknowledged that even unintended civilian destruction can bring about defeat in an arguably just war, whereas in Gaza deliberate civilian destruction was part of Israel's chosen strategy in a clearly unjust war of aggression, occupation, and repression. Where, then, are the double moral standards?

WAS GOLDSTONE RIGHT?

None of the Goldstone Mission's major factual findings have been successfully refuted. On the contrary, very early in 2009, the nature and consequences of the

Israeli attack were made abundantly clear by many U.S., European, and Israeli journalists. Since then, a number of investigations and reports of international and even Israeli human rights groups have supported Goldstone's findings—among them those of several UN agencies, the Red Cross, CARE, Oxfam, Israeli Physicians for Human Rights, accounts by Israeli soldiers, and—especially—the highly detailed reports of Amnesty International and Human Rights Watch.

The uncontestable facts leave no doubt that the Israeli attack on Gaza constituted a grave war crime. Indeed, by accepting that Israel had a case for self-defense and by failing to include a full discussion of previous Israeli attacks on Palestinian and other Arab civilians and infrastructure, the Goldstone Mission actually understated the full range and import of Israeli criminality.

NOTES

1. Peter Beinart, "The Failure of the American Jewish Establishment," *New York Review of Books*, June 10, 2010.

2. The major criticisms can be found in a number of official Israeli government statements as well as in many other attacks, especially Alan Dershowitz, "The Case Against the Goldstone Report," January 2010, http://www.alandershowitz.com/goldstone.pdf; Dore Gold, "The UN Gaza Report: A Substantive Critique," *Jerusalem Center for Public Affairs*, November 2009; Moshe Halbertal, "The Goldstone Illusion," *New Republic*, November 6, 2009 (reprinted here, pp. 346–359); Asa Kasher, "Operation Cast Lead and the Ethics of Just War," *Azure*, no. 37 (Summer 2009); Michael Oren, "Why the Holocaust Still Matters," *New Republic*, October 6, 2009.

3. It is true that Islamic Jihad, a more radical Muslim group than Hamas, fired a few rockets. However, there is substantial evidence that it did so in defiance of Hamas's wishes; in any case, the Hamas authorities quickly put an end to the Islamic Jihad attacks.

4. Jeremiah Haber, *Magnes Zionist*, January 12, 2010. Haber, the pen name of an Israeli-American political philosopher, translated and summarized the letter.

5. For details, see my "A Perfect Moral Catastrophe: Just War Philosophy and the Israeli Attack on Gaza," *Tikkun*, March–April 2009.

6. "I Lost Everything," *HRW Report*, May 13, 2010.

7. Zeev Sternhell, "With a Conscience That Is Always Clear," *Haaretz*, October 30, 2009.

8. Isabel Kershner, "Tough Military Stance Stirs Little Debate in Israel," *New York Times*, December 25, 2009.

5

The U.S. Congress and
the Goldstone Report

Brian Baird

During Operation Cast Lead—and I hate to call it Operation Cast Lead, it sounds so surgical, and it was everything but—there was a picture of three little Palestinian boys who had been killed lying on a little rug, and the father was just grief-stricken. Those boys were about the same age as my twin boys, and I thought, those could be my kids right there. They posed no threat to anybody, and there they were dead. I decided when I saw the picture that someone should go there as witness to what had happened. I carried the photo with me when I went, and I put a picture of those children up during my floor speech about the Goldstone Report. Someone has to speak up for those children and the hundreds of thousands of children just like them who have no voice here in America.

I read the entire Goldstone Report, front to back, and I read it critically. And after all the flak it had taken, I thought, Well, what am I missing here? I didn't have any beef with it at all. In fact, it was absolutely consistent with everything we had seen and heard in Gaza and in Sderot. I found the report and the conclusions to be fact-based, measured, and completely justified. So when a congressional resolution was put forward attacking the Goldstone Report and urging the administration to "unequivocally block any further consideration in any multilateral forum," I was deeply upset and determined both to speak out in support of the report and against the biased and distorted resolution that attacked it.

The sad paradox was that when the congressional resolution came to the floor, so many of my colleagues spoke with such passion about a report they had never read and a place they had never been. Whereas I had read the report, and I had been to Gaza more times at that point than anybody else in the Congress, and I thought it was a perfectly valid report. And it was very disappointing to hear my colleagues go on and on attacking a perfectly valid report and endorsing a terribly biased, unwarranted, and unwise resolution. One might think that if you take a matter seriously and you have someone who actually knows more about the matter than you do, before you go to the floor of the House and speak about it, you might actually ask them very simple questions: You've been there, what did you see? You've read the report, what did you learn?

Well, that did not happen. I talked to Howard Berman (chairman of the House Foreign Affairs Committee) about the bill, because I was so concerned about it. And Howard and I discussed things a little, but it was always proactive on my part. I proactively went to people and said, You need to know about this. This is what we saw when we were there. This is what I see in the report.

Of the people who went down and spoke with the most passion against the Goldstone Report and for that dreadful resolution, not a single one came to me and had a sincere discussion. The majority leader took fifteen minutes to speak against the resolution. Well, to my knowledge, he never spoke to any of us who had been there.

Whenever I got a chance to talk to a colleague about Gaza and the Goldstone Report, I'd say, First of all, the level of destruction is much more than people have seen on television. There was clearly in my judgment—and I think Goldstone concluded as well—a willful intentional, strategic effort to destroy vast areas of civilian infrastructure, including public facilities, but also private industrial capacity. The entire industrial area was devastated. And we met the people who owned the businesses—one gentleman had a Ph.D. from Ohio State—and they talked about the Israelis coming through with bulldozers and tanks and destroying the buildings long after the area was secured. And we asked Israeli leaders about it and their explanations were completely pitiful. For example, when we asked a very senior Israeli official how it made any strategic sense to destroy civilian economic infrastructure, how that would not be more likely to turn civilians against Israel, the answer was "Gaza is Hamastan," as if that mere statement could justify anything at all. I replied that this reasoning was the opposite of the counterinsurgency strategy the United States had found success with at long last in Iraq. If anything, the Israeli strategy seems to be a "pro-insurgency" plan.

Beyond that, strategically it cannot make sense to have 600,000 young people under the age of fourteen essentially living imprisoned in Gaza, unable to come or go for health, education, or economic activity, and through absolutely no fault of their own. Set aside justice for a moment; it just doesn't make sense strategically to do that because in the long run that's going to come back to bite Israel and the United States as well.

Third, I would talk about the justice aspects—for instance, Goldstone's statements about issues like collective punishment. I will tell you that many of my colleagues, several of them prominent supporters of Israel, literally did not understand either that collective punishment is a war crime or why it is a war crime. I actually heard a very prominent member, whom I will not name, say, "Well it is collective punishment because they elected Hamas and Hamas is a terrorist organization." I said in response to this, Are you aware—you've just accused Israel of a war crime? The member said, "I don't think it is a war crime."

Well, it is. And there are reasons to designate it as such. So there's a profound, ultimately willful ignorance of what was done there—and what continues to be done on a daily basis—and why it was not only wrong and counterproductive but unlawful under international law.

A fourth thing that's important is to dispel people's myths about what was done and why. The most prominent myth is that Nothing at all had worked to stop the rocketing, this was the last straw, Israel finally had to do something. The fact that there was a six-month ceasefire is unknown to almost all my colleagues to this day. The other myth of course is that, Gee, Israel out of the goodness of its heart withdrew from Gaza and immediately got nothing but Qassams and Katyushas. And the whole history of blockading the export of tomatoes and letting the crops get destroyed and not allowing freedom of movement, all of that gets lost.

Also virtually unknown by the American public and, sadly, by many of my colleagues in Congress, is that the Arab peace initiative has called for recognition and normal relations with Israel if there can be a two-state solution with '67 borders, a shared capital in Jerusalem, freedom of movement, etc. So many people seem to believe that the entire Arab and Islamic world wants to wipe Israel out, but the fact is the Arab League and the Islamic Conference have endorsed the plan to do just the reverse if a real and just resolution can be obtained.

Finally, I think it is absolutely essential to communicate to people about the day-to-day indignities, injustices, and dangers that the people of Gaza face. And by the way, I don't limit my concerns to Gaza; I think what's happening in the West Bank and East Jerusalem is horrible as well. I'm friends with Tawfik Nasser, the head of the Augusta Victoria Hospital in Jerusalem, and he tells us of a seven-year-old child who has brain cancer, and after weeks of effort is able to finally get to Augusta Victoria, but not in the company of his parents, only with the maternal grandmother, who is quite sickly herself. The Israelis won't let the parents get out.

I look at my colleagues and say, You know, I will tell you what happens to me if my child dies of cancer and I can't be with him, I'm a terrorist after that point. Some seem shocked by this, but speaking personally, it is probably true for me. I ask my colleagues, how would you deal with having your child die without you there because someone else had blockaded your land and refused to let you out? Maybe you're a better person than me and would not respond with rage. But how do you possibly justify doing this to a child and his or her family?

People come up with rationales for everything though. They say, Hamas turned ambulances into car bombs, that's why the Israelis are so careful. So therefore a completely innocent person can't hold their child's hand while they die of brain cancer? And they seem OK with that, and they don't understand what this is doing to the Palestinian people and the U.S. image internationally.

I want to make a really key distinction. It is easy and tempting to speak about our need to respond differently in Gaza, and for that matter East Jerusalem and the West Bank, solely out of nationalistic geopolitical self-interest. And it goes something like: If we don't treat these people better they will become terrorists and they will come kill us, or it will destabilize the region. I get that.

But here's something much more fundamental than that, and that's the golden rule: You should not do this to human beings. The golden rule needs a corollary, which is, Not only do unto others as you would have them do unto you, but do not allow to be done unto others what you would not want to be done unto yourself, and certainly don't facilitate that. We are absolutely complicit in this. And the young boys and girls who I've seen when I visited Gaza deserve a better future, and so do the parents, the teachers, the mental health professionals, the honest businesspeople, the human rights groups, all of them who are fighting against all odds to keep their children positive, to keep them from wanting to be martyrs, to keep them from getting caught up in the hatred. The Palestinian people are among the best educated in the Arab world, among the most progressive when it comes to women's rights, and they're doing everything they can, and the world at large is turning a blind eye. America is abetting these abuses, and Israel is facilitating them on a daily basis.

Israel has for a long time been one of our leading recipients of foreign military aid. And by the way, many of the bombs and phosphorus shells were U.S.-made. The United States didn't cause an earthquake in Haiti, we didn't cause hunger in pick-your-place. But we are contributing to hunger in Gaza. We are contributing to people living in terrible conditions, and we are contributing to a mafia underground that's going to undermine the social fabric of that society.

And let's be clear, these are not black-and-white issues. Rockets do fall on Sderot, and during the second intifada an awful lot of innocent Israelis, including civilians—women and children—were blown to bits by homicide bombers. There are indeed factions in the region who call for the destruction of Israel and the United States for that matter. We have to go into this honestly and unequivocally condemn all of that. And part of what I have tried to do is to be honest about this, and that is an empowering position: By being honest about the shortcomings of U.S. and Israeli policy, I can simultaneously confront people on the other side. Now it's your turn to renounce the hatred, to defend religious pluralism, to support the rights of women; on and on it goes.

I have long been and continue to be a strong friend of Israel; I have great admiration for much of what Israel has accomplished and for the Israeli people. But I think their policies vis-à-vis Palestine are in many cases unjust by any standard of international justice, and they're counterproductive, most importantly to our own security, which must be my primary concern as a member of Congress, but ultimately I think to Israeli security as well.

People always say, Would you speak out if you were not leaving office? Yes, I have in fact been doing so for years. I went to Gaza in February of 2009, and when I spoke out then, I was still planning to run for reelection.

But this question is in itself a really sad commentary. If there's a belief that members of Congress cannot speak openly about a major international issue of justice and national security unless they're not running for office, because a lobby here in America would make it politically untenable to do so, that is a dangerous but real situation. It doesn't apply to me, but clearly it affects the thinking of many, many, many of my colleagues without any question about it.

Which brings us back to the Goldstone Report. Here was one of the world's most preeminent jurists having the courage and integrity to investigate actions by a country he dearly loves. Justice Goldstone conducted a thorough and objective analysis; criticized all sides where criticism was warranted; went out of his way to get to the facts, in spite of Israeli obstruction of his efforts; then issued a report that, again, having been to the region myself, was an accurate account of what occurred and a valid legal analysis of what was done.

What was the response of our Congress? Rather than standing firm for human rights for all people and for the rule of international law, Congress called for the administration to seek to block any consideration of the report in any multilateral forum. The message this sends to the rest of the world, and especially to the Arab and Muslim world and to the Palestinians in particular, who by the way include a great many Christians as well, is simply awful.

The message all the people of the Middle East receive is that the United States will not stand up for human rights and the rule of international law if it means the State of Israel will be challenged for any of its actions. We do not really want investigations; we do not really believe people of the stature of Justice Goldstone should be listened to unless they agree with us and look uncritically at the actions of our ally.

The damage this does to our standing in the world, to our own security, and, more important still, to the cause of justice itself is terrible. For me, it is not only what Congress did that is so troubling, it is also why and how it was done, with such narrow, biased, and shortsighted understanding of the consequences.

Our nation, our Congress, our foreign policy should be better than this.

6

Palestinian Dispossession and the U.S. Public Sphere

Rashid Khalidi

The Goldstone Report is a landmark in the history of how the Israeli-Arab conflict has been perceived in the American public sphere. Its reception reflects the growing recognition that this is not in any way a symmetrical struggle between equals, and that "for decades the lion's share of power has been in the possession of one side, and the lion's share of suffering has been borne by the other."[1] It involves as well the realization that not only have many more lives been lost on the Palestinian than on the Israeli side (this imbalance reached a 100-to-1 ratio during the onslaught against Gaza in 2008–2009) but also that an entire society has been repeatedly assaulted and fractured.

The Goldstone Report serves these purposes in several ways. In 452 pages it clinically documents the humiliations of Palestinians during the war on Gaza, bringing into international discourse the fears they experienced, the terrors of serving as human shields, the repeated public stripping of male prisoners, the way women were dishonored by being confined to pits for hours with no access to sanitary facilities, and many other assaults on the dignity of the Palestinians caught up in this offensive. It does this while giving full voice to the fears and anger of many Israelis. Perhaps most important, the report has furthered the necessary process of bringing historical awareness and a sense of the importance of international legal standards to the public understanding of this conflict. In its historical sections the report lays out clearly the events that led up to Israel's offensive, thereby shredding the flimsy propaganda pretexts for it. Moreover, since the Gaza Strip is under

Israel's full, de facto control, it is still effectively under Israeli military occupation, and this means that Israel retains its responsibility for protection of the civilian population under the Fourth Geneva Convention. Thus most elements of its siege and blockade, because they inflict collective punishment on that population in order to achieve the political aim of bringing down the Hamas government, with no military justification, may sink to the level of war crimes and possibly even crimes against humanity. This is a serious assertion, especially coming from an esteemed international jurist who has carefully considered war crimes and crimes against humanity in many other areas of the world.

The Goldstone Report could not have been written, and would have had little effect, as recently as a decade ago. The fact that it has had such an impact reflects how the report is both a product of an evolving consciousness and a vital contributor to it. Thanks to this evolution, it has had an unprecedented reception, and that in turn has furthered a growing understanding of the complex interaction between Israel and Palestine.

The only way to truly appreciate the historical impact of the Goldstone Report is to look back on the changing ways that Americans have comprehended the history of the conflict since May 15, 1948. That date marked the establishment of the State of Israel. For Palestinians, it also marks the period in which about half the Arab population of Palestine, over 700,000 souls, were dispossessed and became refugees, and the Palestinians were made stateless. Palestinians call these traumatic events al-Nakba, or the catastrophe.

In the American public sphere, and in the U.S. political arena in particular, for most of these sixty-three years it has been possible to talk only of the Israeli aspect of this dual anniversary. The sole event being marked on May 15 was therefore the seemingly miraculous birth of the State of Israel only three years after the revelation of the Holocaust. Any discussion of the dispossession that these linked events entailed for the Palestinian people was considered by some as evidence of borderline anti-Semitism. It is important to stress that most Americans long knew almost nothing about Palestine except the falsifications that had been foisted on them by decades of propaganda stressing the Biblical roots of the modern Zionist enterprise. Thus, for them, looking at just one side of the coin seemed only right and natural.

This carefully crafted propaganda was the work of seasoned professionals like Edward Gottlieb, one of the founders of the modern public relations industry. In order to "sell" the new Israeli state to the U.S. public, Gottlieb commissioned a successful young novelist and committed Zionist, Leon Uris, to go to Israel and write a book.[2] This was *Exodus: A Novel of Israel*.[3] Gottlieb's gambit succeeded brilliantly: *Exodus* sold as many copies as *Gone with the Wind*, up to that point the greatest best-seller in U.S. history. A large proportion of the false ideas Americans still hold about Palestine—drawn from Uris's images of a heroic, modern David facing a backwards, brutal Arab Goliath—can be traced to this persuasive book and to the popular motion picture of the same name, starring the handsome, young Paul Newman as Ari Ben Canaan.

This process of "selling" Israel has continued unabated since then: Indeed, in addition to being successful as an idea, a national movement, and a colonial settler phenomenon, since its beginnings political Zionism has been a resounding public relations success. Even now we can read online the leaked memos to pro-Israel advocacy groups of top-drawer public relations professionals like Frank Luntz, the foremost pollster for the Republican Party.[4] The systematic hoodwinking of the American public by precisely the same means whereby the Republican Party "sold" the Iraq war—namely, through rehashed myths combined with distorted, cherry-picked facts—is thus still ongoing when it comes to "selling" the Israeli narrative to the American public. In many cases precisely the same people are doing the selling.

However, over the past decade or so the limits of this process of indoctrination have become clear. This is especially the case with the younger generation of Americans, a trend that was already clear to the key figures in the Israel advocacy establishment in 2002, when the Jewish Telegraphic Agency published a remarkable piece entitled "Jewish Groups Coordinate Efforts to Help Students 'Take Back Campus,'" indicating that these groups already felt that U.S. campuses had been lost to them, notwithstanding their previously flourishing *hasbara* (propaganda) efforts.[5] The limits are also evident among a growing segment of the American Jewish community. Most of this largely liberal group is out of step with the aggressively right-wing, hawkish, Likud-oriented, pro-settlement, and pro-occupation leadership that dominates the establishment organizations of the American Jewish community—the American Israel Public Affairs Committee (AIPAC), the Conference of Presidents of Major American Jewish Organizations, the Anti-Defamation League, the American Jewish Committee, the Zionist Organization of America, the AIPAC-founded Washington Institute for Near East Policy,[6] the Israel on Campus Coalition, and others. This growing disenchantment with Israel among liberal American Jews was the main burden of a remarkable article by Peter Beinart in the June 10, 2010, issue of the *New York Review of Books*, which caused a firestorm of criticism from the usual suspects. Over time, however, with the impact of the Gaza aid flotilla fiasco and similar disasters for Israel's image, it has seemed increasingly on target.[7]

Beinart and other analysts have speculated as to what has caused this change, especially among liberal youth, whom he identifies as particularly alienated from the leaders of the American Jewish establishment. One theory is that it is due primarily to the skepticism of the younger generation about the hypocrisy of their elders generally, and of politicians and the media specifically. This can be confirmed—entirely unscientifically—from my own observation that students I encounter at lectures all around the country seem to rely more on *The Daily Show with Jon Stewart* for a serious take on the news than on the cable "news" channels and other mainstream media. Another factor is undoubtedly the accessibility of alternative information and views via the internet, which enables technically savvy young people to compile their own view of the world. In doing so they often rely on sources much closer to events than the mainstream media, including blogs, YouTube, and newspapers and satellite TV stations providing information in English and other languages in the Middle East and elsewhere. All of these sources treated the Goldstone Report entirely differently than did the mainstream press, giving it greater, and more objective, coverage than it would otherwise have had.

For whatever reason, in spite of a barrage of lies and distortions by some of the most accomplished propaganda specialists in human history, the reality of Palestine and its history over the past sixty-three years have managed to make their way into parts of the American public consciousness. I exempt from this discussion the American political sphere, which still lives on in an unreal parallel universe in Washington, vigorously policed by AIPAC and its minions. Even the sober conclusions of the fact-finding Mission headed by Justice Richard Goldstone have not managed to break through into that alternative Bizarro world.

The first reality that has managed to establish itself is that Palestinians are a people, and that they are entitled to national, human, and natural rights like any other. One of the high points in the denial of this obvious and seemingly undeniable fact was Joan Peters's *From Time Immemorial.*[8] This book purported to show that the Palestinian people never existed: that they were just a random assemblage of migrants, vagrants, and castoffs, their numbers inflated by statistical trickery. This assertion is ridiculous to anyone who has seen the many-hundred-years-old stone houses in Palestinian villages dotting the West Bank and Galilee. (Those that are still standing: Over four hundred villages were destroyed by the Israeli authorities after being ethnically cleansed of their population in 1948.[9]) Nevertheless, this compilation of nonsense and wishful thinking was initially believed and endorsed by scholars like S. D. Goitein, Bernard Lewis, and Barbara Tuchman. Only after careful examination of Peters's sources revealed what a complete fraud it was did some of those who had praised it slink away in silence.[10]

Remarkably in view of the continuation of such persistent attempts to deny the very existence of the Palestinian people, over time this reality has come to be acknowledged not just by scholars and academics but by the bulk of the American public, media, and even, belatedly, the political sphere, with several recent presidents affirming it. As this shift was taking place, I examined the origins of modern Palestinian national consciousness in the early twentieth century[11] and found that, like all nationalisms, it was a construct made up of preexisting elements and was in part a reaction to other national groups, including, but not restricted to, the nascent Zionist movement. And like all nationalisms, this construct eventually took on a life of its own. Hardships, traumas, and defeats over nearly a century have only served to solidify this sense of identity. Such an outcome should not have been hard to understand, but many of those who denied the existence of this identity were not amenable to any kind of understanding. Mercifully, in recent years this denial has become reduced to an embittered, shrill minority view.

Another set of realities that have begun to penetrate the curtain of distortion and falsification around Palestine relates to the fact that it is Palestinians, and not Israelis, who are the main victims of the conflict between them. These are very difficult concepts to convey given the fact that for nearly two thousand years in the West, Jews were repeatedly persecuted, often murderously. The resulting deeply felt reality of victimization is important to understand as the soil from which political Zionism emerged, and is the essential background to its success from the end of the nineteenth century through the twentieth century.[12]

This tragic saga is well known in the West, where many explicitly make the connection between the lethal impact of anti-Semitism and the impetus for the creation of Israel.[13] As a result, distinctions between Jewish victimhood in the past, on the one hand, and the current power of the State of Israel and its ongoing victimization of Palestinians, on the other, have been exceedingly hard to make. This is especially the case in light of the Western sense of guilt over millennia of anti-Semitism, culminating in the Holocaust. The deaths of many Jews at the hands of the Nazis would have been preventable had Western countries been willing to give refuge to persecuted Jews between 1933 and the war years when the Final Solution was decided upon. Instead, these countries callously closed their doors to those who might have been saved. One form of expiation of this richly merited sense of guilt for many in the West has been unwavering support for Israel, along with suppression of facts reflecting the suffering inflicted on the Palestinians.

Nevertheless, in recent years a series of specific, shocking events has partly overshadowed this sense of guilt and confronted the Western consciousness with the reality of the actual situation between Palestinians and Israelis. There was extensive media coverage of these events, whose dramatic nature overcame the inherent biases of many journalists. They included the deaths of 17,000 people during the ten-week Israeli siege of Beirut and the subsequent Sabra and Shatila massacres in 1982; the brutal repression of the first Palestinian intifada from 1987 until 1991; Israel's massive attack on Lebanon's infrastructure during the summer of 2006, killing over 1,000 people; and its assault on the Gaza Strip over the winter of 2008–2009.[14] This series of prolonged, vivid, and photogenic crises has slowly overwhelmed the deeply held notion that Israel is the eternal victim of aggression, is not responsible for any of its actions, and is thus justified in doing whatever it does under the rubric of self-defense.

The entire sequence of events also increasingly isolated those who still insisted on repeating the traditional Israeli narrative in the face of undeniable facts, arresting images, and all logic. The impact of this avalanche of changes in perception, crystallized by the Goldstone Report, could be seen in the newfound attention to the siege and blockade of Gaza after the fiasco of the Israeli attack on the humanitarian aid flotilla in May 2010.

There have thus been widening breaches over several decades in a heretofore inviolate discursive wall around the Palestine question. The increasing vulnerability of this previously impregnable citadel helps to explain the escalating ferocity of the attacks by partisans of Israel on journalists who report the truth, on politicians who stray from the orthodoxy prescribed for them by AIPAC, and, especially, on dissidents within the Jewish community who dare to break ranks in public. The latest person to experience this savage treatment was Justice Richard Goldstone. And yet there are many hard truths about Palestine that remain to be communicated.

Whatever the partition of Palestine and the establishment in 1948 of a state for the Jewish people in a country that then had a 65 percent Arab majority did for the Jews—whether it resolved the age-old Jewish Question, created a needed homeland, and helped to make up for the crimes of the Holocaust, or whether it created a conundrum for every Jewish community inside and outside of Palestine that, to this day, has not been fully resolved—its effects on the Palestinians were crystal clear.

The 1947 decision to partition Palestine necessarily and inevitably led to the dispossession of the Palestinian people and the denial of their rights. Nearly half of the population in the area allotted to the Jewish state under the partition plan was Arab, and most of the land in that area was Arab-owned. Only rigorous ethnic cleansing and systematic "legalized" theft of land could have created a Jewish state in these circumstances.

For the plan to partition Palestine and to establish Jewish and Arab states was not meant to rectify the injustices of previous decades against the Palestinians.

These injustices were embodied in the texts of the Balfour Declaration and the League of Nations Mandate for Palestine, which gave national rights to what in 1917 was an 8 percent Jewish minority, but which did not even mention by name— let alone provide national or political rights for—the 92 percent majority of the country's population that was then Arab. These internationally sanctioned documents determined how Palestine was governed by the British until 1948, in favor of the Zionist project and against the will and interests of its indigenous population. Rather than righting this wrong, the partition resolution inflicted a new one by seeking to make up (in small part) at the expense of Palestinians for the terrible harm the West had done to Jews, before, during and after the Holocaust.

Proof that this was all the international community, headed by the United States, intended partition to do can be found in its complete passivity when the Palestinian state was aborted before its birth by a combination of five factors:

1. the crushing of the Palestinians militarily by stronger and better-organized Zionist forces in the months before May 1948;[15]
2. collusion between the nascent Israeli state and Jordan, both of which were firmly opposed to the creation of a Palestinian state;[16]
3. collaboration between Great Britain and Jordan for the same reasons;[17]
4. the disunity and weaknesses of the newly independent Arab states;[18] and
5. the fatal errors and weaknesses of the Palestinians, whom Britain had crushed during their abortive revolt of 1936–1939, when 10 percent of the adult male population had been killed, wounded, imprisoned, or driven out of the country.[19]

Indeed, for the great powers, partition was primarily meant to do one thing: create a Jewish state. A Palestinian state was no more than an afterthought, and indeed none of these powers actually favored its creation. In consequence of all these factors, no Palestinian state came into being in 1948 or afterward. And so the past sixty-three years have witnessed an unbroken sequence of Arab-Israeli wars and attendant regional instability, whose root cause was the unresolved Palestine Question.

It is not as if no one foresaw this outcome. In their internal deliberations, senior U.S. military, intelligence, and diplomatic figures warned not only that an Arab-Israeli war would occur, initiating a serious long-term conflict, but that this result would have fateful consequences for the United States for many years to come. These assessments were presented to President Truman, but were ignored.[20] They were entirely correct, although it took many decades before American policymakers could again publicly voice sentiments indicating that this conflict harmed American interests and hinting that perhaps Israel was a strategic burden rather than an unmitigated blessing for the United States. Today, figures like commander of U.S. forces in Afghanistan General David Petraeus, Chairman of the Joint Chiefs of Staff Admiral Mike Mullen, Secretary of Defense Robert Gates, Vice President Joseph Biden, and President Barack Obama speak openly about the cost to the United States of the continuation of this conflict. Underlying such statements is the unspoken sense that it is Israeli intransigence that is costing the United States "blood and treasure."[21] Indeed, according to the *New York Times*, the belief that Israel is a strategic liability "has gained increased traction in Washington—both inside the Obama administration (including the Pentagon, White House and State Department) and outside."[22] Things have thus come full circle in Washington.

Those within the government who foresaw this from 1947 through the 1960s were scornfully described as "Arabists" in a book of the same name, which conveyed the veiled insinuation that they were upper-class WASP anti-Semites.[23] Their successors have been systematically slandered by pro-Israel partisans.[24] Anyone else in the public sphere who points out the same realities—such as John Mearsheimer, Stephen Walt, the late Tony Judt, or President Jimmy Carter[25]— becomes a target of defamation-mongers like Daniel Pipes, Charles Krauthammer, and Martin Kramer.[26] The calumny is amplified by the echo chamber of Fox News, and by the right-wing blogosphere and talk radio. Now the same has been done to Justice Goldstone.

In the past, just a hint of this sort of treatment was enough to intimidate authors, publishers, lecturers, and university officials. The successful—and highly profitable—publication of best-selling books by Carter and by Mearsheimer and Walt shows that something has changed. The vilification campaigns continue against those who speak up about the oppression of the Palestinian people or challenge the reigning orthodoxy on the unlimited virtue of Israel, but now there is push-back at this bullying and intimidation.

Equally insidious are the attempts to exert external pressure on American university campuses, where significant shifts away from wall-to-wall support for Israel are taking place. These campaigns involve the mobilization of the media, the Israel lobby, and cooperative local politicians. At many universities, these pressures have been successfully resisted, as so far has occurred at Columbia, which was a bellwether for such campaigns at many other American universities.[27] But at DePaul University in the case of Norman Finkelstein, administrators caved in when confronted with the attack-dog methods of his detractors. The record shows that administrators will often not stand up to such powerful outside forces on their own, but that they may feel obliged to do so if faculty and students insist on academic freedom, on faculty responsibility for the curriculum and for promotion and tenure processes, and on insulation of the university from insidious external influences.

In conclusion, although there is reason for short-term pessimism both about the outcome of the political process that determines American Middle East policy and about the situation in Palestine and in Israel, there are signs of encouraging positive trends.

Where Palestine is concerned, they include a growing recognition of how harmful most forms of violence are to the Palestinian cause. Similarly, fewer and fewer Palestinians believe in a negotiating process that is not based on international law and that for nearly twenty years has led directly to the consecration and expansion of Israeli occupation and settlement. Instead, there is a growing appreciation of the importance of nonviolent resistance and of similar efforts by civil society groups in initiating a process involving Palestinians, Israelis, and others that can end the occupation—something that neither endless negotiations nor violent "resistance" have measurably advanced. These trends are linked to the alienation of the population from what are perceived to be the bankrupt approaches of both Fatah and Hamas and the feeble Palestinian authorities they control in Ramallah and Gaza respectively. Also encouraging are the endurance and strength of Palestinian society and the Palestinian economy in the face of difficult circumstances, and the flexibility and resilience of institutions of civil society in taking over leadership of the Palestinian struggle despite the paralysis of the political process.[28]

In Israel and among that country's most intelligent supporters, there is a growing sense (outside the Israeli political process, which is currently dominated by the forces of intransigence and chauvinism) that the status quo of ever-expanding occupation and settlement in the West Bank and East Jerusalem and the siege of Gaza are untenable. Some, including senior Israeli political leaders, two of them former prime ministers, have even argued that continuation of these policies carries the seeds of Israel's destruction. In spite of their bluster, many in the Israeli elite realize that Israel cannot in the long run succeed if young Americans, especially in the Jewish community, no longer swallow the old propaganda and if Israel is increasingly seen by U.S. policymakers as a strategic burden rather than an asset. These are not the assessments of fringe analysts: The head of the Mossad, Meir Dagan, expressed such sentiments to a Knesset committee.[29]

This is not a situation that will change rapidly, however. It took generations to establish the myths Israel was built on, and it will take years to deconstruct them, as well as for the generations who believe in them to lose their influence. If we want these changes to continue, much work will be necessary to confront old prejudices and myths, and to help people to get over their fears of intimidation by the forces that are fighting to maintain the status quo. Because issues related to Israel and Palestine have become intertwined with questions of identity, they must be handled carefully and tactfully. This is hard to do in the cut and thrust of political battle, especially given the desperation of those on the other side who see their hard-won power slowly ebbing away.

It may be a long time before the Goldstone Report's forthright conclusions can be brought before an effective international body, and before we can expect an end to Israeli impunity. But the handwriting is on the wall. The system of domination and control through the calculated use of violence and overwhelming power that has obtained in the occupied territories for over forty-three years, and has maintained the dispossession of the Palestinian people for sixty-three years, cannot be hidden forever. The brilliantly conceived discursive artifice, the citadel of lies, that has concealed all of these crimes for so long is crumbling slowly but surely. Given the acknowledgment by Israeli leaders such as former Prime Ministers Barak and Olmert that continuation of the status quo will lead inevitably to Apartheid and possibly worse,[30] the day is nearing when this status quo will pass. It is up to Israelis and Palestinians in the first instance to dismantle this iniquitous system and put in place one that is more just and more stable. However, Americans and other citizens of the world have a heavy responsibility too, since it is the United States and the international community that have upheld this entire discriminatory structure since its erection, going back at least to the partition resolution of November 29, 1947.

NOTES

1. Daniel Luban, "No Direction Home: Maybe American Liberal Zionism Isn't Worth Saving," *Tablet*, June 3, 2010, http://www.tabletmag.com/news-and-politics/35105/no-direction-home/print/.

2. See Arthur Stevens, *The Persuasion Explosion: Your Guide to the Power and Influence of Contemporary Public Relations* (New York: Acropolis, 1985), pp. 104–105; and Jack Shaheen, *Reel Bad Arabs: How Hollywood Vilifies a People* (New York: Olive Branch Press, 1980).

3. Leon Uris, *Exodus: A Novel of Israel* (New York: Doubleday, 1958).

4. Peter Beinart, "The Failure of the American Jewish Establishment," *New York Review of Books*, http://www.nybooks.com/articles/archives/2010/jun/10/failure-american-jewish-establishment/?pagination=false.

5. Rachel Pomerance, "Jewish Groups Coordinate Efforts to Help Students 'Take Back Campus,'" Jewish Telegraphic Agency, August 28, 2002. Pomerance notes that "pro-Israel professionals from the elite consulting firm, McKinsey & Company, offered pro-bono services" to the Israel on Campus Coalition.

6. The poorly hidden fact that the supposedly "independent" Washington Institute was a creature of the Israel lobby was recently spilled by someone present at its creation, M. J. Rosenberg, then an official of AIPAC; see "The Think Tank AIPAC Built: The Washington Institute for Near East Policy," http://politicalcorrection.org/blog/201004130003.

7. Peter Beinart, "The Failure," *New York Review of Books*, June 10, 2010.

8. Joan Peters, *From Time Immemorial: The Origins of the Arab-Jewish Conflict over Palestine* (New York: Harper & Row, 1984).

9. The best reference on the destroyed villages is Walid Khalidi, ed., *All That Remains: The Palestinian Villages Occupied and Depopulated by Israel in 1948* (Washington, DC: Institute for Palestine Studies, 1992).

10. Just like *Exodus*, this book is still selling briskly: http://www.amazon.com/Time -Immemorial-Arab-Jewish-Conflict-Palestine/dp/0963624202/ref=sr_1_1?ie=UTF8&s =books&qid=1275922991&sr=1-1.

11. In *Palestinian Identity: The Construction of Modern National Consciousness* (New York: Columbia University Press, 1997).

12. See Peter Novick's brilliant book, *The Holocaust in American Life* (New York: Houghton Mifflin, 1999).

13. For an example of how this connection is made, see Wendy Brown, *Regulating Aversion: Tolerance in the Age of Identity and Empire* (Princeton: Princeton University Press, 2006), pp. 107–148.

14. After the Winograd report revealed Israel's PR failures during the offensive against Lebanon, major changes were made in its information strategy in order to "sell" the Gaza attack with a meticulously prepared propaganda barrage; see http://www.ynetnews.com/home/0,7340,L-4752,00.html.

15. Rashid Khalidi, *The Iron Cage: The Story of the Palestinian Struggle for Statehood* (Boston: Beacon Press, 2006), pp. 118–139.

16. Avi Shlaim, *Collusion Across the Jordan: King Abdullah, the Zionist Movement and the Partition of Palestine* (New York: Columbia University Press, 1988).

17. Mary Wilson, *King Abdullah, Britain and the Making of Jordan* (Cambridge: Cambridge University Press, 1987).

18. Eugene Rogan and Avi Shlaim, eds., *The War for Palestine: Rewriting the History of 1948* (Cambridge: Cambridge University Press, 2001).

19. Khalidi, *The Iron Cage*, pp. 107–118.

20. See John Snetsinger, *Truman, the Jewish Vote, and the Creation of Israel* (Palo Alto: Hoover Institution Press, 1974), as well as the chapter on Truman in Michael Suleiman, ed., *U.S. Policy on Palestine from Wilson to Clinton* (Normal, IL: Association of Arab-American University Graduates, 1995).

21. At a press conference on April 13, 2010, President Obama stated that continuation of this conflict "ends up costing us significantly in terms of both blood and treasure." See http://www.whitehouse.gov/the-press-office/press-conference-president-nuclear-security-summit.

22. Helene Cooper, "Washington Asks What to Do About Israel," *New York Times*, June 4, 2010, http://www.nytimes.com/2010/06/06/weekinreview/06cooper.html?scp=1&

sq=helene%20cooper&st=cse. See also Anthony Cordesman, "Israel as a Strategic Liability?" Center for Strategic and International Studies, http://csis.org/publication/israel -strategic-liability.

23. Robert D. Kaplan, *Arabists: The Romance of an American Elite* (New York: Free Press, 1995).

24. One such case was the smear campaign that followed on President Obama's nomination of Charles Freeman to head the National Intelligence Council.

25. See Jimmy Carter, *Palestine: Peace Not Apartheid* (New York: Simon & Schuster, 2007); Jimmy Carter, *We Can Have Peace in the Holy Land: A Plan That Will Work* (New York: Simon & Schuster, 2009); John Mearsheimer and Steven Walt, *The Israel Lobby and U.S. Foreign Policy* (New York: Farrar Straus & Giroux, 2007); and Tony Judt's series of articles in the *New York Review of Books* and elsewhere.

26. The U.S. Institute for Peace responded to Pipes's attacks on it as follows: "These allegations were investigated carefully with credible private individuals and U.S. government agencies and found to be without merit. The public criticism [by Pipes] was found to be based on quotes taken out of context, guilt by association, errors of fact, and innuendo." See E.J. Kessler, "Bush Fails to Re-nominate Scholar Opposed by Muslims and Liberals," *The Forward*, January 10, 2005.

27. Columbia, described by its detractors as "Bir Zeit on the Hudson," may have been chosen because it has several Palestinian-American faculty members and is located in a city with several newspapers devoted to gutter journalism and replete with politicians who leap at every opportunity for Arab-bashing and waving the Israeli flag.

28. See Mouin Rabbani, "Palestine 2010: Time for Plan B," http://al-shabaka.org/policy -brief/politics/palestine-2010-time-plan-b?utm_source=Al-Shabaka%20announce ments&utm_campaign=fd278465fb-Policy_Brief_Announcement%206_08_2010_GA& utm_medium=email.

29. See Meir Dagan, "Mossad Chief: Israel Gradually Becoming Burden on US," www.haaretz.com/news/diplomacy-defense/mossad-chief-israel-gradually-becoming -burden-on-u-s-1.293540.

30. "Olmert to *Haaretz*: Two-State Solution, or Israel Is Done For," *Haaretz*, December 29, 2007, http://www.haaretz.com/news/olmert-to-haaretz-two-state-solution-or-israel -is-done-for-1.234201; "Barak: Make Peace with Palestinians or Face Apartheid," *The Guardian*, February 3, 2010, http://www.guardian.co.uk/world/2010/feb/03/barak-apartheid -palestine-peace.

7

Discrediting Goldstone, Delegitimizing Israel

Henry Siegman

At its heart, the controversy over Judge Richard Goldstone's "Report of the United Nations Fact-Finding Mission on the Gaza Conflict" is not about Goldstone. It's about Israel.

Goldstone and his fellow commission members are human, and therefore fallible, and there may well be legitimate grounds for criticizing some specific aspects of the report. Indeed, an expert panel of distinguished international lawyers who convened at Chatham House, the British think tank, to assess procedural criticisms of the Goldstone Mission identified aspects of the report that contributed to perceptions of bias. Nevertheless, they concluded that "the Report was very far from being invalidated by the criticisms. The Report raised extremely serious issues which had to be addressed. It contained compelling evidence on some incidents."[1]

One need not be an expert, but only possess a decent respect for human life, to conclude that any military operation in which the kill ratio is over 100 Palestinians— mostly civilians—to 1 Israeli soldier requires an immediate, honest, and open investigation to determine the reasons for such vast and tragic a disparity.

That Israel's government did not launch such an investigation on its own is a profoundly saddening indication of its growing indifference to the lives of Palestinian civilians. It constitutes an abandonment of the humanism that was so essential a feature of early Zionism and a betrayal of the most fundamental principles of Judaism. Israel's government demands that its neighbors formally recognize the legitimacy of the state's Jewish identity. But nothing threatens to bring the legitimacy of that identity into greater question than the State of Israel's own behavior—i.e., its seeming indifference to the possibility of the loss of innocent life on so vast a scale as occurred in Operation Cast Lead.

According to the prophets of Israel—invoked in Israel's Declaration of Independence as defining the identity and purposes of the Jewish state—the legitimacy of Jewish existence in Palestine is determined by its adherence to the demands of justice. Isaiah declared God's disdainful rejection of the Israelites' religious observances and, indeed, their very presence in the land if they desecrate its holiness by rampant injustice and oppression. That Hamas, which for years had its suicide bombers target innocent Israeli citizens, has a worse record than Israel is hardly a source of comfort for those who saw the rebirth of Jewish independence as signifying something more than the success of one more nationalist enterprise.[2]

Particularly ugly are efforts by Israel's government to discredit Goldstone personally because of his role as a justice in South Africa's Apartheid government. That role may be one for which Goldstone deserves to be criticized. But Goldstone's past failings tell us nothing about the integrity of his report twenty years later, following his distinguished and widely respected contributions as an international jurist—not to speak of the role he played, at President Mandela's request, in helping guide the transition of South Africa's courts from Apartheid to the rule of law in a democratic society.

And if, as oddly suggested by some members of Netanyahu's government whose own political views are decidedly neo-fascist, Goldstone's role in South Africa's Apartheid government compromised his legitimacy, what legitimacy is left for the State of Israel, which secretly collaborated with that Apartheid government in the 1970s and '80s, supplying it with arms and partnering with it in the development of nuclear technology?

Israel's government has charged Goldstone with failing to examine the history and circumstances that justified Israel's decision to launch the war in Gaza. It is a strange accusation.

First, there was nothing in Goldstone's report to suggest that he and his commission considered Israel's actions in Gaza an unjust war (despite evidence, as indicated below, that war might not have been Israel's only option). To the contrary, the report explicitly affirms Israel's right and obligation to protect its citizens from terrorist violence. Indeed, the very rules of war that the report uses to weigh Israel's actions apply specifically to just wars, not to unjust ones. An unjust war should not be waged at all.

Second, Goldstone pleaded with Prime Minister Netanyahu to allow his commission to visit Sderot, the Israeli city that was relentlessly targeted by Hamas's rockets, so that its residents could be interviewed and their stories included in the report. Netanyahu refused. Indeed, he did not even deign to reply to the request. So the decision to discredit and delegitimize the commission and its chair was made by Netanyahu and his government before the commission had done its work—well before there were any findings that Israel could pass judgment on.

The report does omit one salient set of facts from its discussion of the history and circumstances of Operation Cast Lead. But it is an omission that works to Israel's benefit by failing to explore evidence that might have called the legitimacy of even a less lethal Gaza offensive into question.

The historical background to Israel's Operation Cast Lead is not limited to the rocket assaults on Sderot; that is only part of the story. It must also include the role Israel played from the very outset of the Palestinian elections in 2006, which resulted in Hamas's defeat of Fatah.

For all the talk of Israel as "the only democracy in the Middle East," its government set out to undermine and subvert by violent means the outcome of that democratic election. In collaboration with the Bush administration, it mobilized, armed, and funded the Gaza militia commanded by Muhammad Dahlan, at the time Abu Mazen's security adviser, in order to overthrow the newly elected Hamas government. When this plot failed, as detailed in *Vanity Fair*,[3] and Hamas preempted the Israeli- and U.S.-sponsored putsch, Israel sealed off Gaza with the aim of destroying its economy and impoverishing its population. The expectation was that the suffering it is inflicting on Gaza's civilians would turn them against Hamas.

Israel's claim that Operation Cast Lead was its only way of ending Hamas's assault on Israeli civilians was given the lie by Brigadier General (Res.) Shmuel Zakai, former commander of the Israeli Defense Forces' Gaza division.

As reported in *Haaretz* on December 22, 2008, just five days before Operation Cast Lead, Zakai charged Israel's government with having made a "central error" during the *tahdiyeh*, the six-month period of relative truce between Israel and Hamas. He argued that Israel had failed "to take advantage of the calm to improve, rather than markedly worsen, the economic plight of the Palestinians of the Strip. . . . When you create a tahdiyeh, and the economic pressure on the Strip continues . . . it is obvious that Hamas will try to reach an improved tahdiyeh, and that their way to achieve this is resumed Qassam fire. . . . You cannot just land blows, leave the Palestinians in Gaza in the economic distress they're in, and expect that Hamas will just sit around and do nothing."

The truce, which began in June 2008 and was due for renewal in December, required both parties to refrain from violent action against the other. Hamas had to cease its rocket assaults and prevent the firing of rockets by other groups such as

Islamic Jihad (Israel's intelligence agencies acknowledged that this had been implemented with surprising effectiveness), and Israel had to put a stop to its targeted assassinations and military incursions. This understanding was seriously violated on November 4, when the IDF entered Gaza and killed six members of Hamas. Hamas responded by launching Qassam rockets and Grad missiles. Even so, it offered to extend the truce, but on condition that Israel end its blockade. Israel refused. It could have met its obligation to protect its citizens by agreeing to ease the blockade, but it didn't even try. It cannot be said, therefore, that Israel launched its assault to protect its citizens from rockets. It did so to protect the continuation of its strangulation of Gaza's population.

This, too, is part of the history of Israel's Operation Cast Lead. Its omission from the Goldstone Report no more compromises its findings that both Israel and Hamas are guilty of war crimes and possibly crimes against humanity than the omissions that so distressed Israel's government.

NOTES

1. "Report of an Expert Meeting Which Assessed Procedural Criticisms Made of the UN Fact-Finding Mission on the Gaza Conflict (The Goldstone Report)," Chatham House, November 27, 2009, http://www.chathamhouse.org.uk/files/15572_il271109 summary.pdf.

2. Israeli governments and their supporters, whose moral outrage on this subject gets the better of them, need to be reminded that according to Benny Morris, Israel's preeminent historian of the Jewish struggle for statehood in the '30s and '40s, it was Jewish terrorists who were the first to resort to the targeting of Arab civilians. In *Righteous Victims* (New York: Vintage Books, 2001), Morris writes that the upsurge of Arab terrorism in 1937 "triggered a wave of Irgun bombings against Arab crowds and buses, introducing a new dimension to the conflict." While in the past Arabs had "sniped at cars and pedestrians and occasionally lobbed a grenade, often killing or injuring a few bystanders or passengers," now "for the first time, massive bombs were placed in crowded Arab centers, and dozens of people were indiscriminately murdered and maimed." Morris notes that "this 'innovation' soon found Arab imitators."

3. David Rose, "The Gaza Bombshell," *Vanity Fair*, April 2008.

8

Gaza, Goldstone, and the Movement for Israeli Accountability

Ali Abunimah

For many years, Israel has been losing the carefully cultivated liberal and progressive support in Western countries, especially the United States, that has helped shield it from accountability for crimes against people in Palestine, Lebanon, Syria, and other countries. Israel's attack on Gaza in 2008 and the publication of the Goldstone Report mark a dramatic acceleration in this loss of support, and Israel now faces a global campaign for accountability that cannot be silenced with its usual public relations strategies. Some Israelis perceive this mounting pressure as a crisis of legitimacy so severe it constitutes an "existential threat." For Palestinians and others, it offers hope that justice and a better future are closer.

The day after hijackers flew planes into New York's World Trade Center, the Pentagon, and a field in Pennsylvania killing almost 3,000 people on September 11, 2001, Benjamin Netanyahu was asked what he thought this atrocity meant for relations between Israel and the United States. The once and future Israeli prime minister didn't hesitate: "It's very good," he said, before catching himself and adding, "Well, not very good, but it will generate immediate sympathy" and would "strengthen the bond between our two peoples, because we've experienced terror over so many decades, but the United States has now experienced a massive hemorrhaging of terror."[1]

This set the tone for what became Israel's basic narrative: 'We are under attack not because Palestinians are aggrieved at specific material injustices that can be remedied by among other things withdrawal from territory and respect for their human rights. Rather, we are the first victims of, and the vanguard of Western civilization against, a global Islamofascist threat.' To make the case, Israel and its allies have relied on the demonization, denigration, and misrepresentation of Palestinians as wild-eyed religious fanatics and recast the conflict in religious terms: "Judeo-Christians" on one side, and an alien and threatening monolithic "radical Islam" on the other.

This narrative flourished against the backdrop not only of the September 11 attacks but also the failure of President Bill Clinton's July 2000 Camp David summit and the Palestinian uprising that broke out in response to the violence of Israeli occupation. It reached its pinnacle with the 2006 Israeli war on Lebanon, which President George W. Bush's secretary of state Condoleezza Rice notoriously described as the "birth pangs of a new Middle East." Israel's massive, indiscriminate bombardment of Beirut's densely populated southern suburb—the Dahiya—gave birth to the "Dahiya doctrine," later used in Gaza and described in the Goldstone Report (para. 1191).

The savagery of the Israeli bombardment of Lebanon—and the refusal of the Bush administration in the United States and the government of Tony Blair in the United Kingdom to call for a ceasefire—alienated many people in those countries and around the world, especially as the Israeli action appeared to be a practice run for a potential attack on Iran.[2] Israel's humiliation in Lebanon—despite the horrific levels of death and destruction it caused there—heightened doubts about Israel's value as a "strategic" asset to the United States. Israel may have viewed its attack on Gaza as an opportunity to restore the "deterrence" it lost through its failure in Lebanon. But the publication of the Goldstone Report may in hindsight be seen as a key turning point when its post–September 11 narrative started to falter and even backfire as a new wave of global civic mobilization sought justice and accountability for what happened in Gaza.

By posing the Palestine question in religious-civilizational terms and aligning themselves with the neo-conservative and Christian far-right, Israel and its supporters accelerated a long-term erosion of the liberal and progressive support that formed the bedrock of the U.S.-Israeli relationship and, hence, Western support for Israel more broadly. "For the last generation," the Council on Foreign Relations' Walter Russell Mead has observed, "Israel has been losing popularity and support among some groups of Americans. The shift in sentiment is particularly notable among Democrats, among some of the more liberal mainline churches, among African-Americans and among people with graduate and professional degrees."[3]

What Mead terms "liberal gentile Zionism" peaked in and has been on the decline since 1967—the year of Israel's triumphant conquest of the West Bank including East Jerusalem, the Gaza Strip, Egypt's Sinai Peninsula, and Syria's Golan Heights. Mead attributes this loss of support to factors such as the inexorable rightward shift in Israeli politics; cultural changes within Israel that make it less identifiable as a "Western" state; the transformation of perceptions about Israel from embattled refuge for Jews to aggressive occupier; and, significantly, the realization that the "Arab argument that Israel was a colonial imposition like French Algeria or white South Africa gained plausibility with many people." Taken together, these factors have made it seem, according to Mead, "equally less necessary and less moral among liberals to support the Jewish state." Paradoxically, Mead points out, "overall public support for Israel in the United States has been rising, not falling for most of the last generation." Numerous opinion surveys show at the very least that high American public support for Israel, and the relative lack of support for Palestinians, has been fairly stable.

What explains this seeming contradiction is not so much a change in overall support for Israel (at least for now) but, rather, a shift of Israel's support base away from the liberal mainstream toward the nationalist and sometimes racist right. This process is happening in parallel among Jews and non-Jews. A *Rasmussen Reports* survey in March 2010, for example, found that 49 percent of American voters agreed with U.S. President Barack Obama's contentious public demand that Israel should stop building settlements in the occupied West Bank, while 22 percent disagreed and 29 percent were unsure. Support for the president's stance rose to 62 percent among Democrats, with Republicans evenly divided. Even more starkly, while 69 percent of Republicans saw Israel as an ally, that was a view shared by just 46 percent of Democrats. Forty-three percent of Democrats viewed Israel as "somewhere between an ally and an enemy."[4]

Since 2001, leading pro-Israel groups have formed close alliances with right-wing evangelicals, such as Pastor John Hagee, founder of Christians United for Israel, whose conservative and theocratic social agenda American liberals oppose and fear. It is an alliance that may have served short-term goals but further frayed the tenuous ties between Zionism and its liberal-progressive constituency. Rabbi Eric Yoffie, president of the Union for Reform Judaism, warned in 2007 that young American Jews were being driven away from identifying with the Jewish state by "the increasingly right-wing and even reactionary tone that some elements of the organized community have adopted in their pronouncements on Israel."[5] The majority of young, socially liberal American Jews, Yoffie argued, would respond only to a pro-Israel message that chimed with the values of a generation that is "pluralistic in their thinking, and . . . tolerant of difference, especially differences in gender and sexual orientation." Instead, Yoffie, warned, these young Jews—and by implication everyone else—were being offered spokespersons such as Hagee "who is contemptuous of Muslims" and "dismissive of gays." Such alliances have shackled Israel domestically in the United States to a far-right that is increasingly shrill and unabashed in its xenophobia and Islamophobia, especially since the election of Barack Obama as president. In addition, Israel is associated with U.S.-led wars, occupations, and assassination practices in Muslim-majority countries that have generated growing resentment and resistance under the Bush and Obama administrations alike.

The war on Gaza forced the tensions between Israel and its liberal supporters into the open. Haidar Eid, an independent analyst in Gaza, has likened the massacre to the 1960 Sharpeville shooting of black anti-Apartheid protesters by the Apartheid government of South Africa.[6] Sharpeville, he argued, marked the moment that the appeal of South African civil society for boycott, divestment, and sanctions (BDS) started to reach the outside world. A similar opening was seen following the Gaza attack, as the rapid growth of the Palestinian BDS movement showed.

The 2005 Palestinian civil society call for BDS targets Israel's three-tiered system of oppression and disenfranchisement of Palestinians: It calls for widespread academic, cultural, and economic boycotts of Israel until Israel ends the occupation and colonization of all Arab lands occupied since 1967; recognizes the rights of the Arab-Palestinian citizens of Israel to full equality; and respects the rights of Palestinian refugees to return to their homes and properties.[7] It has also shifted the Palestinian struggle in the West ever more firmly onto precisely the pluralistic ground that Zionism claimed to occupy but has gradually abandoned. As Omar Barghouti (one of the BDS campaign's prime movers) put it, the BDS call "appeals to international civil society by evoking the same universal principles of freedom, justice and equal rights that were upheld by the anti-apartheid movement in South Africa and the civil rights movement in the United States."[8]

BDS has mobilized activists in unions, town halls, churches, and especially students on university campuses in Europe and increasingly in North America. Rahul Patel, one of the student senators supporting a divestment bill at the University of California, Berkeley—which passed by a large majority but was then vetoed—put the campaign in this context: "In the 1980s the Student Government was a central actor in demanding that the university divest from South African apartheid. Twenty-five years later, it is a key figure in shaping a nationwide movement against occupation and war crimes around the world."[9] Moreover, adherence to the U.S. civil rights and South African anti-Apartheid movements as models (both made extensive use of boycotts) accords in spirit, at least, with the recommendations

President Obama made to Palestinians in his famous speech to the "Muslim world" delivered in Cairo early in his term.[10] The campaign began to go mainstream as artists of international renown, including Elvis Costello and The Pixies, heeded the Palestinian BDS call and canceled scheduled performances in Israel.

"In their search for justice, victims of serious violations of human rights have often looked for accountability mechanisms in other countries when there were none at home or the existing ones did not offer an effective remedy" (para. 1646). With these words, the Goldstone Report endorsed the use of "universal jurisdiction"— bringing cases in national courts of third countries against those suspected of war crimes and crimes against humanity. Since before the 2008 attack on Gaza, Palestinians had attempted to use universal jurisdiction to bring cases against Israeli war crimes suspects in Spanish and Belgian courts. In an unprecedented move, a London magistrate issued an arrest warrant in December 2009 for Tzipi Livni, the Israeli foreign minister at the time of Operation Cast Lead, who was scheduled to be in the United Kingdom. Livni was not arrested, but the warrant sent a signal that even the most senior Israeli officials would have to carefully weigh or curtail their foreign travel.[11]

The Goldstone Report's idea that civil society could act where official mechanisms of accountability had failed resonated beyond legal proceedings. It inspired another kind of protest that I, as an alumnus of the University of Chicago, participated in along with students from a number of Chicago-area campuses when former Israeli Prime Minister Ehud Olmert was scheduled to give the King Abdullah II Annual Leadership Lecture just weeks after the Goldstone Report was published. The university had been unresponsive to complaints from students about Olmert's invitation and insisted on proceeding with a heavily controlled event designed in students' eyes to suppress rather than foster dissent or debate. In response we decided to make the event ungovernable—the term coined by anti-Apartheid civil disobedience campaigners in South Africa.[12]

The moment Olmert began to speak in the packed auditorium I rose from my seat and called at the top of my voice, "War crimes are not free expression!" I continued to protest as university police escorted me onto the street, where I joined hundreds of demonstrating community members and students. Meanwhile inside, each time Olmert tried to speak again, other students would stand up and protest— some reading out the names of Palestinians killed during the attack on Gaza. Poignantly one young woman rose and, brandishing a thick sheaf of paper, declared, "This is a list of the 1,400 people killed in Gaza. It's 101 pages long!" We considered it a victory that Olmert was not only publicly confronted with the names of some of those killed in military attacks he had ordered but also effectively prevented from delivering a self-justificatory speech unchallenged. For us, the issue was never Olmert's views but his actions, and the university's complicity by giving him a prestigious platform from which to justify them—as well as a large honorarium. "The killings of more than 3,000 Palestinians and Lebanese during Olmert's three years in office," I wrote in *The Chicago Maroon*, "are not mere differences of opinion to be challenged with a polite question written on a prescreened note card. They are crimes for which Olmert is accountable before international law and public opinion."[13] It seemed particularly obscene that anyone could defend Olmert in the name of "academic freedom" when the attacks ordered by Olmert had destroyed or damaged 280 schools in Gaza, destroyed university buildings, and killed 164 pupils and 12 teachers, according to the Goldstone Report (para. 1267).

I quoted these facts and the Goldstone Report's words that "crimes against humanity are crimes that shock the conscience" (para. 293). When institutions with the moral and legal responsibility to punish and prevent such crimes choose complicit silence—or, worse, harbor a suspected war criminal, already on trial for corruption in Israel, and present him to students as a paragon of "leadership"—then disobedience, if that is what it takes to break the silence, is an ethical duty. Instead of condemning them, any university should be proud of its students who have the courage to stand up.

University administrators were publicly unmoved by these arguments, but our action went viral. Within a few days a video taken in the auditorium (in violation of a University of Chicago media ban) had been viewed more than a hundred thousand times on YouTube. When Olmert spoke at the World Affairs Council in San Francisco a week later, he was confronted by similar disruptions and twenty-two activists were arrested—an incident that was also caught on video.[14] These actions became models for regular protests against Olmert, and other former and current Israeli officials and military officers, at institutions ranging from the London School of Economics, Nottingham University, and Manchester University in the United Kingdom to Union College, New York, and the University of Denver, Colorado, in the United States.[15] Eleven students at the University of California, Irvine, were arrested and faced tough disciplinary measures and possible criminal charges for briefly disrupting a lecture by Israeli Ambassador to the United States Michael Oren.[16] Protests became so frequent that the Israeli foreign ministry considered suspending lectures by senior figures around the world, a major victory for the movement.[17]

Israel's response to this upsurge of activism was to paint it all as a campaign to "delegitimize the Jewish state." The Reut Institute, an influential Israeli think tank, even recommended that the government and its intelligence services launch a campaign to "sabotage" and "attack" the global, decentralized, and growing Palestine solidarity movement.[18] Israel's policy of demonization of nonviolent international activism culminated in its May 31, 2010, attack on the Gaza Freedom Flotilla. During this assault, Israeli helicopters and naval commandos killed nine activists and injured dozens of others aboard the *Mavi Marmara*, one of six ships attempting to break the blockade on Gaza with more than seven hundred passengers and ten thousand tons of humanitarian aid.

But the killings on the high seas only boosted BDS activism and increased the global focus on the situation in Gaza. Solidarity actions included a week-long refusal by the Swedish Dockworkers Union to handle any Israeli goods at Sweden's ports. The union's ombudsman, Erik Helgeson, explained that the action was in solidarity with the 1.5 million people—half of them children—living under blockade in Gaza: "The main aim is to keep the pressure on Israel so that the world focus is not turned away. It is not to paralyze their economy."[19] The Swedish dockworkers inspired their counterparts in South Africa, Norway, India, and Oakland, California, to follow suit—precisely the sort of actions that incrementally tightened international pressure on Apartheid South Africa in the 1980s.

A crucial part of Israel's counterattack has been to burnish "Brand Israel." "We must continue to represent the true Israel," wrote Wayne Firestone, president and CEO of Hillel, a national network of pro-Israel campus centers, "as a country that shares America's Western values and contributes to the world in a variety of fields, not the least of which are industry, medicine and arts."[20] Critics have parodied this strategy as "greenwashing" and "pinkwashing" (or "gaywashing")—a transparent public relations effort to paint Israel as a center of environmentalism, social freedoms, and tolerance designed to appeal to Israel's idea of Western liberals. But the strategy met with immediate resistance.

In 2009, the Toronto International Film Festival (TIFF) made Tel Aviv the focus of its "City to City" film series, declaring in its promotional material that "Tel Aviv is a young, dynamic city that, like Toronto, celebrates its diversity." Dozens of film professionals objected to what they charged was a "Brand Israel" effort to "take the focus off Israel's treatment of Palestinians and its aggressive wars." As signatories to the Toronto Declaration, the professionals stated that while they did not oppose the inclusion of Israeli films in the festival, they did object to TIFF "staging a propaganda campaign on behalf of what South African Archbishop Desmond Tutu, former U.S. President Jimmy Carter, and UN General Assembly President Miguel d'Escoto Brockmann have all characterized as an apartheid regime."[21]

Israel's niche marketing to gay communities in North America and Europe also met with resistance. In San Francisco, activists opposed the Out in Israel LGBT

Cultural Festival, saying "We are going to stand up for the rights of all people—queer and straight—and not allow ourselves to be played off against other oppressed people."[22] The group Queers Against Israeli Apartheid (QUAIA) has been a sizable contingent in Toronto's annual pride parade for several years.[23] In 2010, Pride Toronto organizers attempted to ban the use of the phrase Israeli Apartheid, generating a huge protest that eventually forced them to back down. As a result of the controversy, the largest-ever Palestine solidarity contingent marched in the Toronto pride parade.[24] Following Israel's attack on the Freedom Flotilla, organizers of Madrid's pride parade disinvited an Israeli delegation that was sponsored by the Tel Aviv municipality and the Israeli foreign ministry.[25]

However crass, detached, and contradictory Israel's efforts to change the subject, co-opt other communities, and denigrate Palestinians as less civilized may appear, they reflect a realization that the battle for legitimacy in the countries on which Israel has always relied for military, economic, and political support cannot be won at the extremes—it has to be fought on the territory of universal principles, human rights, and equality. This, now, is ground held increasingly firmly by the Palestine solidarity movement, as Israel's base slides out of the mainstream.

Calls for better branding, smarter *hasbara*, or slicker marketing to cover up the crimes documented by the Goldstone Report—or to deny and obfuscate the daily experiences of Palestinians under Israeli blockade and occupation—suggest that too many Israelis cannot see their country in the cold light that others do. The BDS movement seeks to change that, to force the sort of introspection, reassessment, and action that South Africa's Apartheid rulers had to undertake as their country became an international pariah. It is only when those with power begin to perceive their own vulnerability, their own need to listen to the voices of those they marginalize, those who are dehumanized and killed without consequence, that there is a possibility for peaceful transformation. Although the road still appears long, when Palestinians do achieve freedom, justice, and equality it is likely they will look back at the Goldstone Report as one of the catalysts that helped mobilize thousands of people toward that goal.

NOTES

1. James Bennet, "Spilled Blood Is Seen as Bond That Draws 2 Nations Closer," *New York Times*, September 12, 2001, http://www.nytimes.com/2001/09/12/international/12 ISRA.html; accessed May 11, 2010.

2. Seymour M. Hersh, "Watching Lebanon: Washington's Interests in Israel's War," *New Yorker*, August 21, 2006, http://www.newyorker.com/archive/2006/08/21/060821 fa_fact.

3. Walter Russell Mead, "Obama and the Jacksonian Zionists," blog post, March 16, 2010, http://blogs.the-american-interest.com/wrm/2010/03/16/obama-and-the-jacksonian-zionists/); accessed May 11, 2010.

4. "49% Say Israel Should Stop Building Settlements as Part of Peace Deal," *Rasmussen Reports*, March 17, 2010, http://www.rasmussenreports.com/public_content/politics/current_events/israel_the_middle_east/49_say_israel_should_stop_building_settlements_as_part_of_peace_deal; accessed May 11, 2010.

5. Eric Yoffie, "When We Let John Hagee Speak for Us," *The Forward*, May 18, 2007, http://www.forward.com/articles/10732/; accessed May 11, 2010.

6. Haidar Eid, "Sharpeville 1960, Gaza 2009," The Electronic Intifada, January 22, 2009, http://electronicintifada.net/v2/article10232.shtml; accessed May 12, 2010.

7. "Palestinian Call for Boycott, Divestment, and Sanctions (BDS)," Palestinian Campaign for the Academic and Cultural Boycott of Israel, July 9, 2005, http://www.pacbi.org/etemplate.php?id=66; accessed May 17, 2010.

8. Omar Barghouti, "BDS: A Global Movement for Freedom and Justice," Al-Shabaka, May 5, 2010, http://al-shabaka.org/policy-brief/civil-society/bds-global-movement-freedom-and-justice; accessed May 12, 2010.

9. Palestinian Campaign for the Academic and Cultural Boycott of Israel, "UC Berkeley Student Senate Passes Divestment Bill in Response to Israeli Occupation," March 18, 2010, http://www.pacbi.org/etemplate.php?id=1194; accessed May 12, 2010.

10. Obama stated: "For centuries, black people in America suffered the lash of the whip as slaves and the humiliation of segregation. But it was not violence that won full and equal rights. It was a peaceful and determined insistence upon the ideals at the center of America's founding. This same story can be told by people from South Africa to South Asia; from Eastern Europe to Indonesia." See "Remarks by the President on a New Beginning, Cairo University, Cairo, Egypt," The White House, June 4, 2009, http://www.whitehouse.gov/the_press_office/Remarks-by-the-President-at-Cairo-University-6-04-09/; accessed May 12, 2010.

11. "Israel Confirms U.K. Arrest Warrant Against Livni," *Haaretz*, December 19, 2009, http://www.haaretz.com/news/israel-confirms-u-k-arrest-warrant-against-livni-1.2133.

12. See, for example, "ANC Call to the People," 1986, http://www.anc.org.za/ancdocs/history/ungovern.html; accessed May 12, 2010.

13. Ali Abunimah, "Why I Disrupted Olmert," *The Chicago Maroon*, October 22, 2009, http://www.chicagomaroon.com/2009/10/22/why-i-disrupted-olmert; accessed May 12, 2010.

14. See "VIDEO: Citizens arrest, disruption of Olmert in San Francisco Press Release; Northern California Palestine Justice Groups," The Electronic Intifada, October 23, 2009, http://electronicintifada.net/v2/article10851.shtml; accessed May 17, 2010.

15. For examples, see the video of protest during the lecture by Israeli colonel Bentzi Gruber at the University of Denver, May 14, 2010, http://www.youtube.com/watch ?v=SUNCA-Rmqlk; the video of protest during the lecture by Ron Prosor, Israeli ambassador to the United Kingdom, November 10, 2009, http://www.youtube.com/watch ?v=G9ZaodkULH4; and the video of protest against Israeli deputy ambassador in the U.K. at Manchester University, April 14, 2010, http://www.youtube.com/watch?v=53W -ccqHcZk.

16. Jacob Adelman, "UC Irvine Suspends Muslim Group over Disruption," Associated Press, June 14, 2010.

17. Eli Bardenstein, "Foreign Ministry Considering Stopping Lectures," *Maariv* (Hebrew), May 6, 2010, p. 16, http://coteret.com/2010/05/06/maariv-foreign-ministry-considering -stopping-lectures-in-us-and-uk-because-of-heckling/; accessed May 17, 2010.

18. Ali Abunimah, "Israel's New Strategy: 'Sabotage' and 'Attack' the Global Justice Movement," The Electronic Intifada, February 16, 2010, http://electronicintifada.net/v2/ article11080.shtml; accessed May 17, 2010.

19. "Swedish Dockworkers Boycott Israel," *Al Jazeera* (English), June 23, 2010, http://english.aljazeera.net/news/europe/2010/06/2010623114558557329.html.

20. Wayne L. Firestone, "Op-Ed: Fighting the New Divestment Effort on Campus," *Jewish Telegraphic Agency*, May 6, 2010, http://jta.org/news/article/2010/05/06/2394711/ op-ed-fighting-the-new-divestment-effort-on-campus; accessed May 17, 2010.

21. See http://torontodeclaration.blogspot.com/.

22. "Queers Say NO Pinkwashing Apartheid," *QUIT* (*Queers Undermining Israeli Terrorism*), April 13, 2010, http://www.indybay.org/newsitems/2010/04/13/18644638.php; accessed May 17, 2010.

23. See "Queers Against Israeli Apartheid Wins Battle Against Censorship," QUAIA, June 23, 2010, http://queersagainstapartheid.org/2010/06/23/queers-against-israeli -apartheid-wins-battle-against-censorship.

24. Andrew Brett, "A Case Study in Failure: The Israel Lobby at Toronto Pride," July 6, 2010, http://www.rabble.ca/blogs/bloggers/andrew-brett/2010/07/case-study-failure.

25. Yoav Zitun, "Spanish Pride Parade Doesn't Want Israelis," *Ynet*, June 8, 2010, http://www.ynetnews.com/articles/0,7340,L-3901785,00.html.

9

Israel's Siege Mentality

Noam Sheizaf

There are three primary threats facing us today: the nuclear threat, the missile threat and what I call the Goldstone threat.

—ISRAELI PRIME MINISTER
BENJAMIN NETANYAHU

Today Israel can best be described as living under a siege mentality. The Israeli government led by Benjamin Netanyahu and Avigdor Lieberman has exploited a nationalistic mood to promote a growing hostility to human rights organizations and the international community. Perhaps the best way to understand this mentality is to look at Israel's response to the Goldstone Report. Under Netanyahu and Lieberman, Israelis have come to view the Goldstone Report as an existential threat—a direct attack on the very legitimacy of their state's existence. Within a few months from its publication, not only was the report rejected by almost the entire political system, as well as in public opinion, but it brought to a halt the limited debate that had taken place regarding the Israel Defense Forces' conduct in Gaza. The report itself was turned into a tool in the persecution and delegitimization of human rights activists and organizations in Israel, and its actual content was all but forgotten.

To understand this process, it is best to begin with Israel's official responses to recent wars. In April 2007, two years before Justice Goldstone was appointed to head the

United Nations Fact-Finding Mission on the Gaza Conflict, an Israeli committee, led by Justice Eliyahu Winograd, delivered its preliminary report concerning a controversial military conflict, this time at the north of Israel, in Lebanon in 2006. Winograd's commission had been appointed by the Israeli government amidst mounting public pressure and calls for Defense Minister Amir Peretz and Prime Minister Ehud Olmert to resign because of the limited success Israel had in the war.

During the Winograd Committee hearings, several Israeli human rights groups appealed for an investigation of alleged illegal actions carried out by the IDF and violations of international law. The committee mostly chose not to look into these matters, stating that such actions and violations were not part of its mandate and that it didn't wish to be drawn "into issues which are part of a political campaign against the state [of Israel]." The committee added, however, that all claims of illegal acts by IDF should be investigated, and not by the army alone.[1] This issue remained almost unnoticed; however, the tendency to view legal and ethical criticism of the conduct of the IDF as an attack on the very existence of the state would reemerge in the controversy surrounding the Goldstone Report.

Like Israel's other two "war committees"—the Agranat Committee that looked into events leading to the 1973 (October) war and the Cahan Committee that investigated the 1982 massacre in Sabra and Shatila refugee camp in Lebanon—the Winograd Committee was created out of a sense of deep failure on the battlefield and of the unnecessary sacrifice of Israeli soldiers. Pundits and military experts had expressed the concern, reflected in the Winograd Report itself, that Israel's ability to deter its enemies was seriously hurt. When the Israeli attack on Gaza began on December 27, 2008 (a month and a half before general elections), the public expected this military operation to have clear results: limited Israeli casualties and significant damage to Hamas.

While the hope that Israel would topple Hamas was never fulfilled—nor was the desire to rescue captive Israeli soldier Gilad Shalit—the devastation in Gaza was seen for the most part as evidence that the Palestinian military infrastructure and personnel had been severely damaged. Together with the low fatality rate on the Israeli side—10 soldiers and 3 civilians, compared to 121 soldiers and 44 civilians in the Lebanon war—and the fact that the number of rockets launched toward the south of Israel dropped by 90 percent following the operation, most of the public viewed Operation Cast Lead as a success.[2]

The previous inquiry committees were born out of a sense of military failure. As far as Israelis were concerned, this time there was nothing to investigate.

On April 3, 2009, the day his committee was announced, Justice Goldstone sent a letter to Aharon Leshno-Yaar, Israel's permanent representative to the United Nations in Geneva, seeking the cooperation of the Israeli government and the IDF and asking to meet with victims of Hamas's attacks and to visit areas that were affected by rockets. In the opening of his letter, Justice Goldstone attempted to allay Israeli fears:

> I wish personally to assure you that prior to considering the invitation to lead the mission, I satisfied myself that it would be given un-biased and even-handed terms of reference.

Four days later, Ambassador Leshno-Yaar wrote Justice Goldstone that "Israel will not be able to cooperate with the proposed fact-finding mission," due to the "grossly politicized" nature of the United Nations Human Rights Council (UNHRC) resolution that led to the establishment of the committee. This resolution, wrote the ambassador,

> prejudges the issue at hand, determining at the onset that Israel has perpetrated gross violation of human rights and implying that Israel has deliberately targeted civilians and facilities.

The very next day, Justice Goldstone sent another letter to Ambassador Leshno-Yaar, assuring him that his mission would investigate all human rights violations related to the military operation. On April 29 Goldstone wrote again, asking for the third time to meet the Israeli ambassador. On May 4 he wrote directly to Prime Minister Netanyahu, and then again, on May 20, to Ambassador Leshno-Yaar, stating that his previous letters remained unanswered.

The Israeli reply came on July 2, 2009, after the members of the Mission had returned from their second visit to Gaza (entering from Egypt, since Israel wouldn't let them in). Ambassador Leshno-Yaar reiterated his earlier concerns and summed up most of the arguments that later would be repeated again and again by Israeli representatives and their supporters: The findings of the Mission were practically predetermined, Israel was perfectly capable of investigating itself, (the army was currently conducting such an investigation), and the UN Mission members had been manipulated by Hamas officials in Gaza.[3]

Much of the change in attitude between 2002 and 2009 can be attributed to the right-wing government that was formed by Benjamin Netanyahu in February 2009 and the siege mentality that came with it. The foreign office, which normally presented the more welcoming face of Israeli policy to the world, began to demonstrate an aggressive and even hostile manner toward foes and allies alike. Foreign Minister Lieberman accused Norway and Sweden of an anti-Israeli attitude and even of encouraging anti-Semitism; he refused to meet the president of Brazil during his formal visit to Israel, and his deputy minister staged a public humiliation of the Turkish ambassador that caused Ankara to threaten to recall its ambassador without sending a replacement. Later, a crisis even broke out between Israel and the United States, causing Netanyahu to cancel a trip to a nuclear summit that President Obama held in Washington in April 2010.

Israeli suspicions about the international community are the result of two developments: a steady growth over the past decade in the strength of the right-wing and religious parties within Israel, and the Palestinian Authority's decision to pursue the diplomatic front, rather than armed struggle, to force Israel out of the West Bank. Israel had enjoyed considerable international sympathy during the second intifada, when suicide bombers were exploding in the heart of its towns; ironically, the relative quiet that accompanied Netanyahu's first year in office brought back international demands for an Israeli withdrawal. Israelis once again saw themselves portrayed as "the bad guys," when, in their view, they were just recovering from another attempt to destroy them.

In Israelis' eyes, their two recent withdrawals from Lebanon and Gaza had both led to continued attacks and ultimately to war. They saw Cast Lead as establishing a comfortable status quo, when suddenly they were being asked to evacuate more territory, this time at the heart of the country, surrounding Jerusalem and overlooking Tel Aviv and its suburbs. For Israel's leaders, the political price for such a withdrawal would be tremendous, while its benefits, if there were any, were unclear.

In the elections following the Gaza war, a new generation of politicians who rose to power represented these existential anxieties. Senior Israeli officials started making a habit of criticizing international bodies and foreign governments; the public followed with spontaneous calls to boycott companies from "hostile" countries.[4] Several protests were held in front of foreign embassies in Tel Aviv.

Even months after the publication of the Goldstone Report, when the damage this attitude was causing Israel became clear, most of the Jewish public continued believing that Israel should not have cooperated with the fact-finding mission. More than 90 percent of the Jewish public thought the report was biased, and some 80 percent supported the statement that "there were no war crimes in Gaza."

It was not as if the Goldstone Report came as a complete surprise. In the months after the war, two major news stories revealed allegations of war crimes. The first came in March 2009 with the publication of soldiers' testimonies from an event at the Rabin Pre-Military Academy in which at least one soldier described what sounded like the intentional killing of a civilian. Four months later, Breaking the Silence, a veterans' organization that exposes wrongdoings by IDF soldiers in the occupied territories, issued a report accusing the army of using white phosphorus on civilians and deliberately endangering the lives of Palestinian civilians. In both cases, the army dismissed the testimonies as "hearsay evidence."

The Goldstone Report got a similar treatment when it was published in September 2009. The government issued a preliminary analysis of the report, concluding that it sent "a troubling message to terrorist groups . . . that the cynical tactics of seeking to exploit civilian suffering for political ends actually pays dividends." As time passed, the government began to attack Justice Goldstone himself.[5] Even the usually restrained President Shimon Peres publicly called the judge "a small man, devoid of any sense of justice [who was] on a one-sided mission to hurt Israel. . . . If anyone should be investigated, it should be him."

On the diplomatic side, Israel put considerable effort into preventing the report from moving from the UNHRC to the General Assembly and the Security Council. The government threatened to withdraw permission for the operation of a second mobile phone company in the Palestinian Authority unless Mahmoud Abbas asked for the UN to defer a vote on the Goldstone Report. If that wasn't enough, according to a report in *Haaretz* the head of Shin Bet, Yuval Diskin, warned Abbas that "Israel would turn the West Bank into a second Gaza" unless the vote was postponed.

As the damage to Israel's image began to be evident in early 2010, a debate started both in the media and in the government over whether to conduct a formal Israeli inquiry into the events described in the Goldstone Report. Attorney General Menny Mazoz, Minister of Justice Ya'akov Ne'eman, and, surprisingly enough, Foreign Minister Avigdor Lieberman argued before Prime Minister Netanyahu that Israel must present the international community with a reliable report of its own that would present clear answers to the allegations in the report. Senior officials from the Foreign Office and the Justice Department claimed that internal investigations by the IDF wouldn't be seen as reliable enough, and that the Israeli investigation should be led by a known and respected figure, preferably one of the former heads of the Israeli Supreme Court.

On the other side were Israel's security authorities, led by Defense Minister Ehud Barak, who stood firm in opposition to any external investigation, meaning one not led by the army itself. Chief of Staff Gabi Ashkenazi told cabinet ministers that such an inquiry would send soldiers and officers the message that their government didn't trust them.

The official Israeli response to the Goldstone Report was sent to the UN a year after the war ended, and it stated that the IDF was investigating 150 incidents from the war, 36 of which had led to criminal investigations.[6] There was no mention of an external Israeli investigation. Once again, Israeli leaders chose to turn their backs on the international community, partly in avoidance of the domestic political price involved in confronting the army and partly due to a general sense that such an external investigation wouldn't shift international public opinion anyway.

By the end of the winter, the Goldstone Report had become, for many Israelis, the ultimate manifestation of what was perceived as an unjust international hostility toward their country. In the public image, supporting the report, or even elements of it, was no longer an ethical or political question, but an expression of anti-Israeli sentiment and even treason.

On January 29, 2010, *Maariv* newspaper published a cover story by its top po-litical correspondent, Ben Caspit, that accused the U.S.-based New Israel Fund (NIF), the leading foundation supporting civil society organizations in Israel, of being almost solely responsible for the Goldstone Report. Caspit's story was based on a paper by a right-wing watchdog group called Im Tirzu, which did no more than count the footnotes in the Goldstone Report. It found that 92 percent of the negative references regarding Israel that came from Israeli sources were attributed to human rights organizations financed by the NIF, such as B'tselem, Shovrim Shtika, the Association for Civil Rights in Israel, and others. This was no more than an arithmetic manipulation, since NIF organizations were mentioned in only 14 percent of the footnotes in the entire report, but by talking about "negative refer-ences from Israeli sources," Im Tirzu and Caspit were able to create the impression that the NIF was actually behind 90 percent of the Goldstone Report.

Caspit's article drew a straight line from the diplomatic siege on Israel to the Goldstone Report and "the enemy within":

> Israel's image is at an all-time low. International pressure is mounting, and with it the calls for boycott. All this was fueled by the Goldstone report, which was in itself fueled by Israeli sources. The funding for these sources is provided by, amongst others, the NIF. The question is whether the New Israel Fund is indeed for Israel.

Politicians and right-wing groups jumped on the story immediately. Two Knes-set debates followed. In one of them Zevulun Orlev, a member of the Knesset from the right-wing Jewish Home Party, accused the NIF—along with its president, Naomi Hazan—of no less than treason. Member of Knesset (MK) Yulia Shamalov-Berkovich from the centrist Kadima Party also joined the attack:

> We must say to all Israel-haters that enough is enough. We won't sit quietly when our enemies from home try to lead an undemocratic revolution here, encouraging boycott, desertion and pacifistic refusal to serve in the IDF,

based on lies and distortions. We must draw our lines and tell the traitors of
our people that this is enough.

On February 3, the Knesset Constitution Committee formed a sub-committee
to look into the foreign funding of Israeli organizations. That same week *The
Jerusalem Post* informed Hazan that the paper would stop publishing her columns.
Most disturbing was a new Knesset bill, put forward in late April 2010, that, if
passed, would make it possible for the state to shut down any human rights organization "which is involved in activity intended to lead to the prosecution or arrest
of IDF officers and government officials for war crimes." The proposed bill had
broad support and was signed by more than twenty MKs from both the ruling
coalition and the opposition parties.

> *I don't like comparing to South Africa, but towards the end
> of Apartheid, many whites saw anyone who was a member
> of the anti-Apartheid movement as if he was anti–South
> Africa. It was a pity, since we were a movement which sup-
> ported South Africa. Things in Israel are quite similar today.
> People in Israel need to understand that going against gov-
> ernment policy doesn't mean that you are anti-Israeli.*
>
> —JUSTICE GOLDSTONE IN AN INTERVIEW TO
> *HA-IR* MAGAZINE, SEPTEMBER 2009

To a greater degree than anything else that happened during the first year of the Netanyahu government, the events surrounding the Goldstone Report demonstrated
how isolated from the world and betrayed by it Israelis feel right now. Absorbed in
their own fears—however justified—Israelis refuse to listen to or understand the
criticism they face.[7] Realizing that they are unable to win over international public
opinion, they direct their anger and frustration against human rights organizations,
peace activists, and members of the Palestinian minority. More and more often,
criticism of government policy is perceived as an attack on Zionism, and even as
pure anti-Semitism.

As international pressure to lift the siege on Gaza and evacuate the West Bank
continues to mount, this persecution of the enemy within is also likely to intensify.
In the process, the Goldstone Report becomes no more than a symbol. Reject it,
and you are with us; listen to it, acknowledge it, and you are against us. That's all
that matters now.

NOTES

1. "Final Report of the Commission of Inquiry into the Events of Military Engagement in Lebanon 2006," chapter 14, article 9 (my translation from Hebrew). The Winograd Committee did recommend an "authorized" investigation to be carried out regarding the use of cluster bombs by the IDF in Lebanon.

2. A *Haaretz* poll conducted just before the end of the fighting in Gaza found that 78 percent of the public view the military operation as a success; see http://www.haaretz .co.il/hasite/spages/1055752.html. In addition, a Channel 10 News poll conducted in October 2009 (after the Goldstone Report was published) found that 68 percent of the public opposed the idea of an Israeli investigation into Operation Cast Lead.

3. Though the Mission was not allowed to visit Israel, an unofficial Israeli delegation, which included civilians who were hurt in rocket attacks, did testify before the Goldstone committee in Geneva.

4. Following an anti-Israeli story in a Swedish tabloid, an ex-IDF soldier tried to launch a boycott on IKEA. He received considerable media attention, but the boycott itself failed. More successful was a boycott of the popular holy-day resorts in Turkey: Israeli tourists' entries to the country dropped 33 percent in 2009.

5. On May 7, 2010, *Yedioth Ahronoth* published a front-page investigation "into the dark past of Judge Goldstone," citing cases in which he sentenced blacks to beatings and deaths under the Apartheid laws.

6. As of this writing, thirty-six criminal investigations have been conducted by the IDF, one soldier has been tried for stealing credit cards from Palestinians, and two have been charged with carrying out the illegal "neighbor procedure"—using Palestinian civilians to check for charges and booby traps.

7. Sometimes, it feels as though the international community could have done a better job communicating itself to Israelis. Making the Goldstone Report available in Hebrew as well, so that Israelis wouldn't need to rely on pundits and reporters to know what's in it, might have been a good start.

10

The Unholy Assault
on Richard Goldstone

Letty Cottin Pogrebin

I keep thinking the Israel-right-or-wrong crowd can't possibly stoop any lower. But then, astonishingly, they do. Not only do they behave indecently, they behave *unJewishly*.

From the moment the Goldstone Report was released in September 2009, its contents and lead author have been subjected to fierce, well-orchestrated attacks by Israeli and American Jews who purport to be defending the legitimacy of the Jewish state and the safety of the Jewish people. Reasonable people can disagree with the report's conclusion that during the 2008–2009 Gaza war, Israel (as well as Hamas) may have committed war crimes and the IDF soldiers responsible should be prosecuted—if not internally, then in the World Court. Reasonable people can debate whether years of Hamas rocket fire justified Israel's claim of self-defense, or what constitutes a "just war," or whether the UN Mission's fact-finding methods were suspect or its panel members biased. However, all substantive discourse was squelched once Israel declared the report an existential threat and battened down the hatches.

Prime Minister Netanyahu and his right-wing government refused either to investigate the incursion that resulted in the death of more than 1,300 Palestinians, including some 300 children, and 13 Israelis, or to subject its military's behavior to the judgment of an international body. Instead, they went on the attack. Dore Gold, Israel's former ambassador to the United Nations, called the report "the most serious and vicious assault on the State of Israel"[1] since the UN's 1975 resolution equating Zionism with racism. Virtually every American Jewish *macher* (big shot) with the *chutzpah* (nerve) if not the bona fides to speak for "the Jews" was quick to label the report false, libelous, odious. Canadian judge and human rights lawyer Irwin Cotler termed it "tainted to the core."[2]

Rather than discuss the *contents* of the report or the conduct of the combatants, Israel's defenders launched their all-points campaign to bury the report. But their strategy was complicated from the start by an inconvenient truth: Richard Goldstone, the person with ultimate control over the UN investigation and the lead author of the report, was one of them, a Jew. And not just any Jew, an exemplary one. Until 2003, he served on South Africa's highest court. Before that he distinguished himself as chair of his nation's Commission of Inquiry into violence under Apartheid, as chief prosecutor of war crimes in the former Yugoslavia and Rwanda, and as part of the team that investigated the Oil for Food scandal in Iraq. The law schools at Harvard, New York University, and Fordham gave him visiting professorships. The MacArthur Foundation and the American Bar Association awarded him some of their top honors.

Goldstone's Jewish credentials were equally stellar. A proud self-identified Zionist, he served on the governing board of Hebrew University (until, that is, the university quietly stripped him of the role several months after the publication of the report); as chair of Brandeis University's Advisory Board on Ethics, Justice, and Public Life; and president of World ORT, the international Jewish educational organization. He was a dogged investigator of Nazi war criminals in Argentina. Aharon Barak, former president of the Israeli Supreme Court, described him as "a dear friend" with "very deep ties to Israel."[3]

Obviously, it wasn't easy to destroy Richard Goldstone. But for his report to be permanently deep-sixed, he had to be thoroughly discredited—re-portrayed not just as a naïve dupe of the human rights community but as an enemy of Israel, a Nazi in Zionist clothing, a perpetrator of "blood libel," a self-hating Jew. (I Googled "Richard Goldstone self-hating Jew" while writing this essay in May 2010, and 486,000 entries came up.) The attack dogs couldn't kill the messenger but they could tear him to pieces.

"There are three primary threats facing [Israel] today," said Prime Minister Benjamin Netanyahu, "the nuclear threat, the missile threat, and what I call the Goldstone threat."[4] Israeli President Shimon Peres called Goldstone "a small man, devoid of any sense of justice."[5] Others in the government and media piled on, as did the American Jewish establishment, the so-called leaders of the so-called organized Jewish community (though few have been elected). South Africa's chief rabbi, Warren Goldstein, accused Goldstone of "delegitimizing Israel."[6] Uncountable critics labeled him an anti-Semite. Ramping up the rhetoric to outright character assassination, Harvard Law School professor Alan Dershowitz said Goldstone was "an evil, evil man,"[7] "a traitor to the Jewish people,"[8] the UN's "token court Jew,"[9] and a "despicable human being."[10]

There's a Hebrew word for what these people did to him: They put him in *cherem*, a condition some call "Jewish excommunication," though in this case that's an understatement. Someone in *cherem* is not just persona non grata in the eyes of our religious arbiters, he is totally cut off from the Jewish community. From the moment the report was released, Goldstone was treated like a leper—shunned, defamed, disowned—and the worst was yet to come.

In April 2010, the South African Zionist Federation threatened demonstrations outside the Sandton Synagogue if he showed up at his grandson's bar mitzvah. Given the volatile political context, that was tantamount to banning the grandfather from the ceremony. Avrom Krengel, chair of the SAZF, told the *South African Jewish Report* that the Zionist Federation was taking the lead and "coming across most forcefully because we represent Israel." [11] No less an authority than Rabbi Moshe Kurtstag, head of the Beth Din (Jewish court of law), seemed to support the move, calling it "quite a sensible thing to avert all this unpleasantness." Goldstone, he explained, had done "a tremendous disservice not only to Israel but to the Jewish world."[12] In an ironically damning postscript, he added: "I understand that he is a judge, but he should have had the sense to understand that whatever he said [about Israel's role in Gaza] wouldn't be good and he should have just recused himself."[13]

But it wasn't Goldstone who caused the "unpleasantness," or aroused anti-Israel feelings, or stoked anti-Semitism. It was the IDF's shock and awe tactics in Gaza, the government's policies of collective punishment, house demolition, checkpoints, blockades, settlement expansion, and the systematic humiliation and dehumanization of an occupied people. That's what has stained Israel's image. That's what has coarsened Israeli civil society and corroded the Zionist dream.

It strikes me that the smear campaign against Goldstone, appalling enough in human terms, should be condemned on specifically *Jewish* grounds. His opponents have breached our tradition's fundamental moral and ethical standards by slandering a human being who was created "in God's image" and by sacrificing Judaism's justice-based values on the altar of a nationalism gone mad. In short, Judge Goldstone's Jewish aggressors are not fit to kiss the hem of his robes.

Mercifully, a few sane Jewish voices rose above the vitriolic clamor: Thirty-seven American rabbis signed a letter supporting Goldstone. *Tikkun* magazine named him the recipient of its 2011 award of honor. Arthur Chaskalson, retired chief justice of the South African Constitutional Court, said those who would bar Goldstone from his grandson's bar mitzvah "should hang their heads in shame."[14] Albie Sachs, another retired Supreme Court justice, said he "felt sick" about the attacks on his old colleague. "What saddens me today is that any Jew who speaks out with an independent voice especially [about] the conduct of the State of Israel, is regarded as a self-hating Jew. . . . Why should someone be made to choose between being a Jew and having a conscience?"[15]

Why indeed? Those who wear the label *Jewish* leader, and certainly the rabbis among Goldstone's aggressors, had to have known better. Anyone who went to Hebrew school for more than six months learned that callousness and cruelty are forbidden; that *rachmanes* (mercy) and *chesed* (lovingkindness) are commanded; and that Hillel, the illustrious first-century sage who, when asked by a gentile to summarize the entire Torah while standing on one foot, replied without missing a beat, "Do *not* do unto others what you *would not have done unto you*." (Emphasis mine.)

Moreover, the most observant and educated of Goldstone's attackers were doubtless aware that speaking ill of another human being ("hate speech" in current parlance) violates one of Judaism's most sacrosanct laws, the prohibition against *lashon hara* (the Evil Tongue—i.e., gossip), which Maimonides defined as any utterance (true or not!) that might cause a person physical or monetary damage, or shame, humiliation, anguish, or fear.

The Talmud's famous story of the Oven of Achnai goes even further. It establishes that *onaat devarim*—verbal torment or abusive speech—is a *more* heinous infraction than physical assault. (*Devarim* means words; *onaah* means horrific oppression or rape.)

The Talmudic story opens with a dispute among the sages of the Sanhedrin over the ritual purity of a clay oven. Most of the decisors (authorities who decide matters of Jewish law) agree that the oven is unclean, but Eliezer, a respected voice though in this instance a minority of one, insists it is clean and summons four astounding miracles to prove his position. The sages dismiss these divine signs, proclaiming the Torah "is not in heaven"—meaning, the law is to be interpreted by human thinkers on earth—and the majority rules. God apparently agrees since the heavenly voice laughs and, seemingly disarmed by the sages' logic, says, "My sons have defeated Me, My sons have defeated Me." To underscore their victory, the sages set fire to the disputed oven and everything else Eliezer had declared clean, and then vote to excommunicate him. When Eliezer weeps and grieves deeply, God, despite having ruled for the sages, responds to Eliezer's mistreatment by withering harvests across the land, spoiling dough, and incinerating every object Eliezer looks upon. Then the president of the Sanhedrin meets his untimely death, taking the hit for his minions' sin of *onaat devarim*. The gravity of this forbidden activity becomes crystal clear: God nearly destroyed the world because of the "wounded feelings" of Eliezer, an honorable man.

Surely the rabbis who made Richard Goldstone's life miserable were aware of the Eliezer story. Likewise, they had to know that similar behavior caused the calamity of calamities, the destruction of the Second Temple. Tradition holds that the First Temple fell because of three sins: sexual immorality, murder, and idolatry, and for those three, the Israelites were punished with seventy years in exile. But the Second Temple was demolished for only one reason—*sinat chinam* (baseless hatred), Jew hating Jew, an infraction so severe that it merited an exile of two thousand years.

Though presumably knowledgeable, a lot of holier-than-thou Jews violated all sorts of Jewish laws and traditions by politicizing Goldstone's grandson's sacred rite of passage, causing pain to a man and his family, and dumping verbal sludge on a fellow Jew whose only crime was to pursue justice and demand that Israel live up to its founding principles. Yet, Israel's fanatical defenders won't let up on Goldstone until he is irreparably destroyed. Why? Avrom Krengel, of the South African Zionist Federation, unwittingly provided the answer at the meeting the SAZF demanded as a quid pro quo for lifting the threat of demonstrations so that Goldstone could attend the bar mitzvah. "Without your credentials as a Jew and pre-eminent Human Rights Jurist this report would have lacked all credibility and would have failed to gain any traction," Krengel told Goldstone. "Your involvement in this mission and report has lead to potentially devastating consequences for Israel and the Jewish people."[16] Translation: As long as a shred of Goldstone's reputation remains intact there's always a chance that his report will gain traction and Israel will be held accountable for its abuses.

To forestall that possibility, his foes mounted a fresh offensive last spring based on a front-page story in *Yedioth Ahronoth*, Israel's mass circulation daily, that charged that during his years on the Constitutional Court, Goldstone "sided through and through with the racist policies of the Apartheid regime," "sentenced dozens of blacks mercilessly to their death," and should "look long and hard in the mirror and do some soul-searching before he rushes to criticize others."[17] Bingo! The one arena of his life that had been beyond reproach, his judicial record, was now red meat.

Goldstone immediately responded that his decision to accept an appointment to the Apartheid bench was "the most difficult of my career"[18] but he'd said yes in the belief that he could accomplish more by defending the rule of law from within the judicial system. His critics fell over each other exploiting the story and ratcheting up the rhetoric. Danny Ayalon, Israel's deputy foreign minister, said, "I don't want to exaggerate but these are the same explanations we heard in Nazi Germany after World War II."[19] Alan Dershowitz, the Harvard law professor, sank to a new low. "That's what Mengele said, too,"[20] he told an Israeli TV program, referring to Josef Mengele, the infamous death doctor of Auschwitz. According to *The Forward*, Israeli Foreign Minister Avigdor Lieberman ordered *Yedioth*'s story distributed to his diplomatic missions abroad "to be used by official representatives arguing against Goldstone's Gaza findings."[21]

Since Nelson Mandela appointed him to South Africa's highest court *post-Apartheid*, and since he was subsequently named to lead the investigation into state-sponsored terrorism against blacks, one can safely assume that Goldstone, whose decisions, by the way, have been a matter of public record for some thirty years, was considered a fair and honest justice. "I have been judged by my fellow South Africans and by President Mandela for my role both during and after apartheid," he told *The Forward*, "and I find it curious that [prior to the Goldstone Report] no one in Israel ever raised the issue except to laud me."[22]

Jews who claim to espouse Jewish values ought to be outraged by the avalanche of ad hominem attacks on Richard Goldstone, but they should be even more conscience-stricken by the possibility, just the *possibility*, that the IDF committed atrocities in Gaza. Yet at this writing (June 2010), many in our community are still vilifying the judge but almost no one, other than scholars and indefatigable lefties, is talking about his findings: Thousands of Palestinian homes reduced to rubble. Gaza's infrastructure—the Parliament, Ministry of Justice, Ministry of Interior, schools, mosques, courthouses, prisons, Gaza's only flour producer, scores of agricultural fields, water supplies, the main poultry and egg-producing farm, and a sewage treatment plant—in ruins. Women and children burned by white phosphorus bombs. People shot while their arms were shackled. A mother and three daughters shot while carrying a white flag. Twenty-two members of one family killed in Gaza City.

As for crimes committed on the Palestinian side, the report acknowledges, and condemns, the hundreds of Hamas rockets and mortars fired at civilians in southern Israel. Had Netanyahu not personally refused Goldstone's repeated requests for Israeli cooperation, the case against Hamas would doubtless have been more fully documented. Furthermore, it should be noted that the examination of Hamas's behavior was a condition of Goldstone's taking the assignment and that his critique is the first to be made under UN auspices.

Some weeks after the report was released, an American rabbi asked what I thought of it and promised me "confidentiality." Having lived through any number of Jewish political and religious disputes, he knew how perilous it is for a Jew to go public with an opinion that diverges from the "mainstream." He wanted to reassure me that my response would be safe with him.

Thought control, coerced unity, silencing—these, too, are antithetical to Jewish tradition. Virtually all of our inherited wisdom is the fruit of millennia of verbal disputation among smart, contentious rabbis. Shammai taught that we should light eight candles the first night of Chanukah and one fewer candle each subsequent night. Hillel said we should do the opposite. Though Hillel won, Shammai's dissent has come down to us through the ages because the ancients understood there is much to be learned from the minority view.

It would have been "good for the Jews" and for Israel had the report's substance been frankly confronted and debated, but so far the only game in town is "Kill the message, trash the messenger." In that sense, Goldstone is the Eliezer of our age—a judge pledged to defend the law in the face of arrogant opposition, excoriated for holding Jews to their principles, excommunicated for speaking truth to power. One can only hope the contemporary story doesn't end as badly as the one in the Talmud.

NOTES

1. "Justice Richard Goldstone and Former Israeli Ambassador Dore Gold Discuss the U.N. Gaza Report," *Brandeis Now*, November 6, 2009, http://www.brandeis.edu/now/2009/november/gazaforumcoverage.html.

2. Irwin Cotler, "The Goldstone Mission—Tainted to the Core" (Part I–Part II), *The Jerusalem Post*, August 16, 2009.

3. Anshel Pfeffer, "Goldstone: Holocaust Shaped View on War Crimes," *Haaretz*, September 18, 2009.

4. Benjamin Netanyahu, Speech at the Knesset Special Session, December 23, 2009, http://www.pmo.gov.il/PMOEng/Communication/PMSpeaks/speech40sigh231209.htm.

5. Shuki Sadeh, "Peres: Goldstone Is a Small Man Out to Hurt Israel," *Haaretz*, December 11, 2009.

6. Warren Goldstein, "Goldstone's Unjust Rush Job Has Hurt the Cause of Peace," *Business Day*, October 20, 2009.

7. "Dershowitz: Goldstone Is a Traitor," Jpost.com, January 31, 2010.

8. Ibid.

9. Alan Dershowitz, speech at AIPAC Policy Conference, March 21, 2010, http://www.aipac.org/PC2010/webPlayer/sun_dershowitz10.asp.

10. Chris McGreal, "Goldstone Family Drawn into Row over Goldstone Report," *The Guardian*, April 30, 2010, http://www.guardian.co.uk/world/2010/apr/30/richard-goldstone-south-africa-jews.

11. Moira Schneider, "Goldstone 'Barred' from Grandson's Barmitzvah," *South African Jewish Report*, April 16–23, 2010.

12. Ibid.

13. Ibid.

14. Ibid.

15. McGreal, "Goldstone Family Drawn into Row over Goldstone Report."

16. Avrom Krengel, "Richard Goldstone, We Deplore Your Report," *The Guardian*, May 5, 2010.

17. Tehiya Barak, "Judge Goldstone's Dark Past," Ynetnews.com, May 6, 2010, http://www.ynetnews.com/articles/0,7340,L-3885999,00.html.

18. Nathan Guttman, "Israelis Condemn Goldstone's Role in South Africa During Apartheid," *The Forward*, May 12, 2010.

19. "Ayalon Slams Goldstone over Apartheid," *The Jerusalem Post*, May 6, 2010, http://www.jpost.com/Home/Article.aspx?id=174940.

20. Barak, "Judge Goldstone's Dark Past."

21. Guttman, "Israelis Condemn Goldstone's Role in South Africa During Apartheid."

22. Ibid.

11

Messages from Gaza

Laila el-Haddad

When I spoke to my father over Skype the night of January 16, 2009, from Durham, North Carolina, it was with the very real possibility that we might never see or speak to each other again.

He was in his home in Gaza City, in the heart of Israel's assault on Gaza, "Operation Cast Lead."

We tried to stay "off-topic."

He told me he had recently acquired a *hasoon* songbird, a goldfinch, from the farmer who tends his land. It is famous for its stunning melodies. But my father said that ever since the assault on Gaza had intensified, the bird no longer sang. Instead, it was chirping "boom boom." "It's shell-shocked," he joked.

Ending the conversation with a rare moment of laughter during those dark days, we hung up.

Around dawn his time, he sent me a brief e-mail:

> Loved ones:
>
> I thought to take a few moments on the generator to write this email to you. It might be our last communication. The Israeli army has been heavily bombarding everything in Gaza now. They escalated their attack intensively after 4 A.M. Tal El-Hawa is on fire (I will attach photos that I took of smoke from burning buildings). They just fired a missile on one apartment in a huge apartment building in front of our house (Borj Al-Shorook). I guess

> Laila knows it. Phosphorus bombs now are fired everywhere on houses and on people. UNRWA's main stores in GAZA were hit.
>
> Hundreds of people are trapped in burning buildings in Tal El-Hawa and Al-Sabra and everywhere in GAZA. It is clear now that these people decided now to finish everyone and everything in GAZA strip. I still have faith in Allah.

The following morning, he had survived. And a couple of days after that, there was an unfamiliar stillness in Gaza. No F-16s ripping through the sky. No ravaging explosions. There was time to hear yourself think, my father told me. It was all a sort of anesthetic: a pause in a calculated brutality to allow the caged disposables a moment to contemplate their options—to create the illusion they even have options.

"They destroyed anything in their path—people, buildings, streets . . . nothing was left untouched," my father explained the following day. "It is calm, for now. We sleep, for now. But the siege continues."

My father and I made simultaneous back-to-back appearances on multiple media outlets that month. On January 3, 2009, we appeared on CNN, and he summed up what was happening. He spoke calmly, eloquently, in the pitch dark of besieged Gaza, with only the fire of Israeli artillery illuminating his world. "They are destroying everything that is beautiful and living and ordinary," he told the anchor. The list was as seemingly endless as it was familiar: the parliament building down the street from my parents' home, the mosque around the corner, the university my cousin attends, the ambulance our neighbor drives, the pier where we get our fish, the playground my son used to play in, the farm where my friend's father lived (his father was killed too), the restaurant where I had my evening coffees.

His hands were trembling, he confessed, as he and my mother lay on the floor of their home. They had moved their mattress far away from the windows, thunderous explosions ripping through the thick black sky all around them, lighting it up in enormous clouds of fire.

I called my parents every hour; sometimes every few minutes when I saw renewed bombardment on my television screen, my eyes fixed on Al Jazeera English a good part of the day despite my son Yousuf's nagging to switch to cartoons. After a few days he stopped asking, because, tearful and angry, I had told him Gaza is being bombed, that Seedo and Tete are in danger. Sometimes I stayed on the phone with my father until the bombing subsided. Sometimes we didn't say anything at all. We simply held the phones to our ears and spoke to each other in silence. As though I could shield him from the Hell being unleashed around him for those few minutes. However absurd it sounds, we felt safe somehow—reassured that if something were to happen, it would happen while we were together.

Sometimes he would call me for assurance, and even information:

"What's going on? What's going on?" he would repeat in a weary, hypnotic tone. "It just felt like they bombed our street from the inside out. I can't see anything. I don't know what's happening. What's the news saying?" He was desperate for any morsel of information that could make sense of the terror being wrought upon them. "The Apaches are right above our house. It's complete darkness outside, complete darkness," he went on.

Yousuf joined the conversation unceremoniously, popping his head into my laptop screen, my portal to Gaza.

"Seedo? I like the *fatoosh* you used to make! Seedo . . . are you OK?"

"Habibi, when we see each other again—if we see each other again—I'll make it for you," my father promised. The very possibility seemed to comfort him, no matter how illusory.

My parents spoke to Yousuf for a while as I heard the explosions echoing over the speaker, and saw machine-gun fire and the aftermath of phosphorus bombs over the city on my TV. Yousuf complained of an ear infection.

The fear was salient; it was suffocating; it was in the air, friends told me, and no one knew what was to come next. And there was nowhere to turn to except up in Heaven above.

And so many people in Gaza took to doing just that: They were waking up for special pre-dawn prayers, *qiyam il layl,* in the "last third of the night"—a window of time when believers feel especially close to God and when it is said He is especially close to our calls upon Him, and supplications and prayers are most likely to be answered.

And so they trembled, and they waited, and they prayed during this small window to Heaven for the gates of Hell to be closed. And then it was dawn once again.

It was my daughter Noor's birthday on January 1. She turned one year old. I couldn't help but think: Who was born in bloodied Gaza on that day?

My father passed the phone to my mother. She tried to make idle chitchat, asking about when we would celebrate Noor's birthday—though I'd already told her we had a small party.

"Oh that's right, that's right. This war, it makes people amnesic, I swear. Yassine?" she said, addressing my husband, an ophthalmologist, seeking reassurance, seeking comfort, seeking sense. "I don't know what's wrong with me. It's strange, strange. My body is literally trembling from the inside. From the inside. Why do you think that is? It's strange."

After all was said and done, it remained to be asked: Why did this have to happen at all? Why the assault? Why the ongoing siege?

Perhaps Mahmoud Darwish put it best in his poem "State of Siege," written in besieged Ramallah in 2002: "This siege will endure until we are truly persuaded into choosing a harmless slavery, but in total freedom!"[1]

Gaza is an occupied territory that has been subjected to a premeditated, methodical siege since the free and fair parliamentary elections in 2006, which in turn followed a near-hermetic closure for the decade before that. And its residents— already stateless after more than forty years of occupation, and a majority of them refugees from towns and villages surrounding the Gaza Strip—are at once being blockaded and bombarded by land, sea, and sky. Former UN human rights investigator John Dugard has argued that this situation is unprecedented in modern history.

The siege has intentionally deprived an already impoverished and dispossessed people of many of the basic items needed to prosper: electricity, books, and raw materials with which to rebuild. This has forced 97 percent of factories to shut down.[2] It has deprived the residents of Gaza of cattle and fertilized chicken eggs. Notebooks and newspapers. It has also placed them on a forced diet[3] that changes on a weekly basis. Cilantro, cumin, ginger, or fresh milk: On any given week, the import of different food items is abruptly stopped.

But as most any resident of Gaza will fervently tell you, the siege is not about food and sustenance, plenty of which arrives through donor aid and tunnel trade; it is about freedoms: freedom to move in and out of Gaza, freedom to fish more than three miles out at sea, freedom to learn, to work, to farm, to build, to live, to prosper. After all, Gaza was never a place with a quantitative food shortage; it is a place where many people lack the means to buy food and other goods because of a closure policy whose tenets are "no development, no prosperity, and no humanitarian crisis."[4]

And then, on top of all this, Operation Cast Lead. Closed in on all sides, there was no entry and there was no escape. And it had happened before our eyes, with regional and global complicity and blessings.

Into this context came the Goldstone Report, accusing Israel (and the Hamas government) of war crimes and possible crimes against humanity. It didn't just report on the destruction, but called for action, for accountability. It was a vindication of sorts, confirming what people in Gaza had known all along. Validation of the horror they had endured and a step toward impacting Israel in the public and international arena.

For some, the report was simply a marketing opportunity. (In Gaza City, PLO Flag Shop owner Tareq Abu Daya sold hundreds of traditional *kuffiyeh* scarves embroidered with Justice Goldstone's name for $22 each.) For others, the report was one of dozens that have done little more than document what they already know.

Many considered it merely "ink on paper." Just more pages to add to the ever-accumulating pile of reports and resolutions and statements criticizing Israel for its draconian and illegal policies and its assaults against the Palestinians. Another report, but no actual implementation. No action is ever taken to stop the condemned actions, and so the reaction of many Palestinians is "Great, but how will this report change matters on the ground?" "Will it result in the end of Israel's asphyxiating siege of Gaza?" "Will those responsible actually be held accountable in international courts?"

As of today, the Goldstone Report has had no practical impact on the lives of Palestinians in Gaza. Whether it will prove to have been a turning point only time will tell.

Toward the end of January, I asked my father what happened to his bird. He said he had let it go, not knowing if he would be around to care for it, and not comfortable with imprisoning an animal accustomed to freedom the way he was being imprisoned. It was free to defy the siege—and so it did. And so had he, by proxy.

NOTES

1. Mahmoud Darwish, "State of Siege," as translated by Ramsis Amun; available online at http://www.arabworldbooks.com/Literature/poetry4.html.

2. See http://www.gazagateway.org/2009/09/no-development-no-prosperity-no-human itarian crisis/.

3. Dov Weissglass, former adviser to Israeli prime minister Ariel Sharon, was reported to have said the following in explaining the Gaza blockade policy: "It's like an appointment with a dietician. The Palestinians will get a lot thinner, but won't die." See "As the Hamas Team Laughs," http://www.haaretz.com/print-edition/opinion/as-the-hamas-team-laughs-1.180500.

4. See http://www.gazagateway.org/2009/09/no-development-no-prosperity-no-human itarian crisis/.

CONTRIBUTOR BIOS

Ali Abunimah is author of *One Country: A Bold Proposal to End the Israeli-Palestinian Impasse* and co-founder of The Electronic Intifada.

Brian Baird served twelve years in Congress, representing Washington State, and was chairman of the Energy and Environment Subcommittee of the Science and Technology Committee. A licensed clinical psychologist, Baird is a former professor of psychology at Pacific Lutheran University in Tacoma and has worked in state and Veterans Administration psychiatric hospitals, community mental health clinics, substance abuse treatment programs, institutions for juvenile offenders, and head injury rehabilitation programs. He is the author of two books: a guide to internships in the social services and a guide for families on vacation.

Laila El-Haddad is a Palestinian journalist and blogger from Gaza City. She is currently based in the United States and is a frequent contributor to Aljazeera.net, the Guardian Unlimited, the Electronic Intifada, and the BBC and has appeared on CNN, NPR, and Democracy Now. Since November 2004, she has authored the award-winning blog "Gazamom" (formerly "Raising Yousuf: A Diary of a Mother Under Occupation"). The blog covers the trials of raising her children between spaces and identities, displacement and occupation. She is the author of *Gaza Mom: Palestine Politics, Parenting, and Everything in Between* (Just World Books, October 2010).

Moshe Halbertal is a professor of philosophy at The Hebrew University and the Gruss Professor at New York University School of Law. A fellow at the Shalom Hartman Institute, he has a doctorate in Jewish Thought from The Hebrew University and is the author of several books, including *People of the Book: Canon, Meaning and Authority*.

Adam Horowitz lives in New York City, where he is co-editor of Mondoweiss.net. He holds a master's degree in Near Eastern Studies from New York University.

Rashid Khalidi is the Edward Said Professor of Arab Studies at Columbia University. He is a past president of the Middle East Studies Association and the author of six books, including *Sowing Crisis: American Dominance and the Cold War in the Middle East* (2009), *The Iron Cage: The Story of the Palestinian Struggle for Statehood* (2006), *Resurrecting Empire: Western Footprints and America's Perilous Path in the Middle East* (2004), and *Palestinian Identity: The Construction of Modern National Consciousness* (1997).

Naomi Klein is the author of the international best-sellers *The Shock Doctrine: The Rise of Disaster Capitalism* and *No Logo: Taking Aim at the Brand Bullies*. She writes a regular column for *The Nation* magazine and *The Guardian* newspaper that is syndicated internationally by The New York Times Syndicate. In 2004, her reporting from Iraq for *Harper's Magazine* won the James Aronson Award for Social Justice Journalism. Also in 2004 she wrote and co-produced *The Take*, an award-winning feature documentary about Argentina's occupied factory movement. She is a former Miliband Fellow at the London School of Economics and holds an honorary Doctor of Civil Laws from the University of King's College, Nova Scotia.

Jules Lobel is a law professor at the University of Pittsburgh School of Law and vice president of the Center for Constitutional Rights. Through the Center, Lobel has litigated important issues regarding the application of international law in the U.S. courts. Lobel is co-author with Professor David Cole of the award-winning *Less Safe, Less Free: Why America Is Losing the War on Terror* (New Press, 2007) and the author of *Success Without Victory* (NYU Press, 2003) and numerous articles on international and constitutional law in legal publications.

Letty Cottin Pogrebin, a founding editor of *Ms. Magazine* and a past president of The Authors Guild, has published nine books—most recently *Three Daughters*, a novel. Her essays have appeared in many publications including the *New York Times*, *The Nation*, and the *Huffington Post*. She is a past president of Americans for Peace Now, a founding board member of the International Center for Peace in the Middle East, and a veteran of several Jewish-American/Palestinian-American dialogue groups.

Lizzy Ratner is a journalist who has written for the *New York Times*, *The Nation*, the *New York Observer*, and other publications and has worked on staff at the *New York Observer* and Democracy Now. She lives in New York City.

Noam Sheizaf is a Tel Aviv–based Israeli journalist. He has worked for several publications, among them the daily *Maariv* and Ynet.co.il, Israel's leading news portal. Before that, he served as combat officer in the IDF. Sheizaf blogs at www.promisedlandblog.com.

Henry Siegman, director of the U.S./Middle East Project, is a visiting research professor at the Sir Joseph Hotung Middle East Program, School of Oriental and African Studies, University of London. He is a former Senior Fellow on the Middle East at the Council on Foreign Relations and was national director of the American Jewish Congress from 1978 to 1994.

Jerome Slater was a professor of political science at SUNY/Buffalo from 1966 to 2000 and now holds the title of University Research Scholar there. He is the author of a number of books and journal articles on American foreign policy, especially on the Israeli-Palestinian conflict. He blogs on that topic at jeromeslater.com.

Raji Sourani is a human rights lawyer based in Gaza City and the director of the Palestinian Centre for Human Rights (PCHR). Over the years of his work against the human rights violations committed by both the Israeli occupation and the Palestinian Authority, Sourani was arrested numerous times and even subjected to torture for speaking truth to power. He was declared an Amnesty International prisoner of conscience in the 1980s. In 1995, Sourani founded PCHR, which has offices and staff across the Occupied Palestinian Territory. He is a recipient of the RFK Memorial Award for Human Rights, a member of the Executive Committee of the International Commission of Jurists, and vice president of the International Federation for Human Rights.

Desmond Tutu is the archbishop emeritus of Cape Town, South Africa, and a global advocate for justice, peace, and reconciliation. Born and raised in Klerksdorp, Transvaal, in South Africa, he was a leading figure in the struggle to end Apartheid, initially as the first black general-secretary of the South African Council of Churches and then as the archbishop of Cape Town, the highest position in South Africa's Anglican Church. His calls for both nonviolent resistance and economic sanctions earned him the title "South Africa's moral conscience," and in 1984 he was awarded the Nobel Peace Prize for his role in his country's liberation struggle. In 1994, after Apartheid ended, Nelson Mandela appointed him to lead the country's Truth and Reconciliation Commission, which investigated Apartheid-era atrocities and helped smooth the transition toward democracy. Since then he has continued to campaign tirelessly for the rights of the world's oppressed, poor, and marginalized, most notably as the chair of the Elders, a group of eminent human rights leaders. In addition to the Nobel Prize, Archbishop Tutu was awarded the Gandhi Peace Prize in 2005 and the Presidential Medal of Freedom in 2009.

Philip Weiss is a journalist who has written for many different magazines, including *The Nation*, the *New York Times Magazine*, *Harper's*, and *Esquire*. He is the author of two books: a political novel and an investigation of a murder in the Peace Corps. He is co-editor with Adam Horowitz of Mondoweiss.net and lives in the Hudson Valley, New York.

INDEX